JOURNAL FOR THE STUDY OF THE OLD TESTAMENT SUPPLEMENT SERIES
241

Sheffield Academic Press

No Other Gods

Emergent Monotheism in Israel

Robert Karl Gnuse

Journal for the Study of the Old Testament
Supplement Series 241

To Becky (1984–), Jake (1987–) and Adam (1990–)

Copyright © 1997 Sheffield Academic Press

Published by Sheffield Academic Press Ltd
Mansion House
19 Kingfield Road
Sheffield S11 9AS
England

Printed on acid-free paper in Great Britain
by Bookcraft Ltd
Midsomer Norton, Bath

British Library Cataloguing in Publication Data

A catalogue record for this book is available
from the British Library

ISBN 1-85075-657-0

CONTENTS

ACKNOWLEDGMENTS

This manuscript has been in process for many years. Ideas were planted like small seeds in a fertile field nearly fifteen years ago by a colleague, Father Imre Mihalik of Notre Dame Seminary in New Orleans, who unfortunately died before publishing his own manuscript on the subject of evolving monotheism. The actual foundation for this monograph emerged from a seminar paper at Loyola University of New Orleans in 1985. Ever since that time the topic has been growing piecemeal. Some of the ideas found here have appeared as presentations for the national College Theology Society convention and the Yamauchi lecture series of Loyola University as well as journal articles in *Biblical Theology Bulletin, Zygon* and *Journal of the American Academy of Religion* (all to be cited later). This project developed over the years in great part due to the continued encouragement of Walter Brueggemann of Columbia Theological Seminary in Atlanta. Special thanks go to Ms Patricia Doran of Loyola's Inter-library Loan department for obtaining the many resources necessary for writing a work such as this.

This is not a systematic work; rather, it probes in many directions. It offers a summary and critique of contemporary scholarship concerning the emergence of Israel in the land of Palestine in Iron Age I (1200– 1050 BCE) and the evolution of monotheism among pre-exilic Israelites and post-exilic Jews. It seeks to discern the dynamics of emerging monotheism in the biblical tradition in relationship to similar ideas elsewhere in the ancient world and to focus on the ideational and social implications of that emergent monotheism. I believe the best way to characterize the emergence of monotheism is to describe it as both a revolutionary and an evolutionary process, and to this end an appeal is made to contemporary scientific evolutionary paradigms. If such a perception is meaningful, there are then significant theological and social implications that flow from that new perceptual model. This book can only be suggestive in regard to such theologizing and theorizing. My hope is that others will be inspired by some of the suggestions here and use them in their own scholarly and pedagogical work. I am especially thankful to the editors of Sheffield Academic Press for allowing me the privilege of expressing my observations through the medium of one of their publications.

ABBREVIATIONS

AB	Anchor Bible
ABD	*Anchor Bible Dictionary*
ANET	J.B. Pritchard (ed.), *Ancient Near Eastern Texts*
ASORDS	American Schools of Oriental Research Dissertation Series
ATANT	Abhandlungen zur Theologie des Alten und Neuen Testaments
BA	*Biblical Archaeologist*
BARev	*Biblical Archaeology Review*
BASOR	*Bulletin of the American Schools of Oriental Research*
BBB	Bonner biblische Beiträge
BETL	Bibliotheca ephemeridum theologicarum lovaniensium
Bib	*Biblica*
BibB	Biblische Beiträge
BJRL	*Bulletin of the John Rylands University Library of Manchester*
BTB	*Biblical Theology Bulletin*
BZ	*Biblische Zeitschrift*
BZAW	Beihefte zur ZAW
CBQ	*Catholic Biblical Quarterly*
CBQMS	*Catholic Biblical Quarterly*, Monograph Series
CTM	*Concordia Theological Monthly*
EBib	Etudes bibliques
HAR	*Hebrew Annual Review*
HBT	*Horizons in Biblical Theology*
HR	*History of Religions*
HSM	Harvard Semitic Monographs
HUCA	*Hebrew Union College Annual*
IDBSup	*Interpreter's Dictionary of the Bible Supplement*
IEJ	*Israel Exploration Journal*
Int	*Interpretation*
JAAR	*Journal of the American Academy of Religion*
JAOS	*Journal of the American Oriental Society*
JBL	*Journal of Biblical Literature*
JNES	*Journal of Near Eastern Studies*
JQR	*Jewish Quarterly Review*
JSOT	*Journal for the Study of the Old Testament*
JSOTSup	*Journal for the Study of the Old Testament*, Supplement Series
KD	*Kerygma und Dogma*

MDOG	Mitteilungen der deutschen Orient-Gesellschaft
NTOA	Novum Testamentum et Orbis Antiquus
OBO	Orbis biblicus et orientalis
OBT	Overtures to Biblical Theology
Or	*Orientalia*
OTL	Old Testament Library
OTS	*Oudtestamentlische Studiën*
PEQ	*Palestine Exploration Quarterly*
PJ	*Palästina-Jahrbuch*
PTMS	Pittsburg Theological Monograph Series
RB	*Revue biblique*
RelSRev	*Religious Studies Review*
RSR	*Recherches de science religieuse*
SBLDS	SBL Dissertation Series
SBLMS	SBL Monograph Series
SBT	Studies in Biblical Theology
SJOT	*Scandanavian Journal of the Old Testament*
TLZ	*Theologische Literaturzeitung*
TQ	*Theologische Quartalschrift*
TS	*Theological Studies*
TZ	*Theologische Zeitschrift*
VT	*Vetus Testamentum*
VTSup	*Vetus Testamentum*, Supplements
WMANT	Wissenschaftliche Monographien zum Alten und Neuen Testament
ZAW	*Zeitschrift für die alttestamentliche Wissenschaft*
ZDPV	*Zeitschrift des deutschen Palästina-Vereins*
ZTK	*Zeitschrift für Theologie und Kirche*

In his classic 1962 work entitled *The Structure of Scientific Revolutions* Thomas Kuhn described how revolutions in scientific thought occur. When enough data have accumulated in a particular field of research which calls into question the reigning paradigm or theory used by scientists to describe the phenomena they observe, the vast majority of scientists become ready to adopt rather quickly a new hypothesis which explains the observed data in a more coherent fashion. When a reflective individual provides such an over-arching explanation, it then captures the imagination of the scientific community as a better alternative and becomes the new scientific explanation. Although the non-scientific community may perceive that this individual appears to have generated a radical new theory, often the theory provides explanations that many scientists in the field were anticipating in their own research for some years prior to the presentation of the new paradigm. While the masses may sense that a theory suddenly fell by the wayside in revolutionary fashion, actually there had been great pressure upon the scientific community to provide a better theory to explain the new evidence they had accumulated for some time prior to the breakthrough. This pressure led to the apparent acceptance of the new theory, in dramatic fashion, by the scientific community. Kuhn felt justified in describing such transformations of consensus opinions among scientists as 'scientific revolutions'. Examples provided by him included the emergence of new theories which took years or even a generation or two to gain complete acceptance, but even then those periods of time should still be considered rather brief for the opinions of the majority of scientists in a particular field to change over so completely to a new paradigm.[1]

Since the publication of Kuhn's work the intellectual community has been fascinated with using his characterization of such 'scientific revolutions' to describe 'paradigm shifts' not only in the various fields of natural

1.   T. Kuhn, *The Structure of Scientific Revolutions* (Chicago: University of Chicago Press, 2nd edn, 1970 [1962]).

science, but also in the social sciences and the humanities. There are times when the gradual emergence of new and contradictory information in a particular field of study builds to such a point where the specialists finally accept a new theory or paradigm to reconfigure and explain the data more coherently. Such 'paradigm shifts' have occurred frequently in the past few generations in many arenas of human learning.

I

We are at a point in time in particular areas of study in the Hebrew Bible where just such a 'paradigm shift' appears to be underway. Recent archaeological work and deep reflection upon the biblical texts by critical scholars, especially since 1975, has led us to envision the emergence of Israel's identity in very different ways from the textbook models and theological portrayals which were popular from 1945 to 1975. I see 1975 as a signal year because critical works on the historicity of the patriarchal narratives were produced by John Van Seters and Thomas Thompson, both of which contributed significantly to the growing unrest with traditional understandings of Israelite origins and religious identity.[2] Two areas of study in particular have undergone a dramatic transformation: the understanding of the Israelite conquest (1200–1050 BCE) and the emergence of Yahwistic monotheism.

In the past twenty years Hebrew scripture scholars have assessed existing paradigms used not only in scholarship but also in textbooks and found them to be wanting. In this period of scholarly ferment one cannot be too sure where the new paradigms will take us, but a new consensus seems to be emerging on a number of issues, some of which may have significant implications for how Christians and Jews draw out theological and religious meanings from the biblical texts. Two areas of research have drawn my attention for the past ten years: first, how archaeologists have begun to redefine the process by which the Israelites conquered or settled Palestine; and secondly, how historians of Israelite religion have begun to sense that monotheism emerged much more slowly and later than was assumed in the past.

Many biblical theologians have taken their cue for the creation of biblical or 'Old Testament' theologies from the critical scholarly under-

---

2.   T. Thompson, *The Historicity of the Patriarchal Narratives* (BZAW, 133; Berlin: de Gruyter, 1974); and J. van Seters, *Abraham in History and Tradition* (New Haven: Yale University Press, 1975).

standing of these two aspects of biblical study. Although in theory biblical theologians suggest that they theologize from the text, in reality, all theologians craft their theological articulations in the light of the critical historical and textual assumptions they have adopted. The emergence of new scholarly understandings will cause biblical theologians to fine-tune their explications and stress different nuances in the future. This volume is designed to be a tentative probe in suggesting what might be the themes that biblical theologians will stress in the future as they reflect upon the biblical literature of the Hebrew canon.

Formerly, the model so popular for biblical theologians and often expressed in the textbooks envisioned the Israelite conquest in dramatic fashion, as either an invasion from the outside or an internal revolution in Iron Age I (1200–1050 BCE) Palestine. The result was the creation of highland Israel, a group of people with a distinct social and religious identity. In like fashion, the Yahwistic faith was seen to have arisen in some dramatic form among the people in that same era, and often scholars assumed some form of conscious covenanted commitment by the highlanders to a new deity, called Yahweh, brought into the land from the outside. The worship of this deity generated religious and social values in opposition to the traditional Canaanite religion of the land with its mythic beliefs and cultic activity. In subsequent years the Israelite ethos and religion was compromised by the continual contact with Canaanite culture, and its pollution was furthered by the policies of kings, from Solomon onward, who attempted to integrate the culture of highland Israelites and lowland Canaanites for political solidarity in the realm. Scholars called this process syncretism. Reform oriented prophets, zealous kings like Hezekiah and Josiah of Judah, and above all the Deuteronomic reformers attempted to restore pure original Yahwism, and this goal was accomplished finally in the crucible of the Babylonian exile (586–539 BCE) from which true monotheism and its values emerged as the belief system of all Jews. This scenario provided a grand format for textbooks, and professors could draw inspiring parallels with contemporary social and religious situations.

Recently, however, scholars have begun to suspect that the emergence of the highland Israelite identity and monotheistic belief did not occur in such dramatic fashion, but rather the process may have been more gradual and much later than the textbooks taught. Since 1980 archaeologists have suspected increasingly that the origin of those people called Israel was a gradual, internal and peaceful process in highland Palestine.

There was no invasion or revolution, nor even a significant migration of outsiders into the land, as three earlier theories had suggested. Rather, the origins of these people were to be sought in peaceful social dynamics among the indigenous Palestinian populace. Archaeologists have provided a number of variations on this scenario in the past fifteen years, and to date no real consensus has emerged. I attempted to characterize and classify some of these new archaeological theories on the peaceful, internal origins of Israel in two previous articles.[3]

Furthermore, the archaeological evidence began to mount that the Yahwistic religion of the Israelites had much more in common with the Canaanite religion than previously was acknowledged. The prophets and the Deuteronomistic History were describing offensive religious customs within the Yahwistic religion itself and not alien Canaanite religious intrusions brought in by way of some process of syncretism. There really was no great conflict between two religions, Canaanite and Israelite, but rather a gradual evolution of a complex Yahwistic religion from a polytheistic past to the monotheistic values envisioned by the prophetic, Deuteronomic, and Priestly reformers. This monotheistic religion asserted itself completely only in the exile when the common people began to accept the belief system of the reformers.

The implications of this paradigm shift of interpretation among scholars on both issues is truly significant. For years we drew theological and ethical conclusions from the dramatic contrast of Israelite and Canaanite culture. I, too, used such paradigms in writings and lectures.[4] The contrast, of course, was designed to encourage the modern audience, be they church members or students in college and seminary, to emulate the values of the Israelites in comparable ways today and to eschew the values of the Canaanites when they appear in modern garb. The appropriate equation of Canaanite values in modern society understandably was left to the discretion of the preacher or teacher. Unfortunately, that

3. R. Gnuse, 'Israelite Settlement of Canaan: A Peaceful Internal Process', *BTB* 21 (1991), pp. 56-66, 109-117.

4. R. Gnuse, 'But Who is the Thief?', *Blueprint for Social Justice* 36.4 (1982), pp. 1-7; *idem*, *The Jewish Roots of Christian Faith: An Introduction to the Old Testament* (New Orleans: Loyola University Press, 1983), *passim*; *idem*, *You Shall Not Steal: Community and Property in the Biblical Tradition* (Maryknoll: Orbis Books, 1985), pp. 53-85. Other good examples would be the basic textbook presentations in P. Ellis, *The Yahwist: The Bible's First Theologian* (Notre Dame: Fides, 1968), pp. 61-65; and B. Anderson, *Understanding the Old Testament* (Englewood Cliffs, NJ: Prentice–Hall, 4th edn, 1986), pp. 181-93.

mode of weaving biblical theology and ethics, the way of dialectical contrast, can no longer be used.

Now scholars envision the culture and religion of Israel to emerge more gradually and peacefully; we perceive that it achieved its apotheosis in the exile and beyond. The post-exilic era (586 BCE–70 CE), which we so often characterized as a non-creative age, must now be seen more properly as the age when the biblical ethos truly came to fruition. The theologians must now theologize from a model which understands that the Israelite ethos shared much in common with its ancient milieu and only gradually distinguished itself at a later date. What then will be the theological implications?

This volume seeks to provide suggestions for what direction biblical theology might take in the future, what particular assumptions might become important in our theologizing. It is not meant to be a systematic exposition of a new biblical theology, rather it is a probing prolegomena to such a theology. (The book is also a fuller explication of a paper I presented in 1985 which appeared in revised form as an article in 1994).[5] It contains some highly speculative suggestions or theological musings which may inspire a more developed biblical theology or at least be integrated into future biblical theologies. In many ways this volume parallels an earlier work in this series, an excellent text by Leo Perdue, *The Collapse of History: Reconstructing Old Testament Theology*, which also surveyed the new possible directions of biblical theology.[6]

II

I attempt several tasks. The first two chapters review the diverse scholarly observations made by scholars on the issues of the Israelite conquest or settlement of Palestine and the emergence of Yahwistic monotheism. Hopefully, these chapters serve readers by providing summaries and some classifications of complex contemporary scholarship on these

5. R. Gnuse, 'The Development of Monotheism in the Biblical Tradition: Its Social Context' (Loyola University Religious Studies Faculty Seminar, New Orleans, November 8, 1985); *idem*, 'New Directions in Old Testament Theology: The Impact of Current Scholarship upon the Theological Task' (College Theology Society National Convention, New Orleans, June 3, 1990); *idem*, 'New Directions in Biblical Theology: The Impact of Contemporary Scholarship in the Hebrew Bible', *JAAR* 62 (1994), pp. 893-918.

6. L. Perdue, *The Collapse of History: Reconstructing Old Testament Theology* (OBT; Minneapolis: Augsburg–Fortress, 1994).

issues. Although the book is primarily about the development of monotheism, as the title indicates, the consideration of the Israelite conquest is
significantly related to that issue, for the understanding of the settlement
process gives us a deeper insight into the origin of the Israelites, and this
in turn provides us with a foundational awareness of the nature of the
Israelite religion and ethos and how it evolved. In the textbooks of the
past the understanding of Israelites as originating primarily outside the
land of Palestine led readers to view Israelite religion and culture as quite
distinct from that of the Canaanites from the earliest stages of the settlement onward. In my consideration of Israelite religion I do not attempt
to evaluate the religion of Israel as a whole, but rather focus upon the
emergence of monotheism in particular. The former topic deserves the
kind of multi-volume treatment it has most recently received in the
excellent work by Rainer Albertz.[7]

The next three chapters deal in cursory fashion with the nature of
emergent monotheism in Israel's world and summarize the possible consensus which is arising among scholars, biblical theologians and pedago-
gues concerning the development of monotheism among Israelites and
Jews. The expression 'emergent' is used in conjunction with the term
'monotheism' to reflect the basic thesis of this work, that, generally
speaking, monotheism developed over the course of many centuries in
the ancient world and is evolving even today, and that these developmental stages often come in 'bursts' in response to particular social and
religious crises. These chapters touch upon many issues, including monotheistic tendencies in the ancient Near East, the stages of monotheistic
development in Israel, the ethical and social implications of fully emergent
monotheism, and the intellectual paradigms by which we may envision
the process of monotheistic evolution. These topics are so broad as to
merit separate volumes, so I am forced to treat many aspects only in a
superficial fashion. My goal is to expose the reader to the complexity of
the discussion, which is interdisciplinary in nature, especially the wider
religious and social issues connected to the emergence of monotheism.
Too often biblical scholars dare not embark upon such a wide discussion
for fear of not doing justice to the complexity of the materials. This
volume, however, undertakes the challenge of making a sweeping study
of issues connected to the phenomenon of emergent monotheism for the
sake of the general reader. If at times the discussion is not sufficiently

---

7.   R. Albertz, *A History of Israelite Religion in the Old Testament Period*
(trans. J. Bowden; OTL; 2 vols.; Philadelphia: Westminster Press, 1994).

sophisticated to please the critical reader, I apologize.

The two chapters on tradition and process thought provide a discussion of topics which may be a sweeping springboard for further biblical theology. In my opinion our new insights and paradigms have significant implications for modern religious imperatives for social reform and Christian self-understanding of the nature of tradition. In short, the process of emerging monotheism did not end with Israel and the Jews; rather, it is a process which still continues in the greater Judaeo-Christian tradition today. Jews and Christians are called upon to continue developing the implications of monotheism still today in affirming the radical equality and dignity of all people. The monotheistic process is not complete. This is one of the cardinal messages this volume seeks to affirm. Likewise, I also believe, perhaps rightly or wrongly, that the new shape of biblical studies and these new insights concerning the evolutionary advance of monotheism may focus attention more directly upon the theological metaphors offered to us by process philosophy. To that end, a chapter on the congruence of biblical thought in the Hebrew canon and process concepts is provided. This topic also deserves a separate volume to do it better service, so hopefully the reader will have some patience with its brief discussion.

Finally, the last chapter deals with a topic especially close to my heart, the significant parallels between modern scientific evolutionary theories and paradigms in the social sciences. This chapter is a revision of a previously published article.[8] Its inclusion here is merited by the continual use of ideas found within this chapter throughout the volume as a whole, and especially in those discussions about emergent monotheism as both an 'evolutionary' and a 'revolutionary' process. Here is another cardinal thesis of this volume: emergent monotheism may be seen as an evolutionary process which develops over a period of time in preparation for a period of radical revolutionary breakthrough, which is followed by a period of time in which the religious and social implications of that breakthrough unfold and manifest themselves gradually in human culture. As we shall see, this follows a contemporary model of biological evolutionary theory called 'Punctuated Equilibria'.[9] In terms of emergent monotheism

8. R. Gnuse, 'Contemporary Evolutionary Theory as a New Heuristic Model for the Socioscientific Method in Biblical Studies', *Zygon* 25 (1990), pp. 405-31.

9. Leading authors in this area of study include Niles Eldredge, Stephen Jay Gould, Steven Stanley, Elisabeth Vrba and Ian Tattersall, whose works will be listed in the chapter especially dedicated to the study of evolutionary theory.

I see the evolutionary preparations in the stages of religious development in pre-exilic Israel; the radical breakthrough occurs in the Babylonian exile; and the unfolding of the implications of the breakthrough have been occurring now for over two millennia. This is why we may speak of the on-going monotheistic evolutionary/revolutionary process even today.

The last chapter may be the most controversial in several ways, for it seeks to be interdisciplinary by crossing over the line from the social sciences to the natural sciences in speculative fashion. The re-introduction of biological evolutionary categories into the discussion of Israelite and Jewish religion may lead many readers to recall with disdain the old attempts of the nineteenth- and early twentieth-century thinkers to apply the old paradigm of Darwinian gradualism in lock-step fashion to a study of history and religion. The result was the creation of neat stages of progressive development which ultimately seemed to distort the data for the sake of the theory in many fields of historical and social-scientific research. So, there was a negative reaction to using the concept of evolution in our discussions. As one scholar of Israelite religion, Imre Mihalik, candidly observed, we became afraid to admit any gradual development in regard to monotheistic belief, because we were afraid of evolutionary ideas in any form.[10] This volume wishes to alleviate that fear by indicating that there are alternative evolutionary models besides Darwinian gradualism, and these may be used with much greater profit in the discussion of biblical religion or historical phenomena in general.

Not only is the recent model of Punctuated Equilibria a challenge to old Darwinian models, but other biologists are presenting other theories in opposition to the old Darwinian assumptions. Jan Sapp, for example, describes how increasingly since 1980 biologists speak of cooperative 'symbiosis' as the primary force in the evolutionary advance rather than competition for survival.[11] The concept of symbiosis or cooperation rather than conflict should have significant appeal to scholars in the social sciences and the humanities as a foundational principle of how the world works, particularly since so many thinkers reacted negatively to the idea of ruthless competition and survival as a principle to characterize the nature of history and culture.

10. I. Mihalik, 'Some Thoughts on the Name Israel', *Theological Soundings: Notre Dame Seminary Jubilee Studies 1923–1973* (ed. I. Mihalik; New Orleans: Notre Dame Seminary, 1973), pp. 13-14.

11. J. Sapp, *Evolution by Association* (New York: Oxford University Press, 1994).

Theorists in the field of social scientific research are introducing the models of biological evolution into their characterizations. Gerhard Lenski, a noted anthropologist whose writings have influenced me, assumes a model of uneven evolutionary advance in human societies which is immanent and continuous, and he distinguishes between general evolution, which is inexorable in its advance, and specific evolution, which is more multi-directional as a tension by which to explain both the inevitable development in history and human freedom in diverse cultural expressions.[12] I believe that Lenski's ideas combined with the model of Punctuated Equilibria can provide a good model of social and religious development. Elsewhere I attempted to summarize briefly how other historians and anthropologists are using this new model of punctuated evolutionary advance.[13]

III

One of my goals in this volume is to draw together many of the new concepts and terms which are used to describe the process of religious development in the biblical tradition and encourage their usage in scholarship and pedagogical works. Much of what is said here is not original, but it is synthesized into an overview for the readership. Hopefully, many will find at least some of the ideas valuable and useful in their own reflection.

Paramount in my presentation is the use of the concept of evolutionary advance in a punctuated or revolutionary fashion. Essentially, a great social or intellectual advance may be described as both an evolutionary process and a revolutionary breakthrough. Furthermore, a revolutionary breakthrough may be said to last for centuries, both in terms of the preparatory stages and the subsequent unfolding of latent implications.

Another significant paradigm in the study of biblical religion is that proposed by Mark Smith in his work, *The Early History of God*.[14] He wisely suggests that we observe the development of monotheism in Israel resulting from a process of 'convergence' and 'differentiation'. The

12. G. Lenski, 'History and Social Change', *American Journal of Sociology* 82 (1976), pp. 548-64; G. Lenski and J. Lenski, *Human Societies: An Introduction to Macrosociology* (New York: McGraw–Hill, 3rd edn, 1978).

13. Gnuse, 'Evolutionary Theory', pp. 412-18.

14. M. Smith, *The Early History of God: Yahweh and the Other Deities in Ancient Israel* (San Francisco: Harper & Row, 1990).

identity of Yahweh is seen to evolve by absorbing the characteristics of other deities (convergence) while at the same time rejecting certain characteristics and cultic activity (differentiation). I find such a perception quite valuable, and Smith's exposition is excellent.

In a general textbook William Tremmel proposes terminology in his discussion of world religions which dovetails admirably with my ideas. He speaks of how a religion reaches a point where it experiences an intellectual breakthrough or transformation which he describes as a 'kairotic moment'. At this point a religion becomes a truly 'consummate religion'. This corresponds directly with my use of the model of Punctuated Equilibria in the discussion of Israelite monotheism. Tremmel also observes that the majority of the world's religions reached the level of 'consummate' belief during the 'Axis Age' (700–400 BCE), a term that other historians refer to as the 'Axial Age'.[15]

Reference to the 'Axial Age', a term coined by the philosopher Karl Jaspers and developed by social historians such as Shmuel Eisenstadt and others, could be a valuable pedagogical concept for biblical theologians.[16] Use of this term stresses that the biblical religious development occurred as part of a larger worldwide intellectual advance, and that the Israelites and Jews were not some small group developing in isolation and in dialectical opposition to other cultures, as has been assumed at times in past scholarship. The term also focuses upon the time and location of the significant moment of the biblical monotheistic breakthrough—the exile. The Babylonian exile (586–539 BCE) historically was in the middle of the great Axial Age, and the Jews were located in Babylon where they could be stimulated in their own thought by great ideas circulating from many cultures, a key ingredient for all Axial Age breakthroughs. Related to this is the old notion popularized by Max Weber[17] that the Jews were a 'peripheral people', a simple people on the edge of great civilizations like Egypt and Mesopotamia. Such peripheral peoples often draw great ideas from older, change-resistant cultures (which characterizes river

15. W. Tremmel, *Religion, What Is it?* (New York: Holt, Rinehart & Winston, 2nd edn, 1984), pp. 125-45.

16. S. Eisenstadt (ed.), *The Origins and Diversity of Axial Age Civilizations* (State University of New York Series in Near Eastern Studies; Albany: State University of New York Press, 1986); and K. Armstrong, *A History of God: The 4000-Year Quest of Judaism, Christianity and Islam* (New York: Knopf, 1993), pp. 27-78 *et passim*.

17. M. Weber, *Ancient Judaism* (eds. and trans. H. Gerth and D. Martindale; repr.; Glencoe: Free Press, 1952 [1917–19]), pp. xix-xx, 7-10, 206-207, *et passim*.

valley societies) and then reinterpret them for their more basic social setting in a radically new way to effect a social or technological breakthrough. Typically, the Axial Age breakthroughs came from peripheral societies such as Greece, Israel, Persia and Upanishadic India (Ganges River area). By using these concepts biblical theologians could place the emergent monotheism of Israelites and Jews into the greater context of worldwide intellectual and social development.

The old contrast of Israelite thought with mythic Canaanite or ancient Near Eastern thought has been criticized and invalidated by scholars for the past generation. The paradigm of cyclic and mythic pagan thought compared to the linear and historical patterns of exposition in Israel was overplayed by a generation of biblical theologians, especially in the 'Biblical Theology Movement' with its use of 'Salvation History' theology. But now there is a danger of going too far in the other direction and refraining from articulating any comparisons. Emergent monotheism brings social and religious breakthroughs; there is a difference between the attitudes of believers before and after the monotheistic breakthrough of the Babylonian exile. The biblical authors most certainly sensed this as they sought to describe the distinctiveness of Israel in so many of the biblical texts.[18] Therefore, I propose to rehabilitate the old linear and cyclic paradigms used in a former generation (1945–75) in more nuanced fashion. First, the great continuities between Israelite/ Jewish thought and the ancient Near East must be acknowledged. Moral ethics and notions of universalism were around long before Israel, and Israel inherited many ideas from neighboring cultures and merely furthered them along in the existing evolutionary process. Thus, sharp dialectical contrasts can no longer be made. Secondly, the process of emerging distinctiveness in Israel was much later than previously admitted in our scholarship. Often textbooks contrasted Israelite and Canaanite religion and ethics in conjunction with a description of the Iron Age I (1200–1050 BCE) settlement process. Now we must admit that the emergence of a more distinct and conscious self-identity appears only in the exile and beyond. The more distinct identity arises with the creation of the bulk of the biblical literature by post-exilic Judaism. We cannot contrast Israelite and Canaanite thought because in the pre-exilic period

---

18. P. Machinist, 'The Question of Distinctiveness in Ancient Israel', *A Highway from Egypt to Assyria: Studies in Ancient Near Eastern History and Historiography Presented to Hayim Tadmor* (eds. I. Eph'al and M. Cogan; Jerusalem: Magnes, 1990), pp. 420-42.

they are really the same culture. Israelite thought emerged out of the Canaanite milieu and distinguished itself only after a lengthy evolutionary process. We may use the old cyclic and linear paradigms, but they must be tempered severely.

Finally, another expression of value to describe Israelite and Jewish monotheism is the concept of a 'religion from below'. Historians have suggested often that monotheism breeds intolerance and tyranny, that it is used by aspiring world emperors, such as the Persian Zoroastrian Darius or the Roman Christian Constantine, to impose monolithic world order. Following the lead of several authors, most notably Denis Baly and Gerd Theissen,[19] I believe we may speak of 'monotheism from above' and 'monotheism from below'. The former may endorse tyranny, monolithic order and patriarchal oppression, but the latter does not. The Jewish monotheistic breakthrough, as well as the later Jesus movement, represents 'monotheism from below', the religion of the oppressed, not the oppressor. Modern Christianity must decide which it will be in our modern world, and if it chooses the latter, then the true monotheistic revolution will continue.

In conclusion, this work will attempt to build upon the writings and intellectual contributions of many scholars in the field. The copious footnotes will attempt to render credit and respect in some way to the many authors whose ideas have inspired exposition, as well as provide readers resources for further study and reflection. Hopefully, I have drawn ideas together in an edifying synthesis for the readers which may excite further discussion on the nature of emerging monotheism in ancient Israel.

---

19. D. Baly, 'The Geography of Monotheism', *Translating and Understanding the Old Testament: Essays in Honor of Herbert Gordon May* (eds. H.T. Frank and W. Reed; Nashville: Abingdon Press, 1970), pp. 253-78; G. Theissen, *Biblical Faith: An Evolutionary Approach* (Philadelphia: Fortress Press, 1985), pp. 45-81.

Chapter 1

NEW UNDERSTANDINGS
OF THE ISRAELITE SETTLEMENT PROCESS[*]

Scholarly evaluation of the conquest or settlement process of ancient Israel in the Iron Age I period (1200–1050 BCE) in the past century has absorbed the energies of many biblical archaeologists and historians, and a few theologians also. Understanding the dynamics of this process is important due to the significant impact it had upon the shaping of the Israelite ethos. Our understanding of this process also affects dramatically how many authors explain the beliefs of Israel in the form of biblical theology. Models which stress Israelite invasion or revolution tend to suggest that biblical thought was very distinctive and morally superior to the cultures surrounding Israel in that age. The revolutionary model, in particular, has inspired theologies of liberation among contemporary biblical theologians. Models which stress peaceful infiltration or peaceful settlement from within the land emphasize the evolutionary nature of Israel's cultural and religious development. These models might undergird theologies which speak of process.

Introductions used in undergraduate and seminary Hebrew Bible or Old Testament courses readily acknowledge that different theories have been proposed over the years to describe the Israelite settlement process.[1] For years the German theory of peaceful infiltration was placed in opposition to the American model of violent conquest, and then beginning in

---

[*] The substance of this chapter is a revised, updated and shortened version of two articles, summarizing the various theories of the settlement process, which I published in *BTB* 21 (1991), pp. 56-66, 109-17.

1. K. Kuntz, *The People of Ancient Israel* (New York: Harper & Row, 1974), pp. 133-36; W.L. Humphreys, *Crisis and Story: Introduction to the Old Testament* (Palo Alto: Mayfield, 1979), pp. 28-30; L. Boadt, *Reading the Old Testament: An Introduction* (Mahwah, NJ: Paulist Press, 1984), pp. 201-205; N. Gottwald, *The Hebrew Bible: A Socio-Literary Introduction* (Philadelphia: Fortress Press, 1985), pp. 261-76; and Anderson, *Old Testament*, pp. 137-40.

the 1960s a model of social revolution captured the imagination of scholars and students and inspired much theologizing and contemporary imperatives for social reform. In the past fifteen years all three models have waned before the new perception that Israel emerged by a slow internal process. We appear to be in the middle of a 'paradigm shift' as much of the archaeological data and biblical texts is being considered in a new fashion. The new understanding of how Israel emerged as a social entity in the highlands of Palestine also has great significance for the understanding of the emergence of Israelite religion. Therefore, in a volume which evaluates the theological implications of emergent monotheism, we must review the understandings of how Israel initially emerged as a people.

I

A review of the three traditional theories of Israelite settlement (infiltration, violent conquest and internal revolution) will provide a springboard for more clearly understanding the new theories of internal, peaceful origin. Other authors have provided analyses in far greater detail, so I shall give only a brief overview here.[2]

The image of a gradual, peaceful infiltration of Palestine by semi-nomadic Israelites moving from the Transjordan steppe into the Cisjordan highlands was first proposed in detail by Albrecht Alt in the 1920s and 1930s. His views were incorporated in the writings of Martin Noth in the 1940s and 1950s, and they were defended again by Manfred Weippert in the 1970s.[3] More recent advocates include historians, such as Siegfried

2.	M. Weippert, *The Settlement of the Israelite Tribes in Palestine* (trans. J. Martin; SBT NS 21; London: SCM Press, 1971), pp. 5-62; G. Ramsey, *The Quest for the Historical Israel* (Atlanta: John Knox, 1981), pp. 65-98; Gottwald, *Hebrew Bible*, pp. 261-76; W. Stiebing, *Out of the Desert? Archaeology and the Conquest Narratives* (Buffalo: Prometheus, 1989), pp. 149-65.

3.	A. Alt, *Kleine Schriften zur Geschichte des Volkes Israels* (3 vols.; Munich: Beck, 1953), I, pp. 126-92; *idem*, 'The Settlement of the Israelites in Palestine', *Essays in Old Testament History and Religion* (trans. R.A. Wilson; Garden City, NY: Doubleday, 1966), pp. 173-221; M. Noth, 'Grundsätzliches zur geschichtlichen Deutung archäologischer Befunde auf dem Boden Palästinas', *PJ*, 37 (1938), pp. 7-22; *idem*, *The History of Israel* (trans. P. Ackroyd; New York: Harper & Brothers, 1960), pp. 53-84; Weippert, *Settlement*; *idem*, 'The Israelite "Conquest" and the Evidence from the Transjordan', *Symposia Celebrating the Seventy-Fifth Anniversary of the Founding of the American Schools of Oriental Research (1900–1975)* (ed. F. Cross; Cambridge: American Scholars of Oriental Research, 1979), pp.15-34.

Herrmann and Alberto Soggin, and also some Israeli archaeologists, including Benjamin Mazar, the later views of Yohanan Aharoni, Aharon Kempinski and Adam Zertal.[4] This model proposed a two stage process. Pastoralist or semi-nomadic people with their herds moved into the land as a result of their normal migratory movement or transhumance and gradually they settled in the Palestinian highlands to engage in some agriculture. In the second stage these pastoralists increased in numbers and expanded their territory into the lowlands where they came into armed conflict with Canaanite cities, such as Hazor and Luz/Bethel, which they destroyed. This conflict inspired the romantic folk tales in Joshua and Judges, most of which are fictional, containing aetiologies or stories designed to explain place names, customs, and the existence of ruins like the city of Ai (which had lain in shambles for a thousand years before the Israelites arrived). Only gradually did a sense of tribal identity emerge, and final unity came only with David.

In critical response American and Israeli archaeologists and historians in the 1940s and the 1950s challenged the German theories by maintaining that the conquest was a unified, systematic, military invasion by Joshua that may have been more extensive than the biblical book of Joshua indicates. Destruction at Canaanite sites at Debir, Lachish, Luz/Bethel and Hazor were attributed to the late thirteenth century BCE, and the subsequent habitation appeared to be of Iron Age Israelites, which then implied an Israelite conquest even though no biblical account testified to the direct destruction of these cities by Joshua. The Germans were criticized for reliance upon a form-critical study of the biblical texts which denied historicity to the accounts, and the Americans praised archaeological findings as a way to reconstruct the history of Israel. Leading spokespersons included William Foxwell Albright, George Ernest

---

4.   A. Soggin, *Joshua* (trans. R.A. Wilson; OTL; Philadelphia: Westminster Press, 1972), pp. 4, 20, 75, 137, 229; S. Herrmann, *A History of Israel in Old Testament Times* (trans. J. Bowden; Philadelphia: Fortress Press, 1975), pp. 86-111; *idem*, 'Basic Factors of Israelite Settlement in Canaan', *Biblical Archaeology Today* (ed. J. Amitai; Jerusalem: Israel Exploration Society, 1985), pp. 43-75; Y. Aharoni, 'Nothing Early and Nothing Late: Re-Writing Israel's Conquest', *BA* 39 (1976), pp. 55-76, which represents his later views; A. Kempinski, 'Israelite Conquest or Settlement? New Light from Tell Masos,' *BARev* 2.3 (1976), pp. 25-30; and B. Mazar, 'The Early Israelite Settlement in the Hill Country', *The Early Biblical Period: Historical Studies* (Jerusalem: Israel Exploration Society, 1986), pp. 35-48; A. Zertal, 'Israel Enters Canaan: Following the Pottery Trail', *BARev* 17.5 (1991), pp. 28-49, 75.

Wright, Yehezkel Kaufmann, Nelson Glueck, John Bright, Paul Lapp, Yigael Yadin, Yohanan Aharoni (in his early writings) and Abraham Malamat.[5]

Out of this school there arose a third viewpoint in the 1960s and 1970s best articulated by George Mendenhall and Norman Gottwald, which has come to be known as the internal revolution hypothesis, and it has been advocated and developed by a number of significant authors.[6]

5. W.F. Albright, 'Archaeology and the Date of the Hebrew Conquest of Palestine', *BASOR* 58 (1935), pp. 10-18; *idem*, 'Further Light on the History of Israel from Lachish and Megiddo', *BASOR* 68 (1937), pp. 22-26; *idem*, 'The Israelite Conquest of Canaan in the Light of Archaeology', *BASOR* 74 (1939), pp. 11-23; *idem*, *The Archaeology of Palestine* (Baltimore: Penguin, 3rd edn, 1960), pp. 108-109; *idem*, *The Biblical Period from Abraham to Ezra* (New York: Harper & Row, 1963), pp. 24-34; G.E. Wright, 'The Literary and Historical Problem of Joshua 10 and Judges 1', *JNES* 5 (1946), pp. 105-14; *idem*, *Biblical Archaeology* (Philadelphia: Westminster Press, 2nd edn, 1962), pp. 69-85; *idem*, 'Introduction', in *Joshua* by R. Boling (Garden City: Doubleday, 1982), pp. 72-88; P. Lapp, 'The Conquest of Palestine in the Light of Archaeology', *CTM* 38 (1967), pp. 283-300; J. Kelso, *The Excavation of Bethel (1934–1960)* (Cambridge, MA: American Schools of Orinetal Research, 1968), pp. 32, 47-48; Y. Kaufman, *The Religion of Israel: From its Beginnings to the Babylonian Exile* (trans. and abr. M. Greenberg; New York: Schocken Books, 1972), pp. 245-61; J. Bright, *A History of Israel* (Philadelphia: Westminster Press, 2nd edn, 1972), pp. 127-30, which represents his early views; Y. Aharoni, *The Land of the Bible: A Historical Geography* (Philadelphia: Westminster Press, rev. edn, 1979), pp. 200-229, which represents his earlier views; Y. Yadin, 'The Transition from a Semi-Nomadic to a Sedentary Society in the Twelfth Century BCE', *Symposia* (ed. Cross), pp. 57-68; *idem*, 'Is the Biblical Conquest of Canaan Historically Reliable?', *BARev* 8.2 (1982), pp. 16-23; A. Malamat, 'Israelite Conduct of War in the Conquest of Canaan', *Symposia* (ed. Cross), pp. 35-55; *idem*, 'How Inferior Israelite Forces Conquered Fortified Canaanite Cities', *BARev* 8.2 (1982), pp. 25-35.

6. G. Mendenhall, 'The Hebrew Conquest of Palestine', *BA* 25 (1962), pp. 66-87; *idem*, *The Tenth Generation: The Origins of the Biblical Tradition* (Baltimore: The Johns Hopkins University Press, 1973); *idem*, '"Change and Decay in All Around I See": Conquest, Covenant and the Tenth Generation', *BA* 39 (1976), pp. 52-157; *idem*, 'Between Theology and Archaeology', *JSOT* 7 (1978), pp. 28-34; J. McKenzie, *The World of the Judges* (Englewood Cliffs: Prentice–Hall, 1966), pp. 76-120; A. Glock, 'Early Israel as the Kingdom of Yahweh: The Influence of Archaeological Evidence on the Reconstruction of Religion in Early Israel', *CTM* 41 (1970), pp. 558-605; N. Gottwald, 'Were the Early Israelites Pastoral Nomads?', *Rhetorical Criticism: Essays in Honor of James Muilenburg* (eds. J. Jackson and M. Kessler; PTMS, 1; Pittsburg: Pickwick Press, 1974), pp. 223-55; *idem*, 'Domain Assumptions and Societal Models in the Study of Pre-Monarchic Israel', *Congress*

Poor Canaanites oppressed by Egyptian taxation and an oppressive city state system rose in revolt, burned their cities, and fled to the highlands to create an egalitarian state by the process of retribalization. Mendenhall believed that a core of Yahweh worshippers from Egypt crystalized the revolt, so that parasocials (bandits or *'apriu*) already in the highlands and peasants from the lowland cities covenanted together in the highlands to serve the new god, Yahweh. The new egalitarian society of the highlands finally defeated the Canaanites under David, but tragically the absolute monarchy of Solomon betrayed the egalitarian ethos for a new statism.[7] Gottwald de-emphasized the significance of any outside Yahwistic group; rather, he viewed the revolt in the Canaanite cities according to social-scientific categories as an inevitable process of peasant revolution.[8] His use of Marxist categories distanced him from Mendenhall's emphasis upon covenantal religion.[9] Gottwald believed that technology alone

---

Volume (Edinburgh, 1974) (VTSup, 28; Leiden: Brill, 1975), pp. 89-100, 'Israel, Social and Economic Development', *IDBSup*, pp. 465-68; *idem*, 'Nomadism', *IDBSup*, pp. 629-31; *idem*, 'The Hypothesis of the Revolutionary Origins of Ancient Israel: A Response to A.J. Hauser and T. L. Thompson', *JSOT* 7 (1978), pp. 37-52; *idem*, 'Were the Early Israelites Pastoral Nomads?', *BARev* 4.2 (1978), pp. 2-7; *idem*, *The Tribes of Yahweh: A Sociology of the Religion of Liberated Israel 1250–1050 BCE* (Maryknoll: Orbis Books, 1979); *idem*, 'Two Models for the Origin of Ancient Israel: Social Revolution or Frontier Development', *The Quest for the Kingdom of God: Studies in Honor of George E. Mendenhall* (eds. H. Huffmon, F.A. Spina, and A. Green; Winona Lake: Eisenbrauns, 1983), pp. 5-24; *idem*, 'The Israelite Settlement as a Social Revolutionary Movement', *Biblical Archaeology Today* (ed. Amitai), pp. 34-46; *idem*, *Hebrew Bible*, pp. 272-76; *idem*, 'Sociology', *ABD*, VI, pp. 83-84; R. Boling, *Judges* (AB, 6A; Garden City, NY: Doubleday, 1975), pp. 12-18, 64, *et passim*; J. Dus, 'Moses or Joshua? On the Problem of the Founder of the Israelite Religion', *Radical Religion* 2 (1975), pp. 26-41; J. Bright, *A History of Israel* (Philadelphia: Westminster Press, 3rd edn, 1981), pp. 129-43, which represents his later views; M. Chaney, 'Ancient Palestinian Peasant Movements and the Formation of Premonarchic Israel', *Palestine in Transition* (eds. D. Freedman and D. Graf; Social World of Biblical Antiquity, 2; Sheffield: Almond Press, 1983), pp. 39-90; J. Halligan, 'The Role of the Peasant in the Amarna Period', *Palestine in Transition* (eds. Freedman and Graf), pp. 15-24.

7.   Mendenhall, *Tenth Generation*.

8.   Gottwald, *Tribes of Yahweh*, pp. 210-19, 389-587.

9.   Mendenhall, 'Ancient Israel's Hyphenated History', *Palestine in Transition* (eds. Freedman and Graf), pp. 91-103; and B. Anderson, 'Mendenhall Disavows Paternity: Says He Didn't Father Gottwald's Marxist Theory', *BARev* 2.2 (1986), pp. 46-49.

could not explain emergent Israel, ideology must have been a force. His characteristic jargon has captured the attention of his readers for years. Early on he spoke of a 'peasant revolt' which created an 'egalitarian society'; but now he describes Israel as an 'agrarian social revolution' which led to a 'commutarian mode of production' which produces a 'socio-economic leveling effect' vis-à-vis the 'tributary mode of production'.[10] He currently chides contemporary critics of his theory for subordinating the testimony of individual texts to their own historical and archaeological methods and opting for a peaceful evolutionary model as 'an easy social accommodation to conformist satisfaction with the way the world is'.[11] This third model still has compelling rhetoric to attract adherents.

All three theories have been criticized extensively, and this, in part, led scholars to search for a new paradigm. A quick synopsis of the critiques will prepare for an explanation of the new models.

The peaceful infiltration model has been criticized in recent times with the revival of this theory by contemporary advocates. First, the chief weakness of the theory was the inability to demonstrate that a large number of Israelites originated outside the land of Palestine.[12] Secondly, Alt and his followers have been faulted for an inadequate understanding of nomadism, especially in incorrectly assuming that nomadism as a lifestyle naturally precedes a settled life-style, or that nomads naturally would seek land for settlement, or that tribal structures could evolve into state structures, or that overpopulation in the Transjordan would lead to settlement in the Cisjordan (the wilderness may actually hold a large population).[13] Thirdly, the portrayal of the Israelites by Alt and others

10.   N. Gottwald, 'Responses', *The Rise of Ancient Israel* (ed. H. Shanks; Washington: Biblical Archaeology Society, 1992), pp. 70-75; *idem*, 'Sociology', pp. 83-84, and 'Recent Studies of the Social World of Premonarchic Israel', *Currents in Research: Biblical Studies* 1 (1993), pp. 163-89.

11.   Gottwald, 'Recent Studies', pp. 169-85.

12.   C.H.J. de Geus, *The Tribes of Israel: An Investigation into Some of the Presuppositions of Martin Noth's Amphictyony Hypothesis* (Amsterdam: Van Gorcum, 1976), pp. 120-92; N.P. Lemche, *Early Israel: Anthropological and Historical Studies on the Israelite Society Before the Monarchy* (VTSup, 37; Leiden: Brill, 1985), pp. 66-76; I. Finkelstein, *The Archaeology of the Israelite Settlement* (Jerusalem: Israel Exploration Society, 1988), p. 304; and Stiebing, *Desert*, pp. 155-56.

13.   De Geus, *Tribes*, pp. 130-33; Chaney, 'Peasant Movements', pp. 39-90; Lemche, *Early Israel*, pp. 139-40 *et passim*; G. London: 'A Comparison of Two Contemporaneous Lifestyles of the Late Second Millennium BC', *BASOR* 273

ignored the testimony of the biblical text in Exodus and Numbers that the Israelites saw the wilderness or steppe land as an alien and terrifying environment.[14] Fourthly, scholars now sense that Israelite culture has much more in common with Late Bronze Age Palestine (1550–1200 BCE) than previously thought, which makes us less likely to view Israelites as outsiders.[15]

The violent conquest model has received the sternest critique of all three models.[16] First, proponents were chided for their belief that archaeology could be used so readily to verify biblical texts, when material data from the ground is so often ambiguous, capable of different interpretations.[17] Secondly, the destroyed cities in Palestine more likely were destroyed by any one of the many Egyptian military campaigns in this era or the coastal migration of the war-like sea peoples. If the Israelites destroyed these major Canaanite centers, why did they not hold the valley regions in which those particular cities were located?[18] Thirdly, there were chronological problems. Later research discerned that the destroyed cities fell at different times. Cities with which Israelites had contact were not all inhabited at this time in the early Iron Age: Kadesh-Barnea, Arad, Hormah, Heshbon, Dibon, Jericho, Ai, Gibeon and Hebron were uninhabited. Jericho and Ai, the two cities clearly described as falling to Joshua, show no signs of conquest in this era. Advocates of violent conquest somewhat cavalierly lumped together data in the period of 1220 to 1200 BCE to support their theory.[19] Fourthly, the continuity

(1989), p. 39; Stiebing, *Desert*, p. 155-56; and N.A. Silberman, 'Who Were the Israelites?', *Archaeology* 45.2 (1992), pp. 20-27.

14.   Stiebing, *Desert*, pp. 155-56; Silberman, 'Israelites', p. 24.

15.   De Geus, *Tribes*, pp. 156-71; V. Fritz, 'The Israelite "Conquest" in Light of Recent Excavations at Khirbet el-Mishâsh', *BASOR* 241 (1981), pp. 61-73; and G. Ahlström, *Who Were the Israelites?* (Winona Lake, IN: Eisenbrauns, 1986).

16.   Ramsey, *Quest*, pp. 69-73, provides an excellent critique.

17.   Noth, *History of Israel*, pp. 262-82; J. Pritchard, 'Culture and History', *The Bible and Modern Scholarship* (ed. J. Hyatt; Nashville: Abingdon Press, 1965), pp. 313-24; R. de Vaux, 'On the Right and Wrong Uses of Archaeology', *Near Eastern Archaeology in the Twentieth Century: Essays in Honor of Nelson Glueck* (ed. J. Sanders; Garden City, NY: Doubleday, 1970), pp. 64-80; Weippert, *Settlement*, pp. 46-55; Gottwald, *Tribes of Yahweh*, pp. 192-203; London, 'Comparison', pp. 38-39.

18.   Weippert, *Settlement*, pp. 130-32; Ramsey, *Quest*, pp. 69-72; Gottwald, *Hebrew Bible*, pp. 266-67; I. Finkelstein, *Archaeology*, pp. 295-302; Stiebing, *Desert*, p. 153; Silberman, 'Israelites', p. 24.

19.   Ramsey, *Quest*, pp. 64-71; Gottwald, *Hebrew Bible*, pp. 268-69;

of material culture between Canaanites and Israelites speaks against the idea of external origin.[20] Contemporary advocates who wish to salvage the theory, like Amihai Mazar, must suggest that violent and sporadic conflict occurred over many years and was caused by diverse groups both from outside the land and within the land (such as the *'apiru*), who eventually merged and telescoped the memory of their activities together in the book of Joshua.[21]

The social revolution model has received the greatest attention from contemporary critics.[22] First, opponents point out the real lack of concrete evidence for a peasant revolt in ancient Israel, or anywhere in the ancient world.[23] Canaanite cities were not large enough to be 'city states' or have tensions between rich classes and oppressed masses, and the so-called *'apiru* outlaws often had more political power than the city kings.[24] Advocates of social revolution are accused of imposing modern idiosyncratic ideas upon the Israelites; the Israelites appear romantically as revolutionary Americans (Mendenhall) or Marxist inspired peasants (Gottwald).[25] Secondly, the anthropological and sociological models used

I. Finkelstein, *Archaeology*, pp. 295-302; London, 'Comparison', pp. 38-39; Stiebing, *Desert*, p. 152; Silberman, 'Israelites', p. 24.

20. G. Ahlström, 'Giloh: A Judahite or Canaanite Settlement?', *IEJ* 34 (1984), pp. 170-72; *idem*, 'The Early Iron Age Settlers at Khirbet el-Msas (Tel Masos)', *ZDPV* 100 (1984), pp. 35-53; *idem, Israelites*, pp. 1-118; Stiebing, *Desert*, pp. 150-53.

21. A. Mazar, *Archaeology of the Land of the Bible 10,000–586 BCE* (Garden City, NY: Doubleday, 1990), pp. 258-301; *idem*, 'The Iron Age I', *The Archaeology of Ancient Israel* (ed. A. Ben-Tor; trans. R. Greenberg; New Haven: Yale University Press, 1992), pp. 258-301.

22. Ramsey, *Quest*, pp. 93-98, provides an excellent summary of the debate.

23. De Geus, *Tribes*, pp. 184-86; A. Hauser, 'Israel's Conquest of Palestine: Peasants' Rebellion?', *JSOT* 7 (1978), pp. 2-19; Ramsey, *Quest*, pp. 93-94; Fritz, 'Recent Excavations', pp. 70-71; R. Coote and K. Whitelam, *The Emergence of Early Israel in Historical Perspective* (Social World of Biblical Antiquity, 5; Sheffield: Almond Press, 1987), pp. 49-80; Stiebing, *Desert*, pp. 158-59; Silberman, 'Israelites', p. 29.

24. B. Halpern, *The Emergence of Israel in Canaan* (SBLMS, 29; Chico, CA: Scholars Press, 1983), p. 63; D. Redford, *Egypt, Canaan, and Israel in Ancient Times* (Princeton, NJ: Princeton University Press, 1992), pp. 267-69; Thomas Thompson, *Early History of the Israelite People* (Studies in the History of the Ancient Near East, 4; Leiden: Brill, 1992), pp. 51-62; G. Ahlström, *A History of Ancient Palestine* (Minneapolis: Fortress Press, 1993), p. 346.

25. A. Hauser, 'The Revolutionary Origins of Ancient Israel: A Response to

to undergird this theory are weak, because they rely upon the doctrinaire and outdated resources of the 'American School of Cultural Evolution' (Elman Service, Morton Fried and Marshall Sahlins), they reflect little knowledge of nomads and tribal structures, and they misconstrue the relationships between pastoral and sedentary modes of existence.[26] Thirdly, advocates of this model are accused of being insufficiently familiar with Israelite geography, the current scholarly understandings of the *'apiru* phenomenon, and the existence of egalitarian village life found in other regions of Syria and Canaan in the ancient world.[27] Fourthly, the theory relies on paradigms in biblical studies taken from a former generation of scholarship, including the notion of an early covenant and an amphictyonic league.[28]

Out of the discussions a new model is beginning to emerge, which has been inspired, above all, by recent archaeological field research. There are several variations in this new theory, but they share in common the image of an Israelite community which arose peacefully and internally in the highlands of Palestine. William Stiebing classifies these newer theories into two categories: the frontier society model of Joseph Callaway; and the symbiosis or internal nomadic model of Volkmar Fritz and Israel Finkelstein.[29] I would propose the categories of peaceful withdrawal, internal nomadism, peaceful transition or transformation, and peaceful amalgamation or synthesis, which is more developed than my original three-fold distinction outlined in the journal articles several years ago.

Gottwald (JSOT 7 [1978] 37-52)', *JSOT* 8 (1978), pp. 46-49; Ramsey, *Quest*, pp. 97-98; Lemche, *Early Israel*, pp. 35-65, 410; Coote and Whitelam, *Early Israel*, pp. 173-77.

26. Weippert, *Settlement*, pp. 102-126; Lemche, *Early Israel*, pp. 1-34, 84-290; I. Finkelstein, *Archaeology*, pp. 306-314; London, 'Comparison', p. 39; Stiebing, *Desert*, pp. 158-59.

27. Weippert, *Settlement*, pp. 63-102; Hauser, 'Israel's Conquest', pp. 2-19; Ramsey, *Quest*, p. 95; L. Stager, 'Respondents', *Biblical Archaeology Today* (ed. Amitai), p. 85; I. Finkelstein, *Archaeology*, pp. 306-314; London, 'Comparison', p. 39.

28. Ramsey, *Quest*, p. 95; Lemche, *Early Israel*, pp. 297, 411-35; *idem, Ancient Israel: A New History of Israelite Society* (The Biblical Seminar, 5; Sheffield: JSOT Press, 1988), pp. 106-109.

29. Stiebing, *Desert*, pp. 159-65.

II

In the past generation archaeological discoveries have encouraged scholars to generate new ways of understanding the settlement process. The excavation of highland villages (Ai, Khirbet Raddana, Shiloh, Tel Qiri, Bet Gala, Izbet Sarta, Tel Qasileh, Tel Isdar, Dan, Arad, Tel Masos, Beer-Sheba, Har Adir, Horvat Harashim, Tel Beit Mirsim, Sasa, Giloh, Horvat 'Avot, Tel en-Nasbeh, Beth-Zur and Tel el-Fûl) impressed archaeologists with the continuity between lowland urban Canaanite and highland village Israelite culture, especially in regard to pottery, farming techniques, tools and building construction.[30] The peaceful nature of the villages became evident, often they were located far from potential enemies and without any wall defense. Some were too far west to have been settled by people from outside the land, and the rapid population growth implied that people moved up from the lowlands into the highlands.[31] Pottery and particularly the collar-rimmed jar, once described as specifically Israelite, were seen to be derived from Late Bronze Age Canaanite prototypes.[32] Farming techniques were well developed from the early stages of highland settlement, implying experience learned from lowland farming, especially the practices of terrace building to hold run-off water and the construction of lime-coated cisterns.[33] Construction techniques reflected Canaanite origins, including the manufacture of certain bronze

---

30.   A. Mazar, 'The Israelite Settlement in Canaan in the Light of Archaeological Excavations', *Biblical Archaeology Today* (ed. Amitai), p. 61; V. Fritz, 'Conquest or Settlement? The Early Iron Age in Palestine', *BA* 50 (1987), pp. 92-96; R. Greenberg, 'New Light on the Early Iron Age at Tel Beit Mirsim', *BASOR* 265 (1987), pp. 55-80, suggests that some villages were still totally Canaanite in their culture well into the Iron Age; I. Finkelstein, *Archaeology*, pp. 27-234, provides the best overview of the sites.

31.   Stager, 'The Archaeology of the Family', *BASOR* 260 (1985), p. 3; H. Shanks, 'Defining the Problems: Where We Are in the Debate', *Rise of Ancient Israel*, pp. 9, 13.

32.   Weippert, *Settlement*, p. 134; Ahlström, 'Giloh', pp. 170-72; *idem*, 'Khirbet el-Msas', pp. 35-53; Mazar, 'Israelite Settlement', pp. 68-69; London, 'Comparison', pp. 42-50.

33.   J. Callaway, 'Village Subsistence at Ai and Raddana in Iron Age I', *The Answers Lie Below: Essays in Honor of Lawrence Edmund Toombs* (ed. H. Thompson; Lanham: University Press of America, 1984), p. 64; *idem*, 'Respondents', *Biblical Archaeology Today* (ed. Amitai), p. 75; A. Mazar, 'Israelite Settlement', p. 68; London, 'Comparison', pp. 42-50.

tools and building construction, especially the casemate wall, the four-room house and roof supports.[34] The rising consensus among archaeologists is that the distinction between Canaanite and Israelite cannot be drawn in the early period of settlement, for these are the same people, and any significant distinction emerges only in a later era.

Gradually archaeologists began to speak of Israelite settlement as an internal process which was peaceful and gradual. This was like Alt's theory, only it rejected the idea of large numbers of outside pastoralists entering the land. The theory suggests that in some way Canaanites gradually evolved into Israelites as social and political conditions changed at the beginning of the Iron Age. Proponents often point to archaeological evidence which implies a decline in the Late Bronze Age culture and the deterioration of city life caused by Egyptian campaigns, excessive taxation, and perhaps even climate change. However, the actual dynamics of this peaceful change are described differently by various archaeologists and historians. Their theories may be classified into four categories in my opinion, and consideration of these diverse views may be useful for our study.

Peaceful Withdrawal

Joseph Callaway is credited with providing the first observations to undergird this model with his excavations at Ai and Raddana, where he observes that the early Iron Age settlers at these presumably Israelite sites had extensive knowledge of dry farming and other technological skills of the Canaanites, including the use of construction tools (chisels, mattocks and axes), the digging of cisterns, land terracing and house construction abilities (such as the pier technique of roof support). This implies a cultural continuity with the Canaanites in the lowlands to the west and suggests that people moved to Ai and Raddana to avoid conflict in the valleys and chose these sites because they were less crowded than other parts of the highlands. This may be reflected in Josh. 17.16, which speaks of crowded settlements in the hill country while hostile Canaanites dwelt in the valleys. The increase from 23 to 114 villages in the highlands during Iron Age I implies a massive but peaceful withdrawal for Callaway, and he suggests this movement occurred along the entire

34. Callaway, 'Village Subsistence', p. 64; *idem*, 'Respondents', p. 75; A. Mazar, 'Israelite Settlement', pp. 66-68; Stager, 'Family', p. 17; Y. Shiloh, 'The Casemate Wall, the Four Room House, and Early Planning in the Israelite City', *BASOR* 268 (1987), pp. 3-16; London, 'Comparison', pp. 42-50.

Syro-Canaanite coastline.[35] His interpretations are supported by other archaeologists who observe a population decline in Canaanite cities which may have led to the settlement of the sparsely inhabited highlands.[36] The noted sociologist Gerhard Lenski alludes to such a model in his critique of Gottwald's revolution hypothesis, and Lenski describes the notion of peaceful withdrawal into the highlands under the label of 'frontier society' development, a model which emphasizes that peasants under severe economic and social pressure would withdraw to an undeveloped highland frontier to find a more effective mode of subsistence.[37]

David Hopkins provides us with an extensive evaluation of highland Israelite agriculture in Iron Age I (1200–1050 BCE), and the wealth of information he presents must be appropriated by every model of Israelite settlement.[38] Although his evaluations do not directly support a peaceful withdrawal theory, they may be used for that purpose; but more precisely they indicate the peaceful and internal origin of highland Israelites. Hopkins observes that social development occurred along with agricultural intensification of the land. As people cooperated on the clan and familial level, this permitted optimal use of labor, which in turn spread the risk of agricultural disaster over more people and lessened its likelihood. Diversified crops and animal husbandry in shared relationships between various groups and regions of highland Palestine also softened

35. Callaway, 'Village Subsistence', pp. 51-66; *idem*, 'Respondents', pp. 72-78; *idem*, 'A New Perspective on the Hill Country Settlement of Canaan in Iron Age I', *Palestine in the Bronze and Iron Ages: Papers in Honour of Olga Tufnell* (ed. J.N. Tubb; London: Institute of Archaeology, 1985), pp. 31-49.

36. R. Gonen, 'Urban Canaan in the Late Bronze Age', *BASOR* 253 (1984), pp. 61-73; *idem*, 'The Late Bronze Age', *The Archaeology of Ancient Israel* (ed. A. Ben-Tor; trans. R. Greenberg; New Haven: Yale University Press, 1992), pp. 216-17; Stager, 'Family', p. 1; J. Strange, 'The Transition from the Bronze Age to the Iron Age in the Eastern Mediterranean and the Emergence of the Israelite State', *SJOT* 1 (1987), pp. 1-19; Z. Gal, 'The Late Bronze Age in Galilee: A Reassessment', *BASOR* 272 (1988), pp. 70-84.

37. Lenski and Lenski, *Human Societies*, p. 229; G. Lenski, 'Review of N.K. Gottwald, The Tribes of Yahweh', *RelSRev* 6 (1980), pp. 275-78.

38. D. Hopkins, *The Highlands of Canaan* (Social World of Biblical Antiquity, 3; Sheffield: Almond Press, 1985); *idem*, 'Life on the Land: The Subsistence Struggle of Early Israel', *BA* 50 (1987), pp. 178-91. Cf. O. Borowski, *Agriculture in Iron Age Israel: The Evidence from Archaeology and the Bible* (Winona Lake, IN: Eisenbrauns, 1987), who very nicely describes Israelite agricultural techniques until the exile, but unlike Hopkins he does not combine his observations with sensitive critical textual analysis.

the impact of agricultural setbacks. The role of iron, terracing and cisterns was less significant in developing highland agriculture than previous scholars assumed; rather, the cooperation of people in a kinship system more directly led to successful settlement. Community and later state formation arose out of clan cooperation, which permitted population and agricultural growth. Ultimately, no one factor really promoted village development and state formation, but a complex inter-relationship of social and technological factors created the process of development.

Hopkins offers some significant detailed insights into this process. The wide diversity of climate, soils, rainfall and terrain in Palestine encourages diversity of agricultural and pastoral activity, which in turn lowers the 'risk of subsistence failure'. Hence, competition between farmers and pastoralists did not really exist, but both economic pursuits were undertaken creatively by the highlanders.[39] Such diversification spread work over the seasonal calender, thus optimizing the use of labor. Collective labor for harvesting was promoted by the development of clan and kinship structures. Therefore, the rise of tribal structures in the highlands assisted in agricultural intensification. Different clan and tribal units of Israel may have corresponded to different crop growing regions.[40] The agricultural techniques characteristic of Israelite villages reflect their attempt to optimize labor and minimalize the risk of subsistence failure. Terracing prevented water run-off, and because their construction required much labor, they would have been built only after agricultural intensification of the land was fairly advanced (tenth to eighth century BCE). The typical Israelite collar-rimmed jar and storage buildings reflected their need to store produce for periods of shortage—a common phenomenon in the highlands. Fallow year practices described in Exod. 23.10-11 must have been extensive and more complex than implied in the text, since soil conservation and fertility were major goals.[41] Finally, many of these sites (Giloh, Tel Isdar, Izbet Sarta, etc.) are in marginal or remote areas on high ground with natural defenses, and though they often are distant from trade routes, they are located near arable ground. They betray an attempt to leave the valleys behind. Furthermore, the quick growth of these villages indicates a significant population movement. Thus, people were leaving the Bronze Age cities and moving to land which was 'less than optimal', and this caused the need for greater social

39.   Hopkins, *Highlands*, pp. 74, 241-51.
40.   Hopkins, *Highlands*, pp. 83, 213-61.
41.   Hopkins, *Highlands*, pp. 169, 173-85, 191-210, 268-69.

cooperation.[42] Hopkins concludes that the highland villages used the diversity of their environment to produce a wide range of agricultural produce to protect themselves against the variability of the environment, and this demanded great cooperation between families, clans and villages. This impelled them into larger circles of social relationships until the process of state formation began, and the newly emergent state with its system of taxation changed village based subsistence strategies.[43]

Scholars who study the dynamics of state formation and the rise of the monarchy in Israel often characterize the settlement process as one of peaceful withdrawal, too. Frank Frick describes Israelite settlements emerging after an urban collapse of Canaanite cities. Their society then evolved through the socio-political stages of 'segmentary society' (era of the judges) to a 'chieftain society' (Saul) to a 'state' (David). Inspired by Colin Renfrew's model of state formation after social catastrophe, Frick suspects the model of peaceful withdrawal may best describe the appearance of highland Israel with its radical egalitarian ethos.[44] James Flanagan similarly observes that in pre-Davidic Israel people moved from sedentary life in the valleys to a more decentralized existence in the highlands and the Transjordan where they farmed and cared for herds. In effect, the peaceful withdrawal of people moved an agrarian economy eastward.[45]

Gösta Ahlström articulates the model of peaceful withdrawal most clearly in a number of his works, some of which are very extensive. He describes the continuity of the material culture, especially pottery and technology, between the Canaanites and Israelites, and he finds further evidence for this continuity in his assessment of the biblical text.[46] In his scenario Canaanites withdrew from the lowlands due to violence perpetrated by Egyptians and sea peoples. The name Israel reflects this movement, since it is built upon the divine name of El, a Canaanite god. Once in the highlands these people did not 'retribalize', as Gottwald claims,

42. Hopkins, *Highlands*, pp. 159-69, 272.
43. Hopkins, *Highlands*, pp. 272-75.
44. F. Frick, *The Formation of the State in Ancient Israel* (Social World of Biblical Antiquity, 4; Sheffield: Almond Press, 1985), pp. 42-50, 140-41 *et passim*. Cf. his earlier work, *The City in Ancient Israel* (SBLDS, 36; Missoula, MT: Scholars Press, 1977).
45. J. Flanagan, *David's Social Drama: A Hologram of Israel's Early Iron Age* (Social World of Biblical Antiquity, 7; Sheffield: Almond Press, 1988), pp. 288-89.
46. G. Ahlström, 'Another Moses Tradition', *JNES* 39 (1980), pp. 65-69; *idem*, 'Giloh', pp. 170-72; *idem*, 'Khirbet el-Msas', pp. 35-53; *idem*, *History*, pp. 282-390.

they simply built upon the basic familial structure of a non-nomadic type of society. Nor is there evidence of any peasant revolts. Over many years the Israelites simply evolved out of this group of highland peoples. The tribe of Asher, for example, was originally a Canaanite group, and thus is named in Egyptian texts. What sometimes appears as poor technological skill reflects their lack of resources, not the lack of knowledge that outsiders to the land would display. Some foreigners may have entered the land from the south and east, from Edom, to join with these highlanders, and perhaps they brought the worship of the god, Yahweh.[47] In short, Ahlström's writings provide the most important exposition of the position of peaceful withdrawal.

Carol Meyers also utilizes this paradigm of peaceful withdrawal in her discussion of the status of women in Israel.[48] She believes Israel arose in the highlands after war and especially violent plague had ravaged the valleys. Valley population may have declined by eighty percent, and cities may have been burned to limit contagion, a concept first proposed by George Mendenhall.[49] In the highlands of Iron Age I villages expanded from 23 to 114 sites, a growth made possible by withdrawal of many people from the valleys. The increased population required more food, which demanded agricultural intensification, which was helped by terracing and new cisterns, and this in turn produced an even larger population. This spiral effect produced Israel.

Finally, there are some other scholars who appear to use this model in their expositions. Alberto Soggin, who defended the notion of peaceful infiltration in the past, now suggests that peasants fled to the highlands to escape taxation, a novel divergence from the usual explanation of war.[50] John Romer, an Egyptologist, assumes the model in his popular history of the Judaeo-Christian tradition.[51] Robert Boling, who argued

47.   Ahlström, *Israelites*, pp. 6-9, 18-36, 57-64, 83, 92-94, 97; *idem*, 'The Role of Archaeological and Literary Remains in Reconstructing Israel's History', *The Fabric of History: Text, Artifact and Israel's Past* (ed. D.V. Edelman; JSOTSup, 127; Sheffield: JSOT Press, 1991), p. 135; *idem*, *History*, pp. 282-390.

48.   C. Meyers, *Discovering Eve: Ancient Israelite Women in Context* (New York: Oxford University Press, 1988), pp. 64-71.

49.   Mendenhall, *Tenth Generation*, pp. 105-121.

50.   Soggin, *Judges* (trans. J. Bowden; OTL; Philadelphia: Westminster Press, 1981), p. 33; *idem*, *A History of Ancient Israel* (trans. J. Bowden; Philadelphia: Westminster Press, 1984), p. 158.

51.   J. Romer, *Testament: The Bible and History* (New York: Henry Holt, 1988), pp. 64-90.

for a combination of peasant revolution and violent conquest in earlier works, now observes that an increased population in the Transjordan in Iron Age I may reflect a peasant withdrawal from Palestine.[52] In conclusion, many scholars have been attracted to the model of peaceful withdrawal to explain the origins of highland Israel, but in the past ten years there have been some variations proposed which really are separate models worthy of discussion.

These newer theories all assume that the people who became Israel were really indigenous to the highlands already in the Late Bronze Age. David Hopkins's work reflects this scholarly opinion, for more recently he notes that some Canaanites indeed did withdraw from urban centers, but the bulk of the highland village population arose as pastoral nomads who settled the land to produce their own agriculture.[53] Likewise, Lawrence Stager points out that urban population in the Late Bronze Age (about 40,000 people) could not generate all the new highland villages of the early Iron Age. Rather, existing pastoralists settled down in the highlands to farm also.[54] Moshe Kochavi observes that the village settlement pattern in the central highlands of Ephraim, from the north-east to the southwest, implies an Israelite movement from the desert fringe, but not from outside the land.[55] Amihai Mazar also notes the combination of Canaanite cultural elements and the hallmarks of a pastoralist lifestyle, and he suggests Israelites were pastoralists indigenous to the land but always distinct from the Canaanites.[56]

Internal Nomadism

These observations and others have given rise to the model of internal nomadic settlement or the symbiosis hypothesis. Advocates often admit the great continuity between Israelites and Canaanites in material culture, but find certain distinctions, such as the elliptical shape of the village or the four-room house as indicative of a distinctive Israelite pastoral origin.

An author who foreshadowed this new position was C.H.J. de Geus,

---

52. R. Boling, *The Early Biblical Community in Transjordan* (Social World of Biblical Antiquity, 6; Sheffield: Almond Press, 1988), p. 12.

53. Hopkins, 'Life', p. 53.

54. Stager, 'Respondents', pp. 84-85; *idem*, 'Family', p. 3.

55. M. Kochavi, 'The Settlement of Canaan in the Light of Archaeological Surveys', *Biblical Archaeology Today* (ed. Amitai), pp. 55-57.

56. A. Mazar, 'Israelite Settlement', pp. 66-70; Stager, 'Family', pp. 1-35.

who previously had been considered a proponent of the views of George Mendenhall and Norman Gottwald. Throughout his writings de Geus refers to Israel's origin in the land centuries prior to the conquest. From his anthropological perspective Israel's institutions did not reflect an external nomadic existence: 1) The 'house of the father' or *bet-'ab* was an institution of settled society, not nomadic. 2) State formation, as in Israel, did not arise from tribal structures, rather they would inhibit such development. Clans and tribes in Israel were geographic areas, not groups of people. 3) Culturally Israelites had great continuity with the Canaanites, whereas typically nomads would not acculturate so quickly and thoroughly. So, de Geus concludes that the Israelites were ethnically united, sedentary highlanders, who used tribal nomenclature. They were called *'apiru* in Amarna correspondence. They lived between the areas of urban control, interacted with the cities so as to become acculturated, and thus experienced 'cultural symbiosis'. When urban centers decayed, they expanded their control, and eventually settled down to farm. They had been in the land for centuries prior to this expansion as a distinct entity which was 'the not really Canaanite and urbanized part of the population', and they belonged to the 'Amorite Syro-Palestinian culture of the Middle Bronze Age'. From them Israel evolved.[57] De Geus's views foreshadow Israel Finkelstein's theories, even to the point of suggesting Middle Bronze Age (2000–1550 BCE) origins.

Volkmar Fritz seizes upon the word 'symbiosis' to describe his view of the settlement process.[58] Once partisan to Albrecht Alt's view of peaceful infiltration, his excavations in the northern Negev led him to revise his opinions. Israelite culture in the Negev demonstrates a long period of contact with Canaanite culture: 1) The Israelite four-room house was the evolutionary culmination of an architectural form from Canaan. 2) The settlers' familiarity with livestock breeding, metalwork and pottery implied they were not true nomads. Israelites had 'an intensive cultural interchange with neighboring civilizations', and 'this dependence of material culture presupposes an intensive contact of the settlers with the preceding period in the Late Bronze Age'. This contact went far beyond occasional trade, for it was an 'intensive cultural contact that can only have come about through a long period of co-existence'.[59] This form of

57.   De Geus, *Tribes*, pp. 123-87, 210-12.
58.   Fritz, 'Recent Excavations', pp. 61-73; *idem*, 'Conquest or Settlement', pp. 84-100.
59.   Fritz, 'Recent Excavations', pp. 68-71.

symbiosis with Canaanites began as early as the fifteenth century BCE.

When Fritz evaluates the highland settlements of Palestine he suggests the population of those villages could not have come from the old city states. The village architecture goes beyond the old models sufficiently to warrant calling these new settlements the result of a different population group, which had intensive and prolonged contact with the Canaanite culture. Symbiotic contact began before any sedentarization, so that the cultural exchange occurred while the proto-Israelites were still nomadic within the land of Palestine. At some early point these proto-Israelites moved into the land peacefully. They were kin to the Canaanites, but sufficiently separate in ethnic identity, and they brought their own social structures and material culture. An example of this prior cultural identity would be the four-room house, which demonstrates an independent origin arising from tent construction and a long period of independent evolution before being influenced by Canaanite models. Fritz calls these people 'culture-land nomads' who lived in the plains around the cultivated land and searched for pastures, while they also developed trade contacts with the towns. They were more stationary in their movement than normal bedouin, they were 'enclosed nomads' who would never wander too far from local cities, and they were more open to cultural symbiosis than bedouin.[60]

Fritz reconstructs the historical scenario for the evolution of this group of people. They migrated into the land in the fifteenth or fourteenth century BCE, and they may be the *'apiru* and the *shasu* in Egyptian reports. Eventually they evolved into Israel, Moab and Edom. The collapse of Canaanite urban centers between 1225–1175 BCE, caused in part by the sea peoples, encouraged the Palestinian highlanders to expand and engage in farming, which induced the further implementation of the Canaanite economic system and its attendant material culture. The symbiotic relationship with Canaanite cities ended, and these highlanders developed a separate identity as they became Israelites. The further decline of Canaanite cities from 1200 to 1150 BCE led to active Israelite assaults on Canaanite centers. Though the book of Joshua is fictional and aetiological, the accounts in Judges 1 and the Song of Deborah in Judges 5 recall the experiences of this age rather well.[61] Fritz's model is similar to

---

60. Fritz, 'Recent Excavations', pp. 70-71; *idem*, 'Conquest or Settlement', pp. 96-98.

61. Fritz, 'Recent Excavations', p. 71; *idem*, 'Conquest or Settlement', pp. 91, 97-99.

the theories of Albrecht Alt and Martin Noth, except he projects the peaceful infiltration several centuries prior to Iron Age I to account for cultural continuity.

Israel Finkelstein breaks more definitively with Alt's theories by assuming these people were in the land even earlier than Fritz suggests. Finkelstein's particular explication has made him the most well-known proponent of the 'Internal Nomadic' model. He believes Israelites were 'enclosed nomads' who lived in Palestine throughout the Late Bronze Age (1550–1200 BCE) in proximity to urban centers without settling. When Canaanite cities declined, these pastoralists had to engage in agriculture to compensate for the grain and other commodities no longer available from urban centers. They initially settled in greater numbers in the Ephraimite highlands, and from there they spread north and south in the manner described by Alt. In this process they developed horticultural skills (fruit and olives) in addition to their earlier agricultural skills (grain). Increased population caused secondary expansion into the lowlands bringing violent conflict that would last until David's unification.[62] Like Volkmar Fritz, Finkelstein also admits his reliance on Alt's old theories.

Finkelstein affirms the cultural continuity between Canaanites and Israelites, especially in regard to pottery, but he emphasizes the existence of differences more than Fritz and his other contemporaries. Finkelstein believes the Israelites lived within the land as nomads, and that accounts for the differences, but their close economic interaction with urban centers created the cultural similarities. Differences which he highlights include: 1) The shape of many excavated highland villages was elliptical (Beersheba, Tel Isdar, Izbet Sarta), a form which suggests camp formations among nomadic people for defense. This indicates the Israelites had lived in fairly recent pastoral conditions. 2) The extensive use of storage silos in the ground was viewed as a characteristic of nomadic society. The presence of locally stored grain reflects political decentralization and relative local autonomy, typical attributes of nomadic peoples. This would include the collar-rimmed jar, a characteristic Israelite phenomenon, for it primarily functioned for storage. 3) The typical Israelite four-room house was seen to have evolved out of the nomadic tent by Finkelstein.

---

62. I. Finkelstein, 'Respondents', *Biblical Archaeology Today* (ed. Amitai), pp. 80-83; *idem, Archaeology*, pp. 302-306, 352-56; *idem*, 'The Great Transformation: The "Conquest" of the Highlands Frontiers and the Rise of the Territorial States', *The Archaeology of Society in the Holy Land* (ed. T. Levy; New York: Facts on File, 1995), pp. 349-65.

4) Finally, highland surveys of many sites indicate that Israelites settled in areas good for cereal grains and pasturage but not for horticulture, implying a lack of familiarity with more complex agricultural pursuits, which tends to discount the idea that the Israelites withdrew from settled society.[63]

Although Finkelstein admits the impossibility of dating the Israelite settlements he attempts a historical summary. Before the domestication of the camel, pastoralists lived in proximity to cities as 'enclosed nomads',[64] and they exchanged livestock, meat and skins for grain, fruits, olives and finished goods. The proto-Israelite pastoralists were in these relationships already in the Middle Bronze Age II era (1750–1550 BCE) living in the highlands. Highland regions are a 'frontier zone', that is, they are the first to be occupied in times of prosperity, the first to depopulate (or witness the disappearance of villages) in difficult times. In Middle Bronze IIa (1750–1650 BCE) there was prosperity, but in Middle Bronze IIb (1650–1550 BCE) the people left settlements in the highlands, and they swelled the ranks of the pastoralists. The Late Bronze Age (1550–1200 BCE) saw further decline due to Egyptian wars, oppressive tribute, and the sea peoples, and this caused the further decline of villages in both the Cisjordan and the Transjordan. Throughout the Late Bronze Age the Israelites were pastoralists in the highlands in economic and cultural inter-relationships with these declining urban centers, and they left only a few archaeological traces of their existence: 1) Sanctuaries at Shiloh, Deir 'Alla, Amman, Tel Mevorakh, Lachish, Shechem and elsewhere stand alone in the highlands with no apparent surrounding settlements, which implies they served a semi-nomadic population. 2) Cemeteries likewise lack adjacent permanent settlements, which reflects semi-nomads burying their dead, as is recalled in the patriarchal burial narratives of Genesis 12–38. 3) The sophistication of objects found at shrines and cemeteries implies trade connections with the urban centers.

---

63. I. Finkelstein, *Archaeology*, pp. 237-91; *idem*, 'Searching for Israelite Origins', *BARev* 14.5 (1988), pp. 36-38, 45.

64. Finkelstein, like Fritz, relies upon the models of 'enclosed nomadism' and 'dimorphic society' (the relationship of nomads and settled farmers in an economic relationship) developed by Michael Rowton, 'Urban Autonomy in a Nomadic Environment', *JNES* 32 (1973), pp. 201-15; *idem*, 'Enclosed Nomadism', *Journal of the Economic and Social History of the Orient* 17 (1974), pp. 1-30; *idem*, 'Dimorphic Structure and the Problem of the 'Apiru-'Ibrim', *JNES* 35 (1976), pp. 13-20; *idem*, 'Dimorphic Structure and the Parasocial Element', *JNES* 36 (1977), pp. 181-98.

4) Literary references in Egyptian records call these people the *Shasu* or *Sutu* nomads. These people began to settle down in the thirteenth century BCE due to the urban collapse of their trading partners, which broke the 'fragile symbiotic balance'. Unable to obtain grain products, the semi-nomads underwent a sedentarization process, which ultimately led to state formation.[65]

This process was peaceful and gradual. They settled in deserted arable land on the frontier highlands, often clearing forests, seeking land where cereal grains would thrive. Gradually they expanded into other regions, some of which permitted horticulture (grapes and olives), and here they came in conflict with Canaanites. Increased population encouraged agricultural intensification, which in turn created a food surplus and accompanying social stratification, which eventually led to larger political units and state formation. The two stages resemble Albrecht Alt's model of peaceful infiltration followed by violent expansion, and Finkelstein acknowledges his dependence. Using results from many highland archaeological surveys, Finkelstein charts the spread of Israelite expansion. They moved from the central ridge of the Ephraimite highlands north into Galilee, west into the central highlands, and south into Judah. The cultural identity of Israel arose in the eastern part of the central highlands (Shiloh), in a pastoralist mode of existence which betrays long and extensive contact with Canaanite society. Ironically, the same process which caused these people to withdraw into nomadism in the Middle Bronze Age II caused them to resedentarize in Iron Age I—urban collapse. But the difference was that in the former era not all the cities were as devastated as in the later period, when the total collapse of Late Bronze Age society left the nomads with no real urban contacts for trade and agricultural supplies. Also, there was no source of political opposition to prevent the Israelites from settling in the arable land. Thus, Israel was born when pastoralists underwent resedentarization.[66]

Finkelstein's ideas have been debated strenuously in the past ten years. Some authors, like Neil Asher Silberman, quote him approvingly, but a number of critics have challenged his ideas. William Stiebing and Douglas Esse question whether the elliptical village formation and the

---

65.   I. Finkelstein, *Archaeology*, pp. 315-23, 338-48; *idem*, 'Searching', pp. 36, 39-45; *idem*, 'The Emergence of the Monarchy in Israel', *JSOT* 44 (1989), pp. 43-74.

66.   I. Finkelstein, 'Respondents', pp. 80-83; *idem*, *Archaeology*, pp. 302-306, 324-37, 348-56; *idem*, 'Searching', p. 58.

four-room house really reflect nomadic existence. Esse also questions the pattern of land expansion described by Finkelstein, suggesting the pattern was really determined by pastoralists taking the best land first. Stiebing remains unconvinced by Finkelstein's argument that the same phenomenon of urban collapse caused pastoral withdrawal in the Middle Bronze Age II but then pastoral sedentarization in the Late Bronze and early Iron Age I. Why was the fragile symbiotic relationship not destroyed in Middle Bronze Age II? Steven Rosen observes that since pastoralists and nomads really leave more archaeological evidence than Finkelstein assumes, the evidence of their presence in the Late Bronze Age really is too sparse. Robert Boling suggests that since Middle Bronze Age population in the Transjordan increased, the people Finkelstein suspects of withdrawing into pastoralism in that era may simply have moved into the Transjordan.[67] To date, the ideas of Israel Finkelstein on internal nomadic settlement are probably the most well-known and the most hotly debated of the recent theories on the emergence of Israel.

Peaceful Transition or Transformation

A number of scholars see the primary source of highland population resulting neither from urban withdrawal nor from sedentarization of nomads or pastoralists already in the highlands. They believe the existing settled highland population was sufficient to create Israel. They believe the highlands promoted a population increase by human reproduction and lower mortality rates which were possible due to improved agricultural conditions. This would parallel the evolution of the state found in the 'pristine state formation' processes of early Mesopotamia and Egypt (4500–3000 BCE) where a spiral of increased population and agricultural intensification fueled each other. With increased population and agricultural production in the highlands of Palestine a 'peaceful transition' of power occurred, which shifted the center of human activity away from the valleys and into the highlands. This led more easily to the unification of the country, because whereas valley regions tended to be isolated from

---

67. Silbermann, 'Israelites', pp. 29-30; D. Esse, 'Review of Israel Finkelstein, The Archaeology of the Israelite Settlement', *BARev* 14.5 (1988), pp. 6-12; Stiebing, *Desert*, pp. 162-64; S. Rosen, 'Finding Evidence of Ancient Nomads', *BARev* 14.5 (1988), pp. 46-53, 58-59; *idem*, 'Nomads in Archaeology: A Response to Finkelstein and Perevolotsky', *BASOR* 287 (1992), pp. 75-85; Boling, *Transjordan*, pp. 12, 35, 55.

each other by highlands, those who lived in the highland regions were more likely to interrelate with each other economically and politically, especially with significant population increase and agricultural speciali- zation which required trade. With the center of social and economic power in the highlands the possibility of state formation existed for the first time in Palestinian history.

Niels Peter Lemche spends tremendous effort criticizing the theories of George Mendenhall and Norman Gottwald, often in abrasive fashion, for they supposedly subordinate history writing to their religious agenda. He concludes that little may be said of Israel's origins prior to 1000 BCE other than to speak of a gradual process wherein indigenous highlanders increased their population. He questions whether the Davidic empire even existed. Little credence is given to the biblical text in terms of historical credibility prior to 586 BCE; rather, the Hebrew Bible is a very late document from the Hellenistic era with theological fictions for narra- tives. The contrast between Canaanite and Israelite culture is a veiled commentary on conflicts in Judaism between 500 and 200 BCE. There was no real Israelite identity until after the exile, and people who are called Canaanites by the Bible never had any distinct identity in the land of Palestine. The biblical narratives merely invented the identity of Israel for some of the pre-exilic highlanders of Palestine.[68] Essentially, the same population has lived in Palestine throughout the Bronze and Iron Age in fairly unchanged circumstances.

Lemche believes that archaeology and critical historical methods must be used to reconstruct Israel's history.[69] These critical methods lead to 'clear conclusions, which so evidently annihilate the historical value of the account...[and] archaeology can show us concretely that the OT

68.   Lemche, *Ancient Israel*, pp. 119-154, 173-96; *idem*, 'The Development of the Israelite Religion in the Light of Recent Studies on the Early History of Israel', *Congress Volume (Leuven, 1989)* (VTSup, 43; Leiden: Brill, 1991), pp. 97-115; *idem, The Canaanites and their Land: The Tradition of the Canaanites* (JSOTSup, 110; Sheffield: JSOT Press, 1991); *idem*, 'Israel, History of (Premonarchic Period)' (trans. F. Cryer), *ABD*, III, pp. 526-45; *idem*, 'The Old Testament—a Hellenistic Book?', *SJOT* 7 (1993), pp. 163-93; *idem*, 'Is it Still Possible to Write a History of Ancient Israel?', *SJOT* 8 (1994), pp. 165-90; *idem*, 'Kann von einer "israelitischen Religion" noch weiterhin die Rede sein? Perspektiven eines Historikers', *Ein Gott allein? JHWH-Verehrung und biblischer Monotheismus im Kontext der israelitischen und altorientalischen Religionsgeschichte* (eds. W. Dietrich and M. Klopfenstein; OBO, 139; Göttingen: Vandenhoeck & Ruprecht, 1994), pp. 59-75.

69.   Lemche, *Early Israel*, pp. 386-435; *idem, Ancient Israel*, pp. 75-117.

narratives of the conquest cannot be taken at face value in a historical sense'.[70] Pre-exilic people knew of no exodus or conquest traditions, the Psalms and the prophets testify to that, Lemche claims. There was no emergent Israel in Iron Age I, only a gradual transformation of people— the so-called Canaanites became the so-called Israelites, without any ethnic transformation. What occurred was a socio-economic transformation from a valley economy to a highland economy. Peasants of Palestine from the valleys merged with bandits and landless folk, and their numbers increased significantly under successful circumstances in the highlands. Most of these people were familiar with farming techniques already, so they came from the vicinity of urban centers, but outlaw and pastoral elements also joined them in the highlands. Tribes were merely groups of people acting in concert temporarily, and David's kingdom was merely a few such groups banded together for a short time.[71] Hence, Lemche's position is extremely nihilistic compared to other scholars we have considered.

Lemche attempts only a description of the background conditions out of which Israel arose in Iron Age I. The Late Bronze Age was a period of turmoil, especially in 1460, 1400 and 1200 BCE at the hands of Egyptians and sea peoples. War caused economic depression and landless people. As was the case with Dorian Greece, there was no real invasion of new people into Palestine. Eventually conditions in the highlands improved to permit population growth, and this was aided by the technological innovations, such as iron, which made their appearance late in Iron Age I. The population which expanded did not perceive itself to be different from the folks in the Bronze Age cities, that distinction would be invented by post-exilic authors.[72]

Lemche's writings have elicited a significant response from other writers, if only for his bitter denunciations of other scholars. George Mendenhall and Norman Gottwald are chided for reliance upon very dated anthropological sources (Elman Service, Morton Fried and Marshall Sahlins) and for adhering to outdated concepts of evolutionary determinism. Gottwald, in particular, inadequately defines nomadism,

70.   Lemche, 'Israel, History of', pp. 529-30.

71.   Lemche, *Early Israel*, pp. 66-76, 291-377, 386-435; *idem, Ancient Israel*, pp. 75-172. However, in 'Israel, History of', pp. 537-39, he leans toward the 'amalgamation' model.

72.   Lemche, *Early Israel*, pp. 386-410, 423-29; *idem, Ancient Israel*, pp. 75-85, 90, and 'Israel, History of', p. 538.

relies too heavily upon Rowton's very simplistic model of 'enclosed nomadism' (as does Finkelstein), uses Martin Noth's totally discredited amphictyonic hypothesis, fails to understand kinship structures and segmentary societies, and uses bogus dichotomies, such as the Canaan/Israel, peasant/nomad distinctions.[73] In sum, Lemche attempts to overturn completely the resources used by other scholars in this debate with new anthropological models. His contributions and critiques are regarded positively by some, notably Thomas Thompson. Wilfrid Thiel describes Lemche's views as the new 'evolutionary model' and Rainer Albertz calls it the 'evolutionary' or 'digression model' (because it suggests that people digressed by de-urbanization), and both use his observations.[74] But whether Lemche will gain respect in the field with his minimalistic views and his biting rhetoric remains to be seen.

William Stiebing briefly and insightfully proposes a theory of Israel's origins which holds that climatic change was the key factor in the social-historical process. Dry conditions in the Mediterranean area between 1250 and 1200 BCE caused population decline and urban deterioration from Mycenaean Greece to Palestine, which in turn resulted in 'cultural collapse' and 'widespread population shifts'. The end of the Bronze Age resulted from drought; survivors of famine and the resultant political chaos withdrew to the highlands in Palestine, but their numbers were small. The drought abated slightly for a few years (1150–1100 BCE), which enabled refugees to settle in the Palestinian highlands. With the onset of moister conditions after 1000 BCE the highlands witnessed a population increase, which led to the creation of the state. The result was a transition of the population and the centers of power from the lowlands to the highlands. Israel was created not by the movements of people, but by population increase promoted by favorable agricultural conditions.[75]

Robert Drews in his study of Late Bronze Age warfare makes some insightful observations about Israel's emergence. He is convinced that the sea peoples were not migratory families but rather professional mercenaries, formerly in the pay of great powers, who turned their

73. Lemche, *Early Israel*, pp. 1-290, 410-15; *idem, Ancient Israel*, pp. 88-109.

74. Thompson, *Early History, passim*; W. Thiel, 'Vom revolutionären zum evolutionären Israel? Zu einem neuen Modell der Entstehung Israels', *TLZ* 113 (1988), pp. 401-410; Albertz, *Israelite Religion*, I, p. 72.

75. Stiebing, 'The End of the Mycenean Age', *BA* 43 (1980), pp. 7-21; *idem, Desert*, pp. 189-97; *idem*, 'Climate and Collapse: Did the Weather Make Israel's Emergence Possible?', *Bible Review* 10.4 (1994), pp. 18-27, 54.

fighting skills upon the great cities. The small chariot armies of the great states and city states were defeated by the sea peoples' much larger infantry and advanced weapons, including the javelin, a new slashing sword, and a smaller round defensive shield. Their victories caused a transformation in fighting tactics which stressed large, massed infantry forces, and this gave societies like Greece and Israel a military edge. Drews also believes this provided impetus to the development of an egalitarian ethos in those two societies. His model implies that violent conflict may have been an important factor in Israel's emergence.[76] His theories, however, lend more support to the idea of a transition of power. As social systems collapsed and urban centers were destroyed by mercenaries, power shifted to the highlands where population increased. This increased population gave the highlanders more military and social control over the entire country. Drews does not see drought as an important part of this process. However, Stiebing's evidence concerning extensive climate change, drought and famine would dovetail nicely with Drews's suggestions. These natural forces could have been the trigger mechanism which set the mercenaries in motion.

The theories of Stiebing and Drews may fit very well with any of the peaceful, internal models describing Israel's emergence. Their observations may explain the urban collapse or decline that encouraged people to withdraw to the highlands, or forced internal nomads to settle down, or led to the transition of power from lowlands to highlands, or caused the amalgamation of disparate groups in the highlands. Their writings and viewpoints need to be taken much more seriously by biblical historians in the future.

Robert Coote and Keith Whitelam see Israel's emergence as part of a social-historical process that reoccurred for millennia—the alternation of hinterland development and decline. Following French historian Fernand Braudel's focus on long-range social trends, Coote and Whitelam attempt to evaluate the settlement process by placing it within the greater context of six millennia of Palestinian history. Israel's rise was part of the following cycle: hinterland regions develop in periods of economic prosperity to provide more food and to relocate surplus valley population, while in times of economic decline they can absorb population withdrawing from lowland cities. Such a phenomenon should be called 'realignment' and 'transformation' rather than collapse or revolution.

---

76. R. Drews, *The End of the Bronze Age: Changes in Warfare and the Catastrophe ca 1200 B.C.* (Princeton, NJ: Princeton University Press, 1993).

This acknowledges the tremendous cultural continuity between Israelite and Canaanite; in fact, the authors admonish us to be cautious in using either of these terms to describe the culture of that era. Descriptions such as urban and rural are better characterizations of the lifestyles in Palestine. The lowland withdrawal was not as significant a factor in creating Israel as was the expansion of highland population from human reproduction, which was assisted by the transition of highland pastoralists and bandits to agricultural pursuits and trade in a peaceful setting. The birth rate increases when more people are required to work the fields and defend the villages. State formation ultimately becomes inevitable as a result of highland development, the state is not antithetical to the activity of highlanders, as some have suggested rhetorically (George Mendenhall and Norman Gottwald). Once the highlands have been settled rather thoroughly, the increased population has to be more directly organized for agricultural intensification, and they must protect themselves from outside forces which envy this new, increased productivity of the land.[77]

Israel arose as part of a great historical cycle according to Coote and Whitelam. Periods of urban decline transpired in Early Bronze Age II (2650–2350 BCE), Early Bronze Age IV/Middle Bronze Age I (2350–2000 BCE), Late Bronze Age (1550–1200 BCE), the Persian Period (538–332 BCE), and under Ottomon rule (1517–1917 CE). Factors causing population shifts include population, poorer climate, technological change (such as iron and terracing), peasant unrest, change in regional rule by outside empires, and trade. But the collapse of trade was the most significant factor in Israel's emergence. Iron and terracing were not applied extensively in the highlands until the tenth century BCE. Peasant unrest was minimal, since it usually occurs during population expansions, not in periods of depression, for popular unrest requires increased population and tighter state control to ignite the tensions, both of which are the opposite of conditions in the Late Bronze Age (contra Gottwald). Furthermore, conflict between urban dwellers and nomads normally prevents a peasant revolt by bringing poor and rich urbanites together in common opposition to the nomads. Nor could a peasant revolt lead to increased settlement or state formation. Trade, on the other hand, stimulates development or decline in marginal situations. Strong trade connections encourage

77. R. Coote and K. Whitelam, 'The Emergence of Israel: Social Transformation and State Formation Following the Decline in Late Bronze Age Trade', *Semeia* 37 (1986), pp. 121-42; K. Whitelam, 'The Identity of Early Israel: The Realignment and Transformation of Late Bronze-Iron Age Palestine', *JSOT* 63 (1994), pp. 57-87.

urban development and hinterland population growth; the decline of trade reverses the effects. Trade may promote growth and population increase until the land is overburdened and decline sets in; then marginal areas are developed for subsistence farming by the survivors.[78]

The collapse of trade routes caused the highlanders, who became Israel, to engage in 'risk reduction' forms of agriculture. Coote and Whitelam respond to critics, such as Thomas Thompson, who doubt that the breakdown of trade alone could cause a 'systems collapse' in Palestine, by admitting that climatic change, drought and famine could have been the precipitating factors behind trade collapse and thus contributed to the steady decline of urban life. But trade still had to be the important factor in the dynamics of the Palestinian transformation, since the region was a trade corridor.[79]

Therefore, Israel emerged after the decline of Canaanite cities which had been weakened by the loss of 'urban inter-regional trade'. The culture of these highland villages came from the lowland urban centers, according to Coote and Whitelam. The highlands were 're-opened', as had occurred before, and people transformed their wealth into moveable herds rather than grain crops. They were motivated by the simple desire to survive, not some revolutionary ideology. Bandit activity prevented highland development in the Late Bronze Age, but the collapse of trade forced people into the highlands and demanded their cooperation and 'an inter-subregional, inter-group, and inter-tribal stay of conflict'. The actual numbers of lowlanders who retreated into the highlands was small; natural population growth was more significant, resulting from healthier highland climate, lack of state control and taxation which left more produce in the villages, and greater distance from the valley war zones. People already in the highlands switched to agriculture in greater numbers, including even the bandits, for they all required a steady food supply with the demise of lowland centers.[80]

This set in motion the dynamics of state formation. Population increase utilized the available arable land, and then further agricultural intensification was implemented, using devices like labor intensive terracing and iron. But eventually 'environmental circumscripture' occurred because

78. Coote and Whitelam, *Early Israel*, pp. 27-80.
79. Coote and Whitelam, 'Emergence', pp. 119-24; Whitelam, 'Identity', pp. 79-81.
80. Coote and Whitelam, 'Emergence', p. 127; Coote and Whitelam, *Early Israel*, pp. 122-23, 129-35.

of geographic barriers, and this forced a growing population to form a state with its organizational capacities. With highland development, trade returned, further promoting state formation. This development in Palestine led to a chiefdom (minor judges), then a state (David), and this final stage was not antithetical to the concerns of the highlanders, but tried to meet their economic needs. Unfortunately, a state can create financial burdens to be borne by the populace (Solomon) and thus initiate another round of decline.[81]

In conclusion, Coote and Whitelam see Israel created by extensive agriculture, the merger of heterogenous groups, agricultural intensification, revived trade, but above all by the increased highland population which set these forces in motion. The later biblical traditions invented a conquest account to view the Israelites as external to the land, a phenomenon which can be observed in other societies. When members of a society find themselves exiled from their land and need to justify their eventual return, they appeal to their distant ancestors who also had to enter the homeland from the outside. Similarly the biblical traditions invented Abraham and Joshua, who are extensions of David, who in turn symbolized the unified identity of Jews in exile.[82] Their assessment of the settlement views it as a natural process of population increase of Palestinian highlanders, who really had no self-identity at the time of their initial emergence, and that identity was provided only many years later by the biblical texts.

Rainer Albertz appears to favor the ideas of Coote and Whitelam, though he also affirms Lemche's work. Albertz speaks of 'digression', the process by which the collapse of international trade routes forced city dwellers to de-urbanize to highland villages and expand there. Into their developing community the exodus group brought its notions of the god Yahweh.[83] Albertz does not spend great effort developing his own theory of the settlement, because his interest is in discussing the evolution of Israelite religious and familial piety. However, his is a significant work, and its widespread use will popularize his understanding of the settlement and the secondary scholarship upon which he relies.

---

81. Coote and Whitelam, *Early Israel*, pp. 139-66

82. Coote and Whitelam, *Early Israel*, pp. 168-73; K. Whitelam, 'Israel's Tradition of Origin: Reclaiming the Land', *JSOT* 44 (1989), pp. 19-42; *idem*, *The Invention of Ancient Israel: The Silencing of Palestinian History* (New York: Routledge, 1996), pp. 176-237.

83. Albertz, *Israelite Religion*, I, pp. 69-79.

What unifies the viewpoints of Niels Peter Lemche, William Stiebing, Robert Drews, Robert Coote, Keith Whitelam, Rainer Albertz, and others is not only their perception of the settlement and the emergence of Israel as a peaceful and internal process, but also their stress on the development of this people as a distinctly natural highland experience of population growth. What they stress is simply that the highlands developed agriculturally and socially, and this moved the center of power from the valleys to the highland areas. Even more than peaceful withdrawal models it stresses the natural, gradual growth of these people and their society.

Peaceful Amalgamation or Synthesis

In the last five years another model appears to have arisen among scholars, which is a significant variation on the idea of peaceful transition. Some theorists increasingly stress that highland Israel arose as a synthesis or amalgamation of several different groups of people in the highlands. Though that was part of the previous model of peaceful transition, it seems to warrant separate consideration, for it appears to combine elements of peaceful withdrawal, internal nomadism and peaceful transition by stressing the complexity of the synthesis which produced Israel. Authors stress how highland folk absorbed urban refugees, former bandits, highland pastoralists, and those who entered the land, and how all these elements contributed to the development of Israel. The continuity with the lowland farmers in the Late Bronze Age is stressed more than in internal nomadic and peaceful transition theories.

Baruch Halpern's writings contain observations which foreshadowed this model almost fifteen years ago. He was one of the first to describe the settlement process as a complex interaction of several population groups in the highlands. He sternly critiques the peasant revolt model and proposes a scenario which posits that different dynamics were operative in the various regions of Palestine to create Israel. He suggests that only a few of the people came from the lowlands, rather most were descended from highlanders already living in the land combined with some bandit elements and people who indeed entered the land from the outside. Outsiders included a core group from Egypt with the memory of an exodus experience, and they received a sympathetic hearing from people who had experienced Egyptian rule in Palestine. Other larger groups infiltrated down from Syria and came through the Aijalon Pass. They were dispossessed farmers, hence their ability to farm the highlands is evidenced in the earliest settlements. They also brought alien customs, such as circumcision and the rejection of pork. Assyrian expansion in the thirteenth and twelfth centuries BCE may have driven them south, and the memory of the patriarchs may recall their movements. The exodus group from Egypt brought the sacred name of Yahweh, while the Syrian groups created the name of Israel in the land during the thirteenth century BCE. There was some military activity involved with the movement of groups in the Transjordan and later in the process of identity formation in the highlands. By the time of Deborah (1050–1000 BCE) a confederacy existed and the highlanders were conscious of their own ethnic identity in opposition to their neighbors in the lowlands and the Transjordan. Hence, they were clearly a highland phenomenon. They lived too close to cities in the valleys to have withdrawn from them in some antagonistic fashion, nor did they fortify their villages for defense. The actual process of emergence was slightly different in each region. Galilee saw migration from diverse directions, the central hill country was populated by migrants from the upper Euphrates (Syria), and a Yahwistic community from the south Transjordan penetrated the central highlands also. They were pulled together by common economic concerns, especially the need to maintain trade links after the disappearance of Egyptian control. Economic concerns, such as agricultural surplus, also led them to control the lowlands, and this caused the natural emergence of the monarchy.[84] Israel emerged in a process of 'homesteading of pastoral elements already integrated in economic interdependence'.[85] Above all, Halpern stresses we must recognize that, 'Historical Israel is not the Israel of the Hebrew Bible. Rather, historical Israel produced biblical Israel'.[86]

Even though James Flanagan alludes to extensive peaceful withdrawal of the people in the Cisjordan, he also speaks of a symbiosis of those elements with an existing highland population, which in turn created a cultural metamorphosis of highland society. Rejecting notions of conquest, infiltration, and peasant revolt, all of which stress the contrast of sedentarism and pastoralism, he maintains that these two economic lifestyles are merely separate subsistence strategies by the same people, and

84. Halpern, *Emergence*, pp. 47-63, 81-106, 165-83, 209-61; *idem*, 'The Exodus from Egypt: Myth or Reality?', *Rise of Ancient Israel* (ed. Shanks), pp. 86-117; *idem*, 'Settlement of Canaan', *ABD*, V, pp. 1120-43; *idem*, 'Erasing History—The Minimalist Assault on Ancient Israel', *Bible Review* 11.6 (1995), pp. 26-35, 47.

85. Halpern, 'Settlement', p. 1134.

86. Halpern, *Emergence*, p. 239.

we err in trying to recreate two different population groups. Although his concern is to discuss the rise of David and state formation, he believes the biblical traditions provide good insight into the social-cultural processes prior to his reign.[87]

Gloria London stresses the continuity of Canaanite and Israelite cultures. What differences occur result from the economic socio-geographic differences produced by an urban administration in the valleys and a village-familial life setting in the highlands. The so-called Israelite four-room house, collar-rimmed jar and terracing are merely adaptations to hill life. To call these material differences the result of cultural or ethnic differences is wrong. The presence of Canaanite cult objects and figurines in Israelite sites implies this continuity. She sees no evidence for a significant population movement from the lowlands into the highlands. Israelite identity arose through social mobilization; pastoralists synthesized with some urbanites to form a new social identity which gradually redefined itself in opposition to the old lowland culture.[88]

William Dever in the past has stated his sympathy for the peasant revolt model,[89] for the proposals of Coote and Whitelam,[90] and for Fritz's symbiosis model.[91] Yet he does express reservation about the revolt model: 'The emergence of this ethnicity need not have been accomplished by a revolt at all; it may be viewed rather as simply a normal and even predictable historical development in the evolution of society.'[92] Elsewhere he calls the settlement process a 'relatively normal social process of peasant withdrawal and what has been termed "retribalization"'.[93] Dever sees Israelites originating from the farming population within Palestine. There is no Canaanite/Israelite dichotomy, but rather an

87.   Flanagan, *Social Drama*, pp. 119-88, 288-89.

88.   London, 'Comparison', pp. 42-52.

89.   W. Dever, 'The Contribution of Archaeology to the Study of Canaanite and Early Israelite Religion', *Ancient Israelite Religion: Essays in Honor of Frank Moore Cross* (eds. P. Miller, P. Hanson and D. McBride; Philadelphia: Fortress Press, 1987), p. 236; *idem, Recent Archaeological Discoveries and Biblical Research* (Seattle: University of Washington Press, 1990), pp. 79-81; *idem*, 'Israel, History of (Archaeology and the Conquest)', *ABD*, III, pp. 550-53.

90.   W. Dever, 'Archaeological Data on the Israelite Settlement: A Review of Recent Works', *BASOR* 284 (1991), p. 86.

91.   W. Dever, 'How to Tell a Canaanite from an Israelite', *Rise of Ancient Israel*, p. 30.

92.   Dever, 'Contribution', p. 236.

93.   Dever, 'Israel, History of', p. 553.

urban/rural distinction which explains the differences in remains, such as the collar-rimmed jar and pottery. The differences are functional and not ethnic; they result from highland needs. What was truly new was the combination and adaptation of old cultural phenomena, including court-yard houses, silos and terracing. The highlands produced a 'hybrid material culture' to serve the needs of a distinctively new social order which reflected kinship structures. This kinship structure may even be evident in the layout of villages (as noted by Lawrence Stager several years prior). The Israelites already were acquainted with farming tech-niques, they had a sophisticated technology (such as skill at terracing), their pottery had great continuity with Canaanite patterns, and they were even familiar with simple writing, all of which implies that they originated as lowland Canaanites who integrated with existing highlanders and people from outside the land.[94]

Dever's position is more complex than simple peaceful withdrawal. He views the Israelites as a motley crew: urban refugees, social bandits, some revolutionaries, a few nomads, but mostly withdrawn Canaanites. Once they were in the highlands, they transformed themselves, and by the twelfth century BCE they knew that they were different from the Canaanites, and eventually they developed their own ethnic identity in the highlands. They may have begun to develop a sense of social democracy (here Dever shows his sympathy for Norman Gottwald's ideas). What he senses is that an evolution of a complex society occurred in the highlands of Palestine.[95]

Thomas Thompson concludes that little of historical value may be deduced from the biblical narratives, because of their late origin (at least after the fall of Samaria in 720 BCE) and their strong ideological con-cerns which are expressed in story form. He sternly rebukes the models of Albrecht Alt, William Albright, George Mendenhall, Norman Gottwald and Israel Finkelstein for imposing their own theological assumptions upon the text.[96] He maintains that history should be written by using archaeological data as the starting point, not the literary-theological biblical texts. In criticizing the revolt model he stresses there is no evidence of oppressed peasant masses in the Amarna age or thereafter, nor is there

---

94. Dever, *Discoveries*, pp. 39-84; *idem*, 'Archaeological Data', pp. 77-90; *idem*, 'How to Tell', pp. 26-60, 79-85; *idem*, 'Israel, History of', pp. 549-53. He relies upon the data provided by Stager, 'Family', pp. 1-35.

95. Dever, 'How to Tell', pp. 54, 60; *idem*, 'Israel, History of', pp. 554, 557.

96. Thompson, *Early History*, pp. 1-170.

any indication that any city was overthrown—the towns were simply too small for such activities to occur.[97]

Thompson observes that the population of Palestine has been unchanged for millennia; the same people simply move from towns to highlands according to economic needs and fluctuate in numbers according to subsistence strategies. Townfolk would rely upon cereal grains, fruit and wine, while highlanders resort to a combination of herds and grains. There was no massive entrance of a new people, although new population elements came from the north (the Aegean, Syria, Anatolia and some West-Semitic groups) and some Arab peoples from the south and east. Contrary to Robert Coote and Keith Whitelam this transformation did not result from the breakdown of trade; rather, it was a slow natural process of change caused by a multitude of factors, chief of which was climatic change. The central highlanders formed from indigenous folk in the highland villages who were augmented greatly by lowlanders who withdrew into the highlands and the addition of some non-sedentary highlanders, outside pastoralists, and immigrants from Syria, Anatolia and the Aegean area. Furthermore, the unified Israelite and Judahite monarchies were a fiction created by later biblical litera- ture. True political unity did not emerge until the eighth century BCE under the auspices of Assyrian rule. Israelite identity and true economic unity arose only in the post-exilic era with the creation of the fictional biblical narratives and the support of Persian rule. Hence, the Iron Age differed little from the Late Bronze Age; Palestine was an agglomeration of relatively independent city states, one of which was Jerusalem, through- out the so-called period of the monarchies. Thompson's interpretation, like that of Niels Lemche, is extremely critical and more historically minimalist than other authors.[98]

The Egyptologist, Donald Redford, in his history of Palestine sees differences between the highlanders and the lowlanders. Like Finkelstein, he suggests that there were highland pastoralists in the land who settled

97. Thompson, *Early History*, pp. 27-76.

98. T. Thompson, 'The Background of the Patriarchs: A Reply to William Dever and Malcolm Clark', *JSOT* 9 (1978), pp. 35-38; *idem, The Origin Tradition of Ancient Israel*. I. *The Literary Formation of Genesis and Exodus 1–23* (JSOTSup, 55; Sheffield: JSOT Press, 1987), p. 37 *et passim; idem*, 'Text, Context and Referent in Israelite Historiography', *Fabric of History* (ed. Edelman), pp. 65-92; *idem, Early History*, pp. 127-422; *idem*, 'A Neo-Albrightian School in History and Biblical Scholarship?', *JBL* 114 (1995), pp. 683-98.

down to become the bulk of the population, but in addition *shasu* pastoralists came out of the steppe lands of Edom (with Yahweh worship), and here are the beginnings of the Israelite identity. There was little or no peaceful withdrawal in this process. The separation of shrines from the settlements and the aniconic tradition strongly imply their non-Canaanite origins. These outsiders combined with indigenous pastoralists to form a distinctly new group and early memories are preserved vaguely in the book of Judges.[99]

Moshe Weinfeld presents a distinctive view of the settlement process, which involves a process of amalgation of diverse elements in the land. He assumes that certain tribal groups invaded the land and established militant 'camps' from which they fought with neighboring towns and tribal elements ('camp of Shittim', Num. 33.49, Josh. 3.1; 'camp of Gilgal', Josh. 3–4; 'camp of Makkedah', Josh. 10.21; 'camp of Shiloh', Josh. 18.9, Judg. 21.12; and 'camp of Dan', Judg. 18.12). These local groups or 'camps' each had a separate history, and the Joshua group was one of several such 'camps', perhaps arriving later than the others. Eventually they merged with each other and with additional outlaw bands, cities and infiltrating pastoralists to become Israel, and their separate stories likewise were amalgamated together in the books of Joshua and Judges, which thus contain many authentic historical memories.[100]

Other scholars also refer to some form of peaceful and gradual amalgamation of highlanders in their writings. John Gray implies that Israel emerged as a synthesis of internal bandits and external groups of pastoralists.[101] John Dearman describes the settlement process as a merging of highlanders who originated both inside and outside the land.[102]

This last group of scholars tends to be more ecclectic in its interpretation of the materials. They sense the value of observations concerning peaceful withdrawal, internal nomadism and peaceful transition, and so they tend to combine them in a model of amalgamation. As a result, they take into account more of the theoretical observations made throughout

99. Redford, *Egypt*, pp. 268-80.

100. M. Weinfeld, *The Promise of the Land: The Inheritance of the Land of Canaan by the Israelites* (Los Angeles: University of California Press, 1993), pp. 99-155.

101. J. Gray, 'Israel in the Song of Deborah', *Ascribe to the Lord: Biblical and Other Studies in memory of Peter C. Craigie* (eds. L. Eslinger and G. Taylor; JSOTSup, 67; Sheffield: JSOT Press, 1988), pp. 421-55.

102. A. Dearman, *Religion and Culture in Ancient Israel* (Peabody, MA: Henrickson, 1992), pp. 25-35.

the modern history of the debate. But their specific emphasis is upon the
diversity of the people who would become Israel, and that this process
was one of gradual and slow development in the highlands. In my
opinion this last position may be the viewpoint which will prevail, if only
for its inclusiveness in the greater discussion.

In conclusion, the past fifteen years have been revolutionary in terms
of interpreting the Israelite settlement process with new archaeological
information. The old models of peaceful infiltration, violent conquest and
peasants' revolt have faded completely from view. All theories concur
on the peaceful and internal origin of the Israelites. The discussion simply
revolves around the question of the primary origin of these people: were
they refugees out of the old urban centers in the valleys, were they
pastoralists in the highlands who settled down to farm, were they the
result of simple human reproduction in the highland villages, or were
they a complex synthesis of different people resulting from all the factors
mentioned? Regardless of which viewpoint emerges as the consensus,
the notion of a peaceful and internal origin appears to be the rising
scholarly theory.

III

The new models emphasize Israelite settlement as peaceful and internal
in origin, having great continuity with predecessor societies of the Late
Bronze Age. They are in diametric opposition to models favored by
older American scholars, especially violent conquest and social revolution. Those two older models were exciting springboards for biblical
theology, for one could speak of the contrast between Israelite religious
and political values and those of the Canaanites, as well as the rest of the
ancient Near East. The understanding of the conquest or settlement process was pivotal in the doing of biblical theology inspired by the Hebrew
Bible. How scholars and theologians envisioned the Israelite entrance
into the land affected how they envisioned the overall Israelite ethos, and
that in turn affected how they drew upon those biblical texts for ideas to
inspire and sustain their own religious, ethical and social justice themes.
Now use of those old Israelite conquest themes has become inappropriate
for biblical theology and ethics.

In an excellent article Neil Asher Silberman points out that every
generation perceives the nature of the Israelite settlement process through
its own eyes, through the values of its age, or according to the message

which needs to be proclaimed in that age. He suspects that the contemporary models which stress the peaceful and internal origin of Israel in a gradual fashion probably resonate with an age which is trying to learn how to adapt and survive in the face of tremendous change today.[103] Norman Gottwald would concur with Silberman on this observation, but he is very critical of the theological implications which result from this new peaceful, internal model. He suspects they undergird notions of easy accommodation to social injustice and the imperfections of our modern world. Of course, he still prefers the implied theological message of the revolutionary model, which undergirds the call for reform.[104] The model of social revolution was popular in American in an era when religious and political leaders were especially calling for social reform and justice in society, and theirs is still a meaningful message for our age. It may be supported by other portions of the biblical text, even if the con quest narratives no longer avail us, however. The even older violent conquest models used by the *Heilsgeschichte* theologians reflected Neo-Orthodoxy's call to heed the dramatic 'Word of God' and respond to it by living an authentic life in the modern world.[105] It, too, was a truly meaningful message for its age. It was in that theology that I was first trained over 30 years ago. How I viewed the Israelite settlement over the years was determined by the needs of theologians, ethicists and preachers. I certainly would not condemn that process. Rather, we must be aware of it when we consider the writings of significant scholars. When we articulate our own views, we also must be willing to step back and look at our theories as partially an expression of our own contemporary religious and existential needs. We can never escape ourselves and our own intellectual agenda completely, but we can at least be aware of our own limitations. In some respects, how modern thinkers analyze the Israelite settlement even might be a clue as to the direction our theologizing should take, for they might focus unconsciously on the phenomena in a way that reflects what the modern audience needs to hear. It is no coincidence that some authors today still accuse others of importing their own beliefs into the assessment of the texts and the archaeological data. We all do that, even those who so quickly level that charge against others.

103. Silberman, 'Israelites', pp. 22-31.
104. Gottwald, 'Sociology', pp. 83-84.
105. H.G. Reventlow, 'Die Eigenart des Jahweglaubens als geschichtliches und theologisches Problem', *KD* 20 (1974)', pp. 199-200; Redford, *Egypt*, p. 265.

Despite our recognition of our own personal intellectual biases, which will influence even the most objective thoughts we attempt to formulate, we must still ask the key question: What are the implications of these new models of settlement for the greater field of biblical studies and biblical theology? Above all, they tell us something about the Israelite identity. Israelites were part of their ancient Palestinian environment, they were not alien to it. As a result, their social and religious beliefs would have had more continuity with their milieu than we have acknowledged in our biblical theology and textbooks. As we shall see, scholars also suspect a greater degree of continuity between the religion of Israel and the surrounding world than we suspected a generation ago. If the Israelites were for the most part Canaanites who slowly evolved into Israelites, this would explain the nature of the condemnations proclaimed by the classical prophets and the Deuteronomic Reformers. They accused the Israelites of polytheism, and they were most correct in this charge, and the abuses they listed were apt descriptions of the religious life of the people. But this was because the Israelites were really Canaanites who were in the process of converting, or perhaps better stated, evolving into Israelites. The abuses attacked by the Yahwistic party would have been the natural religious expressions of most Israelites, since that was their traditional religion—they were Canaanites. Perhaps, it is best not even to use the words Canaanite or Israelite, since it appears that the former really evolved into the latter. The classical prophets and the Deuteronomic Reformers were not calling people back to a pure Yahwistic past that existed in the wilderness or in the early highland settlements; those days never existed. These reformers were part of the continuing process of transformation. The formation of highland villages was the first part of that transformation, a social process. The later years saw the religious transformation begin, as the prophets and reformers, in effect, caused the emergence of monotheism for the first time. That was the second stage of the transformation of this people. Israel (or the Jews) emerged gradually over six hundred years; the early stages were the social transformations of highland villagers, the latter stages were the intellectual advances of the religious reformers.

Israel or the Jews grew out of the social-cultural context of that first millennium BCE world, they did not arise in violent opposition to their cultural setting. Any presentation of that Israelite experience must emphasize continuity and not contrast in future pedagogy and biblical theology. But what will be the shape of biblical theology as we now try to articulate it with these new insights? The older models of contrast and dialectical opposition dovetailed with Neo-Orthodox theology of the early- and mid-twentieth century; the social revolutionary hypothesis undergirded liberation theology and calls for social reform in our age. The newer models of gradual development and continuity with the environment will inspire a different form of theology, one which affirms the developing traditions of the Judaeo-Christian religion, one that senses that social reform and egalitarianism arise in a developmental process which unfolds for centuries (and is not finished yet), and one that uses the language of process, unity and continuing change in its theological articulations.

Chapter 2

RECENT SCHOLARSHIP ON THE DEVELOPMENT OF MONOTHEISM IN ANCIENT ISRAEL

> The introduction of monotheism into the consciousness of mankind is the greatest single achievement of the ancient Hebrews.[1]

In the Hebrew Bible we may view the foundations for three major religions of our age: Judaism, Christianity and Islam. The Hebrew Bible is a primary source for the development of ethics, social imperatives and our religious understandings of God, people and the purpose of the world. Historians of intellectual development, theologians and biblical scholars often focus upon one significant aspect as the apex of the Hebrew Bible's contributions—the affirmation of monotheism. But immediately the questions arise: What is the nature of true monotheism? How does it first emerge? Was there some form of primordial monotheism which existed prior to that expressed in the Hebrew Bible? Does monotheism emerge by slow evolution, by quick revolution, or by some process which is a complex combination of the two? Finally, at what point did the Israelites or the Jews truly become monotheistic?

In the past generation new scholarship has challenged the old paradigms which were assumed in critical scholarship and used in basic college and seminary textbooks. As is the case with the newer theories concerning the Israelite conquest and settlement, these models for understanding Israel's religious development overturn our older ways of speaking, and they have implications for understanding the emergence of the Israelite and Jewish ethos. In a nutshell the newer models describe Israelite religious development as a slower movement toward the distinctive monotheistic ideas found in the Hebrew Bible, and their final precipitation in the literary texts occurred much later than previously assumed. Likewise, the perception of a gradual emergence of monotheism combines with an

---

1. R. Patai, *The Jewish Mind* (New York: Charles Scribner's Sons, 1977), p. 349.

understanding that stresses Israel's intellectual continuity with the ancient world rather than the older views which placed the Israelite ethos in dialectic with either Canaanite or ancient Near Eastern thought.

I

The nineteenth century saw the full emergence of a critical approach to the study of the Bible. Scholars began to situate the literature within its historical and cultural epoch to more fully understand the message, but especially in order to observe the historical development or evolution of biblical ideas and beliefs. The intelligentsia of the nineteenth century were influenced deeply by the newly articulated theories of scientific evolution, which stemmed from Darwin's *On the Origin of the Species by Means of Natural Selection* (1859) and *The Descent of Man and Selection in Relation to Sex* (1871). These revolutionary works and the writings of like-minded scientific theorists impressed upon thinkers how gradual, slow, evolutionary development with concomitant principles of competition and survival of the fittest appeared to be the paradigm for describing both biological and cultural development. Combined with ideas from the philosophy of George Frederick Hegel concerning the nature of the process of development, this idea of evolution in the broadest sense captured the imagination of many scholars. Historians in all fields began to evaluate human development and cultural achievements with the format of slow, gradual, even inevitable, upward evolutionary advance, which in many fields was called 'progress'. It captured the imagination not only of scholars, but it has become part of our modern commonplace way of viewing reality.

Late nineteenth-century scholars, influenced by these notions of scientific evolution, began to describe the Israelite religious development as a passage through several natural stages of evolution toward increased intellectual sophistication until they attained monotheism and an ethical view of reality. Often these scholars drew terms and concepts articulated by contemporaries in the newly developing fields of anthropology and comparative religions. Hence, Israel's religious odyssey was described with the successive stages of animism, totemism, polytheism, henotheism or monolatry, and finally monotheism. Scholars were tempted to discover evidences for the most primitive of animistic and polydaemonistic thought in biblical texts and to attribute them to early stages of Israel's religious evolution. The first well-developed presentation of this model came with the critical observations of Julius Wellhausen, who undertook a study of Pentateuchal sources as a prolegomenon to writing an intellectual history of Israel.[2] His counterpart in England, William Robertson Smith, also assumed the same gradual, evolutionary scheme of development.[3] Their works marked the beginning of modern critical biblical scholarship, and in particular, their evolutionary assumptions would prevail among biblical scholars for sixty years.

Eventually, however, disenchantment grew with gradual evolutionary paradigms among many scholars in the humanities and social sciences. Students of religious studies chaffed at the way paradigms seemed to straightjacket the data in their fields, and biblical scholars especially began to question whether Israel's religious development occurred as neatly as the paradigms suggested and in the rather short period of seven hundred years (1200–500 BCE). Some authors challenged Wellhausen's assumptions directly and proposed instead the idea of a Mosaic revolution which brought about a developed form of monotheism even prior to the settlement.

The most well-known defender of this viewpoint was William Foxwell Albright in his classic work, *From the Stone Age to Christianity: Monotheism and the Historical Process* (1940), as well as subsequent works.[4] He engaged in an extensive debate with Wellhausen and the supposed Hegelian philosophical assumptions which undergirded his scholarship. (In actuality, it is hard to envision Wellhausen as a true Hegelian, since he viewed post-exilic Judaism as a deterioration and not as an advance or synthesis, as a true Hegelian scheme would suggest.) Albright believed that Moses was a monotheist in the true sense of the word,

> If, on the other hand, the term 'monotheist' means one who teaches the existence of only one God, the creator of everything, the source of justice, who is equally powerful in Egypt, in the desert, and in Palestine, who has

2.   J. Wellhausen, *Prolegomena to the History of Ancient Israel* (repr.; trans. A. Menzies and S. Black; Gloucester, MA: Peter Smith, 1973 [1878]).

3.   W. Robertson Smith, *The Religion of the Semites: The Fundamental Institutions* (repr.; New York: Schocken Books, 1972 [1889]).

4.   W.F. Albright, *From the Stone Age to Christianity: Monotheism and the Historical Process* (Garden City, NY: Doubleday, 2nd edn, 1957 [1940]); *idem*, *Archaeology and the Religion of Israel* (Garden City, NY: Doubleday, 5th edn, 1968 [1941]); *idem*, *History, Archaeology, and Christian Humanism* (New York: McGraw–Hill, 1964), pp. 103-204 *et passim*.

no sexuality and no mythology, who is human in form but cannot be seen by human eye and cannot be represented in any form—then the founder of Yahwism was certainly a monotheist.[5]

Furthermore, after Moses the bulk of the population was monotheistic except for the superstitious, and only 'the ignorant or moronic' were the 'polytheists or henotheists' in that age of monotheism.[6] The prophet Amos was not the first monotheist, as Wellhausen implied, for there 'is not the slightest hint of any such innovation in the poetic addresses which bear his name', rather he merely deepened the social critique that was present already with Elijah.[7] Nor did the Deuteronomic Reformers innovate any aspects of monotheistic faith, they were a nostalgic return to old Mosaic monotheism, who simply were more consistent than the Yahwistic or Elohistic traditions had been in their use of the language about God. Above all, the classical prophets before Second Isaiah all evince monotheism in their critiques.[8] (But notice how Albright indirectly conceded the existence of language in the epic traditions and prophetic polemics which implies that someone in Israel was worshipping more than just Yahweh!) Ultimately, Albright concluded that the monotheism of Moses was of the same ilk as that of the great Pharisee Hillel in 30 BCE,

> The tradition of Israel represents Moses as a monotheist; the evidence of ancient Oriental religious history, combined with the most rigorous critical treatment of Israelite literary sources, points in exactly the same direction. The tradition of Israel represents the Prophets as preachers and reformers, not as religious innovators... Mosaism is a living tradition, an integrated organismic pattern, which did not change in fundamentals from the time of Moses until the time of Christ; Moses was as much a monotheist as was Hillel.[9]

Albright's views on monotheism probably influenced other authors of that age including George Ernest Wright, John Bright, P. van Imschoot, and Edmond Jacob.[10] Albright's protege, George Ernest Wright, also

5.   Albright, *Stone Age*, pp. 271-72.
6.   Albright, *Stone Age*, p. 288.
7.   Albright, *Stone Age*, p. 313.
8.   Albright, *Stone Age*, pp. 315-20, 327-29.
9.   Albright, *Stone Age*, pp. 400-401.
10.   J. Bright, *The Kingdom of God: The Biblical Concept and its Meaning for the Church* (Nashville: Abingdon Press, 1953); P. van Imschoot, *Théologie de l'Ancien Testament* (2 vols.; Paris: Tournai, 1954), I, *passim*; E. Jacob, *Theology of the Old Testament* (trans. A. Heathcote and P. Allcock; New York: Harper & Row, 1958).

contributed significant works in defending the Albrightian position.[11]

The most well-developed defense of early monotheism in Israel was presented by the Israeli scholar, Yehezkel Kaufmann, whose extensive Hebrew work was abridged in the English translation of *The Religion of Israel* (1937–1956/1972).[12] He went even further than Albright in denying polytheism to the masses in Israel. Israelites were so far removed from polytheism that the prophets and biblical authors misunderstood it in their own critiques. The only polytheism really practiced was in the imported cults in the royal courts. The abuses practiced by Israelites themselves who incurred the prophetic critique were the results not of polytheism, for gods other than Yahweh were not worshipped; rather, they were practices connected to fetishism or crass superstitions. Hence, asherim and baalim were not deities but objects crassly used for magic. Since the biblical prophets erroneously misunderstood ancient Near Eastern polytheism to be the mere worship of statues, or fetishism, when they observed something comparable among their own people, they assumed it was full-blown polytheism. (Kaufmann did seem to ignore the plain sense of the biblical text at times.) However, the suggestions of Kaufmann still receive considerable discussion even today.

In general, from 1940 to 1970 significant scholars endorsed the idea of a Mosaic monotheistic 'revolution' rather than the old idea of 'evolution'. This viewpoint exercised considerable influence upon classroom text-books of that era.

If the Israelites were monotheistic under Moses, or at least theoretically so, then the later practices of Israelites which earned condemnation in the biblical literature must have resulted from contact with the Canaanites in the land. Such a conclusion also followed from the rhetoric of the Deuteronomistic History which decried such Canaanite influence. Scholars spoke of syncretism, or the mixing of polytheistic beliefs with pure monotheism, which occurred already in the period of the judges (1200–1050 BCE). The prophets and Deuteronomic Reformers called upon the people to return to the monotheistic faith of the past, but their efforts were not successful until the exile, when all Jews made the final, firm commitment to monotheism. This image of an Israel which was

---

11. G.E. Wright, *The Old Testament against its Environment* (SBT, 2; Chicago: Regnery, 1950); *idem*, *God Who Acts: Biblical Theology as Recital* (SBT, 8; London: SCM Press, 1952); G.E. Wright and R. Fuller, *The Book of the Acts of God: Christian Scholarship Interprets the Bible* (Garden City, NY: Doubleday, 1957).

12. Kaufmann, *Religion*.

originally monotheistic, or at least monolatrous, but lapsed continually into syncretism, was presented in many textbooks and critical studies on the Hebrew Bible in this era. One finds the syncretism model endorsed in significant works by William Albright, George Ernest Wright, Yehezkel Kaufmann, Helmer Ringgren, George Fohrer, Frank Moore Cross, Harry Thomas Frank, and many others.[13]

This portrayal of Israel's religion was also part of a great theological movement from 1945 to 1970, the 'Biblical Theology Movement'. This movement was influenced greatly by continental Neo-Orthodoxy of the early twentieth century, which also reacted negatively to nineteenth-century idealistic liberal thought and the use of simple evolutionary paradigms.[14] The emphasis upon a God who acted in the events of human history, such as the exodus, Sinai, conquest and the ministry of Jesus, was central to biblical theologians in this movement who spoke of the Bible as a history of salvation or a *Heilsgeschichte*. Describing Israel's monotheism as a breakthrough rather than a gradual evolution fit with the theological agenda of these authors, which included many of the aforementioned scholars. It also facilitated a grand pedagogical and theological paradigm: the contrast of Israelite religion with Canaanite or ancient Near Eastern religion. The polytheism of Canaan with its fertility cult was set in opposition to the monotheism of Israel with its ethical demands. As the Israelites were portrayed as vacillating between these two archetypal extremes, one could sense that the biblical theologians were sounding an appeal to contemporary Christians to make a similar decision between great moral options in our own world. The biblical theologians made the Hebrew Bible come alive in relevant fashion in the

13.   Wright, *Biblical Archaeology*, pp. 99-120; Kaufman, *Religion*, pp. 142-47; H. Ringgren, *Israelite Religion* (trans. D. Green; Philadelphia: Fortress Press, 1966), pp. 42, 58, 99 *et passim*; H.T. Frank, *Bible, Archaeology, and Faith* (Nashville: Abingdon Press, 1971), pp. 102-17; G. Fohrer, *History of Israelite Religion* (trans. D. Green; Nashville: Abingdon Press, 1972), pp. 127-30; F.M. Cross, *Canaanite Myth and Hebrew Epic: Essays in the History of the Religion of Israel* (Cambridge, MA: Harvard University Press, 1973), pp. 190-91. Cf. R. Oden, 'The Place of Covenant in the Religion of Israel', *Ancient Israelite Religion* (eds. Miller, Hanson and McBride), pp. 429-47, who observes the the strong emphasis upon covenant by these theologians coincided with their early date for the emergence of monotheism.

14.   Reventlow, 'Eigenart', pp. 199-200; F.-L. Hossfeld, 'Einheit und Einzigkeit Gottes im frühen Jahwismus', *Im Gespräch mit dem dreieinen Gott: Elemente einer trinitarischen Theologie* (eds. M. Böhnke and H. Heinz; Düsseldorf: Patmos, 1985), p. 57; Redford, *Egypt*, p. 265.

classroom and church to inspire Christians to a commitment to biblical religion, social justice and an organic view of the Bible and their own religion. *Heilsgeschichte* themes were sounded most loudly by George Ernest Wright and Reginald Fuller.[15]

The later writings of George Mendenhall and Norman Gottwald with their paradigm of an internal revolution still undergirded *Heilsgeschichte* models, perhaps even more dramatically. They often inspired liberation theologians with their rhetoric, and liberation thought further called Christians to social action with an appeal to images from the Hebrew Bible.[16] Gottwald's discussion of mono-Yahwism and the corresponding exclusive social and religious commitment to the Yahweh movement emphasized the great contrast between the beliefs of Canaan and the revolutionary new thought of Israel, even though Gottwald relinquished Albright's concept of early theoretic monotheism. Now the contrast between Israel and Canaan could be augmented further by adding political and economic aspects.[17] The result was a grand theological and political interpretation of the Hebrew Bible for the modern audience. Unfortunately the *Heilsgeschichte* model has undergone a significant demise and with it the entire Biblical Theology Movement.[18]

15.   Wright, *God Who Acts*; Wright and Fuller, *Book*.

16.   G. Pixley, *God's Kingdom: A Guide for Biblical Study* (trans. D. Walsh; Maryknoll: Orbis Books, 1981); *idem, On Exodus: A Liberation Perspective* (trans. R. Barr; Maryknoll: Orbis Books, 1987); N.K. Gottwald (ed.), *The Bible and Liberation: Political and Social Hermeneutics* (Maryknoll: Orbis Books, 1983); W. Schottroff and W. Stegemann (eds.), *God of the Lowly: Socio-Historical Interpretations of the Bible* (trans. M. O'Connell; Maryknoll: Orbis Books, 1984), are but a few of the works which could be mentioned.

17.   Gottwald, *Tribes of Yahweh*, is the most masterful work in this regard.

18.   B. Albrektson, *History and the Gods: An Essay on the Idea of Historical Events as Divine Manifestations in the Ancient Near East and Israel* (Lund: Gleerup, 1967); B. Childs, *Biblical Theology in Crisis* (Philadelphia: Westminster Press, 1970), pp. 13-87; J.J.M. Roberts, 'Myth versus History: Relaying the Comparative Foundations', *CBQ* 38 (1976), pp. 1-13; H.W.F. Saggs, *The Encounter with the Divine in Mesopotamia and Israel* (London: Athlone Press, 1978), pp. 64-92; J. Barr, *Old and New in Interpretation: A Study of the Two Testaments* (London: SCM Press, 1982), pp. 62-102. The debate is summarized by R. Gnuse, *The Authority of the Bible: Theories of Inspiration, Revelation, and the Canon of the Bible* (New York: Paulist Press, 1985), pp. 66-74; *idem*, 'Holy History in the Hebrew Scriptures and the Ancient World', *BTB* 17 (1987), pp. 127-36; *idem*, 'Reassessing Israel's Intellectual Relationship to the Ancient World: Biblical Foundations for Authority and Theology', *Raising the Torch of Good News: Catholic Authority and Dialogue*

More recently biblical scholars appear to affirm the view that Israelite or Jewish religious development evolved in progressive stages or 'leaps' in the pre-exilic period until its culmination in the absolute monotheism of the Babylonian exile (586–539 BCE). One may still retain the image of a mono-Yahwistic movement in the settlement process, for it can be seen as the first step in the development toward theoretic monotheism. Other significant events that scholars focus upon include the conflict of Elijah and Elisha with the Omrides in Israel, the message of the classical prophets, the refoms of Hezekiah and Josiah, Deuteronomic Reform, and the oracles of Second Isaiah. This position seems to mediate between Albright's idea of early revolutionary monotheism and Wellhausen's gradual evolutionary model by suggesting a series of intellectual revolutions over a period of years which culminated in the exile, the time originally proposed by Wellhausen. Many biblical scholars even use the words 'evolution' and 'revolution' together in their discussions. Hence, since 1980 one senses increasingly the appearance of a different way to describe the emergence of monotheism, one that speaks of an evolutionary process which occurs in revolutionary fashion. Later in this volume I propose a heuristic model taken from modern biology by which to explain this ironic tension of evolution and revolution, called Punctuated Equilibria.

Finally, it should be noted that these new theories concerning Israel's religious development have been augmented by recent archaeological discoveries. As in the case of the shifting paradigms concerning the Israelite settlement process, a precipitating factor to cause many scholars to change their minds is the discovery of individual artifacts from the land of Palestine. In this case, more evidence is being discovered for the diversity and complexity of Israelite cultic practice. Archaeologists are unearthing testimony of extensive Israelite devotion to Asherah, the goddess of fertility, and other gods of Canaan, as well as so-called pagan activities, like sun veneration, human sacrifice and cultic prostitution.

Reference to a few critical examples may suffice. Perhaps the most hotly discussed text comes from Kuntillet 'Ajrûd, a ninth- or eighth-century BCE shrine located on a trade route in the northeastern part of

with the World (ed. B. Prusak; Annual Publication of the CTS (1986), 32; Lanham: University Press of America, 1988), pp. 147-63; *idem, Heilsgeschichte as a Model for Biblical Theology: The Debate Concerning the Uniqueness and Significance of Israel's Worldview* (College Theology Society Studies in Religion, 4; Lanham: University Press of America, 1989).

the Sinai pennisula in the wilderness. It may have been a shrine supported by the northern state of Israel on a trade and pilgrimage route into the Sinai. Scholars date it either to the years 850–837 BCE, when Israel ruled Judah under the extended Omride family (Jehoram, Ahaziah and Athaliah), or to the time of Joash, king of Israel (801–786 BCE), who also dominated Judah, for this would explain Israelite control of an area south of Judah. One inscription may mention Joash's name. Two of the inscriptions, which were discovered in 1975, read as follows, 'I bless you by Yahweh of Samaria, and by his Asherah', and 'Yahweh of Teman and his Asherah'.[19] Teman may be a reference to an older wilderness shrine where Yahweh was worshipped, or perhaps even the archaic cult of Yahweh may have origins there. The most disputed issue is whether the reference is to Asherah as a cultic object in the shrine or an actual deity, the consort of Yahweh.[20] The reference to Samaria also is disputed, for some believe it merely may mean 'guardian', but others suggest the reference to Samaria implies that many Yahwists believed in regional manifestations of Yahweh, as Canaanites also envisioned El.[21]

19.   Z. Meshel, 'Did Yahweh Have a Consort?: The New Religious Inscriptions from the Sinai', *BARev* 5.2 (1979), pp. 24-35; *idem*, 'Kuntillet 'Ajrûd', *ABD*, IV, pp. 103-109; *idem*, 'Two Aspects in the Excavation of Kuntillet 'Agrud', *Ein Gott allein* (eds. Dietrich and Klopftenstein), pp. 99-104; D. Chase, 'A Note on an Inscription from Kuntillet 'Ajrûd', *BASOR* 246 (1982), pp. 63-67; W. Dever, 'Recent Archaeological Confirmation of the Cult of Asherah in Ancient Israel', *Hebrew Studies* 23 (1982), pp. 37-44; *idem*, 'Asherah, Consort of Yahweh? New Evidence from Kuntillet 'Ajrûd', *BASOR* 255 (1984), pp. 21-37; *idem*, 'Ancient Israelite Religion: How to Reconcile the Differing Textual and Artifactual Portraits', *Ein Gott allein* (eds. Dietrich and Klopftenstein), pp. 112-22; J.A. Emerton, 'New Light on Israelite Religion: The Implications of the Inscriptions from Kuntillet 'Ajrûd', *ZAW* 94 (1982), pp. 2-20; J. Day, 'Asherah in the Hebrew Bible and Northwest Semitic Literature', *JBL* 105 (1986), pp. 391-93; J. Hadley, 'Some Drawings and Inscriptions on Two Pithoi from Kuntillet 'Ajrûd', *VT* 37 (1987), pp. 180-213; R. North, 'Yahweh's Asherah', *To Touch the Text: Biblical and Related Studies in Honor of Joseph A. Fitzmyer, S.J.* (eds. M. Horgan and P. Kobelski; New York: Crossroad, 1989), pp. 118-37; B. Margalit, 'The Meaning and Significance of Asherah', *VT* 40 (1990), pp. 274-77, 284-85, all provide discussion of the correct translation of the text, its meanings, and implications for Israelite religion.

20.   Of the aforementioned scholars, Meshel, Dever, Emerton, North and Margalit view Asherah as a consort, and many secondary evaluations follow their lead.

21.   P. Höffken, 'Eine Bemerkung zum religionsgeschichtlichen hintergrund

Another significant inscription comes from Khirbet el-Qôm, a site near Hebron in Judah, dated to the middle of the eighth century BCE. Here a text was discovered which reads, 'Blessed be Uriah by Yahweh and his Asherah'. It, too, implies that Asherah is a deity, a consort of Yahweh, capable of imparting blessing.[22] However, here again, some scholars have disputed the exact translation. Nonetheless, these two inscriptions have been the critical pieces of information to make scholars suspect that polytheistic Yahwism may have been the normative pre-exilic religion of Israel and Judah, and not some syncretistic aberration. As Susan Ackerman states,

> But the evidence from Kuntillet 'Ajrûd and Khirbet el-Qôm would suggest the definition of what constituted Yahwistic worship among the populace in ancient Israel was somewhat broader than prophetic and Deuteronomistic writings would lead us to believe.[23]

Many scholars now concede that the testimony of Kuntillet 'Ajrûd and Khirbet el-Qôm firmly testify to a severely compromised monotheism in the pre-exilic period, if not actual polytheism, as the natural religious expression of the common people in Israel.[24]

von Dtr. 6,4', *BZ* 28 (1984), pp. 88-93; Ahlström, *Israelites*, p. 58; *idem*, 'Role of Archaeological', pp. 128-29; Albertz, *Israelite Religion*, I, p. 83.

22. W. Dever, 'Iron Age Epigraphic Material from the Area of Khirbet el-Kôm', *HUCA* 40-41 (1969-1970), pp. 165-67; *idem*, 'Ancient Israelite Religion', pp. 112-13; A. Lemaire, 'Les inscriptions de Khirbet el-Qôm et l'ashérah de YHWH', *RB* 84 (1977), pp. 595-608; K. Jaros, 'Zur Inschrift Nr. 3 von Hirbet el-Qôm', *BN* 19 (1982), pp. 31-40; Z. Zevit, 'The Khirbet el-Qôm Inscription Mentioning a Goddess', *BASOR* 255 (1984), pp. 39-47; J. Hadley, 'The Khirbet el-Qôm Inscription', *VT* 37 (1987), pp. 39-49; W. Shea, 'The Khirbet el-Qôm Tomb Inscription Again', *VT* 40 (1990), pp. 110-16.

23. S. Ackerman, *Under Every Green Tree: Popular Religion in Sixth-Century Judah* (HSM, 46; Atlanta: Scholars Press, 1992), p. 66.

24. A. Angerstorfer, 'Asherah als "consort of Jahwe" oder Asirtah?', *Biblische Notizen* 17 (1982), pp. 7-16; Jaros 'Inschrift', pp. 31-40; K. Jeppesen, 'Micah v 13 in the Light of a Recent Archaeological Discovery', *VT* 34 (1984), pp. 462-66; P. Miller, 'Israelite Religion', *The Hebrew Bible and its Modern Interpreters* (eds. Knight and Tucker; The Bible and its Modern Interpreters; Chico, CA: Scholars Press, 1985), pp. 206, 217; R. Hestrin, 'The Lachish Ewer and the 'Asherah', *IEJ*, 37 (1987), pp. 212-23; S. Olyan, *Asherah and the Cult of Yahweh in Israel* (SBLMS, 34; Atlanta: Scholars Press, 1988), pp. 23-37; Dever, *Discoveries*, pp. 121-66; *idem*, 'Ancient Israelite Religion', pp. 112-22; W. Dietrich, 'Uber Werden und Wesen des biblischen Monotheismus. Religionsgeschichtliche und theologische Perspektiven', *Ein Gott allein* (eds. Dietrich and Klopftenstein), p. 15; and A. de

Some archaeological finds which lack literary inscriptions are being viewed in retrospect as evidence of deeply ingrained polytheism among the Israelites. One instance is the recently excavated bull shrine in the highlands of Samaria from the early settlement period. Its situation in the heart of Yahwistic highland country indicates to many scholars that the earliest Israelites did not surrender their worship of Baal to become too exclusively dedicated to Yahweh.[25] One final example is the tenth-century BCE cult stand unearthed at Ta'anach in 1968, which indicates that Yahweh was worshipped through the image of the sun and that Asherah likewise was venerated earnestly in Israel.[26]

In the past, biblical scholars would have looked upon such archaeological data as testimony for the syncretism between Israelite and Canaanite religions, which obviously is mentioned in the biblical text. But increasingly it is suspected that an early pure Yahwism may never have existed except in the minds of the Deuteronomistic Historians or among a very small minority of Yahweh devotees (whose religion may not have been really very pure, either). Scholars are beginning to suspect that later Yahwism may have emerged out of a greater Canaanite religion or out of a Yahwism basically indistinguishable from the Canaanite religion. Hence, the artifacts are testimony not to some syncretistic cult, but rather to the normal Yahweh religion for most people in the pre-exilic era.

What this means is not that scholars disbelieve the accounts in the Deuteronomistic History. Rather, they take them more seriously, especially those texts wherein pagan cultic activity is described. Scholars recognize that the biblical authors attest to authentic cultic activity, and that

Pury, 'Erwägungen zu einem vorexilischen Stämmjahwismus: Hos 12 und die Auseinandersetzung um die identität Israels und seines Gottes', *Ein Gott allein* (eds. Dietrich and Klopftenstein), p. 414.

25. R. Wenning and E. Zenger, 'Ein bäuerliches Baal-Heiligtum im samarischen Gebirge aus der Zeit der Anfänge Israels', *ZDPV* 102 (1986), pp. 75-86.

26. G. Taylor, 'The Two Earliest Known Representations of Yahweh', *Ascribe to the Lord*, pp. 557-66; *idem, Yahweh and the Sun: Biblical and Archaeological Evidence for Sun Worship in Ancient Israel* (JSOTSup, 111; Sheffield: JSOT Press, 1993), pp. 24-37; *idem*, 'Was Yahweh Worshipped as the Sun?', *BARev* 20.3 (1994), pp. 52-61, 90; W. Dever, 'Archaeology, Material Culture and the Early Monarchical Period in Israel', *Fabric of History* (ed. Edelman), p. 111; W. Toews, *Monarchy and Religious Institutions in Israel under Jeroboam I* (SBLMS, 47; Atlanta: Scholars Press, 1993), pp. 50-51; J. Hadley, 'Yahweh and "His Asherah": Archaeological and Textual Evidence for the Cult of the Goddess', *Ein Gott allein* (eds. Dietrich and Klopftenstein), pp. 249-53.

they are condemning certain things which did transpire in the religious life of the people. They are not attacking Canaanite intrusions into Yahwism, rather they are attacking early Yahwism. Much in the same way that the Deuteronomistic Historians projected the centralized Temple worship effected by Josiah around 620 BCE back into the very days of Solomon, so also they projected the values of the Yahwism of their own age into the past as a touchstone for critique. In fact, the Yahwism they painted into the past was the Yahwism that they had begun to create by their own reforms. Modern readers must not consider this deceit, but recognize that it was the necessary task of a reforming party to convince the people of its age as to the legitimacy of their position by establishing the antiquity of those beliefs. Had the Deuteronomic Reformers and the Deuteronomistic Historians not done this, they would never have converted the Jews to monotheism. Hence, scholars see the biblical texts describing religious history as it should have been, or from the perspective of a small monotheistic minority. The mass of Israelites, from court member to commoner, were essentially polytheistic Yahwists and did not know that they were in error.

This is the emerging scholarly consensus, but the particulars of this developmental process are vague. Different scholars propose a multitude of theoretically possible scenarios. For my purposes it would be good to look at the scholarly theories of some of the significant authors of our era. I consider first the contributions of theorists who propose in some way the model briefly outlined above. I then briefly consider the loyal opposition, views by scholars who propose radically different models, and the critical response they have received. Finally, I look at some extremely critical models, proposed by scholars who are minimalists in using the biblical text to reconstruct Israel's history or religious development, and who suspect that monotheism was totally post-exilic in all of its developmental stages. It will remain to be seen whether the mainline scholars or the more critical scholars will provide the consensus paradigm of future years. The theological and ideational implications I offer in the later chapters may be intuited from either the mainstream theories or the more critical opinions.

II

A number of critical theories concerning Israel's religious odyssey have been proposed since 1975, and increasingly scholars and teachers in biblical studies have been attracted to the new suggestions. There were, however, a few bold critics before that time who dared to challenge the reigning scholarly paradigms. The following summaries represent a selection of the most significant authors to address the issue of emerging monotheism in Israel over the past thirty years, including some of the early voices of dissent as well as the emerging chorus of contemporary critical scholars.

Denis Baly

In an excellent early essay (1970) Denis Baly lays out parameters for much of the contemporary discussion on the nature of biblical mono-theism.[27] He points out how monotheism emerges not in the desert, as the old stereotypes had it, but in urban settings in the midst of great intellectual struggles over issues such as evil, human suffering, and the universal rule of God. Hence, true monotheism emerged in the Jewish exile in Babylon and the cities of Mecca and Medina with Muhammed. Baly offers a fascinating and valuable typology of monotheistic religious phenomena: 1) 'Primitive Monotheism' occurs among primitive agrarian societies when one deity is elevated well above the hierarchy of close, personal numina. 2) 'Proto-Monotheism' is found among more developed religions when some political or cultural expansion has brought diverse people together, and intelligentsia of the dominant culture try to synthe-size regional deities under the aegis of their own national god. The stress of alien encounters leads them to merge all the gods into one pantheon and ultimately one god. Examples would include the worship of Amun in the New Kingdom period of Egypt, Baal-Shamen of Canaan, Vedantic and Upanishadic thought in India, Persia before Zoroaster, Hellenistic monism, and Arabia before Muhammed. 3) 'Pseudo-Monotheism' occurs when a strong ruler tries to further impose a form of proto-monotheism upon all his subjects for cultural solidarity. Examples would include Akhenaton's cult of Aton in fourteenth century BCE Egypt, the cult of Ashur in imperialistic Assyria, Roman emperor worship, and Zoroastrianism. All three types reflect monotheistic tendencies, but an intellectual breakthrough is necessary to attain the pure monotheism which the Jews secured in the Babylonian Exile.

Until the exile the majority of Jews were polytheistic, but several pre-liminary stages may be observed: 1) The Sinai experience laid the ground-work for monotheism by rejecting the natural world as divine, using the concept of covenant to affirm human equality, refusing to locate Yahweh

27.   Baly, 'Geography of Monotheism', pp. 253-78.

geographically and instead placing the deity in the wilderness, and stressing the absolute power and jealousy of Yahweh. 2) Elijah did not advocate true monotheism, but he affirmed regional monotheism and Yahweh's superiority over the forces of nature. 3) Amos was a universalist and the first 'effective monotheist', although the later classical prophets had to develop his ideas further. 4) Finally, Second Isaiah developed monotheistic belief most thoroughly and then the masses could accept it. Second Isaiah made counterclaims against the image of Ahura-Mazda of the Zoroastrian Persians. Much of Baly's discussion anticipates the later scholarly inquiry, especially with his emphasis upon the various stages of development, the limited nature of Elijah's and Amos's monotheistic understanding, and the possibility of interaction with Persian thought. However, later scholars would not give as much credit to the Sinai experience. Ultimately, Baly's essay is excellent in terms of its methodology.

Morton Smith

One of the first authors to sternly critique the prevailing set of assumptions engendered by William Albright and others was Morton Smith, who stresses that we ought to acknowledge that biblical religion was only one facet of the spectrum of Israelite religious experience prior to 587 BCE.[28] Smith documents the evidence from the Bible itself and archaeological data for the presence of those other religious beliefs. In pungent style he states that we are lacking the testimony of the other pieties in Palestine, such as,

> ...Psalms celebrating the tender mercies of Asherah, stories of the miracles worked by the prophets of Baal or of the zeal of the priests of Anath, histories of the piety and devotion of Manasseh and Jezebel and of the reformation they effected in the national religion...although the cult of Yahweh is the principle concern of the Old Testament, it may not have been the principle religious concern of the Israelites.[29]

28.   M. Smith, 'The Common Theology of the Ancient Near East', *JBL* 71 (1952), pp. 135-47; *idem*, 'The Image of God: Notes on the Hellenization of Judaism', *BJRL* 40 (1958), pp. 473-512; *idem*, 'On the Shape of God and the Humanity of Gentiles', *Religions in Antiquity: Essays in Memory of Erwin Ramsdell Goodenough* (ed. J. Neusner; Leiden: Brill, 1968), pp. 315-26; *idem*, 'Religious Parties among the Israelites before 587', *Palestinian Parties and Politics That Shaped the Old Testament* (New York: Columbia University Press, 1971), pp. 15-56; *idem*, 'The Veracity of Ezekiel, the Sins of Manasseh, and Jeremiah 44:18', *ZAW* 87 (1975), pp. 11-16.

29.   Smith, 'Religious Parties', p. 19.

Smith was the first to propose seriously that the 'Yahweh alone' party was a minority religio-political movement in the pre-exilic period in opposition to the royal cult and all popular or familial forms of religion. Most Israelites belonged to the 'syncretistic party' or the common religion of the masses, while the 'Yahweh alone' movement was small and peripheral in society. There was no monotheistic core of Israelites who entered the land and subsequently fell into paganism, but rather a small group arose and evolved slowly into monotheists. They wrote the biblical texts and projected their beliefs into the distant past to give the impression their monotheism was the norm from which Israelites deviated over the years.

Smith hypothetically traces the development of the movement. 1) In the early years of the pre-monarchical and monarchic periods the cult of Yahweh was not distinguishable from typical West-Semitic religions; Israel shared the common religion of the ancient Near East. Each region had a national deity, and Yahweh was the national god of Israel. Properly speaking, Yahweh was merely the deity of the dynastic rulers in Judah and Israel, and his status was like that of Chemosh in Moab or Milcom in Ammon. Perhaps a few of the nomadic elements that constituted Israel had a proclivity to worship one god, but their impact was minimal. 2) The court of Judah from the time of David (1000 BCE) may have been responsible for popularizing the worship of Yahweh among the masses. Asa is the first king to demonstrate Yahwistic piety (900 BCE), and only during the rule of Jehoshaphat do Yahweh names become common in society (860 BCE). Prior to this time the biblical text admits the presence of names constructed with the names of deities such as El, Baal, Gad, Anath, Am Yam, Zedek, Shalem, Asher and Tsur. 3) A real move toward monotheism began with the Omride conflict in Israel (850–840 BCE) when Jezebel killed Yahwistic prophets. Since her own sons bore Yahwistic names, her victims must have been 'Yahweh aloneists'. However, the overthrow of the Omrides resulted from their foreign connections rather than a desire to elevate Yahweh monotheistically, for the 'Yahweh aloneists' constituted only part of the rebellious movement. The Deuteronomistic Historians unduly stressed the religious dimension of the rebellion years later. 4) Classical prophets and the Deuteronomic Reform movement brought the message of practical monotheism to the masses. Hosea appears to be the first 'Yahweh aloneist' among the prophets (750 BCE). Even by Jeremiah's age (580 BCE), however, monotheism appears to be in the minority, despite the earlier attempts at reform by Josiah (620 BCE), whose actions may have been more political than religious. 5) Finally, in the exile and the post-exilic era the people became monotheists, for then people surrounded by foreign religions had to make a clear decision not to participate in those foreign cults. Such restraint makes a person into a true monotheist.

Smith suggests that the Bible's constant rhetoric about the Israelites turning to idolatry and syncretism is really an admission that the 'Yahweh aloneists' were in the minority. Most Israelites were 'syncretists,' that is, more properly, they worshipped Yahweh as their most important deity along with other gods, and they saw this as perfectly acceptable. For them also it was acceptable to portray Yahweh in iconographic form. The elevation of Yahweh for exclusive veneration in the pre-exilic period was an act of nationalistic expression, as one might find in a time of crisis. Nations around Israel would do the same with their national deities. Perhaps, this was the chief motivation for Hezekiah and Josiah, the so-called monotheistic reformers. The Yahweh movement itself was composed of disparate groups: Levites in the highlands, some Jerusalem priests, nomadic groups like the Rechabites, the Yahweh prophets, and some political groups in Jerusalem. Nor did these groups always work together. Ultimately, in the post-exilic era priestly laws separated the Jews from others and encouraged pure monotheism.

Smith's ideas have been influential and are often quoted by later authors. For some he opened the floodgates of critique and paved the way for new paradigms. Some later authors envisioned an even more critical scenario than he. Morton Smith with his pungent style of presentation was certainly in the vanguard of the contemporary discussion of emergent monotheism.

Gösta Ahlström
Another early scholar who stressed the natural syncretism of pre-exilic Israelite religion was Gösta Ahlström.[30] As early as 1963 he observed

30.   G. Ahlström, *Aspects of Syncretism in Israelite Religion* (trans. E. Sharpe; Lund: Gleerup, 1963), pp. 14-88; *idem*, 'An Israelite God Figurine from Hazor', *Orientalia Suecana* 19-20 (1970-1971), pp. 54-62; *idem*, 'An Israelite God Figurine, Once More', *VT* 25 (1975), pp. 106-109; *idem*, 'King Jehu—A Prophet's Mistake', *Scripture in History and Theology: Essays in Honor of J. Coert Rylaarsdam* (eds. A. Merrill and T. Overholt; PTMS, 17; Pittsburg: Pickwick Press, 1977), pp. 52-57; *idem, Royal Administration and National Religion in Ancient Palestine* (Studies in the History of the Ancient Near East, 1; Leiden: Brill, 1982); *idem, Israelites*, pp. 7-94; *idem*, 'Role of Archaeological', pp. 128-31. Cf. also W.B. Barrick and

that the biblical text does not testify to a 'fallen' version of an early pure Yahwism, but reflects a natural state of religious activity. Asherah worship, the use of idols for other gods, and even the iconographic portrayal of Yahweh were normal religious expressions for polytheistic Israelites, and the monotheists were a small group of dissenters until the exile. We should speak of the various forms of Israelite religion; there was not a normative belief system, but many regional expressions of Yahweh could be found in the various shrines.[31]

In his more recent writings Ahlström uses archaeological data to suggest that Israelite religion was one of a national cult with a high god, Yahweh, served by attendant deities, including Asherah, Baal, Shamash (sun), and Yerach (moon). The religion was a state cult under the royal direction, so the emphasis upon the national deity was determined by each king. Hezekiah and Josiah simply elevated the national deity, Yahweh, for political reasons in Judah. Manasseh was a traditionalist who sought to return to the Judahite practices after his father's disastrous policies. The city and the Temple were the domain of the deity who ruled through the agency of the king.

Different shrines had interpretations of the Yahweh religion (Gibeon, Shiloh, Bethel, Dan, etc.), and the recent discoveries at Kuntillet 'Ajrûd simply unveil another one of those interpretations of the royal cult. Kuntillet 'Ajrûd (800 BCE) represents the beliefs of the northern state of Israel, and in particular the city of Samaria, for the deity was called 'Yahweh of Shomeron'.[32] It was not a Judean shrine even though it was south of Judah. Ultimately, the interpretation of the Jerusalem cult prevailed and influenced the exilic and post-exilic biblical authors.

Yahweh worship came into Palestine with a group from Edom, perhaps the Calebites, Kenites, Jerahmeelites and Kenizzites. The reference to 'Yahweh of Teman' at Kuntillet 'Ajrûd implies an Edomite origin as well as biblical references to Yahweh's coming from Seir (Deut. 33.2; Judg. 5.4). Perhaps, Yahweh was revered first at Gibeon, then rose to prominence with Saul, and was elevated significantly by David, who

---

J. Spencer, 'Parentheses in a Snowstorm: G.W. Ahlström and the Study of Ancient Palestine', *In the Shelter of Elyon: Essays on Ancient Palestinian Life and Literature in Honor of G.W. Ahlström* (eds. W.B. Barrick and J. Spencer; JSOTSup, 31; Sheffield: JSOT Press, 1984), pp. 43-65.

31.　Ahlström, 'God Figurine', pp. 54-62; *idem*, 'God Figurine, Once More', pp. 106-109; *idem*, *Aspects*, pp. 14-88.

32.　Emerton, 'Israelite Religion', pp. 2-20 concurs on this translation.

brought Yahweh to Jerusalem and merged him with El Elyon, a local deity. At Bethel Yahweh merged with Baal, and elsewhere other deities were absorbed ultimately with Yahweh. Essentially the cult of Yahweh spread slowly at first, but as the cult deity of Jerusalem Yahweh was assured of eventual success.

The biblical literature is written from a Jerusalem perspective, which preserved northern traditions only from the cult shrine at Bethel (which gave oral traditions of Elijah, Elisha, Amos and Hosea to the southerners). The books of Samuel and Kings read more like historical novels than real historiography. Ultimately, our record of Yahweh and Yahwism existed only in the later biblical writers' reconstructions of history. For example, Elijah was not an advocate of exclusive devotion to Yahweh, but merely an opponent of the alliance with Tyre and the attendant veneration of Jezebel's Tyrian Baal; and thus Elijah was merely a nationalistic court prophet with pro-Assyrian sympathies. Ahlström's critical portrayal of Israelite religion reflects the general approach of many Scandanavian scholars and foreshadows the very critical approach of the Danish author, Niels Peter Lemche, who will be discussed below.

Imre Mihalik
Imre Mihalik anticipated the critical nature of the discussion on monotheism at a very early date; unfortunately the bulk of his work remains unpublished after his recent death.[33] In an early, bold essay in 1973 he maintains that the 'whole life of Israel was not independent of Canaanite culture; on the contrary it was one manifestation of Canaanite culture'.[34] Mihalik believes that modern biblical scholars are too unwilling to accept an evolutionary model for Israel, even when it provides a good paradigm, a concept with which this author highly concurs.

Mihalik suggests that Yahwism really began to arise only with Elijah, whose very name indicates the new, radical innovation of his movement— 'my El is Yahweh'. Prior to Elijah there were some people in the land of Canaan who viewed El as their high god and others who viewed Yahweh as theirs. El worshippers would have included Samuel and those with whom the name Israel originated. Although the people might have equated the two deities unconsciously, it was not until Elijah that the two deities were equated, and their respective devotees joined ranks in opposition to the Phoenician Baal cult of the Omrides. Furthermore, it was not

33. Mihalik, 'Some Thoughts', pp. 11-19.
34. Mihalik, 'Some Thoughts', p. 11.

until Josiah that a systematic attempt was undertaken to unify the two cults. Throughout the monarchy there was a tendency for the masses to equate the two deities in a naive fashion, and this is evinced by archaic expressions in which either the name of Yahweh or El/Elohim might appear: 1) voice of XX, 2) mouth of XX, 3) face of XX, 4) glory of XX, 5) name of XX, 6) altar of XX, 7) presence of XX, 8) ark of XX, 9) spirit of XX, 10) word of XX, 11) angel of XX, 12) house of XX, and 13) fear of XX. Native Canaanite El worshippers would have identified with Yahweh, who was brought into the land, because the Israelite story of the exodus would remind Canaanites of their own freedom from past Egyptian rule in Palestine. After Elijah's efforts the later classical prophets pushed devotion to Yahweh into the foreground, and eventually they advocated the exclusive worship of Yahweh. While some of Mihalik's ideas are dated, his insights anticipated key issues of the debate years in advance.

V. Nikiprowetsky

In 1975 V. Nikiprowetsky wrote a seminal article characterizing the emergence of ethical monotheism.[35] He sees no evidence of monotheism in the ancient Near East or Israel until the Babylonian exile. What existed in Babylon and elsewhere might be described as 'monarchical polytheism', the elevation of one deity over subordinate deities. What historians observe is either 'affective exaggeration for the sake of adulation' by pious devotees, the creation of a syncretistic deity who absorbs other deities as hypostases or 'parts of his body', or the creation of a collective or abstract deity.[36] The cult of Aton in Egypt came the closest to true monotheism, but it failed for lack of any real followers other than pharaoh's family.

Monotheism emerged among the Jews in exile, as is evidenced by the Deuteronomistic History. Even then, many post-exilic Jews, such as those at Elephantine in Egypt, still were polytheists. There were, however, preliminary stages which prepared for the emergence of monotheism: 1) Jeroboam's division of the nation in 930 BCE indicated to many Israelites that Yahweh could be a national deity of the two nations, Judah and Israel, and this planted the idea of universalism in their minds. 2) Although Elijah did not deny the existence of Tyrian Baal or condemn

35. V. Nikiprowetsky, 'Ethical Monotheism', *Daedalus*, 104.2 (1975), pp. 68-89.

36. Nikiprowetsky, 'Ethical Monotheism', p. 73.

other gods, he declared Baal's impotence before Yahweh (850 BCE). 3) The universalism of Amos and Isaiah (750–700 BCE) further developed ideas which culminated in Jeremiah's implied message that Yahweh is the only deity (600 BCE). 4) Second Isaiah declared most clearly that there is no other god than Yahweh (Isa. 43.10-12, 44.6, 45.6-7). The prophets, in particular, appealed to past traditions which they so idealized that they created a new belief system by projecting their own personal religious experiences into the past. Second Isaiah was a radical monotheist who represented a crystalization of the previous developments. The lateness of true monotheism can be demonstrated by the references to other gods in a work as late as Deuteronomy (Deut. 4.19, 10.17).

The development of monotheism in Israel was inseparable from the vicissitudes of their political experience. The crisis created by contact with the great empires of Assyria and Chaldean Babylon, who succeeded in their political aims while the chosen people suffered, led to a monotheistic faith. So, monotheism did evolve naturally and inevitably, it was an exception in human intellectual history. Monotheism in Israel 'constitutes a particular phenomenon...it does represent a true spiritual revolution'.[37]

H.W.F. Saggs
H.W.F. Saggs, an Assyriologist, has made significant critical scholarly contributions to biblical studies, especially on the Israelite and ancient Near Eastern understandings of God and divine actions in human affairs.[38] He observes that pre-exilic Israelites were clearly polytheistic, and later biblical traditions were 'prescriptive' not 'descriptive' in regard to earlier beliefs, that is, they criticized as abuses those practices which were considered acceptable by the earlier Israelites. Early Yahwists accepted Yahweh prostitutes until Josiah's time. The golden calves were not removed by Jehu or his ally Jehonadab the Rechabite after the revolution inspired by Elijah, and were used for many years thereafter. The asherah images likewise remained in use under subsequent kings Jehoahaz and Joash after Jehu's revolution. An asherah and a bronze snake existed in Judah's cult until Hezekiah removed them. Significantly, the Assyrian king Sargon II listed booty taken from Samaria in 721 BCE which included

37. Nikiprowetsky, 'Ethical Monotheism', p. 86.
38. Saggs, *Encounter*, pp. 64-92 *et passim*; *idem, The Might that was Assyria* (London: Sidgwick & Jackson, 1984), p. 257; *idem, Civilization before Greece and Rome* (New Haven: Yale University Press, 1989), p. 15.

'the gods in whom they trusted', and the Assyrians knew the difference between gods and secondary beings, such as cherubim. In Judah El was worshipped as a separate deity by some people and equated with Yahweh by others. Many objects criticized and destroyed by Hezekiah and Josiah were traditional Yahwistic cult objects. In fact, Hezekiah's activity around 700 BCE attacked so many traditional Yahwistic practices that he alienated the Judahites and made them susceptible to Assyrian propaganda by Rabshakeh in 2 Kgs 18.22.[39] Saggs concludes,

> The whole history of the struggle of the Israelite prophets with syncretism shows that to the ordinary Israelite there was no fixed boundary between Yahwism and those cults of his contemporaries which we refer to as pagan, and that other cults and religious practices and concepts could easily be accepted into the framework of Yahwism. This indicates that in the monarchy period in Israel there was a horizontal (or, if one prefers the term, synchronic) continuum from Israelite Yahwism into the religions of the Canaanites and of Assyria and Babylonia.[40]

Monotheism according to Saggs emerged most clearly with the oracles of Jeremiah and Second Isaiah, and therein he discovers the Jewish contact with Mesopotamian thought. The image of Yahweh as cosmic creator in these two prophets runs counter to traditional Mosaism, so that it can not be part of an internal evolution; rather, it is a response to the Babylonian image of Marduk as world creator. Jeremiah also borrowed the Babylonian idea that the creator deity also had a plan for the entire world. Second Isaiah then related this plan to salvation history, so that Yahweh's care for Israel was a particular aspect of Yahweh's greater concern for the world. In the old El imagery Yahweh was portrayed as creator of the world, and in the old Yahweh traditions Yahweh was said to have saved and elected Israel. Second Isaiah then most effectively combined these two traditions.

Israel articulated nothing radically different from other ancient Near Eastern religions about Yahweh. Israelite religion came to be unique more in terms of 'recognition of what God was not'. God was not in the forces of nature, not to be represented by human or animal form, nor to be found in a multiplicity of forms. The emergence of monotheism entailed the final reduction of conflicting wills in the cosmos to one divine will. It also brought the universalistic perspective that Yahweh cared for other people, and the Jews had to become the channel through

39. Saggs, *Encounter*, pp. 22-23, 197-98; *idem, Assyria*, p. 257.
40. Saggs, *Encounter*, p. 6.

which Yahweh could mediate concern for others. Jews made this leap of thought because their experiences from exodus to exile made them less respectful of the traditions of the ancient world and more ready to reject them in favor of a new intellectual synthesis.[41]

Norman Gottwald

Norman Gottwald's herculean scholarship has contributed greatly to our understanding of the settlement process in Israel, but his grand theories have implications for understanding Israelite religious development as well.[42] By his own admission he steers a middle course between the radical critiques of Morton Smith, Bertil Albrektson and others on the one hand and the traditional *Heilsgeschichte* model on the other. He admits the cogency of Smith's observations about the common theology of the ancient Near East found in Israel's intellectual matrix, but he believes early Israel introduced unique ideas which produced 'mono-Yahwism'.

The cult of Yahweh was an offshoot of Canaanite religion even though it was the ethos of opposition in the Palestinian highlands. After evolving out of many religious sources of its age, this ethos added unique perspectives, including the stress upon the mercy and justice of Yahweh, the concern with egalitarianism, and the representation of Yahweh by egalitarian functionaries. According to Gottwald Yahweh usurped the sacred domain; Israel saw Yahweh as the only 'effective force in all matters decisive to the constitution and functional continuity of the social entity Israel'.[43] Later monotheism was the philosophical elaboration of early 'mono-Yahwism'. In the ancient Near East the functions of various deities might be drawn together in one deity temporarily, but in Israel they came together permanently in the persona of Yahweh.

Gottwald's contributions to the discussion is the concept of 'mono-Yahwism'. This is conceived as a form of monolatry which contains both a radical commitment to one deity and to a new social ethos. It is not true monotheism, because it does not deny the existence of other gods, but in Gottwald's estimation it shares the zeal of monotheism. It is a useful term, even though many of Gottwald's insights would be critiqued by later scholars in the 1980s.

---

41. Saggs, *Encounter*, pp. 43-52, 92, 116, 176, 185-86; *idem, Civilization*, p. 15.
42. Gottwald, *Tribes of Yahweh*, pp. 676-91; *idem*, 'Recent Studies', pp. 83-84.
43. Gottwald, *Tribes of Yahweh*, p. 680.

Fritz Stolz

Fritz Stolz believes that true monotheism is a total religio-cultural system, and for Israel it emerged only in the exile with Second Isaiah, although precursor stages may be observed.[44] True monotheistic reformers, such as Akhenaton, Zoroaster and Muhammed, combined religious and political agendas in an attempt to reorganize the world order. Early pastoral Israel was not monotheistic, nor could it inspire later monotheism. Personal devotion by a family or clan to a single deity is really an attempt to use that deity as a mediator to a higher god. In a more advanced society a deity simply may represent the fullness of the pantheon, as with El at Ugarit or Anu and Enlil in Mesopotamia. Both societies are quite clearly polytheistic, and at best they might exhibit only an occasional urge toward monotheism. Early Israel, too, was polytheistic with Yahweh as one deity among others, and this is implied by the inscriptions at Kuntillet 'Ajrûd and elsewhere.

The seeds of monotheism were planted by the prophetic movement, and Stolz sees several stages of evolution: 1) Elijah engaged in cultural conflict, not a battle for monotheism, for it was a struggle between rival deities, which really assumes polytheism. But his political and religious fight had the zeal of monotheism. 2) A true anti-polytheistic reaction may be seen in the oracles of Amos, Hosea, Isaiah and Micah, who attacked polytheistic elements in the cult, because they sensed the true difference between Yahweh and the world. 3) Second Isaiah was the 'creator' of true monotheism, for it was with him that the central experience of monotheism occurred, the 'moment of exclusion', when the existence of other deities was denied. 4) Deuteronomy and the Deuteronomistic History, which are post-exilic in Stolz's opinion, stressed exclusive worship of Yahweh and a new social worldview. In effect, only post-exilic Jews are true monotheists portraying God as both a distant creator and an active personal deity, whereas polytheists would push the older deity into the background as a *deus otiosus*. As true monotheists they also sought to control the state in order to carry out the social implications of their ideology.

---

44. F. Stolz, *Strukturen und Figuren im Kult von Jerusalem* (BZAW, 118; Berlin: de Gruyter, 1970), *passim*; *idem*, 'Monotheismus in Israel', *Monotheismus im Alten Israel und seiner Umwelt* (ed. O. Keel; BibB, 14; Fribourg: Schweizerisches Katholisches Bibelwerk, 1980), pp. 144-89; *idem*, 'Der Monotheismus Israels im Kontext der altorientalischen Religionsgeschichte—Tendenzen neuerer Forschung', *Ein Gott allein* (eds. Dietrich and Klopfenstein), pp. 33-50.

Othmar Keel

The scholarship of Othmar Keel and his students has been directed especially toward the appreciation of artwork and iconography in ancient Israel.[45] Their study reveals the great continuity Israelite religious art and symbolism had with neighboring cultures, particularly Egypt. The prohibition against images did not prevent the emergence of a generous artistic tradition, including indirect portrayals of Yahweh. For example, Yahweh could be envisioned with traditional imagery taken from the cult of the sun god, who was pictured with the symbol of an empty throne in surrounding cultures. Such solar religious imagery, mediated primarily through the court in Jerusalem, may have given rise ultimately to the aniconic stress in later Yahwism.[46] This continuity with pagan artistic conventions leads Keel to suspect a greater connection with Canaanite (Ugarit) and Egyptian beliefs than biblical scholars have recognized previously. He states that those scholars who argue Israelites only worshipped Yahweh on the basis of personal names, Tigay and Fowler (who will be discussed below), ignore the extensive iconographic evidence for polytheism.

Keel believes that monotheism arose rather late. It is questionable to call Amos and Hosea monotheists, rather Second Isaiah is the first true monotheist. Early contributions to the eventual emergence of exilic monotheism were provided primarily by the activity of the royal courts in elevating Yahweh to the position of being a high god in the heavens.[47]

---

45.   O. Keel, *The Symbolism of the Biblical World: Ancient Near Eastern Iconography and the Book of Psalms* (trans. T. Hallet; New York: Seabury, 1978); *idem*, 'Wer zerstörte Sodom?', *TZ* 35 (1979), pp. 110-17; *idem*, 'Gedanken zur Beschäftigung mit Monotheismus', *Monotheismus*, pp. 12-30; O. Keel and C. Uehlinger, *Göttinnen, Götter und Gottessymbole: Neue Erkenntnisse zur Religionsgeschichte Kanaans und Israels aufgrund bislang unerschlossener ikonographischer Quellen* (Quaestiones disputatae, 134; Freiburg: Herder, 1992), 320, 472, *et passim*; *idem*, 'Jahwe und die Sonnengottheit von Jerusalem', *Ein Gott allein* (eds. Dietrich and Klopfenstein), pp. 269-306. Cf. also S. Schroer, *In Israel gab es Bilder: Nachrichten von darstellender Kunst im Alten Testament* (OBO, 74; Göttingen: Vandenhoeck & Ruprecht, 1987); *idem*, 'Die personifizierte Sophia im Buch der Weisheit', *Ein Gott allein* (eds. Dietrich and Klopfenstein), pp. 543-58, who is a student of Keel's and likewise evaluates the meaning of religious art in Israel.

46.   Keel, 'Sodom', pp. 110-17; Keel and Uehlinger, 'Sonnengottheit', pp. 269-306.

47.   Keel, 'Gedanken', pp. 12-30; Keel and Uehlinger, *Göttinnen*, pp. 320, 472, *et passim*; Keel and Uehlinger, 'Sonnengottheit', pp. 269-306.

Notwithstanding those contributions, the ultimate exilic emergence of monotheism is a revolution, not an evolution or a gradual, inevitable growth of ideas, which brings monotheism out of polytheism as the next logical stage of intellectual development. For this reason Keel condemns the use of old biological models which spoke of gradual human development. He prefers to speak of 'successive revolutions' in religious thought in the pre-exilic era, which finally led to the revolutionary breakthrough of Second Isaiah. Keel's model of 'successive revolutions' is an excellent concept; but what he fails to appreciate, however, is that there are contemporary models of biological evolution which concur with these perceptions of his.

Hermann Vorländer

Hermann Vorländer believes that true monotheism arose only in the exile; prior to that time there was no real distinction between Israelite and Canaanite religion.[48] The emergence of Yahwism began with David's election of Yahweh as the deity of his dynasty. The Yahweh cult was rooted more in the south, and Yahweh veneration spread from Jerusalem to Judah in general.

Although Yahweh was the favorite deity of the people during the age of the divided monarchies, they were still polytheistic. The selection of a personal deity assumes polytheism, for one must select from among the gods one singular deity. The frequent choice of Yahweh in names, as testified to in the biblical text and the archaeological record, implies that individual Israelites took such names to indicate their relationship to this singular deity chosen from among the other gods. At best, Israelites were henotheistic (temporary devotion to one deity, usually during a crisis) or monolatrous (continued worship of one deity), since they never denied the existence of the other gods. This is indicated by the presence of so many deity figurines in Palestinian sites, the many references in the biblical text to other divine beings in direct or subtle fashion (Gen. 31.34; Deut. 32.8; Judg. 11.24; 1 Kgs 11.1, 14.21, 16.31, 19.15; 2 Kgs 17.24-

---

48.   H. Vörlander, *Mein Gott: Die Vorstellungen vom persönliche Gott* (Kevelaer: Butzon & Bercker, 1975), *passim*; *idem*, 'Der Monotheismus Israels als Antwort auf die Krise des Exils', *Der einzige Gott: Die Geburt des biblischen Monotheismus* (ed. B. Lang; Munich: Kösel, 1981), pp. 84-113; *idem*, 'Aspects of Popular Religion in the Old Testament' (trans. G. Harrison), *Popular Religion* (eds. N. Greinacher and N. Mette; Concilium, 186; Edinburgh: T. & T. Clark, 1986), pp. 63-70.

41, 21.7, 23.24; Mic. 4.5), and the post-exilic evidence at Elephantine in Egypt that diaspora Jews also worshipped goddesses like Anat-Bethel, Haram-Bethel, and Babylonian deities such as Bel, Nabu, Shamash and Nergal (all of which may reflect the deities worshipped in pre-exilic Judah). Israelites and Judahites probably perceived Yahweh in the same fashion as other polytheists perceived their deities in countries around Israel. For example, in the Mesha Stela (850 BCE) the king of Moab gave solitary attention to Chemosh, the national god of Moab, in language comparable to that of pre-exilic Israelites.

True monotheism emerged only among the Jewish exiles in Babylon, because they were an ethnic minority there, and religious self-definition helped them to preserve their ethnic identity. Several factors assisted in this transformation: 1) The cult of Yahweh was imageless, so it was easy to transplant it to a foreign land in rustic conditions of exile. 2) The upper classes of Judah primarily were deported to Babylon, and this group had a greater number of intelligentsia ready to make such a monotheistic transformation. Further, a larger percentage of exiles were committed already to the national deity in exclusivistic fashion. 3) These people were receptive to ideas in the land of exile which helped further their own thoughts. Babylonians spoke of Marduk as a universal lord and creator, the Chaldean king Nabonidus elevated his personal deity (Sin) in monolatrous fashion, many Babylonians exhibited exclusive devotion to Nabu, and later in the exile the impact of Zoroastrianism made itself felt. Vorländer attaches great importance to this last factor, for he believes that the Persians must have been impressed with Jewish monotheism, so that the Jews were reinforced positively in their own monotheistic convictions.

Second Isaiah was the first proponent of true monotheism. Subsequent literature was produced which shared this belief and such texts include the Yahwist Epic, the Deuteronomistic History, and the Priestly texts. Vorländer shares with other contemporary critical scholars the tendency to date all Pentateuchal texts to the exile and even later.[49] Biblical

---

49.   Van Seters, *Abraham*; *idem*, *Prologue to History: The Yahwist as Historian in Genesis* (Louisville, KY: Westminster/John Knox, 1992); *idem*, *The Life of Moses: The Yahwist as Historian in Exodus–Numbers* (Louisville, KY: Westminster/ John Knox, 1994); M. Rose, *Deuteronomist und Jahwist: Untersuchungen zu den Berührungspunkten beider Literaturwerke* (ATANT, 67; Zürich: Theologischer Verlag, 1981); E. Blum, *Die Komposition der Vätergeschichte* (WMANT, 57; Neukirchen–Vluyn: Neukirchener Verlag, 1984); *idem*, *Studien zur Komposition des*

narratives were inspired by the historiographic tradition in Babylon. Classic exilic and post-exilic texts espousing monotheism include: Isa. 43.10-13; Deut. 4.35, 39, 6.4, 32.12, 39; 2 Sam. 7.22, and Genesis 1. Monotheism gave strength to the formation of Jewish identity, and it also addressed the question of suffering and its divine causation. This diverse literature combined to portray Yahweh as a universal deity, a creator god, and yet a personal deity at the same time. As a sole god Yahweh became more distant in the heavens, but the exilic cult drew upon aspects of pre-exilic popular religious piety to bridge this gap. All these themes were necessary and natural theological expressions of the exilic experience. The breakthrough to monotheism by the Jews in exile was a significant accomplishment. Even though it was part of a greater first millennium BCE movement away from polytheism toward monism or monotheism occurring elsewhere (Lao Tzu, Confucius, Buddha), the magnitude of the intellectual and religious accomplishment of these Jews ought not be underestimated.

Bernhard Lang
Perhaps the leading author to advocate a new model for understanding the emergence of monotheism is Bernhard Lang.[50] He builds upon the

Pentateuch (BZAW, 189; Berlin: de Gruyter, 1990).

50. B. Lang, 'Vor einer Wende im Verständnis des israelitischen Gottesglaubens?', *TQ* 160 (1980), pp. 53-60, 'The Yahweh-Alone Movement and the Making of Jewish Monotheism', *Monotheism and the Prophetic Minority: An Essay in Biblical History and Sociology* (Social World of Biblical Antiquity, 1; Sheffield: Almond Press, 1983), pp. 13-59; *idem*, 'Neues über die Geschichte des Monotheismus', *TQ* 163 (1983), pp. 54-58; *idem*, 'George Orwell im gelobten Land, Das Buch Deuteronium und der Geist Kirchlicher Kontrolle', *Kirche und Visitation* (eds. E. Zeeden and P. Lang; Stuttgart: Klett-Cotta, 1984), pp. 21-35; *idem*, 'No God but Yahweh! The Origin and Character of Biblical Monotheism' (trans. J.G. Cumming), *Monotheism* (eds. C. Geffré, J.-P. Jossua, and M. Lefébure; Concilium, 177; Edinburgh: T. & T. Clark, 1985), pp. 41-49; *idem*, 'Zur Entstehung des biblischen Monotheism', *TQ* 166 (1985), pp. 135-42; *idem*, *Wisdom and the Book of Proverbs* (New York: Pilgrim, 1986), *passim*; *idem*, 'Afterlife: Ancient Israel's Changing Vision of the World beyond', *Bible Review* 4.2 (1988), pp. 12-23; *idem*, 'Der vergöttliche König im polytheistischen Israel', *Mensch werdung Gottes— Vergöttlichung von Menschen* (ed. D. Zeller; NTOA, 7; 1988), pp. 37-59; *idem*, 'Segregation and Intolerance', *What the Bible Really Says* (eds. M. Smith and J. Hoffman; San Francisco: HarperCollins, 1993), pp. 115-35; *idem*, 'Der monarchische monotheismus und die Konstellation zweier Götter im Frühjudentum: Ein neuer Versuch über Menschensohn, Sophia und Christologie', *Ein Gott allein* (eds.

work of Morton Smith and refines his ideas into an even more critical assessment of Israel's religious evolution. He also critiques the ideas of contemporaries, such as the notion of 'mono-Yahwism' advocated by Norman Gottwald. He believes Gottwald's model is nothing than a 'modern idealization', a 'romantic idea', and 'wishful thinking', rather than a plausible reconstruction.[51] For his own part, Lang believes that the discussion of monotheism can begin no earlier than the ninth-century Elijah and Elisha movement.

Lang suggests that for Israelites Yahweh was merely a national high god, at times (usually in a crisis) elevated above the other deities. One could elevate Yahweh thus and remain a polytheist; in this respect Israel was no different than the neighboring countries. Originally, Israelite religion was a West-Semitic belief system wherein a clan deity, Yahweh, was raised to be a national god. Monolatry of a limited form emerged with Elijah and Elisha in their fight against the Omrides in the north and also in the reforms of Asa and Jehoshaphat in Judah (880–840 BCE). Elijah and Elisha sought the exclusive worship of Yahweh as the national deity over against the imported Tyrian Baal of the Omrides; however, they were not monotheists. The battle was between two groups of polytheists; at stake was the primacy of rival priesthoods and the economic implications of foreign priests and merchants imported into Israel along with close political connections to Phoenicia.

Hosea may have been the first person (750 BCE) to imply that the ancestors worshipped Yahweh exclusively. The message of Amos and Hosea did not entail ignoring other gods, instead it undergirded 'temporary monolatry', or the total allegiance to the national deity in times of crisis. Ultimately this would evolve into 'permanent monolatry', wherein the deity is worshipped exclusively even after the crisis has passed.

Hezekiah's reign saw the Yahweh alone party arise to define Judah's religious identity, especially with the creation of the Covenant Code in Exodus 21–23. Hezekiah even separated Yahweh from some of the old legitimate images associated with Yahweh, such as the bronze serpent and the golden calf.

Josiah's reform went farther in attempting to influence the masses, even to using stern measures upon dissidents, perhaps inspired by the models of Assyrian statecraft, and the agenda of this reform was pro-

Dietrich and Klopfenstein), pp. 559-64.
    51.   Lang, 'Yahweh-Alone', p. 18.

mulgated in the book of Deuteronomy. The age of Josiah saw many customs attacked which had been mainstays of popular piety for years, including the cult of the dead, rival priesthoods at venerable shrines (Bethel), and many other heretofore accepted customs. However, the battle for monotheism was not successful, as Jeremiah's debate with worshippers of the Queen of Heaven indicates in Jer. 44.17. Finally, after 586 BCE polytheism died, and out of its ashes arose Judaism, which was based on the beliefs of the Yahweh alone movement. The revised Deuteronomistic History, generated in the exile, placed the blame for the destruction upon polytheistic Israel and Judah. New religious customs were created for Yahwistic Jews. For example, the Sabbath, formerly devoted also to the Baals, became a day exclusively dedicated to Yahweh. Absolute monotheism was articulated in texts like Deut. 4.35, 39; 1 Kgs 8.60; 2 Kgs 19.19; Isa. 43.10, 45.21-22, wherein the existence of other gods was denied.

The notion of monotheism was arising elsewhere in the world, but the Jews made a quantum leap in the exile. Building upon the ideas of Hermann Vorländer and others Lang believes that Persian Zoroastrianism was a very significant catalyst for monotheistic thought in Second Isaiah. Monotheism arose in the exile to explain the reason for Israel's destruction (it was because of sin, not the gods of the nations) and to redefine the old concepts of kingship, nation and land. Monotheism arose with national destruction to give hope to despairing people, so that 'soteriological monotheism is older than monotheistic dogma'.[52]

Unlike many other scholars Lang believes that the struggle for monotheism continued into the post-exilic period. His consideration of the book of Proverbs[53] convinces him that Dame Wisdom as an image was an attempt by post-exilic scribes to turn a 'school goddess', like the Sumerian Nisaba and the Egyptian Seshat, into a hypostatization of Yahweh, so that the cults of Asherah would be undercut among the Jews. In addition, names of other deities, such as Shaddai, were absorbed into Yahweh, and the heavenly host was turned into angel messengers in the post-exilic era to further combat polytheism.

For Lang the debate whether monotheism emerges by evolution or revolution is difficult to answer, especially since he sees preliminary stages of development in the pre-exilic era, but attributes a major breakthrough to the exile. As I do, Lang appears to hold both concepts in

---

52. Lang, 'Yahweh-Alone', p. 55.
53. Lang, *Wisdom, passim.*

tension. Monotheism, he believes, does evolve, but it is not gradual, unconscious and inevitable. Like Othmar Keel, he sees monotheistic development as a 'chain of revolutions which follow one another in rapid succession' over a period of only a few centuries.[54] He observes,

> The Yahweh-alone idea, it is true, makes its appearance suddenly, but there must always have been people who were concerned about the influence of this new form of belief, who fought against the worship of other gods, and helped the monotheistic cause to gain recognition and, finally, victory.[55]

Norbert Lohfink
Norbert Lohfink believes there always was a latent monotheism or monolatry in the polytheisms of the ancient Near East. The ancients somehow experienced the one, universal deity as a hidden presence, but the full-blown form of monotheism did not emerge until the sixth century BCE. When it did emerge, it arose simultaneously in Zoroastrianism, among the Greek pre-Socratics, and most significantly among the Jews in exile. Basically, the Jewish experience was part of a greater process in the ancient world.[56]

True monotheism in Israel arose after the reforms of Josiah at the earliest, although the worship of Yahweh arose early in Israel's existence. Prior to Josiah Yahwism was primarily a popular familial religion. Even though Israelites had an anti-Canaanite cultural impulse, much of the imagery associated with Yahweh was drawn from the Canaanite religion, such as the image of Yahweh as healer. El and Yahweh basically were merged in the minds of many Israelites from the settlement period onward; Yahweh was an established deity prior to the rise of David. Yahweh was associated with other deities, most of whom were nameless and received no ascription of accomplishments or praise. Yahweh's original lack of connection to other deities in the Canaanite pantheon facilitated these mergers. Over the years the monarchy also introduced rival foreign deities. However, it was Josiah who made Yahwism into the state religion and replaced the earlier syncretism of many deities. With him Yahweh became the high national god of the state. By that time Yahweh had taken over the functions of the most of the other deities. During the later Babylonian exile old oral traditions were drawn together

---

54. Lang, 'Yahweh-Alone', p. 56.
55. Lang, 'Yahweh-Alone', p. 56.
56. N. Lohfink, 'Gott und die Götter im Alten Testament', *Theologische Akademie* 6 (1969), pp. 50-71.

to create Deuteronomy and the historical narratives, and monotheistic assumptions were projected back into Israel's history. Lohfink stresses that religious values arose in conjunction with social values; Yahweh's exclusivity was connected to a sense of social egalitarianism and a struggle for justice, which culminated in the reforms of Josiah and the exilic literature.[57]

Gerd Theissen

In his book entitled, *Biblical Faith: An Evolutionary Approach* Gerd Theissen offers a superb discussion on the use of evolutionary thought to understand biblical faith.[58] His evaluation emcompasses both the emergence of monotheism in the Hebrew Bible and the message of Jesus in the New Testament. He offers a theoretic discussion of the ideational and social dimensions of biblical belief using evolutionary paradigms. Monotheism emerges not as a simple uniform evolutionary experience, rather it is a revolution, or in scientific terms it is an evolutionary mutation. Theissen's understanding of mutation is rooted in contemporary theories of evolution, and he no longer uses the facile and simplistic categories of biological evolution as a slow, gradual process. For Theissen, monotheism is an evolutionary mutation which 'protests' the principles of natural selection, or the brutal competition between peoples. For monotheism calls people to a universalism which encompasses everyone with a humanitarian ethos.

This religious development is part of greater human cultural evolution. Whereas biological evolution proceeds with the selection of species in the struggle of the survival of the fittest, cultural evolution does not require brutal competition or death of the participants for an evolutionary advance. There is 'a hierarchical superiority of cultural evolution to

---

57. N. Lohfink, 'Das Alte Testament und sein Monotheismus', *Der eine Gott und der dreieine Gott: Das Gottes Verständnis bei Christen, Juden, and Muslimen* (ed. K. Rahner; Schriftenreihe der Katholischen Akademie der Erzdiözese Freiburg; Munich: Schnell & Steiner, 1983), pp. 28-47; *idem*, 'The Cult Reform of Josiah of Judah: 2 Kings 22–23 as a Source for the History of the Israelite Religion', *Ancient Israelite Religion* (eds. Miller, Hanson and McBride), pp. 459-75; *idem*, 'Zur Geschichte der Diskussion über den Monotheismus im Alten Israel', *Gott, der Einzige: Zur Entstehung des Monotheismus im Israel* (ed. H. Haag; Quaestiones disputatae, 104; Freiburg: Herder, 1985), p. 25; *idem, Theology of the Pentateuch: Themes of the Priestly Narrative and Deuteronomy* (trans. L. Maloney; Edinburgh: T. & T. Clark, 1994), pp. 35-95.

58. Theissen, *Biblical Faith*, pp. 51-81 *et passim*.

biological evolution in humanity'.[59] Cultural evolution occurs because people have consciousness, while biological evolution works with blind instinctive drives. Cultural evolution results from human cooperation, social interaction and the exchange of ideas. An advance occurs when people combine traditional elements in a new way in art, technology or lifestyles. Change occurs when people transform their way of thinking rather than simply dying. This is 'soft selection', not the 'hard selection' of biological evolution, and the process occurs much more quickly.

Theissen believes that monotheism essentially broke through in human cultural evolution with the teachings of Xenophones in Greece, Zoroaster in Persia, and Second Isaiah among the Jews in exile, and all three movements were roughly contemporary. Taking into account the future which lies before us, Theissen considers this time (500 BCE) to be relatively early in the history of human cultural evolution. Before the Babylonian exile the Jews were basically polytheistic, worshipping separate deities, including El Elyon (Gen. 14), El Shaddai (Gen. 17), Beth-El (Gen. 35), Baal (1 Kgs 2.18), Asherah (2 Kgs 23.7) and the Queen of Heaven (Jer. 44.25). From 1200 to 586 BCE the exclusiveness of Yahweh was established, from 586 to 332 BCE monotheism truly emerged among the Jews, and from 332 BCE onward a reaction against the philosophical monotheism of the Greeks led later Jews and Christians to declare their monotheistic revelations the unique manifestation of God.

Theissen's discussion of the pre-exilic emergence of Yahwistic exclusivity is of interest here. Yahweh was worshipped by Midianites (Exod. 18 and Egyptian texts which refer to the *Shasu-Yhw* land), but it was the Joshua group which brought this deity to the land and merged with the pre-existing entity called Israel (who were ravaged by Pharaoh Merneptah before Joshua's people arrived). Yahweh was elevated to importance by the Davidic dynasty in the tenth century BCE. In the ninth century BCE (Elijah and Elisha) and later in the eighth century BCE (Amos and Hosea) Yahwism became an opposition movement and developed the inclination for exclusivity. Then Hezekiah, Josiah and the upper classes of Judah used Yahwism for political reform, further developing exclusivism. Throughout the pre-exilic era Yahwism was a minority monolatrous movement which became a 'temporary henotheism' during periods of political crisis. Conditions of continual crisis led to 'chronic monolatry', which in turn gave rise to the 'consistent monotheism' of the exile. At this point, the exiles, who were upper class Jews, began to

59. Theissen, *Biblical Faith*, p. 9.

view Yahweh as creator of the world and the director of human history. So, in exile the old national deity of Judah became a personal deity for many individual Jews, and this was a major transformation. (Theissen relies heavily upon Rainer Albertz's understandings of the evolution of personal religion in Israel at this point—Albertz will be discussed later in this chapter.) In the later Hellenistic era the battle was over whether monotheism required conversion to a particular faith commitment to one deity. Those who ultimately became monotheists realized that they had undergone a radical conversion or commitment (or 'mutation' in biological terms) to a new worldview.

Jewish monotheism has its own particular nuances because of its birth in exile. Those who became pure monotheists in the crucible of exile made a difficult personal choice to be separate from their surrounding world, which impressed upon them the radical nature of their commitment. Unlike later triumphalistic monotheistic movements, such as Christianity in the fourth century CE, Jewish monotheism emerged with a deep commitment to peace, because of the experience of its oppressed devotees in exile. Unlike Akhenaton's monotheism, which originated in the royal court, 'from above', this monotheism emerged 'from below', from the common people, and therefore was prone to criticize political structures on behalf of an egalitarian ethos. Unlike the henotheism of Marduk, who surmounted his peers in the divine realm, Yahweh simply had no peers. In response to Marduk's victory in the divine realm, his devotees sought to conquer their neighbors; but Yahweh's devotees saw all peoples unified under one god, and there was no imperative for conquest. Therefore, Judaism eventually could give rise to Christianity, the ultimate missionary religion. With these observations Theissen delineates more clearly the characteristics of Yahwism than did the old *Heilsgeschichte* movement.

I see Theissen's contributions as the most constructive of all the authors' for the greater theological task. His use of evolution as a paradigm will be developed further by me, and his particular characterization of biblical monotheism adds greatly to a revised understanding of the monotheistic worldview.

Christoph Dohmen
Christoph Dohmen describes the rise of monotheism in conjunction with the development of the prohibition against images.[60] He observes the

---

60.   C. Dohmen, 'Heisst *pesel* "Bild, Statue"?', *ZAW* 96 (1984), pp. 263-66;

following historical process: 1) The imageless cult of the early period created a tendency to worship one deity by the early monarchy, but this did not entail the denial of other deities' existence. 2) Initially during the monarchy the prohibition of images implied one could make no images of Yahweh, but one could have images of other gods. 3) The intolerant monolatry of Elijah and Elisha rejected foreign deities and their images, and the prohibition against images outlawed worship of foreign gods altogether—though their existence still was not denied. 4) Hosea sought to exclude all foreign religious practices from the Yahweh cult, so all iconography became suspect. 5) Hezekiah actualized reforms to remove such influence along the lines suggested by Hosea, and biblical prohibitions against images took shape in their early form (Exod. 20.23, 34.17; Lev. 19.4, 26.1). 6) Josiah and Deuteronomic Reform sought exclusive worship of Yahweh through systematic reform, and generated the significant prohibition in Deut. 5.8 and elsewhere (Deut. 4.16, 18, 23, 25). 7) Finally, exilic and post-exilic development saw the emergence of true monotheism among the people and the prohibition against images in Exod. 20.4 and Deut. 27.15. The evolution of the command thus parallels the emergence of monotheism. Hence, Dohmen's model certainly merits consideration with theories on emergent monotheism.

Ernest Nicholson
Ernest Nicholson in his study of the biblical concept of covenant laid out his views on the evolution of monotheistic faith and the new perspectives it engendered.[61] He perceives that Israelite religion grew out of the Canaanite religious milieu and held much in common with it. But at some point a zealous monolatry arose which evolved into a strict monotheism, and he stresses how the prophetic concept of God's righteousness and the demand it placed upon people was most responsible for this transformation.

He outlines the following stages of religious evolution: 1) Initially, Yahweh was a national high god who was revered with other deities, including Shalim, Shamash, Astarte, Baal, Anath and Asherah. 2) The first conflict arose in the days of Elijah, whose name means 'Yahweh is God'. This was an inner Israelite debate over the question of which deity

---

idem, Das Bilderverbot: Seine Entstehung und seine Entwicklung im Alten Testament (BBB, 62; Frankfurt: Athenäum, rev. edn, 1987 [1985]).

61. E. Nicholson, *God and His People: Covenant and Theology in the Old Testament* (Oxford: Clarendon Press, 1986), pp. 191-217.

deserved the highest allegiance—Yahweh or Tyrian Baal. 3) The most decisive stage of development came with the eighth-century BCE prophets and their ideas of covenant and God's righteousness. 4) The culmination of monotheistic thought came in the exile with Second Isaiah.

More important in Nicholson's discussion are the ideational implications of emergent monotheism. He attributes the significant accomplishments to the classical prophets, for he believes they split the divine-human continuum of the ancient world apart by declaring Yahweh to be totally transcendent. Yahweh's distance alienated the other deities, so that they ultimately disappeared for the Israelites, along with all forms of magic which had been the ways of sustaining the universe. Israel's everyday life became rationalized by the demand of Yahweh's righteousness, and human free will was the most important determining event, because the mysterious forces of the world were gone. Nicholson thus rearticulates the dichotomies of *Heilsgeschichte* theologians, but his presentation is more nuanced, and Israel's divergence from the ancient mind is now said to be the classical prophetic movement culminating in the exile.

William Dever

William Dever's scholarship has been primarily in the area of archaeology and history, but his consideration of early Israelite settlement has led him to provide insights on pre-exilic Israelite religion.[62] In particular, he emphasizes the significance of the Asherah cult and Asherah as a consort of Yahweh in the pre-exilic period.

His impression from the discipline of archaeology is that 'the material basis of the early Israelite cult can hardly be distinguished from that of the Canaanite cult of the Late Bronze Age in any significant detail'.[63] Early Israelite religion evolved slowly out of the earlier religious beliefs, and local or regional cult sites flourished at places such as Dan, Megiddo, Ta'anach, Tell el-Far'ah, Lachish, Arad and Beersheba, each with its own mixture of Yahwistic and old Canaanite practice until the end of the

---

62.   Dever, 'Archaeological Confirmation', pp. 37-44; *idem*, 'Material Remains and the Cult in Ancient Israel: An Essay in Archaeological Systematics', *The Word of the Lord Shall Go Forth: Essays in Honor of David Noel Freedman in Celebration of His Sixtieth Birthday* (eds. C. Meyers and M. O'Connor; Winona Lake, IN: Eisenbrauns, 1983), pp. 571-87; *idem*, 'Asherah, Consort', pp. 21-37; *idem*, 'Contribution', pp. 209-47; *idem*, *Discoveries*, pp. 121-66; *idem*, 'Archaeology, Material Culture', pp. 103-15; *idem*, 'What Remains of the House that Albright Built?', *BA* 56 (1993), pp. 25-35; *idem*, 'Ancient Israelite Religion', pp. 105-125.

63.   Dever, 'Contribution', p. 233.

monarchy (586 BCE). There were many different religious parties, including the official cult, familial popular religion or folk religion, the beliefs of the prophets, the beliefs of the Yahwistic priests, and so on. Archaeology especially brings to light many of the old religious beliefs embedded in the popular religion, such as the inscriptions at Kuntillet 'Ajrûd, which speak of 'Yahweh and his Asherah', and also inscriptions at Khirbet el-Qôm. Dever stresses the need to write a history of Israelite religion which fairly combines archaeological discoveries with a critical analysis of the biblical text.

Dever particularly is convinced that Asherah was viewed as a goddess, not as an object or hypostatization of Yahweh. She was a merger of several older fertility goddesses, and she had been the consort of El before Yahweh assumed her when he absorbed El. Sites at Beth-Shan, Megiddo, Ta'anach, Tell Far'ah/Tirzah, 'Ai and Lachish provide us with hundreds of Asherah figures, as well as molds for producing the figures, offering stands for Asherah, and astragali for divination in general. Dever concludes that Yahwism was 'far more syncretistic than the idealized portrait of the literary sources in the Hebrew Bible'.[64] Essentially the Deuteronomistic History and the Priestly editors in the exile reconstructed the nature of the earlier religion from their own perspectives. True monotheism arose only in the exile and post-exilic era.

P. Kyle McCarter

P. Kyle McCarter believes that Yahwism came from Midian at a very early period, so that even the Israel of Merneptah's day was Yahwistic.[65] Early on in the settlement process the Israelites sensed that they were distinct from the folks in the villages down in the valleys. But with the absorption of local Canaanite shrines, religious values were appropriated in each region of Israelite settlement, and the Yahweh religion became slightly different at each subsequent Israelite shrine. Hence, the 'Yahweh of Samaria' testified to in the Kuntillet 'Ajrûd inscription was a national deity, while the 'Yahweh of Teman' was an archaic wilderness shrine portrayal of Yahweh. McCarter classifies the Yahweh shrines into three types: 1) the old desert shrines, 2) adopted Canaanite shrines, and 3) newly

64. Dever, 'Archaeology, Material Culture', p. 113.

65. P.K. McCarter, 'Aspects of the Religion of the Israelite Monarchy: Biblical and Empirical Data', *Ancient Israelite Religion* (eds. Miller, Hanson and McBride), pp. 137-55; *idem*, 'The Origins of Israelite Religion', *Rise of Ancient Israel* (ed. Shanks), pp. 118-41.

created Yahweh shrines, all of which could have a different portrayal of Yahweh. Religious reforms under Hezekiah and Josiah eliminated local shrines and their respective manifestations of Yahweh for the sake of the central shrine in Jerusalem. This caused people to view Yahweh in a more unitary fashion. Thus, between the ninth century BCE and the late seventh century BCE the truly significant move toward monotheism was connected to the transition from viewing the different manifestations of Yahweh to a unified perception of the deity. The biblical writers seem to admit that theirs was a different form of Yahwism than had existed in the various shrines, including even Samaria and Jerusalem.

Baruch Halpern

Baruch Halpern has contributed significant literature in the area of Israelite historiography and also has touched upon the issues of developing monotheism. In his earlier writings he suggests that monotheism may have arisen late in the pre-monarchic period with the emergence of the tribe of Levi. He recognizes the evidence of polytheism among the early Iron Age I Israelites, including the worship of Baal, the stars (Judg. 5.20), and even the patriarchal ancestors (Abraham, Gen. 23.19-20; Rachel, Gen. 35.16-20; 1 Sam. 10.2; Jer. 31.15; Joseph, Josh. 24.32). This essentially Canaanite religion was changed late in the period of the judges with the rise of an 'intolerant monotheism'.[66]

In later writings, however, Halpern offers a more nuanced position.[67] Now he observes that fully developed monotheism arose only in the exile with Second Isaiah, although a tendency to affirm universalism may be observed early in the name Yahweh-Elohim, which could mean 'he causes the gods to be'. This would imply the recognition of other gods in conjunction with the elevation of the high god or national deity, which is a phenomenon found elsewhere in Syria and Palestine. Archaeological and textual evidence indicates the worship of other deities and the presence of pagan practices in pre-exilic Israel. From Kuntillet 'Ajrûd and other sites the inscriptions tell us that Asherah and other 'subsidiary members of Yahweh's assembly' were worshipped, except under

66. B. Halpern, 'Doctrine by Misadventure: Between the Israelite Source and the Biblical Historian', *The Poet and the Historian: Essays in Literary and Historical Biblical Criticism* (ed. R. Friedman; Harvard Semitic Studies, 26; Chico, CA: Scholars Press, 1983), pp. 66-67; *idem, Emergence*, pp. 92, 102, 246-49.

67. B. Halpern, '"Brisker Pipes than Poetry": The Development of Israelite Monotheism', *Judaic Perspectives on Ancient Israel* (eds. J. Neusner, B. Levine and E. Fredrichs; Philadelphia: Fortress Press, 1987), pp. 77-115.

Hezekiah and Josiah, as a normal part of Yahweh worship. Also accepted as a natural part of the Yahweh cult was human sacrifice (Lev. 18.21; 2 Kgs 23.10; Jer. 7.31-32, 32.35; and elsewhere).

Halpern introduces some interesting categories into the discussion. Early Israelites are said to have the components of monotheism with deep loyalty to Yahweh, but they were 'not self-consciously monotheistic', that is, they lacked philosophical monotheism or perhaps they were 'monolatrous henotheists' in 1000 BCE. This 'unselfconscious monotheism' contrasts with the 'selfconscious monotheism' or philosophical monotheism of the exile. In the early age they were part of a widespread phenomenon in the ancient world, but only they attained the advanced stage of monotheistic belief.

How did this process evolve? 1) Solomon tolerated the worship of many deities in Jerusalem under a state policy designed to rule an imperial population, even though Yahweh was the high god. 2) A true reaction to this policy came in the ninth century BCE with xenophobia against a Tyrian Baal (though not against other deities), which then affirmed radical loyalty to Yahweh. 3) The classical prophets critiqued not only foreign elements, but also 'inner-Israelite customs' in the Yahweh cult, including the veneration of Baals theoretically subordinate to Yahweh in the national cult. 4) Their critique led to official stigmatization of the Baals under Josiah's selfconscious monotheistic reform (Deut. 4.19, 17.3; 2 Kgs 17.16, 21.2-5, 23.4, which are passages from Josiah's time and not the exile, as other scholars posit). 5) Second Isaiah joined the monotheism of Josiah with the aniconic tendency of Amos and Micah, which then implied the total separation of the symbol from the one symbolized and the radical separation of Yahweh from the world—the rejection of hypostatization. Halpern attributes more to Josiah's reform in this process than other contemporary scholars in the field do.

There is an evolution from an early monotheistic set of assumptions, which were inconsistent but had occasional 'susceptibility to fits of intolerance' to a later more self-conscious radical monotheism. This transformation was made possible in the social experience of Israel, for 'religion exists only in its implementation by real and varied people, not in some ethereal Platonic form'.[68] Although Halpern seeks to respect the ideas of Yezekel Kaufmann on the understanding of Israelite monotheism, he admits that Kaufmann did not recognize this social transformation from early to later philosophical monotheism.

68. Halpern, 'Brisker Pipes', p. 107.

Mark Smith

A scholar who has contributed the most extensive evaluation on the Israelite understanding of Yahweh before the exile is Mark Smith.[69] He criticizes those who describe belief in Yahweh as monotheistic or monolatrous with occasional lapses in polytheistic syncretism, especially William Albright, Yehezkel Kaufmann, Helmer Ringgren, George Fohrer, Frank Cross, and most particularly the recent work of Jeffrey Tigay, who tries to demonstrate that Israelites were monotheistic on the basis of the large percentage of Yahweh names among the populace.

Smith perceives that Israel's religious emergence is really a breaking with its own Canaanite past and not merely the avoidance of alien Canaanite beliefs, for the worship of Baal and Asherah, as well as many other customs, was a natural part of old Yahweh worship. Yahweh emerged as the sole deity in a process of 'convergence' and 'differentiation'. Yahweh converged with El, absorbed the features of Asherah and Baal (especially evident in poems like Gen. 49; Judg. 5; 2 Sam. 22 = Ps. 18; Ps. 29; and Ps. 68), while at the same time certain practices were eliminated in a process of differentiation, including the cult of the dead, child sacrifice and worship at high places. Differentiation began in the ninth century BCE with the conflict with Baal; then the later classical prophets continued this process by attacking Asherah, sun worship and the objectionable practices mentioned.

Much of this process was part of the natural elevation of a state deity, which may be found in other cultures. Marduk, for example, absorbed the names of fifty other deities in Babylon, and so also Ashur in Assyria and Amun-Re in Egypt took imagery from other gods. Since the elevation of Yahweh was undertaken by kings, especially Hezekiah and Josiah, the state was responsible for emergent monotheism more than any other group: it was not really the villain that sponsored state syncretism against true Yahwism.

Early Israel was composed primarily of Canaanites who evolved into Israelites. Hence, one cannnot distinguish Canaanite from Israelite religion in Iron Age I (1200–1050 BCE), and Asherah, Baal, El and Yahweh were related integrally. Early on El and Yahweh were equated, since both were portrayed as healers, fathers, compassionate, and both dwelt in a tent over

---

69.   M. Smith, 'God and Female in the Old Testament: Yahweh and His "asherah"', *TS* 48 (1987), pp. 333-40; *idem, Early History of God; idem,* 'Yahweh and Other Deities in Ancient Israel: Observations on Old Problems and Recent Trends', *Ein Gott allein* (eds. Dietrich and Klopfenstein), pp. 197-234.

the cosmic waters. El became just another name for Yahweh very early, as indicated by names during the united monarchy. Likewise, Yahweh began to usurp Baal's role as the warrior when he became the national high god under David. Only with the entrance of the Tyrian Baal from Phoenicia in the ninth century BCE did the equation of Yahweh and Baal become problematic. (Judg. 6–7 really reflects this conflict). Throughout the pre-exilic era Asherah was merely a symbol, a pole, generally accepted by Israelites as an emblem of Yahweh. Jeremiah's 'Queen of Heaven' is either the Syrian Astarte or Babylonian Ishtar. Biblical authors critically telescoped the real second millennium BCE deity named Asherah with first millennium BCE Astarte to create Asherah worship where there really was none. The symbol had no reference to a separate deity. Solar imagery was attributed to Yahweh during the monarchy for political reasons—the sun could be equated with both the king and Yahweh, and this enhanced the royal dynasty. There was no true cult of the sun. In conclusion, there were few deities for pre-exilic Israelites, and the same was true in other West-Semitic countries around Israel. A few deities were absorbed into Yahweh throughout the monarchy. By Smith's estimation Israel was not as flagrantly polytheistic as other scholars assume.

Smith believes that the emergence of a state and the centralization of the national state cult caused the emergence of a national high god and accompanying monolatry. So that 'like the monarchy Israelite mono-latry developed out of both adherence to past religious traditions and departure from them, out of both conservation and innovation'.[70] The Yahweh alone party which first appeared in the ninth century BCE supported this state sponsored trajectory. International political conflict created the image of Yahweh's power over other peoples and this added impetus to the idea of universal dominion. Further, there was the tendency of prophets to attack certain modes of behavior in the religion which had been acceptable in earlier years, and the late entrance of religious influence from other countries made the prophets even more critical of old, indigenous cultic activity, such as Baal worship. All these forces together created a monolatrous trajectory which came to fruition in the exile in the oracles of Ezekiel and Second Isaiah.

Smith concludes that although monotheism was not characteristic of Israel's early religion, the process of convergence and differentiation was, and this would be the chief factor in emerging monotheism. Convergence began in the period of the judges, and differentiation became a significant

70. Smith, *Early History of God*, p. 148.

dynamic in the ninth and eighth centuries BCE. Not only the prophets, but also the monarchy, abetted this process. In this regard, Smith criticizes the models of John Bright, George Mendenhall and others who view the monarchy as the opponent of monotheism. Differentiation in the late monarchical period coincided with the literary production of much of the present Bible. Ultimately, monotheism arose as both an 'evolution' and a 'revolution'. It arose slowly out of polytheism (evolution) as Yahweh emerged from Canaanite roots and absorbed El and Baal, but it also differentiated itself from certain aspects radically (revolution), including Baal cultic activity, the cult of the dead, and other practices, as it created new metaphorical contexts for the images appropriated from the past.

Smith's contributions are a significant addition to the debate. His model of convergence and differentiation merits further use by the scholarly community, for it appears to be a good pedagogical tool to explain complex processes in a more nuanced fashion than we had in the past. His attempt to see monotheism's emergence both as revolution and an evolution captures the spirit of what other theorists have sought to express with images such as a 'chain of successive revolutions'.

Andrew Dearman

Andrew Dearman summarizes the contributions of many scholars very nicely in his work. He believes that the early pre-monarchic religion of Israel was monolatry, but it contained elements which would lead to monotheism.[71] Very early on El was identified with Yahweh in an 'integrating or unpolemical monolatry' comparable to the way in which Seth and Baal were merged in Egypt under Ramses III (1175 BCE). Dearman suggests that polytheism is an inappropriate word to use to describe early Israelite belief. Essentially the Yahwistic cult was corrupted by kings during the monarchy with syncretistic practices, including the cultic observances of Asherah (whom he considers an objectionable cult symbol rather than a goddess). This early laxity or naive monolatry in the Yahweh cult began to change in the ninth century BCE struggle against the Omride importation of Baal. This struggle would evolve into the more rigorous monotheism of a later era. Dearman's model is more conservative than those of other scholars, for he attributes much of the monotheistic advance to the earlier stages. But he does recognize an evolutionary process from early monolatry to later monotheism.

---

71. Dearman, *Religion*, pp. 12-122.

Norman Cohn
Norman Cohn provides a thumbnail sketch of the history of Israelite religion in his volume on apocalyptic literature, which assumes that originally Israelites were polytheists and that their high god was El, and Yahweh was subordinate to him (Deut. 32.8). Hosea was the first to advocate the worship of Yahweh alone, and thereafter Yahweh began to absorb El, until the eventual triumph of monotheism in the exile. Israelite thought was not radically different from that of the ancient Near East, for the ancients in general viewed their deities as active in human affairs. However, Israel's portrayal was more consistent and thorough in this regard. Eventually the new Israelite worldview matriculated in the exile and post-exilic era. Cohn also credits Zoroastrianism with providing Jews with significant religious insight.[72]

Rainer Albertz
Rainer Albertz provides us with a grand history of Israelite religion wherein he attempts to trace the development of 'familial religion' or 'popular religion' and its interaction with the official religion of Israel.[73] His work may become a classic in the field, even though many scholars have moved beyond the paradigm which attempts to distinguish between popular and official religion. His theory suggests that the Deuteronomistic History preserves rather well the memory of earlier religious practices of the pre-exilic era. Albertz integrates much of the scholarship already discussed in this chapter into his history.

Albertz believes that the pre-exilic period had many different forms of Yahwism which subsequently were leveled out by the texts of the exile and post-exilic authors. There were forms of religious expression appropriate to the levels of state religion, local or 'place' religion, and family religion, and ultimately this last form of piety was the most significant for the development of Yahwism. The 'popular religion' of Israel may be exemplified best in the patriarchal narratives of Genesis and the familial religion practiced there: devotion to one family deity, use of teraphim, no extensive shrine cultus, merely occasional sacrifice, dream incubation, and the concern with illness, fertility and descendents. This religion was

72. N. Cohn, *Cosmos, Chaos, and the World to Come: The Ancient Roots of Apocalyptic Faith* (New Haven: Yale University Press, 1993), pp. 77-162.
73. Albertz, *Israelite Religion*, I, pp. 1-94, 146-231; II, pp. 399-426; *idem*, 'Der Ort des Monotheismus in der israelitischen Religionsgeschichte', *Ein Gott allein* (eds. Dietrich and Klopfenstein), pp. 77-96.

common to the entire ancient world and basically polytheistic. Although devotion to one family deity might appear monolatrous, it is a far cry from later monotheism.

Yahweh worship came into the land from the outside with a very small exodus group, for whom Yahweh was a symbol of their solidarity. However, early Yahwism should not be viewed as having a nomadic origin. Yahweh displaced El and took over Asherah, El's consort. The exodus group merged into the evolving matrix of the Palestinian highlanders, who evolved into Israel eventually. Yahwism began as a typical ancient Near Eastern religion, as reflected in the inscriptions at Kuntillet 'Ajrûd and elsewhere. As these inscriptions imply, Yahweh took on different forms in the various regions, and the patriarchal narratives reflect this and serve as a source for describing the religion of early Iron Age Israelites.

Monotheism emerged slowly over a period of years as a result of many social and religious conflicts. In the early monarchy Yahweh was elevated to the head of the pantheon by the state religion, and this gave Yahweh an imperial character. The earliest seeds of true monotheism were planted by Elijah, whose ideas were later developed by Hosea. Hosea was the first to condemn activity within Yahwism, such as the bull cult, and differentiate Baal from Yahweh clearly. Hezekiah went further in reforming Yahwistic practices, cultic activity in shrines, and familial piety with the aid of the newly created Book of the Covenant (Exod. 21–23). Josiah brought monotheistic ideas to bear upon society signficantly, to the point of closing provincial shrines and seriously trying to control the familial piety, and Deuteronomy reflects his theological agenda. Ultimately, monotheism prevailed in the early post-exilic era. During the exile Yahwism was separated from state support, and this is what truly permitted Yahwism to emerge as a universalistic and monotheistic faith, for it was no longer connected to the agenda of a political state. From the beginning of the movement it had a special potential to stress the exclusive worship of Yahweh, and this created social conflicts (especially in the age of Elijah) which led to the eventual development of pure monotheism. This sense of exclusivity must go back to an exodus group,

> It is strange that all the reform groups (Elijah, Hosea, Deuteronomy) appeal to the early period as justification for Yahweh monolatry. Taking all idealization into account, this idea could not have been completely plucked out of thin air if it was to have convinced those to whom it was addressed.[74]

74.   Albertz, *Israelite Religion*, I, p. 265.

The full development of monotheism also was connected to a fight against the emergence of social classes. Hence, true monotheism could arise only in the exile after the collapse of society with all the attendant social structures and the political-national religion of Judah. Consistent monotheism appears in the exile with Second Isaiah. Unlike Hermann Vorländer and Bernhard Lang, Albertz believes that no outside stimulus was necessary during the exile to precipitate monotheistic thought; rather, the trajectory was there from the beginning. Yahwism was successful ultimately because it was rooted in pre-exilic familial piety, not in the religious agenda of the Judean state. Albertz downplays Zoroastrian influence, for in Zoroastrian thought monotheism is grounded in the notion of the creation of the world, whereas in Judaism it is grounded in the exodus experience. Nor did Jewish monotheism lay claims to worldwide rule as did Zoroastrianism and later Christian monotheism.

One must sense a general consensus in all of the authors thus far discussed. They sense an evolutionary process which moves through various stages of monolatrous or henotheistic intensity in the pre-exilic era to a form of pure monotheism which arises in the exilic era. Although they describe the process in stages of development, they often stress the radical or revolutionary nature of this trajectory. They see monotheism emerge in a series of conflicts or crises, wherein significant spokespersons articulate insights or undertake actions which advance the movement. These scholars also provide us with new concepts and terminology by which to describe this process. It appears that their views represent an emerging consensus which will manifest itself in scholarship and textbooks within the next generation.

III

Dissenting voices have spoken in opposition to the general thrust of critical scholarship reviewed thus far. Some authors have affirmed the presence of monotheistic belief early in Israel's existence, and they have received a stern critical response from the scholarly guild. Their views, too, merit our brief attention.

Irving Zeitlin gives us a sociological history of the Yahwistic religion written in the tradition of the great sociologist Max Weber and defending the perspective of Yehezkel Kaufmann.[75] He maintains there was no

75. I. Zeitlin, *Ancient Judaism: Biblical Criticism from Max Weber to the Present* (Cambridge: Polity Press, 1984).

syncretism between the faith of Moses and Canaanite cultus, the monotheistic revolution began with Moses, and the suppression of polytheism
was complete among the Israelites from the time of Moses onward. He
especially criticizes the ideas of Julius Wellhausen, Albrecht Alt, Martin
Noth and Gerhard von Rad, while he quotes with great approval William
Albright and Kaufmann. Like Kaufmann he maintains boldly that Israelites
were so monotheistic they could not understand true polytheism, so the
prophetic critique was issued against fetishism and not true polytheism
among Israelites. Zeitlin also defends the historicity of the patriarchs, a
violent conquest under Joshua, the Mosaic authorship of Deuteronomy,
and the general historicity of all biblical narratives; he also critiques all
forms of critical textual analysis.

In general, scholars have ignored Zeitlin. Zeitlin's work, published in
1984, uses sources from before 1970, and his approach is reminiscent
of popular writings in the 1940s. His understanding of archaeological
findings and his use of biblical texts is naive and sometimes in error, as
when he maintains that female fertility figures have not been found in
Israelite sites and there is no evidence for Canaanite religious influence
among the Israelites.[76] Any positive references to Zeitlin's work ignore
these very serious deficiencies.

A much more serious challenge to contemporary critical thought has
been offered by Jeffrey Tigay and Jeaneane Fowler,[77] both of whom
critically evaluate Israelite names on inscriptions and in the biblical text
which use a theophoric element, such as Yahweh, El or Baal. Their
discoveries of the preponderance of the name of Yahweh in personal
names led them to conclude that Israelites for the most part worshipped
Yahweh exclusively and were either very monolatrous or monotheistic.
Tigay maintains that the only polytheism which was extensive in the
land was the religious activity sponsored by the royal court due to its
international connections. Fowler boldly states,

> Hebrew religion was unique in that it was monotheistic, and no sugges-
> tion that it was otherwise can be gained from personal names...there is no

76. Zeitlin, *Ancient Judaism*, p. 29.
77. J. Tigay, 'Israelite Religion: The Onomastic and Epigraphic Evidence',
Ancient Israelite Religion (eds. Miller, Hanson and McBride), pp. 157-94; *idem, You
Shall Have No Other Gods: Israelite Religion in the Light of Hebrew Inscriptions*
(Harvard Semitic Studies, 31; Atlanta: Scholars Press, 1986), pp. 1-96; J. Fowler,
Theophoric Personal Names in Ancient Hebrew: A Comparative Study (JSOTSup,
49; Sheffield: JSOT Press, 1988).

divine consort for the Israelite God, so that titles of female deities are totally lacking in Hebrew.[78]

Tigay, in particular, relies upon Kaufmann's understandings in several ways. The object of prophetic ridicule was not true polytheistic activity, but rather superstition and fetish veneration. Both Tigay and Fowler, however, are much more sophisticated in their presentation than Zeitlin, and thus they have received a critical response from other scholars in the field.

In general, their research seems to indicate rather that the popularity of Yahweh may have increased over the years, since the percentage of Yahwistic names increased by the end of the monarchy. Albertz considers the same data and observes that whereas 25% of early monarchical names used Yahweh in their formation, by the late monarchy it had risen to 80% of the names. Furthermore, notes Albertz, the use of divine names reflects personal or familial piety and not the religious activity of the society as a whole.[79] This may not prove that the Israelites were consistently monotheistic, but rather it may be evidence for the emerging monotheism hypothesized by other scholars. Tigay and Fowler may not be sensitive enough to the concept of a national high deity, who does not exclude the existence of other gods, but does draw the bulk of pious devotion from among the people. Several scholars observe that this evidence only implies the great popularity of Yahweh. Furthermore, some critics quickly point out that in many cultures around Israel the names of popular deities do not occur frequently in personal names, so that in Israel the names of El, Baal and Asherah likewise may be absent in common names. 1) Many deities at Ebla are not represented in personal names. 2) Asherah's name was used rarely in Ugarit where she was very popular. 3) Tannit was popular in Carthage, but her name seldom appears. 4) Similar phenomena may be observed in Egypt with the multitude of deities worshipped there, and yet their names do not appear in human names. 5) Many observe that the archaeological inscriptions in Israel which refer to Asherah do not have a corresponding number of references among the personal names.[80] Basically, people simply tended

---

78. Fowler, *Personal Names*, p. 313.

79. Albertz, *Israelite Religion*, I, p. 187; *idem*, 'Der Ort', p. 82.

80. Olyan, *Asherah*, pp. 35-37; D. Pardee, 'An Evaluation of the Proper Names from Ebla from a West Semitic Perspective: Pantheon Distribution According to Genre', *Eblaite Pesonal Names and Semitic Name-Giving* (ed. A. Archi; Rome:

to prefer certain names, thus little can be concluded from the evidence of Tigay and Fowler. The names in no way indicate the presence of foreign religious practices which were absorbed into Yahwism, nor do they reflect those particular aspects of pre-exilic Yahwistic piety so often attacked by the prophets (solar worship, cult of the dead, bronze serpent, etc.). Also, the presence of Asherah figurines, the presence of Baal names on the Samaria ostraca from the eighth century BCE, and a host of other images from recent archaeological sites make the overall argument of Tigay and Fowler most tenuous.[81] If indeed we could measure religious piety by the names of people, we should see evidence of all the practices of the pre-exilic period in some way, but we obviously do not. Axel Knauf notes that all that can be proven by Tigay's evidence is that the Yahwism of Hosea penetrated Judah's ruling classes by the seventh century BCE, and the 'evidence is insufficient for "monotheism" outside this class and prior to that period'.[82] The only scholar who takes seriously the work of Tigay and Fowler is Johannes de Moor, who believes the high percentage of Yahweh names implies popular monotheism and a reluctance to admit publically the veneration of other gods.[83]

Johannes C. de Moor also advocates that Yahwism arose as a revolutionary breakthrough in Iron Age I (1200–1050 BCE) in reaction to the Late Bronze Age (1550–1200 BCE) 'crisis of polytheism'.[84] There the conflict between El and Baal, and their respective devotees, as well as the debauching of the gods, led to a disdain for the gods and a readiness by people to embrace a new deity, such as Yahweh. This may be seen in the Ugaritic literature. Devotees turned to new gods; in the north of Palestine they revered Baal, in the south they opted for Yahweh-El. Yahweh and El were equated by some as the same god, even before Israelites came into Palestine; for others Yahweh was the Ugaritic god Yam. In the Amarna period Jacob encouraged exclusive worship of this

Missione Archaeologica Italiana in Siria, 1988), pp. 119-51; Smith, *Early History of God*, p. xxi.

81.   Taylor, *Yahweh*, p. 264; Dever, 'Ancient Israelite Religion', pp. 111-12.

82.   E.A. Knauf, 'From History to Interpretation', *Fabric of History* (ed. Edelman), p. 61.

83.   J.C. de Moor, *The Rise of Yahwism: The Roots of Israelite Monotheism* (BETL, 91; Leuven: Leuven University Press/Peeters, 1990), pp. 10-11, 33, 40-41.

84.   J.C. de Moor, 'The Crisis of Polytheism in Late Bronze Age Ugarit', *Crises and Perspectives: Studies in Ancient Near Eastern Polytheism, Biblical Theology, Palestinian Archaeology and Intertestamental Literature* (ed. A.S. Van der Woude; Oudtestamentische Studiën, 24; Leiden: Brill, 1986), pp. 1-20; *idem, Rise of Yahwism*.

deity, Yahweh-El. Yahweh eventually came to be more popular with the entrance of nomads into Palestine in the fourteenth century BCE, who were the *'apiru*. Later nomads were led in by Beya (1203–1197 BCE), a notable person mentioned in Egyptian texts, who would be known ultimately as Moses. These new and aggressive devotees of Yahweh predominated in the south, where Yahweh absorbed the persona of El, and became a single high deity who was jealous of other gods and especially opposed to Baal in the north. De Moor attempts to trace this evolution with a study of the ancient poems in Genesis 49, Judges 5, Psalm 68, Habakkuk 3, and others. Habakkuk 3, for example, reflects the piety of the fourteenth-century BCE *'apiru* religionists. For de Moor monotheism was established firmly among the people before the rise of the monarchy.

Scholars have not critiqued de Moor's hypothesis to date. It is brilliantly argued, but it is incredibly hypothetical. He has reconstructed a detailed history on the basis of apparently archaic sounding poetry in the Bible, a dangerously subjective procedure. His theory is possible, but not probable. Such a theory is difficult to refute, but also impossible to prove. Any hypothesis which increasingly turns literary allusions into specific historical reconstructions becomes less likely to have been the true historical scenario. De Moor's theory runs counter to the direction in which scholars are moving in their understanding of monotheistic evolution, so he will convert few readers to his hypothesis.

The voices of dissent which argue for early monotheism will not carry the day in the current discussion. Increasingly scholars view the emergence of monotheism as a later phenomenon, which evolved in the pre-exilic era and came to fruition in the exile. There is, however, a significant group of scholars who argue for yet another viewpoint. These scholars believe that monotheism emerged totally in the exilic and post-exilic eras, and there were no preliminary stages of development in the pre-exilic period. Their analyses are very detailed, and their scholarship is well established in related areas of critical study, so their ideas may take center stage in the future discussion. Their ideas are radical and thought-provoking, and in many ways an attractive alternative. Therefore, we ought to review their suggestions also.

IV

An extremely critical scholarly view is expressed by scholars who see the biblical literature as being totally an exilic and post-exilic creation, imply that most of the biblical narratives are fictionalized, and suggest the biblical worldview is a Jewish creation in the exile and beyond. Obviously they minimize any significant pre-exilic contributions to the emergence of monotheism, and view it as a creation of the Jewish community in exile and beyond.

Niels Peter Lemche

One of the most critical historians of ancient Israel is Niels Peter Lemche.[85] He believes that the biblical text is a later post-exilic creation from the Hellenistic Period after 300 BCE, and the narratives are mostly fiction. The text is of dubious value for historical reconstruction or as an accurate portrayal of Israelite religion; rather, it reflects post-exilic politics and persons. The biblical narratives set up very stereotypical images of polytheistic Canaanites and monotheistic Israelites, when in reality the pre-exilic inhabitants of Palestine would have recognized neither image as describing them.

The real religion of pre-exilic peoples in Israel and Judah was a typical West-Semitic polytheism, for true monotheism did not emerge until after the exile among the Jews. Worship of the god Yahweh came into the land in the early Iron Age, but the group was not monotheistic, as the destruction of the bronze serpent in 2 Kgs 18.3 indicates. Most Israelites were simply the indigenous people of the land, and their religion was essentially Canaanite, a continuation of the religion of the Late Bronze Age cultus in Palestine. Prior to the monarchy we have no sources by which to reconstruct their religion, but after the rise of the monarchy we may use the Psalms as a source to envision so-called Israelite religion.

This religion differed from shrine to shrine in understanding the cult of Yahweh. The Psalms reflect the beliefs of Yahwists in Jerusalem, who ultimately tried to standardize regional cults under the leadership of Hezekiah and Josiah. In their beliefs Yahweh was the divine king of the city state of Jerusalem, and the king was his adopted son. The covenant was merely between Yahweh and the king, and the land and people were blessed through the mediation of the king, as with the divine pharaoh in Egypt. Yahweh was subordinate to El, equal to Baal (or at times equated with him), and had a female consort deity. In this fertility religion Yahweh eventually emerged as creator, and the other gods were his servants, including Asherah, Shamash (sun) and Yerach (moon). The later prophets

85.   Lemche, *Early Israel*, pp. 386-475; *idem, Ancient Israel*, pp. 155-257; *idem, Canaanites; idem,* 'Israelite Religion', pp. 97-115; *idem,* 'Old Testament', pp. 163-93; *idem,* 'Is it Still Possible', p. 165; *idem,* 'Kann von einer', pp. 59-75.

and Deuteronomic Reformers refined this religion to create an egalitarian covenant between Yahweh and the people, a new perception of Yahweh which stressed righteousness, and a fictional history of exodus, Sinai, conquest and even David. Their attempts would create monotheism in the post-exilic era, and their written literature would take shape only in that era.

Lemche maintains that consideration of biblical religion should focus only upon the post-exilic period,

> Our task is accordingly to explain the reasons why this Israelite religion, although essentially Canaanite in origin, developed into Jewish monotheism of the post-exilic period which is the official religion of the Old Testament.[86]

Lemche sees this post-exilic religious development as an intellectual breakthrough worthy of our consideration. It was indeed unique in its synthesis, even though each of the particular elements was drawn from the ancient world.

Thomas Thompson

Although he is primarily a critical historian, Thomas Thompson has addressed the question of religious development in Israel.[87] Like Niels Lemche, Axel Knauf, Giovanni Garbini and David Jamieson-Drake, all of whom he quotes with approval, Thompson believes we cannot reconstruct a pre-exilic history or religious development of Israel. The literature is a post-exilic fictional creation, although he concedes that some written traditions may be as early as the time of Josiah (620 BCE).

Early Israelite religion was polytheistic, at best occasionally henotheistic. Thompson is very critical of scholars who contrast monotheistic Israel with polytheistic Canaan, especially William Albright. He suggests that monotheism emerged only in the exile.[88] The early roots of monotheism

---

86. Lemche, 'Israelite Religion', p. 113.

87. Thompson, *Origin Tradition*, pp. 37-39, 193-96; *idem*, 'Text, Context and Reference', pp. 65-92; *idem*, *Early History*, pp. 13-24, 415-23; *idem*, 'How Yahweh Became God: Exodus 3 and 6 and the Heart of the Pentateuch', *JSOT* 68 (1995), pp. 57-74.

88. Thompson, *Early History*, p. 89, quotes with approval the recent publication of an older 1968 Danish dissertation of H. Friis, *Die Bedingungen für die Errichtung des davidischen Reiches in Israel und seiner Umwelt* (Heidelberg: Diebner und Nauerth, 1986), *passim*, who maintains that monotheism emerged only in the exile with the literary development of the Davidic traditions.

may lie with the classical prophets who planted the seeds of the idea. Josianic reforms brought 'universalist monotheism' and the values which created the biblical perspective. The Babylonians and Persians both created the post-exilic Judean state by complex movements of people, and the folk displaced into Judah by those world powers subsequently assumed the identity of the Jews, even though they may not have been ethnically descended from Israelites and Judahites. These new, imported people claimed the religious and literary traditions and then developed them even more. Their religious synthesis reflects great Persian Zoroastrian influence. The high god of Syria, Elohe Shamayim, was identified with Yahweh, who really came out of the Israelite cult in Samaria, and further imagery was provided from the Babylonian cult of Sin and Zoroastrian beliefs about Ahura Mazda. Essentially, Jewish monotheism was completely developed in the post-exilic era and really had less continuity with the pre-exilic era than we have assumed.

Giovanni Garbini

Even more critical than Niels Lemche or Thomas Thompson in his reconstruction of Israelite history and religion is Giovanni Garbini.[89] Pre-exilic Israelite religion was a typical agrarian religion: it was polytheistic with strong sexual orientations, and at best it was henotheistic with Yahweh viewed as the national high deity elevated only slightly over the other gods. Yahwism simply grew out of Canaanite henotheism.

Later Yahwism in the exile and post-exilic eras radically critiqued and reformed that earlier religion. It fictionalized a narrative history for the pre-exilic era, and according to Garbini, even the post-exilic Ezra is a theological fiction of a later time in the post-exilic era. The oracles of the prophets were revised by exilic theologians to generate ethical mono-theism and notions such as the divine election of the Jews. To undergird the idea of election the stories of exodus and conquest were invented completely. The first true theologian of the biblical tradition was Second Isaiah, whose monotheism was inspired deeply by the teachings of Zoroaster.

---

89. G. Garbini, 'Gli Ebrei in Palestina: Yahvismo e religione fenecia', *Forme di Contatto e Processi di Trasformazione nelle Societá Antiche* (Rome: Ecole Française de Rome, 1983), pp. 899-910; *idem, History and Ideology in Ancient Israel* (trans. J. Bowden; New York: Crossroad, 1988), pp. 52-132.

Herbert Niehr

Herbert Niehr also provides a very critical historical assessment of emerging monotheism in Israel.[90] For him pre-exilic religion was simply another West-Semitic religion, and the ultimate movement toward monotheism was part of a great tendency in the ancient world. Yahweh was a high god in typical West-Semitic fashion, who was more comparable to Baalshamem (or Baal Shamayim) in Syria, rather than the Canaanite god El. Baalshamem was the 'God of the heavens', whose role diminished in first millennium BCE in Palestine as Yahweh and other deities assumed his roles. Yahweh assumed Baalshamem's functions as presider over the heavenly council, resident on the great holy mountain, creator of the world, victor over the forces of chaos, and source of justice (which is typically assigned to the sun god). Niehr suspects the solar imagery was the truly significant contribution to Yahweh's persona. The equation of Yahweh with Baalshamem was supported by the royal courts in Israel and Judah because of their extensive cultural and political contacts with Phoenicia, where evidence exists that the veneration of Baalshamem was most important in the Syro-Palestinian cultural sphere. This Phoenician influence was greatest under Solomon of Judah and Omri of Israel, when Phoenician artists and merchants were active in the royal courts of Jerusalem and Samaria respectively. Although the royal courts supported the amalgamation of Yahweh's persona with that of Baalshamem, this equation was opposed by the popular Yahwistic minority. This tension between the tendency to absorb Baalshamem's characteristics and the popular opposition to such foreign influence helped to create the ultimate portrayal of Yahweh. Hence, Yahwism evolved out of Canaanite origins in a complex fashion. Niehr's description of this tension is quite similar to Mark Smith's model of 'convergence' and 'differentiation'. This transformation of Yahwism by the Yahweh alone movement was very late, occurring in the post-exilic period when Yahweh became supreme and the other gods became merely angelic messengers. The post-exilic metamorphosis and reinterpretation of religious imagery is called 'archaization', 'remythologization' and 'literary paganism' by Niehr. It took place in the Persian and Hellenistic eras when comparable ideas were emerging among other peoples.

90.   H. Niehr, *Der höchste Gott: Alttestamentlicher JHWH–Glaube im Kontext syrisch-kanaanäischer Religion des 1. Jahrtausends v. Chr.* (BZAW, 190; Berlin: de Gruyter, 1990), *passim*; *idem*, 'JHWH in der Rolle des Baalsamem', *Ein Gott allein* (eds. Dietrich and Klopfenstein), pp. 307-26.

Philip Davies

Philip Davies undertakes a very critical historical analysis of Israel and concludes that the biblical text provides us only with a fictional portrayal of Israel's origins, which scholars have turned into into a 'literary-historical hybrid' by combining archaeological data with fictional narratives.[91] He even doubts whether the Davidic empire ever existed and whether Israel and Judah truly existed as states before the eighth century BCE, and here he relies heavily upon the research of David Jamieson-Drake and others, who interpret the archaeological data to imply that state formation did not occur until that period under the stimulus of Assyrian influence.[92] He suggests that the exiles who returned from Babylon were not Judean in origin, but they made theological claims in order to legitimate their rule and then generated the biblical literature. Old 'Israelian' or 'Samarian' religion and the old Israelite identity were redefined and appropriated by these people whom the Persians settled in Judea. Biblical literature is a post-exilic scribal creation, produced at the request of the state, using little or no oral tradition, and drawn from the perspective of several post-exilic groups.

Yahweh was a synthesis of deities from the pre-exilic age: Elohim, Shaddai, Elyon, El and a deity actually named Yahweh worshipped by some people. The biblical portrayal of Yahweh was created in the Chaldean and Persian periods, when the idea of a single high god was emerging among other intellectuals in the ancient Near East. Yahweh was portrayed in the same manner as were Marduk and Sin among the Babylonians and Ahura Mazda among the Persians. The biblical canon was created in the second century BCE in order to fight Hellenism in the time of the Maccabees. Davies's critical approach shares much in common with Lemche and Garbini.

These critical scholars have envisioned a scenario that moves radically beyond not only the *Heilsgeschichte* models of the Biblical Theology Movement, but even beyond the emerging consensus of so many other scholars. They appear to receive their best audience in European scholarly

91. P. Davies, *In Search of 'Ancient Israel'* (JSOTSup, 148; Sheffield: JSOT Press, 1992), p. 17; *idem*, 'Method and Madness: Some Remarks on Doing History with the Bible', *JBL* 114 (1995), pp. 699-705.

92. D. Jamieson-Drake, *Scribes and Schools in Monarchic Judah: A Socio-Archeological Approach* (JSOTSup, 109; Social World of Biblical Antiquity, 9; Sheffield: JSOT Press, 1991), pp. 48-80; P. Ash, 'Solomon's? District? List', *JSOT* 67 (1995), pp. 70-72, both question whether the Davidic Empire ever existed.

circles, especially among Scandanavian scholars. However, it seems doubtful that their ideas will take root in American circles. One reason is that this critical portrayal which displaces all religious development to the post-exilic era and virtually obliterates the realia of pre-exilic history will not convert easily into useable introductory textbooks for college and seminary courses, nor will it be received too well by church audiences. Furthermore, archaeologists will not be willing to admit that their field research investigates the life and history of a people who have little or no connection to the biblical text. While archaeological finds have contributed to our new critical awareness, archaeologists and biblical historians deeply indebted to them still will seek to write histories of Israel which combine in some balanced, critical and well-integrated fashion the narratives of the Hebrew Bible and the data unearthed from the ground. These scholars will use the biblical texts in critical fashion, but they will not dismiss those texts as fiction and minimal in value as resources for the historical quest. The models of Lemche, Thompson, Garbini and Davies too easily surrender the biblical text as a source in reconstructing the history and religion of Israel in the opinion of many, and thus throw away the baby with the bath water.

V

A great number of specialized studies which consider some aspect of Yahwistic religion increasingly assume that Israelite belief had a great deal of continuity with Canaanite belief. One particular topic of interest is the consideration of the identity and role of Asherah in Israel, especially after the discovery of inscriptions at Kuntillet 'Ajrûd, Khirbet el-Qôm and elsewhere, which pair the name of Asherah with Yahweh as though she were a deity.

Most scholars assume that the average Israelite considered Asherah an actual deity, a consort of Yahweh, and that veneration of her was acceptable throughout most of Israelite and Judahite history.[93] Scholars

---

93.   Ahlström, *Aspects*, pp. 51-88; *idem*, *Royal Administration*, pp. 42-43; *idem*, 'Role of Archaeological', pp. 128-29; Smith, 'Veracity', pp. 11-16; Lemaire, 'Les inscriptions', pp. 595-608; R. Patai, *The Hebrew Goddess* (New York: Avon, 1978), pp. 16-58, who believes that Asherah, Anat and Astarte were separate deities, all worshipped by Israelites; Meshel, 'Did Yahweh', pp. 24-35; D. Biale, 'The God with Breasts: El Shaddai in the Bible', *HR* 20 (1982), pp. 240-56; Dever, 'Archaeological Confirmation', pp. 37-44; *idem*, 'Asherah, Consort', pp. 21-37; *idem*, *Discoveries*, pp. 121-66; *idem*, 'Archaeology, Material Culture', pp. 103-15;

are also quick to point out that in the ninth century BCE, when Elijah, Elisha and Jehu opposed the cult of Tyrian Baal and his Omride supporters, the cult and devotees of Asherah were not suppressed.[94] In fact, it may have been at this time that Yahweh inherited Asherah from Baal in the general piety of common Israelites.[95] However, some scholars suggest that Yahweh already had Asherah as a consort at this time; Asherah became Yahweh's consort when Yahweh absorbed the identity of El who was paired with Asherah previously.[96] Either way the cult of the deity Asherah remained a viable option for Yahwistic Israelites until the reforms of Hezekiah, Josiah and the Deuteronomic Reformers.[97] Then she was absorbed into Yahweh's persona; and Israel as an abstrac-

---

idem, 'Ancient Israelite Religion', pp. 112-22; Garbini, 'Gli Ebrei', pp. 899-910; Dohmen, 'Heisst', pp. 263-66; Höffken, 'Bemerkung', pp. 88-93; Jeppesen, 'Micah', pp. 462-66; Zevit, 'Goddess', pp. 39-47; M.D. Coogan, 'Canaanite Origins and Lineage: Reflections on the Religion of Ancient Israel', *Ancient Israelite Religion* (eds. Miller, Hanson and McBride), p. 119; Theissen, *Biblical Faith*, pp. 79-80; E. Lipinski, 'The Syro-Palestinian Iconography of Woman and Goddess', *IEJ* 36 (1986), pp. 93-95; Nicholson, *God*, p. 200; D.N. Freedman, 'Yahweh of Samaria and His Asherah', *BA* 50 (1987), pp. 241-49; Hestrin, 'Lachish Ewer', pp. 212-23; Schroer, *Bilder*, pp. 21-45; Olyan, *Asherah*; G. Taylor, 'Two Earliest', pp. 557-66; *idem*, 'Yahweh Worshipped', pp. 53-54; B. Margalit, 'Some Observations on the Inscription and Drawing from Khirbet el-Qôm', *VT* 39 (1989), pp. 371-78; *idem*, 'Asherah', pp. 274-77; North, 'Yahweh's Asherah', pp. 118-37; S. Ackerman, '"And the Women Knead Dough": The Worship of the Queen of Heaven in Sixth-Century Judah', *Gender and Difference in Ancient Israel* (ed. P. Day; Minneapolis: Fortress Press, 1989), pp. 109-24; *idem*, *Green Tree*, pp. 6-35; *idem*, 'The Queen Mother and the Cult in Ancient Israel', *JBL* 112 (1993), pp. 385-401, who sees Asherah as a combination of Astarte and Ishtar of Babylon; McCarter, 'Origins', p. 138, which represents his later views; Toews, *Monarchy*, pp. 151-72; Albertz, *Israelite Religion*, I, pp. 194, 211; J. Day, 'Yahweh and the Gods and Goddesses of Canaan', *Ein Gott allein* (eds. Dietrich and Klopfenstein), pp. 184-86.

94.   Patai, *Hebrew Goddess*, p. 29; Saggs, *Encounter*, pp. 22-23; Biale, 'God', pp. 240-56; M. Ottosson, 'The Prophet Elijah's Visit to Zarephath', *Shelter of Elyon* (eds. Barrick and Spencer), pp. 185-98; Freedman, 'Yahweh of Samaria', pp. 214-49; Olyan, *Asherah*, pp. 1-22; Toews, *Monarchy*, pp. 151-72; Hadley, 'Yahweh', p. 242.

95.   Freedman, 'Yahweh of Samaria', pp. 241-49.

96.   Olyan, *Asherah*, pp. 38-69; W. Schniedewind, 'History and Interpretation: The Religion of Ahab and Manasseh in the Book of Kings', *CBQ* 55 (1993), p. 651; Day, 'Yahweh', pp. 184-86.

97.   Olyan, *Asherah*, pp. 70-74; Ackerman, 'Queen Mother', pp. 385-401; Albertz, *Israelite Religion*, I, pp. 194, 211.

tion, or Wisdom, or Torah, took her place as a symbolic consort.[98] There are dissenters to this reigning model. Some scholars still maintain that Asherah for most Israelites simply was a pole or tree, which symbolized the old second millennium BCE goddess, but her identity as a goddess with a distinct persona had been forgotten. The Asherah symbol was an extension of Yahweh or a superstitious fetish.[99] Some will admit that the inscriptions at Kuntillet 'Ajrûd and Khirbet el-Qôm refer to a real goddess, but that these are examples of aberration in the Israelite cult.[100] Or perhaps these inscriptions refer to another outlawed goddess.[101] Still others suggest that Asherah was perceived as a separate goddess in the early years of the monarchy, but she was expelled in the purge of the Tyrian Baal by Jehu.[102] It has been suggested that the veneration of Asherah continued only as an underground religion for women who felt excluded from the male-oriented Yahweh religion.[103] But even most of these scholars will acknowledge that cultic activity connected to Asherah implies pre-exilic Yahwism was not monotheistic.

Scholars who have researched other aspects of pre-exilic Israelite religion also stress the great continuity with Canaanite religion and culture. In his critique of Yehezkel Kaufmann, Jose Faur maintains that pre-exilic prophets and reformers did not deny the existence of other gods; rather, they merely attacked the use of unsanctioned statuary in Israel, that is, illegitimate iconography.[104] David Biale suggests that El Shaddai, whose

98. U. Winter, *Frau and Göttin: Exegetische und ikonographische Studien zum weiblichen Gottesbild im Alten Israel und in dessen Umwelt* (OBO, 53; Göttingen: Vandenhoeck & Ruprecht, 1983), pp. 483-538; M.-T. Wacker, 'Spuren der Göttin im Hoseabuch', *Ein Gott allein* (eds. Dietrich and Klopfenstein), pp. 329-48; M. Klopfenstein, 'Auferstehung der Göttin in der spätisraelitischen Weisheit von Prov 1–9?', *Ein Gott allein* (eds. Dietrich and Klopfenstein), pp. 531-42.

99. Emerton, 'Israelite Religion', pp. 2-20; Jaros, 'Inschrift', pp. 31-40; Lang, 'Yahweh-Alone', pp. 39-40; Winter, *Frau*, pp. 551-60; McCarter, 'Aspects', pp. 147-48, which are his early views; Day, 'Asherah', pp. 393, 397-408, who admits that some references are to a goddess also; P. Miller, 'The Absence of the Goddess in Israelite Religion', *HAR* 10 (1986), pp. 239-48; Tigay, *No Other Gods*, pp. 26-30; Smith, *Early History of God*, pp. 80-103; Dearman, *Religion*, p. 80; Toews, *Monarchy*, pp. 151-72; J. Taylor, 'The Asherah, the Menorah and the Sacred Tree', *JSOT* 66 (1995), pp. 29-54.

100. Miller, 'Israelite Religion', pp. 206, 217; *idem*, 'Absence', pp. 239-48.

101. Angerstorfer, 'Asherah', pp. 7-16.

102. Winter, *Frau, passim*; Miller, 'Absence', pp. 239-48.

103. Winter, *Frau*, pp. 3-92, 539-625; Dietrich, 'Werden und Wesen', p. 28.

104. J. Faur, 'The Biblical Idea of Idolatry', *JQR* 69 (1978), pp. 1-15.

name means 'breasts', originally was a female fertility goddess worshipped by Israelites, who absorbed the fertility imagery of Asherah and the
warrior imagery of Anat, and was merged into Yahweh by monotheistic
Priestly reformers to create the post-exilic portrayal of Yahweh as warrior
and guarantor of descendents.[105] H.C. Brichto, Alberto Green, George
Heider, Susan Ackermann and Jon Levenson conclude that infant
sacrifice was an integral part of the Israelite cult until Josiah's reform,
and it may have involved the worship of an underworld chthonic deity
of healing and fertility, Molek, in a cult of the dead (the Rephaim), or
perhaps infants were sacrificed directly to Yahweh.[106] John Day would
concur with them except for maintaining that we should view the cult as
Canaanite, or more precisely Jerusalem Jebusite, in its origin before the
Judahites adopted it.[107] Hans-Peter Stähli and Glen Taylor see the presence of a cult of the sun which was absorbed by Yahwism in Israel and
Judah, but especially in Jerusalem, in order to describe Yahweh as judge
and protector of world order and to lend legitimation to the status of the
king. These practices were not criticized until the oracles of Ezekiel,
because Yahweh so often was envisioned as the sun in the minds of
many. The sun was not an object made by human hands, and so the
practice was not condemned directly by the second commandment prohibition against images.[108] John Strange observes that Solomon's artwork
in the Temple implies that he tried to create a merger of separate Israelite
deities (El, Baal and Yahweh), and from Egypt images were borrowed in
order to develop the notion of an afterlife (resurrection) connected to

---

105. Biale, 'God', pp. 240-56.

106. H.C. Brichto, 'Kin, Cult, Land and Afterlife—A Biblical Complex', *HUCA*
44 (1973), pp. 1-55; A. Green, *The Role of Human Sacrifice in the Ancient Near
East* (ASORDS, 1; Missoula, MT: Scholars Press, 1977), pp. 156-87; G. Heider,
The Cult of Molek: A Reassessment (JSOTSup, 43; Sheffield: JSOT Press, 1985);
Ackerman, *Green Tree*, pp. 101-163; *idem*, 'Child Sacrifice: Returning God's Gift',
Bible Review 9.3 (1993): 20-29, 56; J. Levenson, *The Death and Resurrection of the
Beloved Son: The Transformation of Child Sacrifice in Judaism and Christianity*
(New Haven: Yale University Press, 1993), pp. 3-52, 111-24.

107. J. Day, *Molech: A God of Human Sacrifice in the Old Testament* (University
of Cambridge Oriental Publications, 41; Cambridge: Cambridge University Press,
1989), pp. 29-71.

108. H.-P. Stähli, *Solare Elemente im Jahwe Glauben des Alten Testaments*
(OBO, 66; Göttingen: Vandenhoeck & Ruprecht, 1985), *passim*; G. Taylor,
Yahweh; *idem*, 'Yahweh Worshipped', pp. 52-61, 90.

divine kingship.[109] John Day and Carola Kloos both conclude that the imagery of Yahweh's conflict with the primordial sea was very significant in Israel's pre-exilic religion, and it reflects extensive Canaanite beliefs which became integral to Yahwism. Day suggests that despite its Canaanite origin (not Babylonian as most have suggested) the battle with the sea was connected to Yahweh's creation of the world and was celebrated in the autumnal New Year's festival.[110] Kloos further opines that this reflects the overall presence of Baal imagery throughout Israelite religion, and thus we can no longer differentiate between 'mythic' Canaanite and 'epic' or 'historical' Israelite religion.[111] Gary Anderson likewise decries the contrast of Canaanite and Israelite religious thought, and he observes the continuity of land fertility concerns in Israelite theology connected to the Temple down into the post-exilic era, including the oracles of prophets like Haggai and Zechariah.[112] John Dearman sternly discourages the use of the Canaanite-Israelite dichotomy in the discussion of legal customs, the concept of property, or the characterization of economic activity,[113] something which I must confess to having done.[114] Choon Seow suggests that Yahwism drew heavily upon the imagery of El and Baal beliefs for its portrayal of the Ark of the Covenant.[115] In Susan Ackerman's broader study of popular religion she concludes that Asherah worship, fertility rites, child sacrifice, the cult of the dead and the worship of several deities were practiced commonly as a normal part of Yahweh religion, and furthermore that necromancy, child sacrifice and fertility rites survived Josiah's reform and endured

---

109. J. Strange, 'The Idea of Afterlife in Ancient Israel: Some Remarks on the Iconography in Solomon's Temple', *PEQ* 117 (1985), pp. 35-40.

110. J. Day, *God's Conflict with the Dragon and the Sea: Echos of a Canaanite Myth in the Old Testament* (University of Cambridge Oriental Publications, 35; Cambridge: Cambridge University Press, 1985).

111. C. Kloos, *Yahweh's Combat with the Sea: A Canaanite Tradition in the Religion of Ancient Israel* (Leiden: Brill, 1986).

112. G. Anderson, *Sacrifices and Offerings in Ancient Israel: Studies in their Social and Political Importance* (HSM, 41; Atlanta,: Scholars Press, 1987), pp. 7-23 *et passim*.

113. Dearman, *Religion*, pp. 1-149.

114. Gnuse, *Steal*, pp. 53-85.

115. C. Seow, *Myth, Drama, and the Politics of David's Dance* (HSM, 44; Atlanta: Scholars Press, 1989), pp. 7-144, 205-210.

into the post-exilic era, as evidenced by oracles in Isaiah 57 and 65.[116] She concludes,

> the ancient cult allowed for greater latitude in religious beliefs and prac-
> tices than the exilic and post-exilic editors of the biblical text would admit.
> We have thus come to doubt the rather homogenous picture presented by
> the biblical writers.[117]

Axel Knauf believes that prior to Hosea El was considered superior to Yahweh, and it was Hosea who created the Yahweh alone movement—he was the true Moses of Israel. Furthermore, Jeremiah was the first monotheist, for he proclaimed Yahweh to be a creator deity, and only in the post-exilic period did Jews become monotheistic as a people.[118] Wesley Toews concludes that Yahweh and El were worshipped as the same deity in the pre-monarchic period, and other deities were worshipped as well, so the efforts of Jeroboam I of Israel were merely a conservative attempt to preserve this pattern of piety.[119] Jacques Berlinerblau observes that pre-exilic Israel had many popular religious groups, not just one; so that the cults of Asherah, Baal and Yahweh were separate but inter-acting religious devotions, and the non-Yahwistic pieties were not just one pagan religion as the biblical texts envisioned.[120] Frederick Cryer's study on ancient Near Eastern and Israelite divination concludes that magical practices and divination in Israel were indigenous, not foreign imports as claimed by the Deuteronomistic Historians, and these customs were widespread and accepted throughout pre-exilic Israel.[121] Meindert Dijkstra suggests that the Deir 'Alla inscription from the Transjordan dates to 800 BCE, which speaks of the prophet Balaam who serves the god El and the goddess Shagar-and-Ashtar, may reflect peripheral Israelite religion rather than Canaanite or Ammonite religion.[122] Hence, a number of specialized, scholarly studies are coming to the conclusion

116. Ackerman, 'Women Knead', pp. 109-24; *idem, Green Tree; idem,* 'Queen Mother', pp. 385-401.

117. Ackerman, *Green Tree*, p. 388.

118. Knauf, 'From History', pp. 26-64.

119. Toews, *Monarchy*.

120. J. Berlinerblau, 'The "Popular Religion" Paradigm in Old Testament Research: A Sociological Critique', *JSOT* 60 (1993), pp. 3-26.

121. F. Cryer, *Divination in Ancient Israel and its Near Eastern Environment: A Socio-Historical Investigation* (JSOTSup, 142; Sheffield: JSOT Press, 1994).

122. M. Dijkstra, 'Is Balaam Also among the Prophets?', *JBL* 114 (1995), pp. 43-64.

that the pre-exilic religion of the Israelites was polytheistic by nature, and the portrayal of the Deuteronomistic History represents the position of a minority who are projecting their values back into the historical experiences of the people.

Finally, there are a great number of general studies and overviews of Israelite religion and history which increasingly assume that polytheism was the natural piety of Israel until the monolatry of the Deuteronomic Reformers and the more stringent monotheism of Second Isaiah. They perceive that Yahwism was really another form of West-Semitic religion, which grew out of the greater ancient Near Eastern religious milieu.[123] Susan Ackerman summarizes nicely the current consensus of many scholars,

> despite the biblical witness neither the priestly nor the prophetic cult was normative in the religion of the first millennium. Rather, a diversity of beliefs and practices thrived and were accepted by the ancients as legitimate forms of religious expression.[124]

Critical scholars now stress that in the future we ought to stress the continuity that Israelite religion had with Canaanite culture.[125] Some further

123. H. McKeating, *Amos, Hosea, Micah* (CBC; Cambridge: Cambridge University Press, 1971), p. 92; H. Wildberger, 'Der Monotheismus Deuterojesajas', *Beiträge zur Alttestamentlichen Theologie (Festschrift für Walther Zimmerli)* (eds. H. Donner, R. Hahnhart and R. Smend; Göttingen: Vandenhoeck und Ruprecht, 1977), pp. 506-30; Soggin, *Judges*, pp. 218, 304; Angerstorfer, 'Asherah', pp. 7-16; Jaros, 'Inschrift', pp. 31-40; Jeppesen, 'Micah', pp. 462-66; D. Gowan, *Ezekiel* (Knox Preaching Guides; Atlanta: John Knox, 1985), pp. 4-5, 40; Hossfeld, 'Einheit', pp. 57-74; Miller, 'Israelite Religion', pp. 207-208, 212; M. Hutter, 'Das Werden des Monotheismus im alten Israel', *Anfänge der Theologie* (ed. N. Brox; Graz: Styria, 1987), pp. 25-39; T. Mettinger, *In Search of God: The Meaning and Message of the Everlasting Names* (trans. F. Cryer; Philadelphia: Fortress Press, 1988), pp. 203-205; C. Kennedy, 'Isaiah 57:5-6: Tombs in the Rocks', *BASOR* 275 (1989), pp. 50-51; M. Polley, *Amos and the Davidic Empire: A Socio-Historical Approach* (New York: Oxford University Press, 1989), pp. 58-64; M. Weippert, 'Synkretismus und Monotheismus: Religionsinterne Konfliktbewältigung im alten Israel', *Kultur und Konflikt* (eds. J. Assman and D. Harth; Frankfurt am Main: Suhrkamp, 1990), pp. 143-79; B.A. Nakhai, 'What's a Bamah? How Sacred Space Functioned in Ancient Israel', *BARev* 20.3 (1994), pp. 18-29, 77-78.

124. Ackerman, 'Women Knead', p. 109.

125. Reventlow, 'Eigenart', pp. 199-217; M. Rose, 'Yahweh in Israel—Qaus in Edom?', *JSOT* 4 (1977), pp. 128-34; W. Dever, 'Material Remains and the Cult in Israel: An Essay on Archaeological Systematics', *The Word of the Lord Shall go Forth: Essays in Honor of David Noel Freedman in Celebration of his Sixtieth*

maintain that we must assess critically our definitions of monotheism in Israel and how we speak of its emergence both in theory and in our pedagogical literature.[126] What we have in much of the biblical text is 'monotheistic language inside of a polytheistic reference system', that is, language which may sound monotheistic to us, but which is spoken to people who consciously or unconsciously were still polytheists.[127] Such language is rhetorical, designed to move people forward in their religious piety, but it does not reflect theoretical monotheism as much as it is the language of an evolutionary process moving toward monotheism. We must understand the biblical language in its evolutionary context to appreciate its depth of meaning. It is to this end that I seek to make a small contribution.

Michael Coogan proposes a fine methodological suggestion for the future when he says 'it is essential to consider biblical religion as a subset of Israelite religion and Israelite religion as a subset of Canaanite religion', so that the biblical faith may be seen as a 'reconstruction' out of the matrix of Canaanite religion.[128] This suggestion encapsulates the paradox

Birthday (eds. C. Meyers and M. O'Connor; Winona Lake, IN: Eisenbrauns, 1983), pp. 571-87; *idem*, 'Contribution', pp. 209-247; *idem*, *Discoveries*, pp. 119-66; W. Schmidt, *The Faith of the Old Testament: A History* (trans. J. Sturdy; Philadelphia: Westminster Press, 1983), pp. 1-4, 138-40, 171-72, 177-80, 184 *et passim*; Miller, 'Israelite Religion', pp. 201-37; Nicholson, *God*, p. 196; Coogan, 'Canaanite Origins', pp. 115-24; J. Holladay, 'Religion in Judah and Israel under the Monarchy', *Ancient Israelite Religion* (eds. Miller, Hanson and McBride), pp. 249-99; Lohfink, 'Reform of Josiah', pp. 459-75; McCarter, 'Aspects', pp. 137-55; B. Peckham, 'Phoenicia and the Religion of Israel', *Ancient Israelite Religion* (eds. Miller, Hanson and McBride), pp. 79-99; Thompson, *Origin Tradition*, pp. 37-38; Flanagan, *Social Drama*, pp. 251-57; Mettinger, *In Search*, pp. 203-205; R. Hendel, 'Worldmaking in Ancient Israel', *JSOT* 56 (1992), pp. 3-18; Berlinerblau, 'Popular Religion', pp. 3-26; Toews, *Monarchy*, pp. 68-69.

126. Halpern, 'Brisker Pipes', pp. 77-115; D. Petersen, 'Israel and Monotheism: The Unfinished Agenda', *Canon, Theology, and Old Testament Interpretation: Essays in Honor of Brevard S. Childs* (eds. G. Tucker, D. Petersen and R. Wilson; Philadelphia: Fortress Press, 1988), pp. 92-107; Michael Fishbane, *The Garments of Torah: Essays in Biblical Hermeneutics* (Bloomington: University of Indiana Press, 1989), pp. 49-63; Dearman, *Religion*, pp. 35-50; F.J. van Beeck, 'Israel's God, the Psalms, and the City of Jerusalem: Life Experience and the Sacrifice of Praise and Prayer', *Horizons* 19 (1992), pp. 219-39.

127. G. Braulik, 'Das Deuteronomium und die Geburt des Monotheismus', *Gott, der Einzige* (ed. Haag), pp. 117, 145-47.

128. Coogan, 'Canaanite Origins', pp. 115-16.

upon which biblical scholars should build in the future. Israel's religion was part of the milieu of the ancient world. The religion of the biblical text has far greater continuity with the ancient world than scholars have acknowledged in the past, yet at the same time it reflects a sophisticated evolutionary advance over the predecessor religion of pre-exilic Israel. This advance is due to a particular recombination of elements from the old belief system. In the future scholars must struggle to express this tension in nuanced fashion to respect what we have observed in the biblical text and the archaeological finds.

VI

Inspired by Coogan's proposal and comparable suggestions by other scholars discussed in this chapter I make the following generalized typology:

1) Biblical religion is a narrow aspect and subsequent interpretation of the broader polytheistic pre-exilic Yahwism of Israel and Judah. It was created by exilic and post-exilic Priestly and prophetically inspired theologians in a negative reaction to that earlier cultus. Biblical religion demonstrates a significant evolutionary advance because of its conscious formulation by those theologians, even though it used the concepts and beliefs of the earlier religious phenomena. This summarizes what many of the previous scholars have opined.

2) Israelite religion is part of a family of national cults which are found in Palestine, including at least the religious beliefs of Ammon, Moab and Edom, and perhaps even the Philistines at the periphery. The continuity between pre-exilic Yahwism and these national cults of neighboring states is probably much greater than authors have recognized in the past. Some scholars, in particular, have acknowledged significant connections between Yahwism and the religion of the Edomites, who may have worshipped the same god as the Israelites.[129]

The differences between regional expressions of Yahwism within Israel and Judah may be as great as the overall differences between Yahwism and the religions of the Transjordan. Certainly many of the peasants in these regions had a set of beliefs which would impress modern observers

---

129. Weippert, *Settlement*, pp. 105-106; J.R. Bartlett, 'The Brotherhood of Edom', *JSOT* 4 (1977), pp. 2-27; *idem*, 'Yahweh and Qaus: A Response to Martin Rose (JSOT 4 [1977] 28-34)', *JSOT* 5 (1978), pp. 29-38; Rose, 'Qaus', pp. 28-34; Ahlström, *Israelites*, pp. 58-60.

as synthetic or syncretistic. In reality, scholars observe a spectrum of changing beliefs and practices across the land of Palestine, much as we observe in Syria and Phoenicia also. This, for example, may be suggested to explain the Deir 'Alla inscription from an eighth-century BCE Transjordanian site. It may reflect a form of Yahwism on the periphery of Israelite settlement, which is the natural religious expression for that region, for it would be the natural transition or bridge between the Israelite and Ammonite territories. It would be part of the gradual spectrum of religious change that would occur as we move from one major region to another.[130]

3) The religious tradition of Palestine is then part of the greater spectrum of West-Semitic religious activity found in Syria, Phoenicia and Palestine or Canaan. Yahwism and the religions of the Transjordan are the southern component of this greater Syrian tradition. Many scholars have suggested such a distinction in the past, implying that perhaps while Baal devotion was strong in the north (Syria and Phoenicia), devotion to El and subsequently Yahweh prevailed in the south (Palestine). Such a distinction seems reasonable.

4) The religion of greater Syria-Palestine then should be considered as a type of ancient Near Eastern Semitic religious experience. It appears to have its greatest continuity with the Semitic religious traditions of Mesopotamia, but it also shares distinct continuity with the Semitic and African religious synthesis of Egypt. So, one may see a spectrum of religious beliefs and practices across the Near East.

I propose, in general, a vision of a 'nested hierarchy' (a term taken from biology) for understanding the religion of the biblical text, which involves acknowledging five levels of religious expression: the biblical religion of monotheism; the pre-exilic Israelite religion; the religious traditions of Palestine; the West-Semitic religious traditions; and the religious experience of the greater ancient Near East. The lines between these categories are rather artificially drawn and somewhat pedantic. For as we move from Syria into Mesopotamia, the beliefs and customs of the people form a gradual spectrum. Artificial though this typology may appear at first, I believe it has heuristic value as a pedagogical tool and

130. H.P. Müller, 'Die aramäische Inschrift von Deir 'Alla und die älteren Bileamsprüche', *ZAW* 94 (1982), p. 239; E. Puech, 'L'inscription sur plâtre de Tell Deir 'Alla', *Biblical Archaeology Today* (ed. Amitai), p. 362; B. Levine, 'The "Balaam Inscription from Deir 'Alla": Historical Aspects', *Biblical Archaeology Today* (ed. Amitai), p. 333.

for scholarly discourse in biblical studies. The typology of these five levels is arranged from the perspective of biblical studies, from the 'bottom' upward, rather than a 'top' down taxonomy of ancient Near Eastern religions. The purpose of this 'nested hierarchy' is to assist biblical theologians in their perception of biblical and Israelite religion in relationship to each other and their greater milieu. Hopefully, it might be helpful in the future discussions of how biblical religious beliefs reflect continuity with the ancient milieu and function as part of a great evolutionary advance for humanity at the same time.

I would argue that the paradigm of a 'nested hierarchy' of religious traditions offers some advantageous new perceptions for viewing biblical traditions.

1. Whereas formerly biblical theologians contrasted monotheistic Israelite beliefs with typical ancient Near Eastern or so-called Canaanite beliefs, this new perception stresses the real contrast may be between monotheistic Yahwism of the exile and beyond with the earlier Yahwism of the pre-exilic era. Biblical authors who created the Deuteronomistic History, the Priestly edition of the Pentateuch, and the collected prophetic oracles were in bitter dialogue with the practices of polytheistic Yahwism. If we wish to use the models of comparison and contrast to illustrate how biblical beliefs stand out in contrast to earlier concepts, we need to recognize that we are contrasting earlier Yahwism with later Yahwism, and the so-called Canaanite or ancient Near Eastern thought systems stand in a very peripheral relationship to the discussion. In effect, we will sense in our comparisons that we are discussing a process of evolution from early to later Yahwism rather than an on-going conflict between people and their values.

2. This model really does not distinguish pre-exilic Israelite religion from Canaanite religion. The typology admits the existence of national religious traditions, such as Ammonite, Moabite and Edomite. Perhaps we should add Israelite and Judahite as two separate entities, since the differences between these two regions may be as great as the distinctions between them and Transjordanian national religions. In general, pre-exilic Israelite and Canaanite religions may be virtually the same phenomenon. Scholars characterized Canaanite religious beliefs on the basis of Phoenician texts, which really describe the religious experience of another region. Or they used the texts of Ugarit which come from the previous millennium (not to mention the region of Syria, even farther north than Phoenicia). Scholars too often contrasted second millennium BCE religion

(mythic Canaanite) with first millennium BCE religion (Israelite), when in reality the latter evolved into the former. The early first millennium BCE religion of the Cisjordan was polytheistic Yahwism throughout most of the populace, and one could consider that either Canaanite or Israelite depending on your modern perspective, but the original devotees of that piety probably knew no such distinction. To be sure, there were regional differences, the biblical texts certainly admit diversity in pre-exilic Yahwism. These regional differences might include a preference for Yahweh among some highland population elements and a preference for Baal among lowlanders, but if we were alive in that era, we might be unable to delineate two separate religious traditions with all the complexities and regional variations before us. Basically, the average Israelite or Judahite saw Yahweh as the national deity and Baal in charge of vegetation, and beyond that the nuances of difference varied from region to region. First millennium BCE Canaanite religion and polytheistic Yahwism might be considered the same greater religious tradition of the Cisjordan.

3. Stressing that biblical religion and especially Israelite religion has closer kinship with the religions of Ammon, Moab and Edom than with the other religions of the ancient Near East will orient scholars to a closer consideration of those religious traditions and a more nuanced treatment of their beliefs. Already sensitive treatments of the religion of Edom may foreshadow future evaluations that will be fueled by increased archaeological discoveries coming from the Transjordan. Scholars will observe the great continuity of religion in the region and common themes which unite Israel and the Transjordan rather than classifying the latter in the greater mix of ancient Near Eastern religion and seeking ideas of these neighboring religious traditions to place in opposition to Israelite belief or to accuse of being the source of syncretism in Israel.

4. Placing the Palestinian, or Canaanite, or south Syrian religious traditions together and artificially distinguishing them from the West-Semitic traditions of Phoenicia and Syria may be a useful model in the light of our present knowledge, for some scholars suspect the existence of differences in these two larger geographic regions. Perhaps, the south was closer to Egypt and more influenced by Egyptian culture in the later second millennium BCE, while the north was closer to the cultural centers of Mesopotamia. Certainly there are linguistic differences between the two regions, and the respective areas may have revered Baal and El with proportionately different zeal. It acknowledges the commonality of

all the West-Semitic religious pieties from Syria down to Egypt, but it also admits a special kinship among the religious traditions of Canaan.

5. Recognition of the connections between biblical religion and Israelite religion with the greater West-Semitic religious tradition will be useful also. Because of the great number of Mesopotamian and Egyptian texts scholars have been tempted to compare Israelite belief directly with them. This new perception will enable many to see that Israelite religion is related to Mesopotamian and Egyptian beliefs through the greater family of West-Semitic religions, which historically was a cultural bridge between Egypt and Mesopotamia. We may observe that Israelite and biblical religions share certain things in common over against Egyptian and Mesopotamian beliefs. For example, West-Semitic religion and polytheistic Yahwism both tended to have a reduced pantheon in contrast to Mesopotamian and Egyptian religions. The evaluation of similarities and differences would be much more accurate once we work with the model that sees Israelite religion as part of a great West-Semitic religious tradition.

6. The use of this model which attempts to fix Israelite and later biblical faiths in a 'nested hierarchy' may help us to be more precise in our use of the comparative method. We shall more accurately describe the real differences between biblical beliefs and the earlier Israelite, West-Semitic and ancient Near Eastern thought out of which they evolved. We shall also more clearly see the continuities, many of which have been overlooked in the past. We may notice that biblical faith may have certain connections with West-Semitic beliefs, which in turn may be found in the rest of the ancient Near East. These would be examples of beliefs shared in common with part of the ancient milieu, but not all. The model of 'nested hierarchies' then would enable us to admit and observe themes which might be both distinctive and shared with contemporary cultures.

7. Above all, the model will help us understand the evolutionary advance of the biblical worldview. Biblical faith evolves out of the pre-exilic Israelite religion. That means it shares much in common with its predecessors, but it is also different. The degree of shared aspects lessens and the degree of difference increases as we view biblical beliefs in the wider panorama of the 'nested hierarchy' of religious traditions. We sense a continuity through each level between biblical faith and its various antecedents. We may sense the difference between biblical beliefs and those in Mesopotamia by considering the progression through West-Semitic and Palestinian belief structures. Ultimately, biblical faith arose

out of its milieu and became something distinct, for biblical authors were certainly conscious of their differences of belief, even if they overstated them. Biblical faith was something new, even though it had great continuity with the past and used the old elements of belief. It used these elements in a new, creative reconstruction or reconfiguration, which stressed themes in a different way. Monolatry became monotheism, and monotheism was the lynchpin in the total belief system. With this as the central principle all the old elements absorbed into the theology appeared radically different, even though they were not. The use of the model of 'nested hierarchies' may enable us to focus more clearly on those elements which were taken over and reconfigured in the new belief system. We may observe how they were continuous with the old religious belief structures, and at what level in the 'nested hierarchy' they were continuous, while at the same time we shall observe more clearly how they functioned differently in the newly emergent monotheistic faith.

So far in this chapter we have observed the new scholarly opinions concerning the emergence of monotheism in Israel. Monotheism, which may have emerged in either Josiah's reform or in the exile, appears to have been the constitutive element in the new reconfiguration of thought. A former generation placed emerging monotheism earlier than the present generation of scholars does. An earlier generation of scholars made sweeping generalizations about the impact of emerging monotheism, but the present generation strives to be more cautious in its articulations. Nonetheless, monotheism in its radical form may be the key to understanding the evolutionary advance of biblical faith. For that reason we must consider monotheism in Israel from a broader perspective in the next chapter.

Chapter 3

MONOTHEISM IN ANCIENT ISRAEL'S WORLD

> ...ethical monotheism was not a 'natural' and universal *fait accompli*,
> destined for all mankind from the very beginning... It simply represents
> the culmination of a historical process belonging to Israel and Israel alone.
>
> V. Nikiprowetsky[1]

This bold statement ultimately sums up the position of the vast majority
of scholars. Although one may observe monotheistic tendencies and the
seeds of monotheistic thought in the ancient world, the clarity with
which monotheism and its related values appear in Israelite and Jewish
culture still impresses the students of intellectual and religious history. In
the biblical literature monotheistic faith is a breakthrough or culmination
of the intellectual and religious development of the ages. It reflects not
only the final stage of six centuries of pre-exilic Israelite religious speculation but perhaps in some way the contributions of nameless thinkers
from the ancient Near East for millennia prior to ancient Israel's
existence as a people. Although it was a breakthrough in a revolutionary
way, it did not arise *creatio ex nihilo*; there was a period of preparation
in the historical process, both in the ancient Near East and Israel, which
led up to the emergence of monotheism in the exile. The Jews did not
make the leap of faith because of some inevitable historical process.
They could have gone the route as in east Asia where the reflective
religious thinkers opted for some form of philosophical monism rather
than religious monotheism. So, Nikiprowetsky speaks correctly when he
maintains that credit should be given to the Jews for this profound intellectual breakthrough. Furthermore, when monotheism truly emerged in
Israel, it brought with it attendant moral values, and so Nikiprowetsky
maintains that the term 'monotheism' must be prefaced with the word
'ethical', for fully developed monotheism is truly ethical monotheism. It
was this form of religious expression that the Israelites and Jews attained
and contributed to our western culture.

1. Nikiprowetsky, 'Ethical Monotheism', p. 69.

I

In an excellent essay David Petersen put forth in lucid fashion the questions which a study of monotheism should address: 1) Did monotheism arise by evolution, devolution or revolution? 2) Did monotheism truly exist in the ancient Near East before Israel? 3) Did the monotheism or proto-monotheism of the ancient Near East influence Israel? 4) When did monotheism arise in Israel? 5) How ought we define our terms such as henotheism and monolatry? 6) What are the implications of monotheism? How does it affect the human psyche? Does it promote violence? Is it sexist? Does it produce equality? Does it support tyranny and hierarchical classes in society? What type of literature does it produce? How do thinkers attribute the contradictory actions of the divine realm to one divine person?[2] These are all excellent questions, and in this volume I attempt to provide some insights and answers to several of the questions.

In brief summary the following observations appeal to me on the basis of scholarly reflections in the field of religious studies:

Monotheism emerges both by evolution and revolution, it is not an either/or proposition. Contemporary biological models see a species' evolution occurring in rapid transformations which have a long period of prior mutational preparation and a subsequent period of unfolding the latent implications of the genetic breakthrough. The same model may describe the monotheistic breakthrough. Tendencies toward monotheism in the ancient world were dramatic indeed, but it is an overstatement to view them as true monotheistic expressions. The ultimate breakthrough in Israel came in revolutionary fashion, yet at the end of a long evolutionary process in the ancient world.

The extent to which prior religious expressions may have influenced Israelite and Jewish thinkers cannot be determined, for we cannot peer into the minds of Israelite and Jewish authors to determine the extent of influence the reading of foreign texts might have had upon their creative articulations. We cannot do that with living thinkers today, nor can we even be sure exactly what in our own personal educational experiences may have wrought the greatest influence upon us. All we can say is that ancient texts and ideas were probably available to the ancient Israelites and Jews, especially in exile, and they might have used some of that material. Ultimately they were part of an ancient world culture, and we

2.   Petersen, 'Israel and Monotheism', pp. 92-107.

must assume some intellectual interplay and cross-fertilization of ideas. But when a biblical author expresses himself or herself in a text, the ideas really belong to that individual no matter how they might have been taken or cannibalized from other sources.

Since critical scholars now view the Babylonian exile as the time of the monotheistic breakthrough, the question is the degree to which significant pre-exilic religious and intellectual development may have contributed to the final emergence of monotheism, or if there was any at all. Increasingly scholars are very critical of the old idea that monotheism arose in the simplicity of the nomadic or semi-nomadic conditions in the wilderness or their highland settlements.

The romantic ideas of yore that monotheism should be connected to the desert, especially in the case of Muhammed and Islam, have been thoroughly discredited.[3] Monotheism is much more of an urban phenomenon in the ancient world, or if it is connected to pastoral regions, they are usually in close proximity to urban areas with which they interact extensively. For it takes the concentration of intelligentsia in an urban center to generate, sustain and communicate the new ideas of a monotheistic faith. It takes an organized and concentrated worshipping community in such centers to accept the beliefs and then propagate them along the networks of trade and communication which link cities. So, monotheistic Yahwism more likely arose in the urban centers of Mesopotamia during the Babylonian exile; Zoroastrianism spread from pastoral and agricultural regions of northwest Persia and Bactria into the urban centers of power in the Achaemedian Persian Empire; Christianity arose in the well-organized Roman Empire in Jerusalem and spread through the cities of the east Mediterranean; and Islam emerged in the trade centers of Mecca and Medina before spreading to all Arabia and eventually the entire Near East. Denis Baly has critiqued the idea of desert origins for monotheism by noting that monotheism rejects an apotheosis of the natural order and the difficult physical environment of the desert makes the separation of God or the gods from natural forces most difficult in the minds of its inhabitants.[4]

Monotheism emerges and develops most fully in the context of serious intellectual struggles, such as the question of theodicy and the presence of evil in the world, or the need to keep the high god from becoming

---

3.   Baly, 'Geography of Monotheism', pp. 254-56; Halpern, *Emergence*, p. 249; Albertz, 'Der Ort', p. 86.

4.   Baly, 'Geography of Monotheism', pp. 254-55.

too distant—the high god can be both transcendent and immanent when he or she is the only deity in the heavens. The discussion of such issues is facilitated by a dialogue setting in which there are a number of intelligentsia to discuss these issues, and they all have been freed from the backbreaking labor of village farming and pastoral herding. Such are the conditions of urban settings where a hinterland region produces agricultural and other material raw resources for the maintenance of a city, and that city is large enough to support a class of scribes, government officials, priests and other potentially reflective individuals. It requires that almost worldwide a large enough human population develops in many urban centers to produce well-developed trade networks along which goods and ideas might flow. Human population and centers of civilization throughout the Old World reached such a critical mass during that period of time which has been called the 'Axial Age' (800–400 BCE).[5] Israelites and the later Jews were very much part of this process in the Babylonian exile, when they would have had contact with new foreign ideas and the chance to dialogue with those ideas. This process would have accelerated in the later years of the exile when the economic conditions of many exiled Jews began to improve. This would be the time of Second Isaiah, the person to whom much credit is given for the monotheistic breakthrough.

The problem in describing the various stages of religious development prior to the monotheistic breakthrough has forced scholars to use terms like henotheism, monolatry, incipient monotheism, latent monotheism, among others. To be sure, henotheism and monolatry probably mean the same thing in theory, and according to Raffaele Pettazzoni and David Petersen we inherited the word 'henotheism' from the philosopher Friedrich Schelling and the classicist Friedrich Welcker, whereas the term 'monolatry' may have been coined by William Robertson Smith to describe early Semitic religion.[6] However, I am not so sure we really

5. Baly, 'Geography of Monotheism', p. 255; Reventlow, 'Eigenart', pp. 213-15; S. Eisenstadt, 'The Axial Age Breakthroughs—Their Characteristics and Origins', *Axial Age Civilizations* (ed. *idem*), pp. 1-25; *idem*, 'The Axial Age Breakthrough in Ancient Israel', *Axial Age Civilizations* (ed. *idem*), pp. 127-34; Halpern, 'Brisker Pipes', p. 106.

6. F. Welcker, *Die griechische Götterlehre* (3 vols.; Göttingen: Dietrich, 1857–62), obtained the term 'henotheism' from Schelling and used it to describe the primordial monotheism of Greeks who supposedly worshipped only Zeus, quoted in R. Pettazzoni, 'The Formation of Monotheism', *Reader in Comparative Religion: An Anthropological Approach* (ed. W. Lessa; Evanston: Row, Peterson & Co.,

need to obtain a consensus definition of these terms. Each author discussed in the previous chapter had a characterization for each level of development, and the scholars simply chose words to summarize briefly their characterizations. The nuances they used in describing those various stages of development were more important than the particular labels they might have used. To arrive at a consensus now would be too late, since so many books and articles are already in print. One can appreciate Morton Smith and others who followed him in the use of the 'Yahweh-alone' expression, for it avoided much of the jargon completely. We must simply be sensitive to the fact that there is an irregular development of religious ideas and beliefs leading up to monotheism, and it really is rather difficult to provide neat and clearly defined labels for all of them. Such is the nature of evolution in all human institutions and belief systems.

A scholar who has introduced very useful language into the discussion in this regard is William Tremmel, who does not address biblical studies directly in his writings, but rather evaluates phenomena in all the world's religions. He uses the term 'consummate religion' to describe the point at which monism (as in Hinduism and Taoism) or monotheism (as in Zoroastrianism and Judaism) emerges within a religious tradition. It also may describe the point at which a religion attains a level of sophistication and philosophical reflection. A consummate religion 'is one in which the concept of universe has been accomplished, and God is no longer attached to a specific place, or limited power'.[7] Thus, pre-exilic Israel saw Yahweh as a god of Palestine, but post-exilic Jews viewed Yahweh as a universal deity. Tremmel speaks of the 'kairotic episode' as that point in a religion's development when it becomes a 'consummate religion'. He also views the 'Axis Age' (the expression he uses rather than 'Axial Age') from 800 to 400 BCE as a 'kairotic episode' throughout the Old World, when significant religious and intellectual breakthroughs occurred in China, India, the Near East and east Mediterranean world.[8] This terminology may be used as a fresh new attempt to articulate the nuances necessary to describe the phenomena of the monotheistic breakthrough, for it recognizes that there is evolution but also emphasizes the dramatic and revolutionary time of change when the evolutionary process comes

1958), p. 43 = Pettazzoni, *Essays on the History of Religions* (trans. H.J. Rose; Leiden: Brill, 1954); Petersen, 'Israel and Monotheism', pp. 97-98.

7.　Tremmel, *Religion*, p. 129.
8.　Tremmel, *Religion*, p. 129.

to fruition. The imagery resonates well with the concerns of this book.

A discussion of the implications of emergent monotheism would entail the consideration of many topics, many of which are beyond my ability to consider. I shall, however, focus upon the tendency of monotheism to produce humanitarian values and to set in motion a tradition of egalitarianism. To be sure, certain interpretations of monotheistic faith have legitimated tyranny in the past, but this would appear to be contrary to the spirit of a monotheistic faith. I shall maintain that the Judaeo-Christian monotheism is a religious breakthrough with social egalitarian implications which are still being worked out in our own age.

II

Traditional Jewish and Christian belief read the narratives in Genesis and so assumed that originally people, descended from Adam and Eve, all worshipped one god in the heavens. At some early point in time human perversity led people to turn from the worship of one true god and revere instead the demons, even making idolatrous statues of them. Such was the opinion of Augustine who said that 'all the gods of the Gentiles are demons' (*City of God*).[9]

In the past four centuries the modern critical mind has looked for other ways of explaining emerging monotheism. Historians have noted that three different options have been articulated by authors: devolution, evolution and revolution.

Advocates of devolution say that originally all people worshipped one deity, but at some point this belief devolved into crass superstition, and the one high god was broken up into many separate deities who were worshipped as numina of the various forces in nature. Ironically, this sounds like the view presented in the biblical text, but it was frequently advocated by deists and post-enlightenment thinkers who considered the phenomena of religion among primitive peoples. Within the past century the position received the catchy title, 'Urmonotheism', because it spoke of a primordial monotheism behind early polytheism.

The earliest spokespersons for this view were the deistic Herbert of Cherbury (1582–1648) and the rationalistic Voltaire (1694–1778). Voltaire saw the worship of one god to be a natural and rational assumption of any people, so that originally monotheism was the religion of all humanity, and only the weakness of the human mind led to its demise. This theory

9.   Pettazzoni, 'Formation of Monotheism', p. 45.

fell out of favor with rationalists, especially in the nineteenth century. Although one still finds it later in the assessment of Greek religion by the classicist Friedrich Welcker, who felt that a primordial worship of Zeus evolved into the worship of diverse deities.[10] Late in the nineteenth century the theory had a revival. Andrew Lang, a student of the religion of the aborigines in Australia, hypothesized that a supreme being played an important role in the beliefs of primitive peoples.[11] Wilhelm Schmidt (1868–1954) developed the ideas even more in his works,[12] and it was his discussion of 'primitive monotheism' which gave rise to the term 'Urmonotheism'. The theory has drawn the attention of many authors in the twentieth century.[13] In the field of biblical studies it attracted the attention of Marie-Joseph Lagrange, who believed that the primitive Semites worshipped only El originally and later El separated into the various numina of nature. William Foxwell Albright also believed that the deep recognition of one high god led many peoples in the ancient Near East and Hellenistic world to articulate strong sounding monotheistic statements, even though they fell short of Israel's monotheistic beliefs.[14]

However, the notion of primitive monotheism has fallen into disrepute in the past two generations. Scholars sense that a view of a primordial high god is not the same as monotheism. Primitive peoples may assert that their ancestors worshipped a high god before the present time in which they now worship many gods, but there is no real evidence that any of those ancestors actually did so. More likely the primitive people thus interviewed are creating a fictional past, an 'Urzeit', which never really existed, just as their envisioned future age, the 'Endzeit', never really comes, either. Perhaps, they are describing indirectly a cosmogony, wherein a primordial deity is said to have begotten or created the gods of a later age. This is not true monotheism; it is polytheism. Above all,

10.   Welcker, *Götterlehre*.

11.   Lang, *The Making of Religion* (New York: Longman, Green & Co., 1898).

12.   W. Schmidt, *The Origin and Growth of Religion* (London: Methuen & Co., 1931); *idem*, *High Gods in North America* (Oxford: Clarendon Press, 1932); *idem*, *Primitive Religion* (London: Herder, 1939).

13.   Albright, *Stone Age*, pp. 170-71; Pettazzoni, 'Formation of Monotheism', pp. 41-43; Lang, 'Yahweh-Alone', pp. 13-14; Petersen, 'Israel and Monotheism', p. 93. The concept of primitive monotheism was evaluated by W. Mühlmann, 'Das Problem des Urmonotheismus', *TLZ* 78 (1953), pp. 705-18; and P. Radin, *Monotheism among Primitive Peoples* (New York: Bollingen, 1954).

14.   M.-J. Lagrange, *Etudes sur le religions semitiques* (EBib; Paris: Lecoffre, 1903), *passim*; Albright, *Stone Age*, pp. 170-71, 217, *et passim*.

one does not discover rhetoric among these primitive peoples which denies the existence of all gods save one, or admits that their ancestors ever did. They simply say that once in the distant past people worshipped one god who was close to the earth. That could be nothing more than henotheism. We modern Westerners, then, are merely importing our understandings of monotheism into their beliefs. As a result, scholars no longer speak of 'Urmonotheism' as an acceptable option.[15]

Many critical scholars over the years have chosen to use another model, evolution, to describe the rise of monotheism, both in Israel and among humankind in general. The earliest advocate was David Hume, who saw polytheism as the natural, earliest stage of human religion.[16] He was followed in this viewpoint by Jean-Jacques Rousseau, who felt that people could not attain to monotheism until they could think more abstractly.[17] Both men were influenced by the writings of early travelers and ethnographers, including men like Father Lafitau who studied American Indians,[18] and Charles de Brosses who observed African cultures.[19] In the nineteenth century a significant advocate was Auguste Comte, the well-known positivist philosopher, who proposed an evolutionary sequence of fetishism, polytheism and then monotheism for the development of religion.[20] His ideas inspired the famous anthropologist Edward Burnett Tylor, who speculated that the evolutionary schema was animism, polytheism and then monotheism.[21] With the exception of those who advocate 'Urmonotheism' most critical scholars in the field of anthropology have retained the evolutionary model in describing the emergence of religion.[22]

The best known advocates for describing Israel's religious development in evolutionary terms are Julius Wellhausen and William Robertson

15. Pettazzoni, 'Formation of Monotheism', p. 44; Lang, 'Yahweh-Alone', p. 14.

16. D. Hume, *The Natural History of Religion* (London: Millar, 1757).

17. J.J. Rousseau, *Emile* (Amsterdam: Néaulme, 1764).

18. F. Lafitau, *Les moeurs des sauvages Ameriquains compares aux moeurs des premier temps* (Paris: Saugrain, 1724).

19. C. de Brosses, *Du culte des Dieux Fetiches, ou parallele de l'ancienne religion de l'Egypte avec la religion actuelle de la Nigritie* (Paris: de Brosses, 1760).

20. A. Comte, *Cours de philosophie positive* (Paris: Bachelier, 1830–42).

21. E.B. Tylor, *Primitive Culture* (repr.; New York: Harper & Brothers, 1958 [1871]).

22. Pettazzoni, 'Formation of Monotheism', pp. 40-41; Petersen, 'Israel and Monotheism', pp. 93-94.

Smith, discussed in the previous chapter. Their model of evolution was a movement through stages of polytheism, henotheism and monotheism, and this paradigm dominated scholarly discussion for two generations, until it received severe criticism from William Foxwell Albright and others in the years after 1940.

More recently contemporary scholars have revived a more nuanced view of an evolutionary scheme with more stages of development. Perhaps the most well-known authors, or at least those who have written most extensively, are Morton Smith, Bernhard Lang and Herrmann Vorländer, all of whom were evaluated in the previous chapter. They have proposed a gradual process of evolutionary development for Israel involving as many as five stages of intellectual advance, and more importantly, they acknowledge the unevenness of the advance—often intellectual leaders are more sophisticated than their audience (the 'prophetic minority' principle). These contemporary authors also recognize that true evolutionary advances take centuries, or even millennia, so that Israel's historical experience is really too brief in six short centuries to process through all the stages of the paradigm as Wellhausen and Smith envisioned. Rather, Israelites and Jews were part of a greater intellectual movement in the ancient Near East, and the five or more stages of religious development in Israel are part of the last major phase of monotheistic evolution in the ancient world, a process whose earliest phases began as early as 3000 BCE with literacy.

These contemporary authors have attempted to define more nuanced expressions to describe Israel's pre-exilic religious attitudes. George Widengren used the term 'affective monotheism' to characterize the devotional attachment of a pious individual to a particular deity both in the ancient Near East and Israel.[23] Johannes Lindblom spoke of 'dynamic monotheism' in the pre-exilic prophets, for they focused on Yahweh and ignored the question of the theoretic existence of other gods.[24] The terms 'temporary henotheism' or 'temporary monotheism' were coined

---

23.   G. Widengren, *The Accadian and Hebrew Psalms of Lamentation as Religious Documents: A Comparative Study* (Uppsala: Almquist & Wiksell, 1936), pp. 54-55, used the term 'affective monotheism,' which stressed the devotional attachment exclusively to one deity. He took the term from J. Hehn, *Die biblische und die babylonische Gottesidee* (Leipzig: Hinrichs, 1913), pp. 96-99.

24.   J. Lindblom, *Prophecy in Ancient Israel* (Philadelphia: Fortress Press, 1973), pp. 332-35.

by Adrianus van Selms, and used by Bernhard Lang and others.[25] 'Latent monotheism' is an expression used by Norbert Lohfink, Bernhard Lang and others.[26] Other terms frequently used include 'incipient monotheism' and 'implicit monotheism'. All of these terms are the scholarly way of saying that the intelligentsia of Israel were on the verge of pure monotheistic thought for some years before the exilic breakthrough. This departs radically from the thought of Wellhausen who supposed that the biblical thinkers moved from an early polytheism through the stages to a later pure monotheism. The common peasants in Israel might have moved through all these stages, but the religious leaders were in touch with the intellectual advance that had been occurring in the ancient Near East for some centuries. Hence, modern authors present a far more nuanced view of evolution than the one critiqued by Albright in the 1940s.

There is yet a third model which deserves mention, and its best advocate is Raffaele Pettazzoni, whose writings deserve greater attention among biblical scholars (especially in the opinion of David Petersen).[27] Pettazzoni strongly maintains that true monotheisms, that is, Yahwism, Zoroastrianism, Christianity and Islam, all emerged as radical revolutions of thought under the leadership of a significant prophetic individual. True monotheism arises out of an existing polytheism and then rejects it completely. Monotheistic revolutions take the old gods and turn them into demons. The new high god does not evolve out of the collective totality of the old gods. By definition monotheism cannot be said to 'evolve' out of something it so dramatically rejects. Furthermore, since one individual, rather than many people over the space of many years, was responsible for the monotheistic articulation, again one must admit that this is best described by the concept of revolution, not evolution. Hence, Pettazzoni speaks of the dramatic accomplishments of Moses, Zoroaster, Jesus and Muhammed in their revolutionary religious role,

25. A. van Selms, 'Temporary Henotheism', *Symbolae Biblicae et Mesopotamicae Francisco Mario Theodoro de Liagre Böhl dedicatae* (eds. M. Beck, *et al.*; Studia Francisci Scholten Memoriae Dedicata, 4; Leiden: Brill, 1973), pp. 341-48. Cf. Petersen, 'Israel and Monotheism', p. 95.

26. Lohfink, 'Gott und die Götter', pp. 50-71; *idem*, 'Das Alte Testament', pp. 28-47; *idem*, 'Zur Geschichte', pp. 9-25; Lang, 'Yahweh-Alone', p. 54.

27. Pettazzoni, 'Formation of Monotheism', pp. 40-46; *idem, The All-Knowing God: Researches into Early Religion and Culture* (trans. H.J. Rose; London: Methuen, 1956), *passim*; *idem, Der allwissende Gott: Zur Geschichte der Gottesidee* (Frankfurt: Fischer, 1957), *passim* (which is a different work from the previous source); *idem, Essays*, pp. 1-10.

and their accomplishments within a single lifetime cannot be described by the image of gradual evolution.[28] Pettazzoni boldly states,

> The affirmation of monotheism always is expressed by the negation of polytheism, and this negation is never anything but the verbal symbol of a combat in which no quarter is given, the combat between a faith in its death agonies and a new religious consciousness affirming itself... Far from developing out of it by an evolutionary process, monotheism takes shape by means of a revolution. Every coming of a monotheistic religion is conditioned by a religious revolution.[29]

The ideas of Pettazzoni have been quoted with approval by some scholars in biblical studies,[30] and others have paralleled his thoughts in their own discussions.[31] Erik Hornung, for example, speaks of how monotheism does not arise within polytheism by a slow accumulation of characteristics, but requires a complete transformation of thought patterns.[32]

Norman Gottwald's portrayal of 'mono-Yahwism' among the Israelite highland settlers of Iron Age I (1200–1050 BCE), discussed in the previous chapter, bears striking resemblance to Pettazzoni's model even though Gottwald works out his ideas differently. For Gottwald, and those who follow him, 'mono-Yahwism' was a revolutionary movement of people who clearly excluded the values of the culture out of which they arose, the Canaanite social system. Like Pettazzoni's monotheism, Gottwald's 'mono-Yahwism' negated the environment out of which it grew. Ironically, however, Gottwald's 'mono-Yahwism' is not monotheism, but rather a monolatry or henotheism. Otherwise the rhetoric of the two scholars is quite similar.

Gerd Theissen likewise speaks of revolution rather than evolution in the emergence of monotheism. Since he views the process of evolutionary development of religious thought in terms of thousands of years of human cultural evolution, six centuries of religious development in Israel is a short period of time, thus worthy of being called a revolution.[33] I concur heartily with Theissen's perceptions and seek to integrate this

---

28. Pettazzoni, *All-Knowing God*, p. 117; *idem*, 'Formation of Monotheism', pp. 44-46.

29. Pettazzoni, 'Formation of Monotheism', pp. 45-46.

30. Lindblom, *Prophecy*, p. 333; Theissen, *Biblical Faith*, pp. 64-65.

31. Keel, 'Gedanken', pp. 20-21.

32. E. Hornung, *Conceptions of God in Ancient Egypt: The One and the Many* (trans. J. Baines; Ithaca, NY: Cornell University Press, 1982), p. 243.

33. Theissen, *Biblical Faith*, pp. 51-81.

very concept into the overall thesis of this book.

At this point some critique of Pettazzoni should be provided. While his model is excellent, there are some problems with it. 1) He facilely equates each religious revolution with a specific reformer, but this is too simplistic. In the case of Moses and Yahwism scholars now recognize rather consistently that monotheism came much later than Moses, either with the classical prophets or in the Babylonian exile. Zoroastrian scholars concede it is extremely difficult to know what the historical Zoroaster really taught, whether it was monotheism, dualism or something else. Thus, in half of the examples Pettazzoni gives, we do not really know the individual responsible for the monotheistic emergence, or even if there was truly one particular individual. 2) His model takes no account of preparatory stages of religious and intellectual development. There have to be some preparatory evolutionary experiences among the intelligentsia in the prophetic reformer's audience, or else no one can hear the message of the great prophet and understand the various aspects and implications of the message. This, perhaps, is part of the reason for Pharaoh Akhenaton's failure in the fourteenth century BCE. 3) Pettazzoni boldly states that monotheism takes the old gods and negates them, but he too starkly overgeneralizes the process. One of the gods usually is appropriated in the monotheistic process and rehabilitated to become the new high deity. Often that deity assumes many of the characteristics of various defeated deities, so that they live on by being absorbed in the newly emergent single deity. Yahweh, Ahura-Mazda and Allah were names applied to particular gods by polytheists before monotheism emerged. The old gods did not all die, at least one survived in every 'revolution', and others endured in submerged fashion. 4) Pettazzoni is also quite strict in how he wishes to define monotheism. He includes Yahwism, but apparently not Judaism. He dismisses the thought of Xenophanes of Colophon and Antisthenes as merely 'monotheistic intuitions',[34] when many authors are willing to concede these thinkers higher status. Gerd Theissen is willing to call Xenophanes (or Xenophon) a revolutionary in the same sense of which Pettazzoni would speak, and even comparable to Second Isaiah.[35] Perhaps Pettazzoni's narrow definition permits him more easily to define monotheism as a revolution which consciously negates previous religious beliefs. 5) Finally, Pettazzoni does not understand evolutionary theory, for he equates evolution with

34. Pettazzoni, 'Formation of Monotheism', p. 46.
35. Theissen, *Biblical Faith*, p. 65.

simple, unilinear, gradual advance.[36] Contemporary evolutionary theory sees progress as an uneven process which entails many preparatory stages for moments of significant evolutionary breakthrough, after which a period of adjustment to the environment or biological stasis occurs. Such a model is really not so far from what Pettazzoni actually describes in his model.

However sharp my criticism of Pettazzoni may be, his contributions to the discussion are very valuable. Much of the process of emerging monotheism is revolutionary and the term deserves use in the discussion. Pettazzoni has highlighted certain dynamics in the monotheistic process which are worth retaining in the portrayal of monotheism. Likewise, the rhetoric of Gottwald's 'mono-Yahwistic' revolution is valuable, for he uses language comparable to Petazzoni to describe an evolutionary process which was prior to the exilic breakthrough and the attainment of abstract monotheism. Gottwald's paradigm also demonstrates the value of Pettazzoni's language in a refined context. The chief redefinition of Pettazzoni's scheme in regard to Israel is the dating of the breakthrough to the exile rather than to Moses.

In conclusion, in the great discussion of whether monotheism emerges by devolution, evolution or revolution, it would appear that the position of evolution is winning in the contemporary discussion. But I would propose a twist in the discussion by maintaining that monotheism emerges both by evolution and by revolution.[37] Such a paradigm would seem to summarize where contemporary theorists are moving, it would reflect the testimony of the biblical text rather honestly, and it would correspond to perceptions in the field of contemporary scientific speculation.

The general tenor of critical biblical scholarship suggests significant stages of pre-exilic religious development connected especially to the activities of Elijah and Elisha in the ninth century BCE, the proclamations of the classical prophets in the eighth century BCE, especially Hosea, and the reform activities of kings Hezekiah and Josiah. Yet almost all scholars acknowledge the truly significant accomplishment of Second Isaiah, and some include his near contemporaries Jeremiah and Ezekiel. This summary of Israel's religious history has led Othmar Keel and Bernhard Lang, for example, to speak of 'a chain of revolutions which follow one

---

36. Pettazzoni, 'Formation of Monotheism', p. 46.

37. Smith, *Early History of God*, p. 156, also hints at the idea of using both evolution and revolution as a model for Israel's religious development.

another in rapid succession'.[38] For them monotheism evolves, but it is not gradual, nor inevitable, rather it comes in spurts as great religious spokespersons speak to a crisis. The greatest crisis was the exile and it caused the greatest quantum leap: a radical monotheistic message which categorically denied the existence of other gods, and it is best exemplified in the oracles of Second Isaiah. In fact, Pettazzoni's categories of the radical monotheistic reformer fit Second Isaiah far better than Moses in respect to his emphasis upon monotheism's total negation of the other gods. At any rate, the rising perception among scholars is that monotheism occurs in stages, each of which is radical.

One might go farther in characterizing the process. While there may have been several significant leaps associated with Elijah, Hosea, Hezekiah, Josiah, and whomever else you include in the sequence, it is ultimately the final leap which is most important. For without the exilic theologians, and especially Second Isaiah, the emergence of abstract monotheism would not have occurred. The earlier stages would have gone for naught; all that would have resulted would have been another nicely nuanced high monolatry in the history of ancient Near Eastern monotheistic-like experiments. Historians might be looking more to Zoroastrianism or some other religion as the source of ethical monotheism. The shape of Christianity would be hard to envision. Second Isaiah's contribution, as well as those of his contemporaries who promoted his thought, is the culmination and the most significant aspect of the emergence of monotheism. The evolutionary and revolutionary paradigm must focus upon this.

Bernhard Lang, Othmar Keel, Rainer Albertz, Albert de Pury and others propose a model of successive revolutions in an evolutionary process, and this is an excellent paradigm in which to discuss the biblical tradition. Lang especially speaks of the revolutionary process of monotheistic emergence occurring in the relatively 'short' period of six centuries.[39] This clever piece of rhetoric acknowledges rightly that six hundred years is indeed a short period of time in relationship to ten thousand years of human civilization from the neolithic agricultural revolution beginning in 8000 BCE until the present, or the three million years of human cultural evolution, or the vast eons of times involved in the evolution of life. God would appear quite patient in these greater processes, and six centuries is quite rapid for a breakthrough as important

38. Keel, 'Gedanken', p. 21; Lang, 'Yahweh-Alone', p. 56.
39. Keel, 'Gedanken', p. 21; Lang, 'Yahweh-Alone', p. 56; Albertz, 'Der Ort', p. 93; de Pury, 'Erwägungen', p. 416.

as ethical monotheism in Israel. Gerd Theissen speaks quite comparably in his attempts to use evolution as a paradigm for biblical thought.[40] To incorporate all the contributions of many individuals over the period of six centuries and to call the entire era one great revolutionary experience is a fine model. To see a six hundred year era as a revolution is certainly preferrable to the approach of Julius Wellhausen and others who sought to condense ten thousand years of evolutionary polytheism, henotheism and monotheism into that same length of time.

Above all, this model is sensitive to the grand sweep of history and human intellectual evolution. It tends to view Israel more in the context of ancient Near Eastern development as well as the even greater sweep of human cultural advance. This is the thrust of the new approach to history taken by the French *Annales* School, best represented by the writings of Fernand Braudel,[41] and introduced into biblical studies by several scholars, most notably Robert Coote and Keith Whitelam.[42] One may observe that there are stages of development in Israel's religious history, which may be termed 'evolutionary', but within the grand scope of human history the entire process was relatively a revolution.

There is good reason to stress the final stage in this process, Second Isaiah's response to the crisis of the exile, as the leap without which the entire monotheism 'revolution' would have been to no avail. This then brings the perception of Israel's monotheism very close to the model of a species' evolution in biology. Contemporary evolutionary theory views the evolution of an individual species as a breakthrough, not the inevitable or gradual culmination of small biotic changes. Rather, small mutations over a long period of time are stored as recessive genes in the matrix of a species, and at some point they emerge in tandem to become dominant genetic factors to produce an evolutionary breakthrough, a new species more adapted to the ecological crisis which the old species may have confronted and failed to master. The heart of the evolutionary advance for the species is the final breakthrough prompted by the ecological crisis, the preparatory build-up of genetic mutations means nothing and goes nowhere unless those genetic factors emerge in the final stage

40. Theissen, *Biblical Faith*, pp. 51-81.

41. F. Braudel, *Civilization and Capitalism 15th–18th Century* (trans. S. Reynolds; 3 vols.; New York: Harper & Row, 1981, 1982, 1984); *idem*, *A History of Civilizations* (trans. R. Mayne; New York: Penguin Books, 1994), pp. 3-573.

42. Coote and Whitelam, 'Emergence', pp. 107-47; *idem*, *Early Israel*; Whitelam, 'Israel's Traditions', pp. 19-42; *idem*, 'Identity', pp. 57-87.

to generate a new species. Then the new species stabilizes and continues to unfold the implications of the new genetic factors in subsequent generations. The exile is like the ecological crisis, and Second Isaiah and his contemporaries are the dramatic genetic transformation that creates the new species, pure monotheism. There are preliminary stages of development, and one might refer to the entire process as a revolution, but it is the final stage which must be stressed as the most crucial part of the breakthrough.

In retrospect, there really are two ways of applying the evolutionary model to a discussion of emergent monotheism. First, one might propose that the preliminary genetic mutations of a biological species may be compared to the pre-exilic activities of Elijah, Hosea, Hezekiah, Josiah and the rest. But the actual breakthrough comes with Second Isaiah and the victory of the prophetic minority, which is like the surfacing of recessive genes to become the dominant genes in a new species. In fact, historians always have recognized that it is best to call these people Jews after the exile, whereas previously they were Israelites or Judahites. This indicates a past awareness of the significant transformation that occurred in the exile. Scholars now may speak of them as a new mutation or new species in human history. The entire six century process of monotheistic emergence may be called both an evolution, because of the pre-exilic stages of preparatory development, and also a revolution, because six centuries is finally a very short period of time in the sweep of human history. Or we may choose to speak of the preparatory pre-exilic stages as the evolutionary process that led up to the exilic transformation, which was the revolution or evolutionary breakthrough. Both ways of speaking focus upon Israel's religious developmental process by itself.

A second way of using the biological evolutionary model is to view the emergence of monotheism from the perspective of the entire ancient world. One then could speak of the religious mutations created by all the monolatrous movements in the ancient Near East as early attempts which bequeathed an intellectual awareness and appropriate language to the Israelites. Like small genetic mutations these religious experiences of many peoples may have in some way prepared for the quantum leap to monotheism taken by the Jews in exile. Again, one could speak of the evolutionary preparation in the ancient Near East which led to the final evolutionary breakthrough or revolution of the Jews. Some readers might prefer to envision the process in terms of simultaneous monotheistic breakthroughs to 'consummate' religion which occurred in several cultures in the Axial Age (800–400 BCE), including the rise of mono-theistic Zoroastrianism, the speculations of Xenophanes of Colophon and other Greek thinkers, as well as the Jewish exiles. In effect, the ancient world was preparing mutations which would lead to breakthroughs in several places, because the great religious crisis of the Axial Age was a worldwide phenomenon, not just the exilic experience of Jews. Either way the model describes the preliminary attempts at monolatrous belief throughout the ancient world as mutations which prepared for the mono-theistic breakthrough of the Jews or the Jews and their contemporaries.

The reader may decide which model is most intellectually satisfying. Ultimately, the significant question is how much Israelite and Jewish thought may have been influenced by religious currents in the ancient world prior to their existence. If one feels such contact was minimal, the first approach which confines itself to a discussion of just Israel's religious experience will be preferable. If one believes that the biblical tradition was influenced heavily by the surrounding intellectual milieu, the second approach with its consideration of religious insights in other cultures will be useful. I find both models to be valuable pedagogical tools. These very speculative variations on the application of biological evolutionary theory to the process of emergent monotheism are provided for the consideration of the reader, who may find one approach more insightful and helpful than the others. The reader may wish to view monotheism from the perspective of Israel's development or the entire ancient world, the reader may wish to view the entire developmental process as revolu-tionary or merely the final breakthrough, and the reader may wish to see the breakthrough as confined only to the Jews or occurring in several cultures in the same era. Regardless of these options, I hope that some value may be found in the application of this evolutionary paradigm.

The old debate as to whether monotheism emerged by evolution or revolution was a valuable intellectual exercise, but now scholars increas-ingly tend to view monotheism as a result of both evolution and revolution. Perhaps the use of biological evolutionary models will help us to envision the process now with an even wider angle of vision.

A final aspect of Pettazzoni's discussion needs to be addressed at this point. Not only did Pettazzoni affirm the revolutionary nature of mono-theism, but he stressed the importance of a single reform oriented individual. How does the new paradigm of revolutionary evolution affect this idea of Pettazzoni's?

First of all, historians now sense that in some instances they do not know which individual to credit with the monotheistic reform. Biblical scholars no longer look to Moses as the founder of monotheism, but more likely stress the contributions of Second Isaiah or perhaps the later Ezra, who so dogmatically promulgated reform in post-exilic Jerusalem in an official capacity with a fixed Torah. At any rate, it is difficult to discern who should be given the credit for monotheism, since there were probably many nameless individuals in the exile and post-exilic era who contributed mightily to the emergence of monotheism among the general populace of the Jews. The same is true for Zoroastrianism, for scholars in Zoroastrian studies are not sure when to date the prophet Zoroaster, or whether even to say he was a monotheist. Those scholars who now date Zoroaster back into the second millennium BCE often doubt whether he was monotheistic in any sense.

This leads to a second observation. Individuals function within a community of like-minded people who support and disseminate the views of the spokespersons. A great thinker may have great insights, but his or her experience was inspired by mentors in an intellectual or religious community which was moving in that new direction of thought already. Often contemporaries of a great reformer were thinking and expressing the same ideas as the great reformer, but they did not get the attention or the credit as did the great reformer. Most important of all, the great reformer must have an audience who understands the message, accepts it, and is willing to communicate it to others, especially after the prophet dies.[43] Later monotheistic evolutionary and revolutionary trajectories require a community of sensitive thinkers to preserve, reflect upon and communicate the message of those who achieve the breakthrough.

Pettazzoni's emphasis upon the great reforming individual is a little naive. Yes, there were individuals, and perhaps more than one in each monotheistic faith, but they all functioned within a greater community of people that helped give birth to their new ideas. The evolutionary and revolutionary model I propose views emergent monotheism either as a six century long revolution or a revolutionary breakthrough which actualizes six prior centuries of development, and requires many great thinkers and disciples along the way. The image of a lone prophet ought best be replaced by the image of several great thinkers working in a community, and the community itself is in an evolutionary process.

---

43. H. Bardtke, 'Altisraelitische Erweckungsbewegungen', *Near Eastern Studies in Honor of William Foxwell Albright* (ed. H. Goedicke; Baltimore: The Johns Hopkins University Press, 1971), pp. 17-34.

III

In David Petersen's fine essay a number of questions were asked about the social and ideational implications of monotheism. He asked whether monotheism engendered violence, tyranny and sexism. A number of authors over the years have considered these issues. Monotheistic thought in general may be seen to introduce both intolerance and openness into the communities through which it spreads.[44] Many authors would stress primarily the connection between monotheistic thought and the development of social and religious egalitarianism, the exact opposite of what other critical scholars have proposed. Other questions are concerned with the literary symbols and literature that a monotheistic movement would create. Finally, there is interest also in the intellectual and religious values, including the philosophical tensions which must be attributed to a single divine being, which ultimately emerge from a monotheistic faith over the years. I attempt to address some of these issues in the remainder of this volume, but a complete discussion of all the questions raised by Petersen lies beyond the scope of this work.

A number of historians have suspected that monotheism can reinforce a form of tyranny. The elevation of one deity in the heavens is akin to elevating one ruler on the earth, who rules everyone. Futhermore, the statement that there is only one true god, and that this deity is yours, will incline you to go out and convert other people. Projected onto the national level it means that a monotheistic state would be driven to absorb other people into its own political and religious structures. Monotheism then would reinforce national energies directed at imperial conquest. Examples in world history where an empire expanded with both political and religious monotheistic imperialism would include the Achaemedian Persian Empire (550–330 BCE) and the Sassanian Persian Empire (100–600 CE) with Zoroastrianism, and the various Arabic Empires (630–1918) with Islam. Christian kingdoms can be listed also in the history of Europe, from as early as the time of Constantine the Great of Rome in the fourth century CE up through all the colonial expansions of Europe and America into the Third World of the past five hundred years. It would indeed

---

44.   See the articles in Geffré, Jossua and Lefébure, *Monotheism, passim.* A. Michaels, 'Monotheismus und Fundamentalismus: Eine These und ihre Gegenthese', *Ein Gott allein* (eds. Dietrich and Klopfenstein), pp. 51-57, tries to assess judiciously the aspects of intolerance and openness which any monotheistic faith would produce.

appear that empire and monotheism go together.

Some authors directly compare polytheism and monotheism in this regard. Polytheism with its diversity in the divine realm can encourage the toleration of social diversity in the human realm, whereas monotheism breeds the dual intolerance of devotion to one deity and commitment to one particular worldview to which others must be converted for their own good.[45] Monotheism brings the desire to oppose the beliefs of others, the need to convert and conquer them, and the urge to encourage human violence throughout the world.[46] Genghis Khan reputedly said, 'In heaven there is no-one but the one God alone; on earth no-one but the one ruler Genghis Khan'.[47] Jürgen Moltmann observes that if religious monotheism indeed combines with absolutism in the church and state, true tyranny results, and ironically then only atheism can rescue human freedom.[48]

Pagans would speak sooner of a general providence than of a single deity and thus admit partial truth to be found in many religions. This spirit was characteristic of the late Roman Empire according to Paul Veyne and Garth Fowden.[49] Joseph Comblin even speaks of the irony in monotheism—if you worship a universal deity, you condemn the religion of others, conquer and convert them, but this proves that in reality you fight for a particular religion and a particular deity and not a truly universal god of all people. In fact, he further maintains that there is no such thing as true polytheism or monotheism, all religions are something in between those two polar extremes.[50]

45.   This is best expressed in the writings of A. de Benoist, *Vu de droite: Anthologie critique des idées contemporaines* (Paris: Copernic, 1977) *passim*; *idem, Comment peut-on etre païen?* (Paris: Michel, 1981), *passim*, whose ideas are critiqued by A. Dumas, 'The New Attraction of Neo-Paganism: A Political, Cultural and Spiritual Phenomenon or Epiphenomenon' (trans. D. Smith), *Monotheism* (eds. Geffré, Jossua and Lefébure), pp. 81-90.

46.   P. Ciholas, 'Monotheisme et violence', *RSR* 69 (1981), pp. 325-81.

47.   J. Moltmann, 'The Inviting Unity of the Triune God' (trans. R. Nowell), *Monotheism* (eds. Geffré, Jossua and Lefébure), p. 51.

48.   Moltmann, 'Inviting Unity', p. 51.

49.   P. Veyne, 'The Roman Empire', *A History of the Private Life. I. From Pagan Rome to Byzantium* (ed. P. Veyne; trans. A. Goldhammer; 5 vols.; Cambridge, MA: Belknap, 1987), p. 216; G. Fowden, *Empire to Commonwealth: Consequences of Monotheism in Late Antiquity* (Princeton, NJ: Princeton University Press, 1993), pp. 37-60.

50.   J. Comblin, 'Monotheism and Popular Religion' (trans. D. Livingstone), *Monotheism* (eds. Geffré, Jossua and Lefébure), p. 91-99.

Many historians who suggest that monotheism undergirds cultural and political imperialism point to the Roman Empire under Constantine and his successors. By the fourth century CE the Roman Empire required an ideology to promote unity and authority. Only a monotheistic and universalist religion could do this, because polytheisms were unable to transcend regional cultural concerns. In its struggle with Sassanian Iran, which had the unifying monotheistic faith of Zoroastrianism, Rome turned to Christianity for religious and political unity. Unfortunately, the divisions caused by the Nestorians, Arians, Monophysites and others threatened to weaken this use of Christianity, and so the need arose for royal sponsorship of the council of Nicea in 323 CE to bring about greater Christian unity. Ironically, neither Zoroastrianism nor Christianity would match the success of Islam in uniting the Near East culturally.[51] Furthermore, literary sources from this era imply the attempt to use Christianity in this fashion was a conscious decision in the minds of fourth-century Christian leaders. Eusebius, the court historian for Constantine, linked monotheism and the justification of the Roman Empire to facilitate the spread of Christianity. For him one ruler on earth equated with one ruler in heaven, one empire under emperor and God meant peace, and polytheism with its diverse pluralism was to be rejected.[52] Given this, one should not be surprised by the edicts of Emperor Theodosius the Great, who outlawed all pagan religions in 386 CE and mandated that everyone should henceforth be Christian. Truly, this form of Constantinian Christianity appears to meet the criteria for a good example of imperialistic and totalitarian monotheism. But is this true for all forms of monotheism, and is it fair thus to characterize biblical monotheism as the inspiration of territorial imperialism and tyranny?

Critics point out that not all monotheistic expressions lead to intolerance, violence and tyranny. Christian Duquoc notes that this is certainly not the case with Hellenistic philosophical monotheisms and Hindu monism, both of which exhibited toleration of religious diversity.[53] But

---

51. Moltmann, 'Inviting Unity', pp. 53-54; Fowden, *Empire*; R.J. van der Spek, 'Assyriology and History: A Comparative Study of War and Empire in Assyria, Athens, and Rome', *The Tablet and the Scroll: Near Eastern Studies in Honor of William W. Hallo* (eds. M. Cohen, D. Snell and D. Weisberg; Bethesda: CDL, 1993), p. 116, who maintains that Constantinian Christianity and not Assyrian religion was the first truly imperialistic religion.

52. G. Ruggieri, 'God and Power: A Political Function of Monotheism?' (trans. P. Burns), *Monotheism* (eds. Geffré, Jossua and Lefébure), p. 17.

53. C. Duquoc, 'Monotheism and Unitary Ideology' (trans. R. Nowell),

that does not excuse the biblical tradition from potential charges of intolerance.

One might point out that Christianity was used by Constantine and others for political purposes, but that was not the true spirit of Christianity. Yet many Christians in Constantine's day certainly applauded his actions, since they appeared to help their movement greatly. One then would have to admit that such combined political and religious imperialism is frequent in Christian history; so much so, that clearly Christian leaders have been too willing to allow their faith to be used by political leaders for repression in return for political favors to those religious leaders. Certainly we have seen such scenarios in this century in Nazi Germany, Eastern Europe and Latin America. We would have to plead that this is not the true use of Christian belief. But an alien to our planet would not be convinced by our argument until this pattern of behavior in the Christian tradition began to change. Christians must become sensitive to the heavy-handed use of their religious beliefs against other people and learn to act more compassionately, in the spirit of the very message they proclaim.

Perhaps a better argument would be to observe that there are different forms of monotheistic expression, even within the same religious tradition. Biblical scholars have noted that the monotheism of the Jews lacked pretensions to political empire, but rather encouraged solidarity with all of humanity. The prophets spoke of a universal deity over all people whose call was to worship without national borders in a state of peace and prosperity,[54] thus the famous oracle in Mic. 4.3-4 and Isa. 2.4,

> He shall judge between the nations, and shall arbitrate for many peoples; they shall beat their swords into plowshares and their spears into pruning hooks; nation shall not lift up sword against nation, neither shall they learn war anymore, but they shall all sit under their own vines and under their own fig trees, and no one shall make them afraid.

The biblical monotheism expressed here is a monotheism 'from below,' from the voice of a conquered people who knew the evils of imperialism. There are monotheisms which are imperialistic, such as that created and used by Constantine, and there are monotheisms which call for peace and human unity. There are monotheisms 'from above', which are defined by a pharaoh, emperor, king or tyrant, and there are monotheisms 'from below', from the people crying for peace. Gerd Theissen says it well,

Monotheism (eds. Geffré, Jossua and Lefébure), p. 61.

54. Lang, 'Yahweh-Alone', p. 55; Theissen, *Biblical Faith*, p. 71; Albertz, *Israelite Religion*, II, p. 425; Dietrich, 'Werden und Wesen', pp. 25-27.

I do not want to claim that anti-polytheistic monotheism is intrinsically oriented on peace. But the Jewish monotheism which came into being in the situation of a defeated people ravaged by war, embraced the unique vision of an overcoming of war. When everyone recognizes the one and only God, there can be no more wars; this is a logical notion, if wars are wars between different gods. It is evident that this logic does not govern the behavior of Jews, Christians, and Moslems.[55]

Perhaps the spirit of early Judaism still has to permeate the total consciousness of those believers who belong to the three monotheistic faiths which are descended from the exilic monotheistic breakthrough. I have spoken of an evolutionary trajectory in the monotheistic process. In biology when a new species finally emerges, it takes some time for the genetic matrix to stabilize, up to ten thousand years for a typical species, and it will endure after that for as long as ten million years. Perhaps we should perceive that the monotheistic breakthrough of ancient Israel is being worked out yet today; we are still in the formative stages of monotheistic evolution in terms of developing the implications which flow from the experience of more than two millennia past. When religion is no longer used as a call to arms, then monotheism will have actualized another significant component of its ideological matrix. Then we shall look back and see that imperialistic monotheisms were merely an evolutionary dead end in the monotheistic breakthrough. The monotheisms 'from below' which unite people by the power latent within the human spirit rather than by the sword will be seen as the true genetic heirs to the monotheistic breakthrough of the ancient Israelites and Jews.

Related to this is the question of monotheism and equality. Many biblical theologians in recent generations have seen the connection between monotheistic faith and equality. The old *Heilsgeschichte* school of biblical studies affirmed this, and it became the central tenet in the expositions of George Mendenhall and Norman Gottwald. The latter spoke of how 'mono-Yahwism' was the sociological corollary to radical egalitarianism which stood in dialectical opposition to the multiple social strata of polytheistic societies. From a literary perspective contemporary thinkers in literary theory see that psychologically monotheism encourages not only freedom of the deity, but also freedom and equality of human beings in the literature which is produced.[56] I discuss these topics

55. Theissen, *Biblical Faith*, p. 71.
56. R. Alter, *The Art of Biblical Narrative* (New York: Basic Books, 1981), pp. 129 *et passim*.

in Chapter 5, but for now there is an important issue to be addressed.

Some anthropologists and historians have maintained that monotheism suppports a hierarchical society. This flows from the previous discussion in which monotheistic religions are seen at times to support authoritarian rulers. If so, the hierarchical social structures would be legitimated also. Guy Swanson has provided sociological support for this argument in his study of more than fifty primitive societies in which monotheism supported a hierarchy of three or more classes.[57] It must be admitted that certainly in our own age Christian and Muslim countries have rigidly stratified societies despite the theoretic claims of equality voiced by religious leaders in those world religions.

However, our response must be similar to those views stated above. Monotheistic revolutions are still working out all their implications in our world today. The rhetoric of equality is there, it is upon the lips of religious leaders, but it has not yet been heeded by the leaders of state and many people. One cannot blame a religion for what individuals do in the name of that religion, especially when the suspicion is great that leaders too often pay only lip service to their beliefs and pay true service to their political agenda. Christian preachers have claimed that to be the case for years and often have disavowed their so-called Christian society. Consider the indictment of Christian Europe issued in word and deed by St Francis of Assisi or the entire monastic movement in general. True equality and egalitarianism emerge slowly in our human culture. Monotheism has been the greatest force to drive this social change forward. Simply because the monotheistic revolution is not yet finished in its transformation of society is no reason to blame it for the woes and the oppression it opposes.

A particular response should be made to Swanson's study of why there are so many hierarchical monotheistic societies, and that response should come from Raffaele Pettazzoni. Since Swanson studied the so-called 'monotheism' of fifty primitive societies, Pettazzoni would reply accordingly,

> The theory of primitive monotheism is founded on an equivocation and on an error. The equivocation consists in calling by the name of monotheism what is nothing of the kind, mistaking for true monotheism the savage peoples' idea of Supreme Beings. The error consists in supposing

---

57.   G. Swanson, *The Birth of the Gods: The Origin of Primitive Beliefs* (Ann Arbor: University of Michigan Press, 1960), *passim*, quoted in Petersen, 'Israel and Monotheism', p. 100.

that to be primitive which is not so, in transforming to the most archaic religious culture the idea of God which properly belongs to our Western civilization.[58]

Pettazzoni would scoff at the attempt to call so many societies mono-theistic, and he is probably correct to do so. It is to be doubted that the fifty forms of monotheistic expression may be compared to the mono-theistic traditons of the Jews which ultimately became manifest in later Rabbinic Judaism, Christianity and Islam, especially in regard to their social implications. All three high religions thus mentioned proclaim rhetoric which affirms human equality. Cultures touched by those religi-ous traditions have provided democratic expressions in theory and practice. One cannot deny monotheism its connection to theoretic egali-tarianism. If perhaps Swanson's fifty societies are capable of being seen as monotheistic, then surely they are either proto-monotheistic or mono-theisms which are extremely undeveloped as of yet, for they have not unfolded an inherent component of true and radical monotheistic faith—the equality of all people.

IV

Historians of thought, ancient Near Eastern specialists, and biblical theo-logians often have turned to the consideration of ancient Mesopotamian and Egyptian texts to perceive the glimmerings of some form of mono-theistic belief. Though there is much disagreement, generally scholars concede that what appears to be monotheistic belief in the texts usually falls short of the articulations found in the Bible. If there is any exception to this, it usually is given for the fourteenth-century BCE reform move-ment of Akhenaton, which appears to be extremely close to true mono-theism. For this study a brief consideration of these monotheistic and near-monotheistic expressions of the ancient Near East will be valuable.

With the emergence of territorial states in the ancient Near East after 3000 BCE, especially in Egypt and Mesopotamia, there was a tendency to organize political structures and laws for the new governments, particu-larly when their rule began to incorporate larger areas and a wider range of people. This propensity to organize the affairs of this world also extended to the divine realm, so that the gods in the heavens were placed into hierarchies by different priestly guilds in the various cities to parallel the structures of the governmental bureaucracy. Needless to say,

---

58. Pettazzoni, *All-Knowing God*, p. 2.

the patron deities of victorious city-states and territorial states were placed
at the apex of the pantheon generated by priests in the victor's capital
city or sacred center.

Sometimes new myths were created or old myths radically transformed as the deity of a victorious state displaced an older god from the
central role in a mythic narrative. Hence, Anu and Enlil in Sumer, Re in
Old Kingdom Egypt, Amun-Re of Thebes in New Kingdom Egypt,
Marduk in Babylon, and Ninurta and Ashur in Assyria rose to become
central deities in mythic narratives, patron deities of the king, and even
proclaimers of a national manifest destiny in later years.[59] For example,
in the second millennium BCE narrative of creation, the *Enuma Elish*,
Marduk of Babylon played the central role, perhaps replacing an earlier
god such as the Sumerian Enlil, because in that millennium Marduk's
Babylon ruled much of Mesopotamia under the aegis of either Amorite
or Kassite dynasts. Mesopotamians believed that events in the divine
realm influenced political events on the earth, so that a victorious city
was merely repeating the accomplishments already achieved by the patron
deity in the realm of the gods; but in reality the events on earth really
created the way Mesopotamians envisioned the divine realm above.

The tendency for a city or country to elevate its deity over the rest of
the pantheon or to absorb the various deities into its patron god increased
dramatically in the first millennium BCE when the Assyrians and the
Chaldean Babylonians elevated Ninurta, Ashur and Marduk at various
times.[60] This, of course, was contemporary with emergent monotheism
in ancient Israel, and scholars have been tempted to assume some sort of
influence, especially during the Babylonian exile of the Jews. James
Henry Breasted observed years ago that universal political domain 'led
to ideas of monotheism' and that 'monotheism was but imperialism in
religion'.[61] This may be an exaggeration, but it contains an element of
truth, for forms of henotheistic expression came from such religio-political
texts in the ancient world. Such texts were clearly political propaganda
created by scribes at the behest of rulers who sought legitimation for

---

59. J.H. Breasted, *The Dawn of Conscience* (repr.; New York: Charles
Scribner's Sons, 1961 [1933]), pp. 272-302; Albright, *Stone Age*, pp. 177, 192;
T. Jacobsen, *The Treasures of Darkness: A History of Mesopotamian Religion*
(New Haven: Yale University Press, 1976), pp. 234-36.

60. Jacobsen, *Treasures*, pp. 234-39.

61. Breasted, *Development of Religion and Thought in Ancient Egypt* (repr.;
New York: Harper & Row, 1959 [1912]), p. 315; *idem, Dawn*, p. 275.

their imperial sway. But such propaganda, expressed frequently, indeed could influence the piety of the people and exercise a great impact upon the religious development of the ancient world.

Therefore, we find many texts in which one deity is so highly and exclusively lauded that the god almost appears to be worshipped monotheistically. Some historians see these texts as reflecting a latent monotheism. Assyriologist Wilfrid Lambert notes that Mesopotamians always were prone to merge the gods into one person for hyperbole, but in some late Babylonian texts Marduk does emerge almost monotheistically. The attempt to unify the pantheon into Marduk was an attempt to have a unified view of the cosmos, but according to Lambert, it failed to win any popular support.[62] William Albright and Norbert Lohfink speak of how the ancients experienced the one, universal deity as a distant presence behind each particular god they worshipped, and this would have prepared the way for true monotheism among the Jews. For Albright the evolutionary development culminated with Moses in the thirteenth century BCE, but for Lohfink it came only in the sixth century BCE, and then monotheism or monism arose not only among the Jews, but also among the Zoroastrians and pre-Socratics.[63] Johannes de Moor speaks positively of how certain deities were elevated as sole deities, including Amun-Re in Egypt and Marduk in Babylon, in a way that was radical henotheism or almost monotheism, and these movements, especially combined with the influence of Akhenaton's reform in Egypt, had very direct impact upon the development of monotheism in Israel.[64] Giovanni Pettinato speaks confidently of how the texts from Ebla attest to a henotheism already in the third millennium BCE.[65]

62. W.G. Lambert, 'The Historical Development of the Mesopotamian Pantheon: A Study in Sophisticated Polytheism', *Unity and Diversity: Essays in the History, Literature, and Religion of the Ancient Near East* (eds. H. Goedicke and J.J.M. Roberts; Baltimore: The Johns Hopkins University Press, 1975), pp. 197-98.

63. Albright, *History*, pp. 147-48; Lohfink, 'Gott und die Götter', pp. 58, 63. Cf. Dietrich, 'Werden und Wesen', p. 18, who also speaks of the common tendency toward monotheism in the ancient Near East; and Stolz, 'Kontext', p. 43, who believes the Mesopotamian lists which equate gods of Sumer and Akkad indicate the earliest movement toward monotheism.

64. De Moor, 'Crisis of Polytheism', pp. 1-20; *idem, Rise of Yahwism*, pp. 42-63.

65. G. Pettinato, 'Polytheismus und Henotheismus in der Religion von Ebla', *Monotheismus* (ed. Keel), pp. 32-48.

Most scholars, however, are fairly negative in ascribing monotheism to ancient Near Eastern peoples. Mesopotamians often used hyperbole in addressing one deity or elevating a deity to temporarily absorb the other gods as a form of exaggerated praise, but scholars suspect that true exclusive worship of one god is not be found.[66] A devotee might worship a particular deity with exclusive language one week and a different deity with the same rhetoric the next week. Furthermore, the elevation of one god to a supreme position in the pantheon may not have made much impression upon the common people. H.W.F. Saggs points out that the hierarchy of deities found in the texts is a literary creation by scribes writing with political agendas; when in reality, the everyday devotees were not even conscious of the systematically arranged pantheon, they worshipped most directly their own regional and specialized deities without regard for whether they were high or low gods.[67] Likewise, Egyptologists stress the fluid concept of the divine held by Egyptians— the one and the many could merge easily. Each deity was but an extension of the divine, and the individuality of each god stood in a harmonious tension with the totality of all the other gods, the fabric of the divine. Hence, one god could represent the totality of the divine, or two deities, such as Re and Amun, might merge for Egyptian thinkers to produce one high god. This could vary from region to region in Egypt and from age to age. The Egyptians did not exclude deities, they amalgamated them in ever changing fashion.[68] Only with Akhenaton's reform are Egyptologists prone to speak of monotheism. We can further observe these phenomena by considering the various texts of the ancient Near East, and here we may observe a nuance of difference between Egypt and Mesopotamia which merits separate consideration.

66.   J. Finkelstein, 'Bible and Babel: A Comparative Study of the Hebrew and Babylonian Religious Spirit', *Commentary* 26 (1958), pp. 431-44; Lambert, 'Historical Development', pp. 191-99 admits that most texts fall into this category; Jacobsen, *Treasures*, pp. 234-36; Nikiprowetsky, 'Ethical Monotheism', pp. 68-76; Schmidt, *Faith*, p. 69.

67.   Saggs, *Assyria*, p. 201.

68.   K. Koch, 'Wort und Einheit des Schöpfergottes im Memphis und Jerusalem: Zu Einzigartigkeit Israels', *ZTK* 62 (1965), pp. 251-71; S. Morenz, *Egyptian Religion* (trans. A. Keep; Ithaca, NY: Cornell University Press, 1973), pp. 139, 149; Hornung, *Conceptions*; Schmidt, *Faith*, p. 69; B. Couroyer, 'Le "Dieu des Sages" en Egypte, II', *RB* 95 (1988), pp. 70-91.

Mesopotamia

Mesopotamia has texts of different genres which display monotheistic tendencies. Consideration of these different texts will reveal some interesting insights.

A special category of literature which receives a lot of attention is the wide range of prayers, lament hymns and private letters in which a petitioner will address a particular deity, often Marduk or Ishtar, as though that deity were the only god in the heavens. At times the petitions even seem to deny the existence of the other gods. Examples of prayers and petitions in our possession contain such exclusivistic language addressed to Marduk, Ashur, Nergal, Ninurta, Shamash, Ishtar, Nabu, Enlil, Sin, and Anu.[69] The wide range of names, including some which never had any claim to being the high god or the patron deity of an imperial state, suggests that any human individual could address any particular deity as though that deity were the apotheosis of the divine without necessarily denying the existence of the other gods. We may call it temporary henotheism or monolatry, or just 'harmless hyperbole', but it is still part of a polytheistic worldview.[70] The other deities simply became part of that addressed god for the moment of prayer. The petitioner engaged in such exaggerated rhetoric to praise and flatter the deity, and thus obtain divine favor and response, in what V. Nikiprowetsky calls 'affective exaggeration for the sake of adulation'.[71] Benedikt Hartmann uses the word 'henolatry' to describe this activity. As monolatry (practical worshipping monotheism) is to pure monotheism, so henolatry is to henotheism (the worship of one god exalted above the rest). Henolatry is practical henotheism, that is, the worshipper acts as though the addressed deity is superior to the other deities, when in actuality, the petitioner is still a polytheist.[72] Some examples of such hymns of praise or petitions include the following,

69. Albright, *History*, pp. 147-48; B. Hartmann, 'Monotheismus in Mesopotamien?', *Monotheismus* (ed. Keel), pp. 57-61; H.-W. Jüngling, '"Was anders ist Gott für den Menschen, wenn nicht sein Vater und seine Mutter?" Zu einer Doppelmetapher der religiöse Sprache', *Ein Gott allein* (ed. Haag), pp. 365-86, who observes how hymns to Marduk stress him as the fullness of the pantheon with parental images.

70. J. Finkelstein, 'Bible and Babel', pp. 431-44; Lambert, 'Historical Development', p. 194; Saggs, *Encounter*, p. 185; Hartmann, 'Mesopotamien', p. 61.

71. Nikiprowetsky, 'Ethical Monotheism', p. 73.

72. J. Finkelstein, 'Bible and Babel', pp. 442-44; Lindblom, *Prophecy*, p. 333; Hartmann, 'Mesopotamien', pp. 50-81.

Hymn to Ishtar

'Praise the goddess, the most awesome of the goddesses. Let one revere
the mistress of the peoples, the great of the Igigi... Who—to her in great-
ness can be equal?... She is sought after among the gods; extraordinary is
her station... All of them (gods) bow down before her.

Hymn to the Moon-God

In heaven who is exalted? Thou! Thou alone art exalted. On earth who is
exalted...O Lord, in heaven as to dominion, on earth as to valor, among
the gods thy brothers, thou hast not a rival.

Prayer of Ashurbanipal to the Sun-God

Thou art uniquely brilliant; no one among the gods is equal with thee...
The attention of all the gods is turned to thy bright rising.[73]

Sometimes these prayers in the ancient Near East reflect the anxiety of
people who wish help from a god and they will say anything to obtain it.
As today, there are 'no atheists in foxholes', so also then, people with
illness and tragedy were not just simple polytheists, but rather they turned
directly and radically to a specific deity for the help they thought that
particular god could provide. Therefore, scholars rightly dismiss these
texts as evidence of monotheism, for though the deep piety may seem
monotheistic at times, it could never evolve into true monotheism.[74]

Another category of texts includes a wide range of hymns and descriptions of the divine realm which organize the deities into a hierarchy.
These scribal creations often subsume various deities under one god, and
the deities become hypostases of that deity. This could be done in one of
two ways: the deities could be merged into that god and become symbolic
parts of his or her body, or the specific functions of various deities in the
universe became the actions performed by that one deity under the
name of each of the absorbed deities. A great god could become a repository of the other gods or even a divine abstraction. Marduk of Babylon
and Ashur and Ninurta of Assyria have hymns of this sort attributed to
them. Various texts make these associations in interesting ways. In a
Chaldean text Marduk was equated with aspects of various deities: Uras
is the Marduk of planting, Lugalidda is the Marduk of the abyss, Ninurta
is the Marduk of the pickaxe, Nergal is Marduk of battle, Zababa is
Marduk of warfare, Enlil is Marduk of lordship and consultations, Nabu
is Marduk of accounting, Sin is Marduk who lights up the night, Shamash

73. *ANET*, pp. 383-87.
74. J. Finkelstein, 'Bible and Babel', p. 444; Albertz, *Israelite Religion*, I,
p. 252.

is the Marduk of justice, Adad is the Marduk of rain, Tispak is the Marduk of troops, and Suqamuna is Marduk of the container. Each deity preserves his or her own function as Marduk absorbs them all.[75] The god Ninurta of Assyria has different deities equated with his bodily parts in another text: Enlil and Ninlil are the eyes, Gula and Belili protect the eyes, Ishtar is the chin, Anu and Antum are the lips, Pabilsay is the tongue, Ea and Damkina are ears, Adad is the skull, Shala is the forehead, Marduk is the neck, Sarpenitum is the throat, and Nabu is his chest.[76] These hymns elevate a deity in political fashion also; note how Ninurta is subordinated to Marduk in the first hymn and Marduk is part of Ninurta in the second hymn, thus reflecting the respective views of Babylonian and Assyrian scribes. Again, this is hardly monotheism.

When Assyrians, for example, defined a god of theirs such as Ashur as a deity so powerful he could defeat other gods, they expressed this by having Ashur absorb Marduk into his persona. This has been called 'monarchical polytheism', a form of political and often military propaganda. It may reflect also the attempt on the part of the military leader to gain the favor of the deity for the impending battle or campaign. Hence, the Assyrian king Tukulti-Ninurta I (1234–1197 BCE) prayed to Ashur for help against the Babylonian king Kashtiliash III and called Ashur the 'lord of lords' and 'king of all the gods', including Marduk of Babylon.[77] Or again, Nabonidus in Chaldean Babylon attempted to elevate the moon god Sin of Haran and Ur around 550 BCE by attributing to this deity the traditional titles of Marduk, 'king of kings' and 'god of the gods'. Whatever his political and religious goals might have been, he failed in short fashion, because the priests of Marduk threw their support to the invading Persian king, Cyrus the Great.[78] Other instances could be mentioned, but in all of these examples we observe a form of political henotheism undertaken by a leader at a particular time to obtain some form of power or control. The texts may reflect the ruler's desire to flatter and manipulate the deity or to convince his human

---

75. J. Finkelstein, 'Bible and Babel', pp. 442-43; Lambert, 'Historical Development', pp. 197-98.

76. Albright, *Stone Age*, pp. 217-18.

77. Albright, *Stone Age*, p. 215.

78. H. Tadmor, 'Monarchy and the Elite in Assyria and Babylonia: The Question of Royal Accountability', *Axial Age Civilizations* (ed. Eisenstadt), pp. 220-21; Saggs, *Civilization*, p. 16, even suggests that Nabonidus's reforms may have been inspired by Jewish thought.

supporters of the strength of his political cause.

In all of these texts the modern reader may notice a certain caution on the part of the ancients when speaking about the elevation of one deity over the others. When a synthesis of gods or their subordination is expressed, the old language could not be altered, one still had to to respect the prerogatives and roles of the deities thus absorbed. If an innovation involved the rejection of existing beliefs or religious formulas, there would be a violent reaction, as when the Assyrian king Shalmaneser V and the Chaldean king Nabonidus of Babylon undertook religious change on behalf of their personal deities which infringed too much upon the other gods and their cultic guilds.[79] There were rules, and if your deity absorbed other deities, those other gods had to be treated fairly and their identities respected. This is not monotheism, and it can barely be called monolatry. It is a type of henotheism or monarchic polytheism, and I would like to call it merely 'political henotheism'.

A third category of texts in Mesopotamia also might be mentioned briefly. In letters, personal names, royal inscriptions, wisdom literature, and in some hymns and prayers, there is only reference to a generic deity, and this leaves the impression that there is but one god in the heavens. However, scholars suspect that here it is merely an unnamed personal deity to which the person refers, and the existence of other gods is not in question.[80] As with prayers and lament hymns the devotee regards his or her given god in such a way as to piously flatter the deity. As a lover only has eyes for the beloved, so the devotee has only one god of importance, even in discourse to other humans.

Therefore, in Mesopotamian texts scholars are certain that traditional definitions of monotheism or even monolatry cannot be met, since even in these texts which sound so appealingly monotheistic, there is no intent to deny the cult or existence of the other gods. Taken altogether the various texts with their henolatry or political henotheism all can be described as the 'momentary worship of one deity', and thus we can use another term, 'momentary henotheism' in a polytheistic setting. Such momentary henotheism might worship a different deity on a different

---

79. Albright, *Stone Age*, p. 213; W. von Soden, *Leistung und Grenze sumerische und babylonischer Wissenschaft* (Darmstadt: Wissenschaftliche Buchgesellschaft, 1965), pp. 58-59; Lindblom, *Prophecy*, p. 333; Nikiprowetsky, 'Ethical Monotheism', pp. 73-74; Saggs, *Encounter*, pp. 46-47, 185; Schmidt, *Faith*, p. 69; Tadmor, 'Monarchy and the Elite', p. 221.

80. Hartmann, 'Mesopotamien', pp. 65-67.

day with the same language. The best singular devotion we might observe in the ancient world would be the lifetime devotion of a single person to one particular deity with unlimited passion, but it is hardly monotheism in our sense of the word.[81] Johannes Lindblom generously refers to this as a monotheism which never breaks the boundaries of polytheism.[82]

Perhaps the language of the Mesopotamian prayers and laments might have played some role in the eventual emergence of monotheism. It has been suggested that this literature smoothed the way for emergent monotheism. For if petitioners flatter each deity as though that god were the only god, they speak of the incomparability of that deity and transfer the attributes of other gods to that deity. This may have created available monolatrous language for the later emergent monotheistic movement among the Jews, especially as they came into contact with Mesopotamian thought in the exile.[83]

H.W.F. Saggs believes that, at best, the later Mesopotamians perceived a cosmic unity in the divine, they sensed that the gods were rooted in one great divine level of existence, but they never made the breakthrough to pure monotheism. If monotheism means belief that all divinity is one, some Assyrians were certainly monotheistic, according to Saggs. But the Assyrians also accepted the multiplicity of the various divine manifestations as gods.[84] Likewise, their neighbors to the south, the Babylonians, could become disgruntled with polytheism, but all they could muster 'was a gradual, bland drift towards the idea that all gods were but aspects of the one'.[85] Only Israel stood out in the ancient Near Eastern Semitic world with its movement toward monotheism.

Egypt
More so than their Mesopotamian counterparts the Egyptian thinkers have been given credit for developing concepts and beliefs that appear monotheistic. Wisdom literature especially has drawn attention because of the propensity of Egyptian sages from the Old Kingdom era (2900–

81. Hartmann, 'Mesopotamien', pp. 78-80.
82. Lindblom, *Prophecy*, p. 333.
83. D. Sperling, 'Israel's Religion in the Ancient Near East', *Jewish Spirituality: From the Bible through the Middle Ages* (ed. A. Green; World Spirituality: An Encyclopedic History of the Religious Quest, 13; New York: Crossroad, 1986), p. 24.
84. Saggs, *Assyria*, p. 204.
85. Saggs, *Civilization*, p. 15.

2400 BCE) to speak of a god in the singular, who was viewed as the creator and sustainer of world order and thus the guarantor of success for the hard-working wise person.[86] However, critical scholars have pointed out that in such didactic texts there is usually one god in particular, often Thoth, who is being addressed directly, and the existence of other gods is not denied. The singular term for god, *NTR*, so often used, is a word for addressing one particular god on a specific occasion, not a proof of monotheistic faith.[87] Didactic and liturgical texts often speak in the singular of a creator god. But again critics point out that in different texts it might be a different deity each time; it is often difficult to determine which deity. Various gods were addressed as the creator of the world, including Re, Ptah, Amun and Khnum, so it is impossible to say whether any deity might be considered consistently by Egyptians to be the creator of the world. Texts are vague in their reference so that different devotees might be allowed to address their own special god as the world creator. Very often faithful devotees in Egypt tended to revere one god in a particular worship setting, usually of their choosing according to the city or shrine in which they worshipped and the particular religious need they had. The singular address in so many texts is no evidence of monotheism.[88]

Some authors have pointed to particular texts or schools of thought as evidencing monotheistic tendencies. The Old Kingdom is highlighted as a significant era in this regard due to the dominance of the cult of the sun god, Re. Scribes in the city of Heliopolis spoke of Re as ruling universally and connected his rule to that of the authority of pharaoh and the state. A number of years ago James Henry Breasted saw the Heliopolitan cult as a proto-monotheistic movement whose ideas would culminate in the later efforts of Akhenaton. Heliopolitan texts were said to proclaim one god, a righteous king, and one moral order—two thousand years before Judaism and Zoroastrianism. The sun god Re appeared to absorb other deities and the result was a 'solar henotheism' or 'solar pantheism', which was close to monotheism.[89] Other texts from the Old Kingdom also have been isolated as evidence of early monotheism. The so-called

86. Breasted, *Dawn*, pp. 308-35.
87. Morenz, *Egyptian Religion*, p. 139; Hornung, *Conceptions*, pp. 42-60; Couroyer, 'Le Dieu, II', pp. 70-91.
88. Koch, 'Wort und Einheit', pp. 251-71; Morenz, *Egyptian Religion*, p. 149; Hornung, *Conceptions*, pp. 57-59.
89. Breasted, *Development*, pp. 43, 298; *idem, Dawn*, pp. 145, 273.

Memphite Theology reflected in texts from Memphis praise the deity Ptah as a great creator. He is lord of the Memphite Ennead of gods and creator of eight deities, two of whom spawned Atum, the demiurge who made the world. Ptah was seen as a deity who continued to create, even through the manifestations of other deities. In various texts he is said to have created by 'spitting' or 'masturbating' or by the 'word of his mouth'. He then became an impersonal high creator deity.[90] William Albright compared these texts to the philosophical *Brahmanas*, early Vedic texts in India. The Egyptian thinker was poised between dynamism, pantheism and monotheism; and had they personalized the deity, monotheism would have resulted. Albright believed that an 'impersonal dynamism' prevailed because it would be centuries before a 'more personal stage of mentality' could arise. Nonetheless, he saw these texts as moving close to monotheistic thought.[91] Hence, an extremely early date is isolated as a time when proto-monotheism arose or when henotheism came close to monotheism.

Recent evaluations, however, have not been kind to the exuberant evaluations of earlier scholars. It often is noted that the Old Kingdom texts have especially strong political agendas. The praise of Re or Ptah and their elevation is connected to the royal house of pharaoh, also located in Memphis, and we may be dealing with religious hyperbole designed to undergird the royal patron of these deities. Furthermore, the sophistication attributed to these texts, especially the creation texts associated with Ptah, may be due to their later literary origin or redaction by scribes in the first millennium BCE.[92] So we may be reading the piety of scribes contemporary with Israelites and Jews.

The cults of other deities have received attention by scholars because those gods were elevated by their royal devotees in dramatic fashion, especially by dynasties in the Late Kingdom or Empire period (1550–1100 BCE). A number of authors have pointed out that the god Amun-Re appears to have been regarded as supreme over the other gods and ruler of the entire world, and this phenomenon may be observed even

90. Albright, *Stone Age*, pp. 179-80; F. Moriarity, 'Word as Power in the Ancient Near East', *A Light unto My Path: Old Testament Studies in Honor of Jacob M. Myers* (eds. H. Bream, R. Heim and C. Moore; Philadelphia: Temple University Press, 1994), pp. 350-53.

91. Albright, *Stone Age*, pp. 182-85; *idem, History*, pp. 152-53.

92. M. Lichtheim, *Ancient Egyptian Literature* (3 vols.; Berkeley: University of California Press, 1973, 1976, 1980), I, pp. 51-57.

before Akhenaton's reform as well as after. Perhaps, some of Akhenaton's radical monotheistic language may have been appropriated from the older cult of Amun-Re. Even as late as Pharaoh Pianky (740–713 BCE) Amun was elevated over the other deities in a strong henotheistic fashion.[93] In a hymn to Amun-Re around 1400 BCE, during the reign of Amenhotep III, the father of Akhenaton, that deity is praised as a universal god of all people,

> Hail to thee, Amon-Re... Who made mankind and created the beasts, Lord of what is, who created the fruit tree, made herbage, and gave life to cattle... Who made what is below and what is above... The chief one, who made the entire earth. More distinguished in nature than any other god, in whose beauty the gods rejoice... The gods fawn at his feet, according as they recognize his majesty as their lord... Who gave commands, and the gods came into being... Thou art the sole one, who made all that is, the solitary sole one, who made what exists, from whose eyes mankind came forth, and upon whose mouth the gods came into being... Hail to thee, who did all this! Solitary sole one, with many hands... Hail to thee, who made all that is! Lord of truth and father of the gods... Maker of all mankind, Creator and maker of all that is.[94]

In a hymn from the nineteenth dynasty, the period after the time of Akhenaton, another hymn also praises Amun-Re in radically exclusive terms,

> The first to come into being in the earliest times, Amon, who came into being at the beginning, so that his mysterious nature is unknown. No god came into being before him; there was no other god with him, so that he might tell his form. He had no mother, after whom his name might have been made.[95]

In the *Tale of Wen-Amon*, a text from the eleventh century BCE, the hero says to the Canaanite prince of Byblos,

---

93.   Breasted, *Development*, pp. 315-17; Albright, *Stone Age*, pp. 214-17; *idem*, *History*, pp. 152-53; Baly, 'Geography of Monotheism', p. 262; E. Hornung, 'Monotheismus in pharaonischen Agypten', *Monotheismus* (ed. O. Keel), p. 91; D. Redford, *Akhenaten: The Heretic King* (Princeton, NJ: Princeton University Press, 1984), p. 163; *idem*, 'The Monotheism of the Heretic Pharaoh: Precursor of Mosaic Monotheism or Egyptian Anomaly?', *BARev* 13.3 (1987), p. 29; B. Kemp, *Ancient Egypt: Anatomy of a Civilization* (New York: Routledge, 1994), p. 263.

94.   *ANET*, pp. 365-67.

95.   *ANET*, p. 368.

> There is no ship upon the River which does not belong to Amon! The sea is his, and the Lebanon is his... Now as for Amon-Re, King of the Gods—he is lord of this life and health, and he was lord of your fathers.[96]

Yet despite all the grand praise and glorious rhetoric, the existence of the other gods is not denied. Amun-Re is the first of the gods, he begot the gods, he is lord over the other gods, and so those other gods clearly exist. The reader can observe also the great continuity between the language of these texts and the Amarna hymns of Akhenaton.

Another deity who was elevated by devotees was the god Seth. Under the Ramesside dynasts (1300–1100 BCE) of the nineteenth dynasty, Seth was identified with Baal, the god of the Canaanites and Hittites, and he was called Sutekh-Baal. William Albright described this movement as the climax of universalist tendencies in an international age. By the end of this era Egypt had reached a level of piety which was 'the highest point ever reached by any pre-Israelite faith with which we are acquainted'. Albright further believed the cults of Amun-Re, Aton and Sutekh-Baal with their portrayals of international creator deities had influence upon Moses.[97]

Although the New Kingdom or Empire period deities have far better texts and a stronger claim to monotheism than their Old Kingdom counterparts of Ptah and Re, critics are not convinced. These deities and their attendant glorifications and attributions of universal domain provide religio-political legitimation for their pharaonic patrons who likewise claimed the right to universal rule. It must be emphasized that in all the liturgies the existence of other Egyptian deities is not denied, even down to the time of Pianky in the eighth century BCE. Erik Hornung stresses this, and he also points out that pharaoh Neferhotep I glorified the god Osiris in very similar hymnic fashion during the Middle Kingdom (2100–1800 BCE), yet no one makes the claims for those hymns that have been made for the New Kingdom hymns.[98]

The tendency for Egyptians to merge deities is sometimes observed as a monotheistic urge. But this reflects no real attempt to simplify the divine realm; rather, it is the result of regional ecclesiastical politics. One merges a local deity with a high god to obtain respect for that local deity. The merger of two high gods, like Amun and Re, is political expediency at the highest levels of government, an attempt by pharaonic

96.   *ANET*, p. 27.
97.   Albright, *Stone Age*, pp. 224, 227, 270.
98.   Hornung, 'Agypten', p. 91.

dynasties to rule over the disparate regional religiosities of greater Egypt. Erik Hornung calls it the equalization of religious politics at this higher level of synthesis. Gods who are merged at either regional or national level do not disappear, they continue in this union until a later generation may merge a deity with a totally different divine partner for new religious and political reasons.[99] This syncretism or merging of separate gods is not monotheism, in fact, it 'rather forms a strong counter current to monotheism' by keeping the emphasis upon one particular deity from turning into henotheism, monolatry or monotheism. Merging deities helps to preserve them, it keeps all the old gods around—it is true polytheism in the Egyptian scheme of things.[100] The gods' identities were quite fluid in the Egyptian practice of merging them throughout Egypt's history, because there was only one true divine reality, and the gods were extensions of that reality or plenum.[101] Therefore, tendencies to organize the pantheon do not reflect henotheism or monotheism. Monotheism does not arise by the slow accumulation of characteristics, but it requires a complete transformation of thought patterns. Henotheism or monotheism requires 'a complete revolution in thought' to effect that transformation, and that never really occurred in Egypt. To negate polytheism, one must negate the entire system of the complementarity of the gods in Egyptian thought.[102] While this never truly happened in Egyptian thought, one movement came close—the reforms of Akhenaton, whose activities have received the attention of many critical scholars.

Akhenaton

The heretic Pharaoh Akhenaton, Akhenaten or Ikhnaton (1350–1334 BCE) was the son of the great Pharaoh Amenhotep III (1386–1349 BCE) and he began his reign with the royal name of Amenhotep IV. Very early in his reign he began to show deep interest in the sun cult which had begun to develop already during his father's reign, and evidence exists of interest in the cult even under Thutmosis IV (1419–1386 BCE).[103] Artistic changes began to occur during his reign in the city of Thebes: there were no physical portrayals of the sun god, Re, and the falcon headed god, Horus, was replaced with a picture of a sun disk with stick-

---

99. Hornung, *Conceptions,* pp. 66-99.
100. Hornung, *Conceptions,* p. 98.
101. Hornung, 'Agypten,' pp. 92-93.
102. Hornung, *Conceptions,* p. 243.
103. Breasted, *Dawn,* pp. 275-77; Albright, *Stone Age,* pp. 218-19.

like arms that terminated in human hands.[104] As early as the fifth year of his reign the young pharaoh banned the worship of the entire Egyptian pantheon, especially Amun, and ordered temples throughout the land closed. This must have been a traumatic experience for priests and laity alike. Then Akhenaton undertook the bold move of taking his royal court to the newly created city of Amarna where he could create a religious setting dedicated to the worship of Aton, or Aten, the sun disk in a very iconoclastic fashion. Here he commissioned an artistic tradition which excluded the portrayal of other gods and envisioned pharaoh and his family in idiosyncratic form, as though they were subject to a severe glandular disorder. Scholars have speculated extensively the possible physical ailments Pharaoh Akhenaton may have possessed.[105]

Aton appears to have received exclusive worship and is portrayed as a universal deity who rules over all the lands of the world. The stark symbolic portrayal of Aton as the solar disk almost suggests that the deity transcended portrayal by any graven image.[106] Aton is praised with classic hymnic language generated at Amarna's court, and hints of universalism and monotheism pervade the hymns. The following lines are excerpts from the famous *Hymn to Aton*,

> When thou are risen on the eastern horizon,
> Thou hast filled every land with thy beauty.
> Thou are gracious, great, glistening, and high over every land;
> Thy rays encompass the lands to the limit of all that thou hast made;
> O sole god, like whom there is no other!
> Thou didst create the world according to thy desire,
> Whilst thou wert alone;
> The countries of Syria and Nubia, the land of Egypt,
> Thou settest every man in his place,
> Their tongues are separate in speech,
> and their natures as well;
> Their skins are distinguished,
> As thou distinguishest the foreign peoples.
> The lord of every land, rising for them,

104. Redford, *Akhenaten*, pp. 171-73; *idem*, 'Heretic Pharaoh', p. 24.

105. R. Johnson, 'The Dazzling Sun Disk: Iconographic Evidence that Amenhotep III Reigned as the Aten Personified', *KMT: A Modern Journal of Ancient Egypt* 2.2 (1991), pp. 14-23, 60-66, creatively suggests that the sun disk Aton was really Amenhotep III, the father of Akhnaton, still living in Thebes, and the cult was dedicated to bringing about the rebirth and rejuvenation of his father.

106. C. Aldred, *Akhenaten: King of Egypt* (London: Thames & Hudson, 1988), pp. 239-40; Kemp, *Egypt*, p. 263.

The Aton of the day, great of majesty.
All distant foreign countries, thou makest their life [also].
The world came into being by thy hand,
According as thou hast made them.
When thou hast risen they live,
When thou settest they die.
Thou are lifetime thy own self,
For one lives [only] through thee.[107]

Aton is described by Akhenaton as unique in the heavens, as though he were a new, unique, mysterious solar deity. In actuality, the cult had antecedents in past Egyptian solar cults, particularly in the Heliopolitan cult of Re, the sun god.[108] Scholars have sensed also the influence of the cults of Ptah and Amun, and the portrayal of Aton's activity makes him appear to be a synthesis of Re and Horus. Horus was portrayed as a falcon carrying a sun disk, and with Aton the sun disk simply stood alone.[109] Yet Akhenaton's hymns speak of Aton as though he were a radically new deity.

Akhenaton dramatically turned his back on other cults, and he especially snubbed the powerful priesthood of Amun or Amun-Re (the synthesis of Amun and Re). Some scholars suspect that a powerful economic and political struggle underlay this entire Amarna episode, and that Akhenaton really sought to break the power of the priesthood. Some even suggest that the young pharaoh was the tool of others in the struggle.[110] Eventually the priesthood of Amun-Re prevailed, however.

Akhenaton's total lack of reference to other deities was unique in Egyptian religious history. Much of what he said about Aton would not have offended most Egyptians, but his total disregard for the other deities scandalized many Egyptians and most likely led to the demise of his dynasty. Some Egyptologists opine that his disregard for the other deities merits him the epithat of atheist, which is certainly what ancient

107. *ANET*, pp. 369-71.
108. Breasted, *Development*, p. 336; *idem*, *Dawn*, p. 22; A. Erman, *Die Religion der Agypter* (Berlin: de Gruyter, 1934), pp. 107-109; Albright, *Stone Age*, p. 219-23; A. Gardiner, *Egypt of the Pharaohs* (New York: Oxford University Press, 1966), p. 227; C. Aldred, 'Egypt: The Amarna Period and the end of the Eighteenth Dynasty', *The Cambridge Ancient History*. II.2. *History of the Middle East and the Aegean Region c. 1380–1000 BC* (eds. I.E.S. Edwards *et al.*; Cambridge: Cambridge University Press, 1975), pp. 50-53; Redford, 'Heretic Pharaoh', p. 25.
109. Redford, 'Heretic Pharaoh', p. 29; Aldred, *Akhenaten*, p. 29.
110. Albright, *Stone Age*, p. 220.

Egyptians would have called him.[111]

Akhenaton's radical elimination of other gods and their cults as well as the statements about Aton's universal rule has led many authors to call him a monotheist. This is reinforced by his command to erase the names of other deities, especially Amun, from monuments all over Egypt, including the sacred temple at Karnak. Nor did he build any shrines to other deities at Amarna. Such activity smacks of the zeal of a monotheist.[112] For him the other gods had somehow ceased to be or function, and his was the sole deity. Although his ideas were not new, he proclaimed them with the authority of a zealous reformer.[113] Akhenaton denied the complementarity of the one and the many, the relationship of any one deity to the great force of the divine, an assumption among Egyptians that enabled them to treat their many gods in fluid fashion. To Erik Hornung this change in logic was the core of Akhenaton's revolution, and it 'anticipated western modes of thought'.[114] James Henry Breasted in his famous quip boldly called Akhenaton the first individual in history.[115] William Albright blunted stated,

> it is absurd to deny the term 'monotheism' to a faith which rejected all the gods except the solar disk, even though it was far from reaching the abstract level of Hebrew, Christian, or Muslim monotheism.[116]

Often scholars point to the elimination of myths and rituals from the Aton cult, which set it apart drastically from earlier religious movements with monotheistic tendencies. This reform separated the sun disk from Re, Horus, or Amun-Re completely. Akhenaton had no mythology, symbolism or rituals; the only thing required was the simple act of an offering upon the altar.[117] It appears to be iconoclastic monotheism, but it certainly would have been uninspiring for the masses with its rugged

---

111. Redford, *Akhenaten*, p. 234; Aldred, *Akhenaten*, pp. 243-45.

112. Breasted, *Development*, pp. 319-43; *idem*, *Dawn*, pp. 277-302; Albright, *Stone Age*, pp. 13, 218-23; *idem*, *History*, p. 153; Gardiner, *Egypt*, p. 227; Aldred, 'Egypt', p. 89; Hornung, *Conceptions*, pp. 243-50; *idem*, 'Agypten', pp. 84-97; Redford, *Akhenaten*, pp. 157-58, 'Heretic Pharaoh', p. 27; *idem*, *Egypt*, p. 382; Theissen, *Biblical Faith*, p. 71.

113. Redford, 'Heretic Pharaoh', pp. 27-29; Aldred, *Akhenaten*, p. 245.

114. Hornung, *Conceptions*, p. 249.

115. Breasted, *Development*, p. 339.

116. Albright, *Stone Age*, p. 13.

117. Albright, *Stone Age*, pp. 218-19; Redford, 'Heretic Pharaoh', p. 28; Kemp, *Egypt*, p. 263.

simplicity. Egyptologists in general praise the movement as being monotheistic.

There are, however, authors who would deny the status of monotheism to Akhenaton's movement, especially among scholars outside the field of Egyptology. Denis Baly calls the movement 'pseudo-monotheism', a belief system imposed from above, an imperialistic religion. Furthermore, since the pharaoh is divine in Egypt and the only true mediator between Aton and the world, this religion appears to be dualism rather than monotheism. Finally, Aton is the sun, and not a truly transcendent deity. In one sense it is just another form of nature worship, either veneration of the sun or the solar rays. Some even would call it a form of pantheism, since the sun gives life to the entire natural realm.[118] V. Nikiprowetsky notes that since only Akhenaton truly could worship Aton, it is hardly a religion much less a monotheistic faith. All it did eventually was secure the victory of the Amun-Re priesthood and discourage the ultimate emergence of monotheism in Egypt.[119]

Even the scholars who are prone to call Akhenaton's reform monotheistic are ready to acknowledge the limitations of the movement.

1. The cult of Aton undergirded the divine status of pharaoh and so the political importance of Akhenaton himself. The deity was portrayed as a king and the pharaoh was portrayed as a deity—an obvious syncretism used by Akhenaton to his advantage. He alone was the mediator to this new deity; his was a monarchist view of Aton. In fact, the only true festival celebrated in this new religion was the royal jubilee, a rite to strengthen the religious legitimation of the pharaoh. The universalism proclaimed in the hymnody was very limited, for Egypt and the pharaoh are the center of the universe. In reality, the Aton cult contains veiled nationalism and imperialism to undergird Akhenaton's Egyptian rule over the world.[120] The sun disk was 'simply the hypostasis of divine kingship, a pale reflection of his own on earth'.[121] The deity was concerned only with Akhenaton, not the people, nor the poor; the cult

---

118. Baly, 'Geography of Monotheism', pp. 259-62; B. Uffenheimer, 'Myth and Reality in Ancient Israel', *Axial Age Civilizations* (ed. Eisenstadt), pp. 166-67.

119. Nikiprowetsky, 'Ethical Monotheism', p. 76.

120. Gardiner, *Egypt*, pp. 229-30; Hornung, 'Ägypten', pp. 84-97; Redford, 'Heretic Pharaoh', p. 29; Aldred, *Akhenaten*, p. 240; K. Luckert, *Egyptian Light and Hebrew Fire: Theological and Philosophical Roots of Christendom in Evolutionary Perspective* (Albany: State University of New York Press, 1991), pp. 107-109.

121. Redford, *Akhenaten*, p. 178.

lacked a sense of justice and compassion.

2. The movement was intellectually arid and sterile despite its appearance of superficial sophistication. The movement had no myths, symbols or rituals, all of which were necessary to capture the imagination of the people. Akhenaton denied the other gods to elevate his own; the essence of his monotheism was a principle of denial, not affirmation. The sun disk did not absorb ideas, it sought to annihilate them. Truly creative theologians in Egypt, such as the Memphite theologians, and the later Israelite and Jewish thinkers knew how to creatively adapt myths in a new and nobler fashion. Nothing truly new would be found in Akhenaton's cult, for even its best ideas, such as the sun disk, were taken from the older cults of Re, Ptah and Amun. Atonism was too rarified for the people, and even many of the upper class intellectuals. Above all, the common people could not worship this god directly.[122] As Donald Redford states, Akhenaton was 'no intellectual heavyweight', for he failed completely to understand the meaningful role that cult and mythology could play for believers.[123]

3. The cult lacked concern for the people, it had no ethics or moral teachings to inspire people, and it especially omitted any rhetoric for social justice, which is to be found in the earlier Egyptian religious and wisdom literature. Monotheistic religious traditions have the power to critique the political establishment, but the Aton cult could not, for it was the political establishment in an ultimate sense, and its concern was only for the royal family. This was monotheism 'from above', not monotheism 'from below', from the masses, like that of Judaism.[124]

4. Most importantly, the movement caused social, religious and economic havoc. Akhenaton attacked the Amun-Re priesthood especially, but also many other segments of society. His rejection of other deities affected artists and architects who worked on temples for the diverse gods, suppliers of food and materials for closed temples, and many other common workers. The ouster of other deities often hurt people psychologically. Osiris offered the hope of an afterlife, but the cult of Aton gave no answer to this question. People devoutly attached to the cult of a

122. Albright, *Stone Age*, p. 222; Redford, *Akhenaten*, p. 233; *idem*, 'Heretic Pharaoh', pp. 27-32; *idem*, *Egypt*, p. 379; Aldred, *Akhenaten*, pp. 245-47.

123. Redford, *Akhenaten*, p. 233.

124. Albright, *Stone Age*, p. 222; Gardiner, *Egypt*, p. 229; Theissen, *Biblical Faith*, p. 71; Uffenheimer, 'Ancient Israel', pp. 166-67; Redford, 'Heretic Pharaoh', pp. 30-32.

particular deity were offended most directly. Finally, all Egyptians had to be pained by the arbitrary dismissal of the many deities who had been worshipped for countless generations. The movement failed because it was forced upon the people from above without offering them a message to unite them in a new, meaningful belief system.[125]

Eventually the Amun-Re priesthood found allies in the army, and the eighteenth dynasty was replaced by general Haremhab (1321–1293 BCE) who founded the nineteenth dynasty. Amarna was demolished as the capital once more was in Thebes. The priests destroyed Akhenaton's movement by carefully returning the gods to their proper positions of respect in order to restore once more the harmony of the cosmos.[126]

Donald Redford even sees something sinister in a cult with such a weak, effete, indulgent pharaoh, who venerated the sun, a symbol of oppressive heat in the desert-like conditions of Amarna, where he held court in the hot, open areas which exposed his courtiers to the blasting heat of the sun,

> He was the champion of a universal, celestial power who demanded universal submission, claimed universal truth, and from who no further revelation could be expected. I cannot conceive of a more tiresome regime under which to be fated to live.[127]

Critical scholars believe that though his regime collapsed, his city was demolished, and his dynasty shortly ended after his death; nonetheless, his ideas lived on in Egypt, and perhaps even in Israel. Ideas promulgated by the Aton movement in Amarna may be observed in the thirteenth-century BCE hymns to Amun-Re, which proclaim that Amun-Re is the good shepherd and a universal deity over all peoples. Influence in the later wisdom tradition, especially the *Teachings of Amen-em-ope*, have been noted also.[128] William Albright suggested that the cult of Seth of the Ramesside period also was influenced by Amarna doctrines.[129]

Israel, too, may have been the recipient of some of the teachings of Aton. Of course, no one ever seriously accepted the theory of Sigmund

---

125. Breasted, *Development,* pp. 6, 340-43; Aldred, 'Egypt', p. 89; *idem, Akhenaten,* pp. 245-48.

126. Hornung, *Conceptions,* p. 250.

127. Redford, *Akhenaten,* pp. 234-35.

128. Breasted, *Development,* pp. 344-56; *idem, Dawn,* pp. 308-35; Albright, *Stone Age,* p. 13; Hornung, 'Agypten', p. 95.

129. Albright, *Stone Age,* p. 223.

Freud that Moses was a former priest of Aton from Amarna.[130] More probable is a connection through the Phoenician scribal tradition, which would have had access to Egyptian texts and ideas, and may have passed them along to the Israelites.[131] Many have noted the affinities between the famous Amarna *Hymn to Aton* and Psalm 104, which seems to have been descended from it in some way.[132] In particular, Psalm 104 praises the creator's majesty which is manifest in the sun and the power of life brought to all the creatures of the world. Many commentators, however, stress the influence of Canaanite or Phoenician intermediaries in bringing this song to the Israelites, for the Psalm also contains strong storm-god imagery.[133]

Although Israel may have obtained some ideas from the Aton cult, most authors maintain Israel's basic independence from Atonism in generating monotheism. Often significant differences are highlighted by scholars. The cult of Aton lacked rituals and ethics; Yahwism had both. Aton was a solar deity, Yahweh was a storm god with occasional solar attributes. Yahweh was a warrior god, a deity who chose a people, who acted in human affairs, and was personal, but Aton did none of this and was really more timeless, universal and impersonal. Yahweh had relationships with many peoples, Aton had only Akhenaton.[134] Yet there are some similarities: Yahweh was portrayed on occasion as the sun or as a king, and Moses' role as mediator did resemble that of Akhenaton. On the whole, one must conclude, however, that the influence of Atonism upon Yahwism was minimal, and this is remarkable considering the close proximity of Egypt to Canaan, and the considerable political influence exercised by the former upon the latter.

130. S. Freud, *Moses and Monotheism* (repr.; trans. K. Jones; New York: Vintage Books, 1967 [1939]).

131. Morenz, *Egyptian Religion*, p. 251; Hornung, 'Agypten', pp. 95-96; Redford, *Akhenaten*, pp. 232-33; *idem*, 'Heretic Pharaoh', p. 27.

132. Baly, 'Geography of Monotheism', p. 262; Schmidt, *Faith*, p. 69; Redford, *Akhenaten*, pp. 232-33; *idem*, 'Heretic Pharaoh', p. 27; J. Eaton, *The Contemplative Face of Old Testament Wisdom in the Context of World Religions* (Philadelphia: Trinity Press, 1989), pp. 121-23; de Moor, *Rise of Yahwism*, p. 67; P. Dion, 'Yahweh as Storm-God and Sun-God: The Double Legacy of Egypt and Canaan as Reflected in Psalm 104', *ZAW* 103 (1991), pp. 58-65; Kemp, *Egypt*, p. 263.

133. De Moor, *Rise of Yahwism*, p. 67; Dion, 'Yahweh', pp. 48-58; G. Taylor, *Yahweh*, pp. 225-30.

134. Schmidt, *Faith*, p. 69; Redford, 'Heretic Pharaoh', p. 32; *idem*, *Egypt*, pp. 380-82.

Where does all this discussion of ancient Near Eastern monotheism lead us? Ultimately, it appears that those intellectual and religious movements in Egypt and Mesopotamia which flirted with henotheism, monolatry or monotheism still fell short of the developing monotheistic movement in Israel. These movements and the texts preserved for us never made a radical disclaimer of the other gods, except for Atonism. Unfortunately for Atonism it did not reach or convert the masses. Though Akhenaton's accomplishments are remarkable, they did not result in a viable monotheistic religion. As a result, our overall assessment of the ancient Near East must be negative.

However, I shall not dismiss the accomplishments of Israel's predecessors. In a certain sense they paved the way for the Israelite and Jewish achievements. These movements provided the language that could evolve into monotheism, and they created the potential of exclusive devotion to one deity. The Jews added the disclaimer concerning the other gods' right to exist.

V

The paradigm we wish to advocate in this book would allow some credit to go to the ancient world. According to the historical approach of Fernand Braudel and the French Annales School we must take the long view of historical and intellectual development. Israel and the Jews were part of a long trajectory of religious and intellectual evolution which had begun in the ancient river valleys of Egypt and Mesopotamia. These prior attempts were intellectual endeavors, which though fated to fall short of monotheism, were necessary evolutionary steps before the Jews could make the monotheistic breakthrough. Although the Jewish experience was a radical breakthrough, necessary and preliminary advances had to be made for centuries prior. Modern biological theory also views evolutionary advance as a series of preliminary steps which finally culminate in a 'leap' or breakthrough to a new species.

The preliminary steps toward ethical monotheism began millennia before Israel was born. Perhaps, the first significant stages may be traced to the emergence of the state and the creation of a complex system of writing around 3000 BCE.[135] Literacy may be a major step for the

_____

135. W. Graham, *Beyond the Written Word: Oral Aspects of Scripture in the History of Religion* (Cambridge: Cambridge University Press, 1987), pp. 11-20; D.M. Lewis, 'The Persepolis Tablets: Speech, Seal and Script', *Literacy and Power*

intelligentsia in disassociating themselves from the mythic matrix of their cultural worldview. The ability to write a mythic account down on clay tablets or stone walls may provide a scribe with the realization that he has power over the narrative. Writing gives people the feeling of control over the universe. The great mythic worldview began to break down from that point onward. Perhaps, it is no mean coincidence that human sacrifice ended in Egypt and Mesopotamia a few centuries after writing and literacy emerged. Also, scribes began to arrange a hierarchy of the gods in the third millennium BCE. Scribes began to sense that they could be the intellectual masters of their world with this new skill of writing.

Furthermore, the rise of territorial states and empires also may assist in breaking down the mythic worldview of a culture. Encountering other people broadens one's horizons and leads sensitive thinkers to portray their chief god as a high deity over all other peoples and ultimately over other gods as well. So, tendencies toward henotheism and monotheism received impetus from social and political realia as well as intellectual factors.

Both aforementioned forces exercised considerable influence upon religious evolution in the ancient Near East after 3000 BCE. A long trajectory was in progress before Israel was born, and its ideas would come to fruition in exilic Judaism. Perhaps, these ideas came to a culmination also among Persian Zoroastrians and Greek pre-Socratics at the same time. This would indicate clearly that Israelites and Jews did not have a monopoly on the trajectory; it was the common property of the intelligentsia in many places.

This again returns us to the model: Israelite and Jewish emergent monotheism was a breakthrough in human intellectual history—even if other people arrived at similar conclusions. This breakthrough required preliminary steps, many of which were achieved in the ancient Near East. One also must speak of the necessary preliminary stages of development in the pre-exilic period of Israel which culminated in the monotheism of the exile. Many small steps are needed before the big leap.

This perception of the monotheistic process will have implications for the way in which we speak of Israel's intellectual and religious relationship to the ancient world. So often in the past we compared the worldview of the ancient Near East with Israel and found the former lacking. The mythic or cyclic worldview of the ancient world was placed in

in the Ancient World (eds. A. Bowman and G. Woolf; Cambridge: Cambridge University Press, 1994), pp. 17-32.

contrast with the historical or linear worldview of Israel. Our new perceptions would admit that we had compared unfairly the worldview of
ancient Mesopotamia and Egypt from 3000 BCE with the views of
Judaism around 500 BCE.[136] The so-called contrast between the ancient
Near East or the Canaanites and the Israelites led us to envision an intellectual and religious conflict in Palestine between Canaanites and Israelites
in the pre-exilic era. Our new perceptions would admit that what really
occurred was more of an evolutionary process wherein Yahwism slowly
emerged out of earlier Canaanite beliefs, and this was part of a greater
phenomenon of the first millennium BCE. There was not so much
conflict as there was evolution.

This is not to say that linear-cyclic comparisons should be eliminated,
for they still may play an important pedagogical role for us. Our new
paradigms, however, call upon us to recognize that we are not contrasting contemporary cultures, but rather observing how human culture
evolved from 3000 to 500 BCE. We are comparing the two poles of a
great intellectual trajectory. I do not wish to diminish the role of Israel or
the Jews in the evolutionary process. They are the culmination of the
monotheistic trajectory in the ancient world, and at the same time they
are the beginning of the monotheistic revolution which still is unfolding
for us today.

Therefore, as we compare the beliefs of the biblical tradition with the
ancient world, we should do so in a new and nuanced fashion, recognizing that evolution and not dialectical contrast is the focus to maintain.
Further, we now sense that Israel did not attain monotheism in the time
of Moses or the pre-exilic era, but rather in the Babylonian exile. Finally,
we recognize that Israelites or the Jews did not stand apart from the
ancient Near East, but were part of the ancient world and its intellectual
advance—they were the culmination of a long journey.

136. Gnuse, *Heilsgeschichte*, pp. 73-83, lists a number of scholars in this regard.

Chapter 4

HISTORY OF MONOTHEISM IN ISRAEL

The new paradigm shift has caused scholars and theologians to view
biblical passages in a new perspective, which sometimes means they allow
them to say things which were ignored in the past. In the Deuteronomistic
History, from Joshua to Kings, there was clear evidence of Israel's
polytheistic roots, but readers often viewed the material as evidence of
backsliding from original monotheism, because they followed the intimations provided by the final editors of these books. The editors were trying
to promulgate monotheism in their own exilic age by projecting their
religious values in idealized fashion back into the past. Some scholars
went beyond the idealized portrait of the Deuteronomistic and Priestly
editors and envisioned a religion more ideal and ethical than even those
biblical editors suggested; Yehezkel Kaufmann's work would be a good
example.

I

The Deuteronomistic Historians crafted a historical narrative which interpreted six hundred years of Israelite and Judean life from the perspective
of Josiah's reform and the exile. They viewed their past through a
Yahwistic lens and saw their history not only as it was but very much as
they felt it should have been. The guidelines by which they measured
their past included strict allegiance to Yahweh, rejection of other deities,
rejection of native Yahwistic cultic activities (such as the golden calves,
asherim and the bronze serpent), centralized worship in the Temple, and
a great deal of egalitarianism and social justice in society. Their criteria
for evaluating the past are laid out very nicely in their great manifesto,
the book of Deuteronomy. They evaluated the past as though their
spiritual ancestors, the prophetic minority, were the true leaders meant
to define the religious life of Israelites from the time of Moses onward,

when in reality they were but a progressive minority within society. Therefore, beguiled by the rhetoric of the redactors of the biblical text, readers sometimes missed the truly dramatic story in the Deuteronomistic History: the great struggle of the progressive thinkers in the 'Yahweh-alone' movement who gave birth to a new value system over the years and helped an entire people evolve toward monotheism.

The Deuteronomistic Historians were not liars; they did not deceive more than historians of any age. All historians seek to craft a narrative of the past by selecting those aspects which they unconsciously or consciously consider most valuable in order to communicate a meaningful message to the present so as to shape the direction of the future. That process of selecting and presenting the memories of the past is a subjective art, and the truly significant factor in the presentation is the value system of the historian. The Deuteronomistic Historians were theologians and preachers who wished to achieve significant religious goals with their interpretation of history; they were, above all, preachers, and the Deuteronomistic History is primarily a sermon. Were it merely a brute rendition of historical events with no interpretative meaning to connect the accounts, it certainly would not belong in our Bible, for it would have no religious meaning. The Deuteronomistic Historians also wrote in the historical style of their age, they did not stress the presentation of events in the concrete, literal and detailed fashion in which modern readers wish to have history told. Rather, they shaped their narratives to accentuate the religious message they wished to proclaim. We should not be put off by their lack of concern with historical accuracy and objectivity, for that was not their agenda. Furthermore, we deceive ourselves if we believe that we write with absolute accuracy and objectivity in our modern historiography. No historian can do that! No historian can burden the reader with all the possible details of the past. Every historian must winnow and select what he or she believes is significant, and present that in organized fashion to the reader. The Deuteronomistic Historians covered six centuries in a very short document by comparison to our modern standards of history writing, and they were more interested in the meaning of the events in those years rather than in a rendition of brute facts. Therefore, to say that the biblical authors reinterpreted the traditions of the past by the monotheistic values of their own age is not to accuse them of dishonesty, but to acknowledge that they engaged in the subjective craft of history writing appropriate to their age. Scholars have stressed that to admit biblical authors wrote with ideological or theological agenda does not discredit their writing as legitimate historiography, but rather acknowledges that indeed they were historians, crafting their texts as historians have done in any age.[1]

After having said that we then must acknowledge that the Deuteronomistic Historians did not hide the facts completely. The biblical narratives provide us with enough information to realize that in reality the Israelites and Judahites were basically polytheistic throughout the pre-exilic period and Yahwism was a complex religion with indigenous polytheistic cultic activities. Scholarly paradigms of the recent generation still use the biblical text as a resource for reconstructing the evolution of Israel's religion, but now we simply read the text more slowly and perhaps 'read between the lines'. Some might call this a 'hermeneutic of suspicion'. We are led to be suspicious of the surface meaning of the text; we look more deeply for the dynamics which might lie behind the text, especially with the aid of archaeological research and sociological models. But more importantly we are suspicious of ourselves; we are suspicious of our past easy interpretations, whether they come from traditional conservative Christian interpretation or out of the scholarly writings of a past generation. We are reading the text more carefully and critically. In this way we will learn to appreciate the theological message of the Deuteronomistic Historians more than if we viewed them merely as archivists recording brute facts, and we might discover something about who we are and what role we play in the emergence of radical monotheism.

As we now return to those biblical passages to consider Israel's religious development, we may see more clearly what is being recalled for us, especially since archaeological finds have provided us with a wider view of the religious practices of that age. The description of Israel's idolatry is not of some backsliding experienced by some foolish Israelites, but rather it testifies to the everyday religious life of Israel which the prophets and reformers were trying to change. Their appeal to an idealized earlier monotheism was part of the rhetoric necessary to gain a hearing among their contemporaries and slowly change their values. The passages which describe Israel's idolatry are resources for us to write a religious history of this people, which speaks of the evolutionary struggle of a

---

1. I. Provan, 'Ideologies, Literary and Critical: Reflections on Recent Writing on the History of Israel', *JBL* 114 (1995), pp. 585-606; M. Brettler, *The Creation of History in Ancient Israel* (New York: Routledge, 1995); W. Holladay, *Long Ago God Spoke: How Christians May Hear the Old Testament* (Minneapolis: Fortress Press, 1995), pp. 88-103.

new intellectual worldview awaiting its birth or breakthrough.

Past textbooks of Israelite religion described Canaanite religion as the 'other' religion in Palestine. Future textbooks ought to see those Canaanite practices and beliefs as early Yahwism, out of which later Yahwism would emerge. The biblical authors did not deceive us, they left us memories of early Yahwism, the religion they sought to move beyond. In our new perspective we recognize that there were not two religions struggling for the soul of a people. There was one religion undergoing a transformation, like a butterfly in its cocoon undergoing change until it would burst out and fly. The struggle in early Yahwism in the pre-exilic period would lead to the bursting out of monotheism in the exile.

II

As we now consider those biblical texts we recognize that they do not describe the 'other' religion in Palestine, or the 'syncretism' of Canaanite and Israelite belief. Rather, they describe the complex and varied customs of pre-exilic Israelites, customs which varied from age to age in the pre-exilic era and differed by region, but which nonetheless taken together describe early Yahwism.

There are passages which admit the existence of other deities. Many are vague and speak of the other gods as subordinate to Yahweh, perhaps as the 'heavenly host' who serve Yahweh as messengers or assistants in divine war. Both post-exilic Jews and modern Jews and Christians have learned to read these as references to angels to thus preserve the monotheistic identity of Yahweh. But pre-exilic Israelites would have understood these messengers, angels or *aides-de-camp* as gods, as the frequently used Hebrew word in such instances, *elohim*, truly implies.

Some notable passages occur in both Pentateuchal and Deuteronomistic texts. Yahweh speaks to Moses about executing judgment upon the gods of the Egyptians in Exod. 12.12 and Num. 33.4, which would be difficult to do, if those beings did not exist.[2] Joshua refers to the gods served by the ancestors in the region beyond the river and the gods of the Amorites as though they were capable of receiving homage in Josh. 24.2, 14-24. Jephthah speaks to the king of Ammon as though his deity, Chemosh, really exists in Judg. 11.24. (Although strangely enough, Chemosh is the god of Moab not Ammon; either Jephthah or the historian is confused about someone's identity.) David speaks as though other gods exist in

2.   Uffenheimer, 'Ancient Israel', p. 145.

1 Sam. 26.19, '...they have driven me out today from my share in the heritage of the Lord, saying, "Go, serve other gods"'. Solomon built shrines for Astarte of Sidon, Milcom of Ammon, Chemosh of Moab and Molech of Ammon according to 1 Kgs 11.1-8, which suggests he might have thought they existed. 2 Kgs 17.29-41 describes how inhabitants in Samaria worshipped many gods, several introduced by recently settled deportees, and presumably accepted as real deities by native Israelites.

Evidence of polytheism in Israel prior to the fall of Samaria is provided by records of Sargon II, who took booty from Samaria which included 'the gods in whom they trusted', obviously referring to idols. Since the Assyrians knew the difference between gods and mere sacred objects, like cherubim, these must have been real Israelite gods.[3] In Judah at this same time, the late eighth century, the prophet Micah states, 'For all the peoples walk, each in the name of its god, but we will walk in the name of the Lord our God forever and ever' (Mic. 4.5). He could have been speaking of the northern state of Israel, too. Passages in the Psalter frequently speak of other beings in the heavenly realm, which presumably would have been seen as separate deities by many Israelites, including, 'Ascribe to the Lord, O heavenly beings, ascribe to the Lord glory and strength' (Ps. 29.1). Some texts envision Yahweh as the national god of Israel while the other deities rule the other nations. Yahweh may be seen as leader of these gods and hence all the nations. Particularly blunt statements are found in Psalm 82, in which Yahweh sits in the divine council 'in the midst of the gods he holds judgment' (v. 1) and condemns the other deities for their injustice, 'You are gods, children of the Most High, all of you; nevertheless you shall die like mortals' (vv. 6-7). After this Yahweh shall rule the nations over which those other deities had charge (v. 8). This certainly sounds like a transitional statement you would make to former polytheists who slowly are becoming monotheists; you imply that Yahweh deposed or killed the other gods. Another passage which some scholars have isolated as indicative of polytheism is Deut. 4.19 where Yahweh allots various deities to the nations of the earth.[4]

> And when you look up to the heavens and see the sun, the moon, and the stars, all the host of heaven, do not be led astray and bow down to them and serve them, things that the Lord your God has allotted to all the peoples everywhere under heaven.

---

3.   C.J. Gadd, 'Inscribed Prisms of Sargon II from Nimrud', *Iraq* 16 (1954), p. 179; Saggs, *Encounter*, p. 23.

4.   Uffenheimer, 'Ancient Israel', p. 145.

The passage which has received the most attention is one in which Yahweh is envisioned as a subordinate deity to El and receives Israel as an allotment, Deut. 32.8-9, 12. This reverses the imagery of Psalm 82 where Yahweh was the chief deity over other gods. Deut. 32.8-9, 12 may be the best indication of an old acceptable Israelite polytheistic perception of the universe.

> (8) When the Most High (Elyon) apportioned the nations, when he divided humankind, he fixed the boundaries of the peoples according to the number of the gods; (9) the Lord's own portion was his people, Jacob his allotted share…(12) the Lord alone guided him; no foreign god was with him.

Here Yahweh receives Israel from Elyon or El, the high deity. In its present monotheistic setting of Deuteronomy the reader could read Elyon as another name for Yahweh, to be sure, but originally the passage would have spoken of separate gods and Yahweh appears to have been portrayed as a son of Elyon or El (like Baal and Mot in the Ugaritic literature).

A special category for consideration would be the various names of deities found in the patriarchal narratives of Genesis 12–50. The patriarchs revered god(s) by the following names: 1) El-Elyon (Gen. 14.19-24), 2) El-Shaddai (Gen. 17.1), 3) El-Bethel (Gen. 35.7), 4) El-Roi (Gen. 16.13), and 5) El-Olam. These names appear to be typical names that Canaanites would use to worship local manifestations of the high god El. The possibility that these names all refer to separate deities or numina revered by the many various ancestors of the Israelites is reinforced by the revelation to Moses in Exod. 6.2-3, where Yahweh states that El Shaddai was his earlier name. Commentators suggest this passage acknowledges that early Israelites were El worshippers and these names reflect regional El deities revered by various peoples who eventually coalesced into Israel. Even the name Israel implies El worship when the name was formed. Thus, biblical authors used the Moses call narrative to draw the various religious traditions together into one pre-Yahweh cult. But the honest recognition of these diverse names may be good evidence of pre-exilic polytheistic El worshipping Israelites who would someday elevate Yahweh over the other gods, absorb El into Yahweh, and eventually make Yahweh the only deity.[5]

5. Mihalik, 'Some Thoughts', pp. 11-19; K. Koch, 'Saddaj: Zum Verhältnis zwischen israelitischer Monolatrie und nordwest-semitischem Polytheismus', *VT* 26 (1976), pp. 299-332, observes Yahweh's ability to absorb other deities in connection

The archaeological find at Kuntillet 'Ajrûd speaks of 'Yahweh of Teman' which leads us to suspect that some Israelites worshipped regional manifestations of Yahweh just as they had revered local manifestations of El. Perhaps this is the nuance in the words of Absalom in 2 Sam. 15.7-8, which may imply a shrine dedicated to 'Yahweh of Hebron'.

> (7) Absalom said to the king, 'Please let me go to Hebron and pay the vow that I have made to the Lord. (8)...then I will worship the Lord in Hebron.

1 Sam. 1.3 implies that Yahweh was worshipped at Shiloh as 'Yahweh of the hosts'. David says that Yahweh cannot be worshipped by him in other lands in 1 Sam. 26.19, which likewise implies a regional devotion and perhaps also regional shrines. It is also possible that Deut. 6.4 speaks against the idea of regional manifestations of Yahweh when it says, 'Hear, O Israel, the Lord our God is one'.[6] Several critical scholars suggest that Yahweh may have been interpreted differently in each of the regional shrines in Palestine. This regionalization of Yahweh may have been the real target of Josiah's attempts to close down shrines outside of Jerusalem.[7] Furthermore, the different iconographic portrayals of Yahweh in various parts of the country may be testimony to such regional portrayals of Yahweh. Archaeologists seldom find an image which portrays Yahweh, and this supports the notion of a strong aniconic tradition from an early date. But there are instances in archaeological sites and perhaps the biblical text where such an image occurs. These include, among others, a cult figurine from Hazor, the bull figurine from the Ephraim highlands, the pictures at Kuntillet 'Ajrûd, the Ta'anach cultic stand, numerous seals, and the cultic image described in Judges 17–18.[8]

with the deity, Shaddai; Smith, *Early History of God*, p. 8; Dietrich, 'Werden und Wesen', pp. 17-18, sees this tendency in Yahweh's equation with El, Baal, the sun and Baal-Shamem; Day, 'Yahweh', pp. 188-93, suggests that the sun, Resheph and Molech were separate deities in Yahweh's entourage; Niehr, 'JHWH', p. 320.

6. Höffken, 'Bermerkung', pp. 88-93; Braulik, 'Deuteronomium', pp. 119-22.

7. McCarter, 'Aspects', pp. 141-43; Ahlström, 'Role of Archaeological', pp. 128-29; Albertz, *Israelite Religion*, I, p. 83; *idem*, 'Der Ort', p. 85; Dietrich, 'Werden und Wesen', p. 21.

8. Smith, 'Image of God', pp. 473-512; *idem*, 'Shape of God', pp. 315-26; M. Haran, 'The Divine Presence in the Israelite Cult and the Cultic Institutions', *Bib* 50 (1969), p. 264; *idem*, *Temples and Temple-Service in Ancient Israel* (Oxford: Clarendon Press, 1978), p. 35; Ahlström, 'God Figurine', pp. 54-62, and 'God Figurine, Once More', pp. 106-109; G. Taylor, 'Two Earliest', pp. 557-66.

With these new understandings of Israelite religion scholars look at all the passages mentioned above and now see evidence of Israelite poly-theism. Previously scholars might have dismissed these biblical references as simply a way of speaking or merely references to angelic messengers, but now they observe them as references to deities with whom Yahweh was associated.

The biblical text repeatedly mentions particular deities and cultic customs associated with them. The frequent reference to these persons leads scholars to suspect that they were part of the greater national piety of pre-exilic Yahwism rather than syncretistic aberrations or foreign imports.

First of all, the frequent references to the asherim stand out promi-nently in the biblical text. Asherim are said to have been erected by Israelites in the early days of the settlement (Judg. 3.7), Jeroboam I (1 Kgs 14.15), Rehoboam (1 Kgs 14.23), Queen Maacah (1 Kgs 15.13), Ahab (1 Kgs 16.33), Manasseh (2 Kgs 21.3, 7), and Israelites in general (2 Kgs 17.16); they were tolerated by Jehoahaz (2 Kgs 13.6); and they were torn down by Hezekiah (2 Kgs 18.4) and Josiah (2 Kgs 23.6, 14). As noted in a previous chapter scholars have debated whether Asherah was a goddess consort of Yahweh or merely a symbol or emblem of Yahweh (a pole or a tree), but with the recent inscriptional evidence unearthed in the past generation scholars lean toward the former opinion increasingly. One likewise suspects asherim were a native Yahwistic cultic phenomenon considered acceptable for most of Israel's history. Elijah did not seem to oppose the disciples of Asherah when he fought the Tyrian Baal supporters, nor did Jehu destroy them in his purge. Perhaps, some of the classical prophets, including even Hosea, accepted her presence. Only later with Hezekiah and Josiah is animosity expressed against the asherim by Yahwists. Then the Deuteronomistic History may have connected Baal to Asherah instead of Yahweh in order to discredit her.[9] Thus, only after Hosea do we observe such an attack on cultic

9.   Ahlström, *Aspects*, pp. 51-88; *idem*, 'King Jehu', pp. 53-61; Smith, 'Veracity', pp. 11-16; Patai, *Hebrew Goddess*, pp. 16-58, who believes that Asherah and Anat-Astarte were separate, and the latter was the Queen of Heaven for Jeremiah; Saggs, *Encounter*, p. 22; Meshel, 'Did Yahweh', pp. 24-35; Biale, 'God', pp. 240-56; Dever, 'Archaeological Confirmation', pp. 37-44; *idem*, 'Asherah, Consort', pp. 21-37; Day, 'Asherah', p. 393; Lipinski, 'Iconography', pp. 87-96; Freedman, 'Yahweh of Samaria', pp. 241-49; Hestrin, 'Lachish Ewer', pp. 212-23; Smith, 'God and Female', pp. 333-40; Olyan, *Asherah*, pp. 70-74; G. Taylor, 'Two Earliest', pp. 557-66; Ackerman, 'Women Knead', pp. 109-24; *idem*, *Green Tree*,

phenomena closely attached to Yahweh, and the asherim provide a good example.[10]

If Asherah was a consort of Yahweh, and if she is to be associated with the 'Queen of Heaven', as some suggest, then material in Jeremiah's oracles testify to the tenacity of this cult. For Jeremiah encountered stiff resistance by devotees to this goddess who believed that forsaking her worship brought woe upon Judah. The passage in Jer. 44.17-19 speaks for itself,

> (17) 'Instead we will do everything that we have vowed, make offerings to the queen of heaven and pour out libations to her, just as we and our ancestors, our kings and our officials, used to do in the towns of Judah and in the streets of Jerusalem. We used to have plenty of good, and prospered, and saw no misfortune. (18) But from the time we stopped making offerings to the queen of heaven and pouring out libations to her, we have lacked everything and have perished by the sword and by famine.' (19) And the women said, 'Indeed we will go on making offerings to the queen of heaven and pouring out libations to her; do you think that we made cakes for her, marked with her image, and poured out libations to her without our husbands' being involved'?

This is testimony of a late and strident veneration of a goddess by Judeans—clear testimony that polytheism did not die easily among the Jews.

Even in exile and beyond, the veneration of a female deity endured.[11] The fifth-century BCE papyri texts from Jewish colonists in Elephantine in Egypt indicate that Jews worshipped the Queen of Heaven under the name of Anatyahu, a combination of the Canaanite goddess Anat and Yahweh.[12]

In conjunction with Asherah one must also mention Baal. Altars to Baal were erected by Ahab (1 Kgs 16.32), Manasseh (2 Kgs 21.3) and

---

pp. 6-35; *idem*, 'Queen Mother', pp. 385-401; Margalit, 'Some Observations', pp. 371-78; North, 'Yahweh's Asherah', pp. 118-37; J. Taylor, 'Asherah, the Menorah', pp. 29-54, suspects that Asherah was portrayed with the almond tree; and Hadley, 'Yahweh', pp. 240-42, suggests that finally Deuteronomistic Historians connected Asherah to Baal to discredit her.

10. Saggs, *Encounter*, p. 23; Toews, *Monarchy*, pp. 151-72. However, McKeating, *Amos*, p. 92; Hadley, 'Yahweh', p. 255; and Dever, 'Ancient Israelite Religion', p. 113, think Hosea, and perhaps other classical prophets accepted the asherim.

11. Patai, *Hebrew Goddess*, pp. 99-179, sees this figure endure in the later Jewish images of the Shekinah, the Matronit and the Kabbala Tetrad.

12. Patai, *Hebrew Goddess*, p. 58; Nikiprowetsky, 'Ethical Monotheism', p. 77.

Israelites in general (2 Kgs 17.16), while altars were torn down and priests were killed by Jehoida and Jehoash (2 Kgs 11.18) and later Josiah (2 Kgs 23.4-5). Scholars, however, have sensed that there was a distinction between native Baals and foreign Baals. Elijah, Jehu, Jehoida and Jehoash opposed the cult of the Baal of Tyre, while they may have accepted the local Baal cults. Only with Josiah is there a total war against all Baal cults. Until that time most Israelites seemed to worship Baal with great frequency (Hos. 11.2, Jer. 11.13-17), and for many he may have been a national deity like Yahweh.[13]

Other cultic objects may have been accepted for a long time as good Yahwistic objects only to be condemned and destroyed by the later zealous 'Yahweh-alone' movement. The most famous object thus destroyed was the bronze serpent of Moses, which Hezekiah eliminated according to 2 Kgs 18.4,

> He broke in pieces the bronze serpent that Moses had made, for until those days the people of Israel had made offerings to it; it was called Nehushtan.

An object with higher orthodox credentials, created by Moses, could not be found. But it was destroyed, testimony that an internal transformation of Yahwism was occurring, now that once acceptable images were being destroyed.

Although not as dramatic, the comparable proscription of the ephod and the teraphim likewise represents the removal of once acceptable Yahwistic cultic objects.[14] Even Hosea said nothing against these objects. But according to 2 Kgs 23.24 Josiah again was responsible for their removal.

Although most readers of the Bible assume that the golden calves erected by Jeroboam I at Bethel and Dan were symbols of Baal, many scholars suspect they were really old, traditional symbols of Yahweh. The calves either were the footstool of an invisibly throned Yahweh, or they were an emblem of Yahweh (a personified symbol of his power), or perhaps in the minds of some northern Israelites they actually held the divine presence of Yahweh. The calves were accepted by Yahwists,

---

13. Ahlström, 'King Jehu', pp. 53-57; Hossfeld, 'Einheit', pp. 72-73; Wenning and Zenger, 'Baal-Heiligtum', pp. 75-86; Lang, 'König', p. 18; Smith, *Early History of God*, pp. 14-15; Dietrich, 'Werden und Wesen', pp. 17-18; A. Lemaire, 'Déesses et dieux de Syrie-Palestine d'aprés les inscriptions (c. 1000–500 av. n. é.)', *Ein Gott allein* (eds. Dietrich and Klopfenstein), p. 149.

14. McKeating, *Amos*, p. 92; Nikiprowetsky, 'Ethical Monotheism', p. 77.

including Elijah and Jehu in the ninth century BCE. Not until Hosea was there a real criticism of the calves. Again, this was a critique of an internal Yahwistic custom not a foreign or pagan intrusion. The Deuteronomistic Historians honestly recalled that the calves were not purged by early prophetic reformers, but in the Deuteronomistic editorializing the calves were closely connected to Baal devotion and the kings of the northern state of Israel were criticized for sponsoring the cult.[15]

Veneration of the sun appears to have been a phenomenon limited primarily to the royal court of Judah, because solar imagery had been associated with royal symbols for years in Egypt and Palestine to undergird the institution of kingship. Increasingly scholars suspect that it was not so much a foreign custom imposed upon Judahites by the Assyrians as it was a natural and indigenous religious activity connected to the cult of Yahweh. Especially with the discovery of the Ta'anach cult stand from the tenth century BCE with its solar imagery one suspects that Yahweh was equated with the sun from the earliest periods for some Israelites. Perhaps the emergence of kingship under David and Solomon in Jerusalem encouraged the first serious use of these motifs. Evidence for solar devotion can gleaned from biblical texts also. Psalm 104 may be influenced in part by Akhenaton's hymn to Aton, the sun disk, and it certainly portrays Yahweh as demonstrating power through the life-giving rays of the sun. Joshua may have addressed Yahweh as the sun at Gibeon in Josh. 10.12-14 when he said,

> (12) 'Sun, stand still at Gibeon, and moon, in the valley of Aijalon.'...
> (14) There has been no day like it before or since, when the Lord heeded a human voice.

More likely the memory of this victory by Joshua was preserved at the shrine in Gibeon, where Yahweh may have been venerated with solar imagery, and so the account was told to portray Yahweh as being in the sun in subtle fashion. Its nuanced subtlety enabled the narrative in this form to slip past the critical eye of the Deuteronomistic Historians into our text. Perhaps comparable concepts are found in 2 Kgs 20.8-11 when the sun moved as a sign during Hezekiah's illness. Not until the age of Josiah was solar imagery purged from the Yahwistic cult. Josiah also removed the horses dedicated to the sun according to 2 Kgs 23.11, which were probably part of this Yahwistic solar cult. Ezekiel in later years criticized solar devotion in the Temple which continued after

---

15. Saggs, *Encounter*, pp. 22-23; Toews, *Monarchy*, pp. 151-72.

Josianic reform (Ezek. 8.16-18). It escaped criticism for so long because sun veneration did not involve an image made with human hands, as did the asherim and the calves, and thus it avoided the critique of those who were devoted to the values affirmed by the second commandment's prohibition against images. In fact, it may have helped to affirm the aniconic tradition associated with Yahweh. Furthermore, the sun god was associated with justice, and this was a very acceptable image to draw into Yahweh's persona.[16]

Another cultic activity which may have been chiefly the prerogative of kings was human sacrifice, particularly that of first-born children. Previously scholars assumed that child sacrifice was a Canaanite custom, but increasingly they suspect that it, too, was a natural part of the Yahwistic religion practiced by kings in times of crisis.[17] Exod. 22.29-30 states, 'The firstborn of your sons you shall give to me. You shall do the same with your oxen and your sheep'. The passage implies that sacrifice of the child should be undertaken as surely as the sacrifice of the animals. However, Exod. 13.13 and 34.19 provide for the replacement or 'redemption' of the child with an animal sacrifice. The omission of any reference to redemption in Exod. 22.29-30 leads scholars to suspect that some Yahweh devotees indeed sacrificed their children as burnt offerings to Yahweh, and this may be the earliest legislation on the custom.

The Deuteronomistic History recalls the memory of people who sacrificed their children: Jephthah, whose sacrifice of his daughter appears to have been honorable, though tragic, according to the narrative (Judg. 11.34-40); Hiel of Bethel who built Jericho at the cost of his youngest son (Josh. 6.26; 1 Kgs 16.34); the king of Moab, who sacrificed his son and heir to the throne and by this act forced the kings of Israel, Judah and Edom to retreat, thus implying that they viewed this as a meaningful and terrifying religious act (2 Kgs 3.27); Ahaz (2 Kgs 16.3); and Manasseh (2 Kgs 21.6). It is not until Josiah's reform that the Topheth in the valley of Hinnom, where sacrifice occurred, was destroyed (2 Kgs 23.10). The

16. Keel, 'Sodom', pp. 110-17; Stähli, *Solare Elemente*, pp. 177-78; Smith, *Early History of God*, pp. 20, 115-34; Ackerman, *Green Tree*, pp. 93-99; J. Taylor, *Yahweh*, pp. 24-37, 114-18, 147-72, 183; *idem*, 'Yahweh Worshipped', pp. 52-61, 90; Dietrich, 'Werden und Wesen', p. 17; Keel and Uehlinger, 'Sonnengottheit', pp. 269-306; Niehr, 'JHWH', pp. 307-326

17. Green, *Human Sacrifice*, pp. 156-87; Heider, *Molek*, pp. 223-408; Day, *Molech*, pp. 29-71; Kennedy, 'Isaiah 57', pp. 50-51; Smith, *Early History of God*, pp. 137-38, 146; Ackerman, *Green Tree*, pp. 101-63; *idem*, 'Child Sacrifice', pp. 20-29, 56; Levenson, *Death*, pp. 3-52, 111-24.

practice endured for a long time in Israelite and Judahite history.

The story of Abraham and Isaac in Genesis 22 is clearly an aetiology to explain why Israelites should not sacrifice their children. Yet Alberto Green and Jon Levenson caution us to recognize that Abraham indeed is blessed by Yahweh for his willingness to offer such a sacrifice, and the permission to sacrifice an animal instead of Isaac does not necessarily vitiate the principle of human sacrifice.[18] Exod. 34.20 appears to command a replacement animal sacrifice for first-born sons, but the command is very terse and somewhat vague.

It is not until the classical prophets that condemnation of infant sacrifice begins to surface. Hos. 13.2 may condemn human sacrifice, but the Hebrew is vague. Mic. 6.7 asks hypothetically, 'Shall I give may first born for my transgression', and presumably the answer should be no! But some authors suspect that the text merely implies that this is the most powerful sacrifice which people can offer Yahweh. Isa. 30.33 alludes to the custom indirectly in a judgment oracle against Assyria, saying that Assyria will receive this punishment. But the custom is not directly condemned here, either. The first truly acerbic assault upon the custom comes only with the later prophets. Jeremiah condemns the practice in several oracles. In Jer. 2.23, 19.6, 11-14, and 31.40 he refers to the Topheth or the Hinnom valley in negative terms, and in Jer. 7.31, 19.5, and 32.35 he explicitly condemns the sacrifice,

> (7.31) 'And they go on building the high place of Topheth, which is in the valley of the son of Hinnom, to burn their sons and their daughters in the fire.' (19.5) '...and gone on building the high places of Baal to burn their children in the fire as burnt offerings to Baal, which I did not command or decree, nor did it enter my mind.' (32.35) 'They built the high places of Baal in the valley of the son of Hinnom, to offer up their sons and daughters to Molech, though I did not command them, nor did it enter my mind that they should do this abomination, causing Judah to sin.'

Jeremiah's overly strong statement that Yahweh did not command this sacrifice may reflect the possibility that some Israelites and Judahites thought it to be so. Ezekiel similarly condemns the practice in Ezek. 16.20-21, 20.26, and 23.37-39,

> (16.20-21) 'You took your sons and your daughters, whom you had borne to me, and there you sacrificed to them [idols] to be devoured... You slaughtered my children and delivered them up as an offering to

18. Green, *Human Sacrifice*, pp. 156-59; Levenson, *Death*, pp. 13, 21-22, 111-42.

them.' (20.26) 'I defiled them through their very gifts, in their offering up
all their firstborn in order that I might horrify them, so that they might
know that I am the Lord.' (23.37-39) '...and they even offered up to
them [idols] for food the children they had borne to me... For when they
had slaughtered their children for their idols.'

Remarkably, Ezekiel implies that Yahweh had commanded this practice
in Israel's history to punish the people, unless Ezekiel is speaking with
extreme sarcasm. Ezekiel, like Jeremiah, appears to be disavowing a
custom seen by many as acceptable Yahweh worship, and this would
explain the vehemence with which both Jeremiah and Ezekiel spoke in
condemning the custom. In retrospect, the reference in Micah might be
seen to suggest that such sacrifice was done to Yahweh. A post-exilic
prophetic reference occurs in Isa. 57.5 against those 'who slaughter your
children in the valleys, under the clefts of rocks', and presumably it speaks
to post-exilic Jews, who by that time would worship only Yahweh. It
would seem that only with the Deuteronomic and Priestly legislation was
the custom truly condemned. The Priestly legislation in particular appears
to reject the cult of the dead because of purity concerns. In fact, purity
concerns in Priestly legislation were a major factor in undergirding
monotheistic belief and practice in the exilic and post-exilic eras.[19]

Did Yahweh receive the sacrifice of children? Some commentators
suspect this to be the case, but others suggest that another deity affiliated
with Yahweh may be the recipient of such sacrifices. The deity most likely
to be associated with human sacrifice is the god Molech. For years
scholars debated whether this word refers to a sacrifice or the actual deity,
and opinion has swung predominantly in favor of the latter option in the
past generation. Laws in Lev. 18.21 and 20.2-5 forbid Israelites to sacrifice their children to Molech, and these archaic laws were codified only as
late as the exile. The post-exilic oracle in Isa. 57.9 mentions Molech, while
not connecting him directly to the sacrifice. Scholars suspect Molech was
a real deity to whom children were sacrificed directly, not Yahweh. This
is reinforced by Ps. 106.37-38 which impies demons received the sacrifice,

(37) 'They sacrificed their sons and their daughters to the demons; (38)
they poured out innocent blood, the blood of their sons and daughters,
whom they sacrificed to the idols of Canaan; and the land was polluted
with blood.'

19. W. Houston, *Purity and Monotheism: Clean and Unclean Animals in
Biblical Law* (JSOTSup, 140; Sheffield: JSOT Press, 1993), pp. 218-58; Smith,
'Yahweh', pp. 222-23.

Ps. 23.4 may refer to the sacrifice in the valley of Hinnom, when it speaks of the valley of the shadow of death. Molech may have been the god of the underworld, like the Ugaritic deity Mot, and sacrifice to him may have insured fertility for the land and a special place in the divine realm for the sacrificial victims. The cult was practiced under the nose, literally, of the Judean kings and the Temple priests in Jerusalem. Increasingly, scholars believe that the cult, though dedicated to Molech, was seen as part of the greater Yahwistic cult, because Molech was part of Yahweh's entourage. Only late did prophets and reforming kings really attack it, especially Josiah, Jeremiah and Ezekiel.

This quick review of the biblical texts connected to the devotion to Asherah/asherim, Baal/baalim, the Nehushtan, golden calves, the sun, and Molech or human sacrifice is intended to show that from a new perspective these may be seen as normal religious practices of pre-exilic Yahwism. Previously these practices would have been called Canaanite intrusions into Israelite religion, but now scholars think differently. What stands out significantly is that the criticism of these objects and customs comes so late in Israel's history. Hosea and Hezekiah in the eighth century BCE opposed the calves, the baalim, and the Nehushtan. But not until the seventh and sixth centuries BCE were condemnations forthcoming for the asherim, sun veneration and human sacrifice, even though these practices existed from early times onward. Previously, modern authors seemed to overlook the truly late emergence of the critiques with Josiah, Jeremiah, Ezekiel and the Deuteronomic reform. Sometimes it was assumed that phenomena like solar veneration and human sacrifice were late introductions in the age of Assyrian imperialism. Now we sense these practices were always present in some form. The lateness of the prophetic critique indicates these must have been acceptable Yahwistic customs for many years. Only when the emergent monotheistic movement was entering its revolutionary stage during the chaos of national revival under Josiah and subsequent national collapse did reformers seek to purge the religion of the old traditional elements.

Furthermore, these observations could lead one to conclude that the so-called Canaanite religion was not really a separate religion from Yahwism and in dialectical opposition to it. Rather, as noted earlier in this chapter, these observations imply that Yahwism was the common religion of Palestinians in the pre-exilic period, it merely encompassed a wide range of activity which would be condemned in later years.[20] One

20. G. Anderson, *Sacrifices*, pp. 1-25; Mettinger, *In Search*, pp. 203-204.

could reinforce this argument by pointing to the great commonalities shared by the so-called Canaanite religion and Yahweh religion. When one senses that the above mentioned customs are perhaps natively Yahwistic, then the cultic phenomena traditionally attributed to Canaanite religion in order to distinguish it from Yahwism suddenly disappears; then those things held in common by Canaanite and Yahwistic devotees suddenly become more significant.

This is not to say that the religion of all Palestine was uniform. There were indeed regional variations, as indicated by the recalled differences between the cults of Samaria and Jerusalem in the biblical text. Perhaps throughout most of the pre-exilic period it would be fair to assume that highlanders might prefer to call upon the deity Yahweh in worship, while lowlanders preferred the names of El or Baal. One might observe some differences that would become significant over the years as classic Yahwism became differentiated. Mark Smith's model of Yahwism's gradual differentiation of religious beliefs from the mainline culture is an excellent way to envision the rise of classic Yahwism. But we must continue to stress that essentially there was no stark distinction between a specifically Canaanite or Israelite religion in the early years of settlement down through most of the monarchy; commonalities far outweighed any emerging differences. There were differences, to be sure, but we modern biblical theologians magnified them until they outshone the common religious heritage shared by all who lived in Palestine. Perhaps the most important characterization which could be made is to say that the average Israelite Yahweh devotee may not have sensed that he or she was religiously different from the so-called Canaanite population. That sense of difference is imported into the texts by much later generations. Further, the differences between Yahwistic cults in the various regions of Palestine could be as great as any difference between Yahwists and their non-Yahwist neighbors. If we could do a socio-religious study of early first millennium BCE Palestine, we probably would devise a spectrum of religious positions and arrive at no clear sense of where to draw the line between Yahwists and non-Yahwists.

With that in mind it is worth observing some of the truly significant similarities shared by the entire religious population of Palestine. In the very important area of cultic sacrifice Canaanite texts and the Hebrew Bible have the following common vocabulary: 1) slaughtered offering, *zebah*; 2) annual slaughtered offering, *zebah hayyamim*; 3) tribute offering, *selamim*; 4) vow, *neder*; 5) gift offering, *minhah*; 6) holocaust offering, *kalil*; 7) priest, *kohen*; and 8) cultic functionary, *qadesh*.[21] The common identity shared by El and Yahweh is impressive. Granted, biblical theologians speak of how Israel absorbed the persona of El into Yahweh, but this was possible only because the perception of El and Yahweh was so similar originally. Yahweh's personality may have changed and thus became capable of absorbing El only because Yahwists were part of the Canaanite scene. In the various texts El and Yahweh are both portrayed as: 1) father figures, 2) judges, 3) compassionate and merciful, 4) revealing themselves through dreams, 5) capable of healing those who were sick, 6) dwelling in a cosmic tent, 7) dwelling over the great cosmic waters or at the source of the primordial rivers, which is also on the top of a mountain, 8) favorable to the widow, orphan and the poor, 9) kings in the heavenly realm exercising authority over other gods, who may be called the 'sons of the gods', 10) warrior deities who led the other gods in battle, 11) creator deities, 12) aged and venerable in appearance, and most significantly 13) capable of guiding the destinies of people in the social arena.[22] The gradual synthesis of El and Yahweh was made possible also by particular religious crises in the land, including the entrance of a handful of zealous Yahweh devotees in the thirteenth or twelfth century BCE who merged with some El worshippers when they took for themselves the name Israel, and the later intrusion of the Phoenician or Tyrian Baal cult in the ninth century BCE which brought devotees of the local El cult and Yahweh devotees together in alliance. But ultimately the synthesis was possible only because of so many shared common beliefs.

The commonality between so-called Yahwists and so-called Canaanites is great when one considers the shared sacrificial vocabulary and views of the high god. If the customs attacked by the Deuteronomistic Historians and the later prophets were truly part of Yahwism, then any modern attempt to contrast pre-exilic Yahwism with Canaanite religion is bogus. Ezekiel spoke most truthfully when he said of the Judeans in Ezek. 16.3, 'Your origin and your birth were in the land of the Canaanites: your

21. Smith, *Early History of God*, p. 2. Cf. Schmidt, *Faith*, pp. 177-78; Sperling, 'Israel's Religion', p. 8.

22. Mihalik, 'Some Thoughts', pp. 11-19; Saggs, *Encounter*, pp. 197-98; T. Mullen, *The Assembly of the Gods: The Divine Council in Canaanite and Early Hebrew Literature* (HSM, 24; Chico, CA: Scholars Press, 1980), pp. 5, 201, 233, 282; Lang, 'König', p. 18; Smith, *Early History of God*, pp. 8-10; Day, 'Yahweh', pp. 181-84; R. Simkins, *Creator and Creation: Nature in the Worldview of Ancient Israel* (Peabody, MA: Henrickson, 1994), pp. 187-88.

father was an Amorite and your mother a Hittite'. Contemporary biblical scholars are beginning to appreciate the true depth of meaning in that statement, and how it should be the starting point for a discussion of Israelite religion.

III

New scholarly perception looks at the biblical texts and sees evidence of a complex early Yahwism which has far more continuity with the Canaanite milieu than formerly we had been wont to admit. How then do we presently write our histories of Israelite religion? We must stress more the continuity with typical West Semitic religious activity and no longer describe certain practices as Israelite and Canaanite respectively. We must sense the evolving nature of the Israelite religion as it slowly differentiated itself from the surrounding culture. We must acknowledge that it made the truly significant moves toward becoming a 'consummate religion' only late in the pre-exilic period and primarily during the exile and beyond. We must perceive how slow evolutionary changes led up to the revolutionary breakthrough in the exile. Ultimately, we must admit that monotheistic Yahwism became a reality only after the exile in the Second Temple period, and our past stereotypes of that age as dull and legalistic must give way to characterizations which stress its brilliance and creativity.

What basic outline might be given for survey of how Israelite or Jewish monotheism emerged? It is not my place in this short volume to write a history of Israelite religion. But a brief outline may be provided based upon the directions suggested by the critical scholars discussed in this volume.

Worship of a god under the name of Yahweh appears to have emerged outside the land of Palestine many years before the appearance of Israel. Egyptian texts in the second millennium BCE refer to the land called *Shasu-seir* and *Shasu-yhw*, which appears to be in the area of later Edom. Biblical traditions reinforce this by describing Yahweh's theophany coming from Seir in the wilderness of Paran (Deut. 33.2; Judg. 5.2). The exodus traditions imply that Yahweh was worshipped by Midian (Exod. 18). The kinship that early epic traditions attribute to Israel (Jacob) and Edom (Esau) in Genesis may reflect a common religious identity. Scholars suspect that the deity Qaus of Edom may be the same as Yahweh. When the inscription at Kuntillet 'Ajrûd speaks of 'Yahweh of Teman', this may be an old archaic name which further implies a wilderness origin in Edom.[23] So, where the biblical narrative traditions describe the theophany of Yahweh to Moses at Sinai in the wilderness, and the old poetry speaks of Yahweh's victorious military procession into the land with the people, many biblical scholars assume there is an old authentic historical memory of the the origin of the Yahweh cult or at least the name of Yahweh outside the land of Palestine.

According to the biblical narrative Joshua brought the worship of Yahweh into the land, and critical scholars believe that indeed some external, small group of immigrants from the south did enter the central Palestinian highlands of Ephraim and Manasseh bringing the name of Yahweh. They were probably more peaceful than the book of Joshua implies, and their real mode of gaining a foothold in the land was through alliances with other highland groups in Palestine, to which the book of Joshua also gives testimony, as with the alliance made with the people of Shechem (Josh. 24). Their entrance was essentially gradual and peaceful, and violence was quite limited—the book of Joshua actually indicates that they only took a few cities directly in the small tribal region of Benjamin and these narratives have been glorified greatly in the opinion of most commentators. Once in the land they amalgamated with their Canaanite neighbors, and took for themselves the Canaanite name Israel, which is compounded upon the divine name El. Likewise, whatever this early cult of Yahweh might have been, it quickly merged into the greater Palestinian religious scene. These outsiders became Canaanites. The emergence of the Israelite identity portrayed in the Bible would not develop until centuries later and then would be projected back into these stories by the biblical historians.

People already in the Palestinian highlands, including pastoralists and outlaw parasocials, would slowly melt together over the years to evolve into the people later called Israel. As they underwent this transformation, they probably did not have a clear sense of who they were other than the differences which separated them from lowlanders. Many had fled the lowlands and had an antipathy toward powerful city states and the enduring Egyptian presence in the lowlands. This could have given rise to an early exodus tradition about escape from Egypt, which only a very few might have experienced—but most would have seen in that tradi-

23. Bartlett, 'Edom', pp. 2-27; *idem*, 'Qaus', pp. 29-38; Theissen, *Biblical Faith*, pp. 52-53; Ahlström, *Israelites*, pp. 58-60; H. Shanks, 'Frank Moore Cross: An Interview', *Bible Review* 8.4 (1992), pp. 24-28, 61-62.

tion the memory of their withdrawal from the lowlands. Yahweh slowly became envisioned as the patron deity of many of these people, perhaps due to the connection with such an exodus story. However, other gods were not denied, and there was very little common religious or ethnic identity in the early years.[24]

Since Yahweh was a deity who originated outside the land, the stories about him naturally lacked certain elements. Yahweh was not part of a cosmogonic myth, he was not descended from a high god, nor was he associated with other gods in any clear way. He was a storm deity, a warrior god, and above all a loner in the divine realm. These aspects would be most important in the formation of later Yahwism. His isolation from the traditions of the West Semitic divine pantheon would be the early seeds which would later evolve into notions of Yahweh's exclusivity. The pressure of certain socio-historical circumstances, and especially the exile, ultimately would generate monotheism from these initial aspects of Yahweh's divine nature. Furthermore, the early Yahweh cult either lacked good icons by which to represent Yahweh or used them sparingly, and this may have been reinforced by an aniconic tradition connected to Yahweh by those early immigrants who brought him into the land of Palestine. Perhaps, their wanderings made such images an encumbrance or poverty made them impossible. The old traditions about the Ark of the Covenant and the Tent of Meeting in Exodus and Numbers may recall vaguely the poor and rustic worship of this traveling warrior deity.

Once in the land, Yahweh was portrayed sometimes by the bull image, so common for warrior deities in Syria and Palestine, and this is evidenced by the bull shrine found in the central highlands dating to the early Iron Age. Yet at some point Israelites became cautious about portraying Yahweh, and eventually disavowed all symbols for their chief deity. It is difficult to say how or when this aniconic thrust began to express itself seriously in the land of Palestine, for there is evidence that Yahweh was portrayed in physical form by some Israelites during the pre-exilic era.

An aniconic emphasis in the religion also carried with it social and economic implications. An aniconic cult reduces the power of the priests, who normally would control the icons; it limits the power of the rich, who could afford to contribute resources for making the icons. Indirectly a general equality of all devotees would be promoted. Different scholars propose a wide range of dates for the emergence of such assumptions in

24. Sperling, 'Israel's Religion', pp. 27-28.

the history of Israelite religion.[25] At any rate, it would seem that the tendencies toward exclusive worship and aniconic portrayal of Yahweh may be early. But these emphases do not indicate monotheism, for the gods of the nations are not rejected necessarily by such assumptions. Here we have the emergence of latent genetic mutations which will lie dormant in Israel's gene pool until a crisis will bring them together in the formulation of the 'consummate religion'—pure monotheism.

In the land of Palestine the equation of Yahweh with El or Baal would be natural, and often the bull image could be associated with any of the three. The equation with El would be the easiest in this regard, but whether Yahweh was similar to El before entry into the land is difficult to determine, since we can never be sure how much the old poetic traditions actually reflect any pre-settlement memories of Yahweh. But perhaps the old storm god image of Yahweh mellowed as images of the gracious and merciful El were absorbed into Yahweh's persona. One could say that Yahweh was absorbed into the West-Semitic pantheon of Palestine and ultimately absorbed all the deities in a process of gradual 'convergence'.

Over the years Yahweh was portrayed differently in the various shrines throughout the land, thus explaining why Absalom could refer to the 'Yahweh in Hebron' or Kuntillet 'Ajrûd spoke of the 'Yahweh of Teman'. In these regional cults maybe different portrayals resulted from how Baal and El images were found in varying degrees in Yahweh's persona. Over the years Yahweh gradually emerged out of the greater Palestinian matrix of deities and beliefs, but Yahweh retained specific characteristics of El and Baal according to religious needs and the res-

---

25. H.P. Müller, 'Gott und die Götter in den Anfängen der biblischen Religion: Zur Vorgeschichte des Monotheismus', *Monotheismus* (ed. Keel), p. 137; Lang, 'Yahweh-Alone', pp. 35-56; Schmidt, *Faith*, pp. 70-71, believes the concepts of divine exclusivity and aniconic beliefs laid the foundation for total development of Israel's religion (cf. his earlier work, *Das Erste Gebot*, [Theologische Existenz Heute, 165; Munich: Chr. Kaiser Verlag, 1969], *passim*); Miller, 'Israelite Religion', p. 212, believes the early demands of the Decalogue encouraged exclusive worship of Yahweh in aniconic fashion; Sperling, 'Israel's Religion', p. 27; R. Hendel, 'The Social Origins of the Aniconic Tradition in Early Israel', *CBQ* 50 (1988), pp. 365-82, believes an early aniconic emphasis created the anti-royal bias; T. Mettinger, 'Aniconism—a West Semitic Context for the Israelite Phenomenon?', *Ein Gott allein* (eds. Dietrich and Klopfenstein), pp. 159-78, believes an early aniconic tradition came to Israel from Tyre and other ancient Near Eastern cultures, which had the imagery of an invisible deity portrayed by an empty throne.

ponses to particular social-religious crises. This is what Mark Smith refers
to with his model of 'convergence' and 'differentiation' in the history of
Yahweh. Characteristics of the gods converged in Yahweh, while at the
same time Yahweh became differentiated from them into a position of
primacy. Yahweh's personality drew primarily upon El aspects, but to a
lesser degree upon the imagery of Baal and the fertility goddesses,
Asherah or Astarte.[26] In effect, there were two processes. The early
Yahweh quickly merged into the Palestinian religious melting pot, but
then slowly emerged years later stealing the attributes of those other
deities.

In his monumental work, *The Tribes of Yahweh*, Norman Gottwald
popularized the notion of 'mono-Yahwism' to describe the religion of
the newly emergent, revolutionary cadre of highland Israelites in Iron
Age I (1200–1050 BCE). Gottwald characterized these people as exclusively dedicated to Yahweh (although they were clearly not monotheists),
ignoring other gods, because such dedication went with their commitment to radical social egalitarianism in the new socio-religious communal
villages of highland Israel. In a similar vein, George Mendenhall in his
book, *The Tenth Generation*, speaks of the deep covenant commitment
of Israelites to Yahweh and the egalitarian religious beliefs connected to
his veneration. In recent years enthusiasm for their models of internal
social revolution and religious egalitarianism has waned, especially since
archaeologists now sense that Israelite identity arose in the highlands
slowly and peacefully, and any common identity was probably very
loose, limited and amorphous. The sense of unity probably did not begin
to take shape until the rise of David, and no true psychological unification ever brought Judah and Israel together. 'Mono-Yahwism' seems to
be a nice, but outdated, scholarly theological construct. Bernhard Lang
calls the model a 'modern idealization of Israel's origins, the romantic
idea of an ancient peasant revolt' and it is 'wishful thinking rather than a
plausible reconstruction'.[27] Perhaps the model of 'mono-Yawhism' went
too far in creating the image of a society that conforms to our modern
sociological paradigm of a peasant society. Nonetheless, there may be
truth in the model for describing the emergence of early highland
Israelites, and this author is tempted to retain the category.

As the highlanders developed their simple village life styles and sub-

---

26. Mullen, *Assembly*; Schmidt, *Faith*, pp. 138, 177-78; Smith, *Early History of
God*; Albertz, *Israelite Religion*, I, pp. 85-87; Day, 'Yahweh', pp. 187-88.

27. Lang, 'Yahweh-Alone', p. 18.

sequently interconnected with each other through trade networks, they slowly evolved a common identity. People attracted to this highland group may have been so for many reasons, including food, but some must have sought the egalitarianism which simple village life would bring. 'Anyone who sought to achieve social justice and security through economic independence joined this progressive new group', notes Gloria London, a leading advocate of the current model of highland settlement.[28] For this reason the exodus traditions might have spoken to deep psychological needs in those early settlements. Over the years Israelites developed a common identity in which they distinguished themselves from the lowlanders, and they portrayed the lowlanders in negative stereotypes 'in an attempt to mask the common bonds between the two communities'.[29] They differed from the lowlanders in economics, tribal and kinship structures (which were fictionally created by the highlanders), and ultimately in religion. The acceptance of Yahweh, the deity from the outside, as their clan and tribal deity, in ways reflected in the patriarchal narratives, became one of those modes of forming a new, cohesive identity.[30] The acceptance of this deity by the diverse highland groups was gradual but significant. Although they did not deny the existence of other gods, nor cease observing their rites, nonetheless Yahweh became their tribal deity—their patron god. In a sense, this is 'mono-Yahwism', their new emerging social existence was closely connected to a deity by the name of Yahweh, and gradually a special identity would develop around the worship of that deity. Although their religion probably did not appear very similar to the later biblical worldview, it was the first truly significant step in the direction of the future monotheistic revolution. Therefore, the concept of 'mono-Yahwism' is worth retaining, for it characterizes a people who had many gods, but one was truly significant for their emerging identity.

The earliest significant regional emergence of Yahweh may have been facilitated by the rise of David in the tenth century BCE. We now sense that David's kingdom was not as well-developed or in such total control of the Palestinian country as a quick reading of the biblical text might imply. His was not an empire in the true sense of that age, nor was it even a state; rather, it was probably a well developed chiefdom—a political entity held together by military strength and occasional raids

28. London, 'Comparison', p. 51.
29. London, 'Comparison', p. 51.
30. Dever, *Discoveries*, pp. 79-81.

against foreigners. This would explain his dependence upon a personal military cadre of mercenaries rather than a professional army, his inability to build a temple or even take a good census, and his need for a fortified city state, Jerusalem, to protect him from foreign invasion and most especially his own people (consider the number of rebellions he faced). Archaeological evidence indicates that a true state did not really emerge in Palestine in either Israel or Judah until the eighth century BCE.[31] The biblical text again has not deceived us so much as we have not read it clearly, for the aforementioned limitations of David's rule are recorded in the narratives of 2 Samuel.

David's policy of rule apparently included the elevation of Yahweh as the national deity. This did not exclude the worship of other deities, of course, otherwise Solomon could not have erected so many shrines to foreign deities. But it provided significant impetus for Yahweh to emerge above El and Baal and set Yahweh on the course to become the national high god for most Palestinians.[32]

It was a common phenomenon for petty states, chiefdoms and groups of people in Syria and Palestine to revere a relatively small number of deities in their pantheons along with one high god, who was the national deity of the political entity. Often the emergence of a national high god paralleled state formation, and this may have provided much of the impetus for Yahweh's emergence as the chief god, especially with the accelerated process of state formation in Israel and Judah in the eighth and seventh centuries BCE. Surrounding the high deity would be several other gods in the typical pantheon of Syria and Palestine, far fewer than the enlarged pantheons of Egypt and Mesopotamia. Some scholars suspect the tendency to revere fewer gods was occurring all over the ancient Near East in the first millennium BCE. At any rate, as a typical West Semitic deity Yahweh would have four or five compatriot gods in attendance as he became the national high god. Theoretically this could have included the following: a consort fertility deity (Asherah or Astarte), the sun god (unless Yahweh was one and the same), Baal (unless these baalim were merely spirits of the earth), the moon god, the god of the

---

31. Jamieson-Drake, *Scribes*, pp. 48-80 *et passim*; Davies, *Search*, pp. 67-70; Thompson, *Early History*, *passim*; Whitelam, 'Identity', p. 65; Ash, 'Solomon's? District? List', pp. 70-72; Lemche, 'Kann vor einer', pp. 65-66.

32. Vorländer, 'Krise des Exils', pp. 101-102; *idem*, 'Popular Religion', p. 67; Lang, 'Yahweh-Alone', p. 21; Theissen, *Biblical Faith*, p. 54; Ahlström, *Israelites*, pp. 93-94; Smith, *Early History of God*, pp. 55, 147-48.

underworld and human sacrifice (possibly Molech), and El (who probably was equated with Yahweh in the minds of many). Thus, there may have been between three and six subordinate deities, all possibly included in the expression, 'the heavenly host'. This was a typical West Semitic pantheon, comparable to the divine lordship of Chemosh over Moab, Milcom over Ammon, and Qaus over Edom, all of whom may have used the same names as Israel did for the subordinate deities. As these subordinate deities in Israel were polemicized over the years, their attributes were absorbed by Yahweh (convergence) who gradually emerged to receive exclusive devotion (differentiation).[33] The royal court began the process of elevating Yahweh even though it was polytheistic.[34]

Outside of the sponsorship of the royal court there was no social or intellectual force to push Yahweh as the sole god until specific religious crises caused the impetus for religious evolution. Biblical texts offer a very selective view of the pre-exilic era, so scholars may never reconstruct all the significant steps in the religious evolution of Israelite belief and the emergence of monotheism. But on the basis of meagre evidence scholars suspect that significant change came with the following stages: 1) the revolt of Elijah, Elisha and Jehu; 2) the oracles of Hosea; 3) the reform of Hezekiah; 4) the reform of Josiah; 5) the oracles of Jeremiah and Ezekiel; 6) the Deuteronomistic History, completed in exile; and 7) the expression of 'consummate' monotheism in Second Isaiah, the final revolutionary breakthrough and culmination of the evolutionary process. Each of these may be seen as a step in which ideas crystalized and individuals inspired a group which subsequently transmitted this thought and sometimes implemented programs of reform. The dynamic of advance requires both a significant individual thinker(s), and equally important, a community to preserve, develop and communicate those new ideas.[35]

In the ninth century BCE the devotion to Baal of Tyre was introduced into Israel by the Omride dynasty and zealously promulgated by Jezebel,

---

33. Smith, *Early History of God*, pp. xxiii-xxiv, 25-26, 145-46 *et passim*, also notes that since El was not polemicized, El must have been absorbed into Yahweh at an early date, p. 8. Day, 'Yahweh', pp. 188-93; and Niehr, 'JHWH', p. 320, speak of how Yahweh must have presided over a pantheon.

34. Baly, 'The Geography of Monotheism', p. 268; Vorländer, 'Krise des Exils', pp. 101-102; Lang, 'Yahweh-Alone', p. 21; Halpern, 'Brisker Pipes', p. 84; Smith, *Early History of God*, p. xxiv.

35. Bardtke, 'Erweckungsbewegungen', pp. 17-34.

wife of Ahab and the high priestess for Baal of Tyre, as well as being the daughter of the king of Tyre. Scholars think that Israelites sensed this Baal was different from the Baal or baalim native to Canaan. It is possible that foreign intrusion awakened Israelite national religious consciousness and even brought El worshippers and Yahweh worshippers together in common opposition to the Phoenician Baal. Maybe Elijah's name, 'Yahweh is my El', is a title he assumed, if his real name was Micaiah-ben-Imlah, to proclaim the equation of El and Yahweh against the foreign Baal. It has been noted that after Elijah's victory at Carmel the priests of Baal were killed but not the attendant priests of Asherah (1 Kgs 18.19, 40). When Jehu's rebellion overthrew the Omrides and the foreign Baal devotees, this so-called radical Yahwist did not remove the golden calves, the asherim, or even the native baalim, other cultic objects considered to be odious by the later Deuteronomistic Historians (2 Kgs 9–10, and especially 10.29-31). This has led critical scholars to conclude that Elijah, Elisha and Jehu engaged in a crusade only to exclude foreign deities, and their actions were more nationalistic in focus than a mono-theistic reform movement. To be sure, the Deuteronomistic Historians tended to stress the exclusive devotion to Yahweh in the revolution, but they were reading the events of the ninth century BCE though the eyes of sixth-century BCE thinkers. Nonetheless, the attack on foreign deities awakened Israelite religious consciousness and unified some of the diverse groups of religious devotees in Palestine. This planted more seeds, or shall we say 'created latent genes', which would lead further to the emergence of monotheism.[36]

Hosea (750–720 BCE) may have been the first classical prophet to attack internal religious elements as unacceptable to the Yahwistic religion, especially the golden calves. If so, this was a significant advance from the days of Elijah. Hosea may have been more responsible than his pre-decessors for actualizing the notions of Yahweh's exclusivity and image-less portrayal. Either those trajectories began with him or he significantly

---

36. Nikiprowetsky, 'Ethical Monotheism', pp. 80-82; Ahlström, 'King Jehu', pp. 52-61; Stolz, 'Monotheismus in Israel', pp. 175-76; Lang, 'Yahweh-Alone', pp. 19, 26-30; *idem*, 'König', p. 18; *idem*, 'Segregation', p. 120; Ottosson, 'Elijah's Visit', pp. 185-98; G. Hentschel, 'Elija und der Kult des Baal', *Gott, der Einzige* (ed. Haag), pp. 54-90; Halpern, 'Brisker Pipes', p. 92; Smith, *Early History of God*, p. 150; Weippert, 'Synkretismus', p. 161; Schniedewind, 'History and Interpretation', pp. 649-61; J. Jeremias, 'Der Begriff "Baal" im Hoseabuch und seine Wirkungsgeschichte', *Ein Gott allein* (eds. Dietrich and Klopfenstein), p. 458.

advanced them. His critique may have blossomed in the later classical prophetic movement. Yet it must be admitted that he did not appear to deny the existence of other gods. He was not a radical monotheist, nor were the other classical prophets. But his critique of internal religious phenomena laid the groundwork for the eventual shape of later monotheistic Yahwism. He and the other classical prophets may sound monotheistic at times, but the evolutionary trajectory was still in the early stages. They may be rightly called Yahweh-aloneists, but they were not yet theoretical monotheists.[37] From this point onward, the intelligentsia were tempted to see Yahweh in more universal terms, as Israel and Judah became involved increasingly in the international politics of that age. Political conflict of that era led them to view Yahweh's might over other peoples (as in Amos) and this evolved into later ideas of universal dominion. Monotheism's ultimate development may have been affected greatly by Assyrian religious imperialism, which caused the classical prophets to respond with their own rhetoric about the universal rule of Yahweh, especially with later prophets like Zephaniah and Nahum.[38]

Hezekiah's reform appears to reflect Hosea's agenda in the southern state of Judah a generation later (710–700 BCE). By removing the bronze serpent or *Nehushtan*, Hezekiah eliminated an old Yahweh symbol which might have been used as an image of Yahweh. Other activities also make him appear to be a forerunner of Deuteronomic reform under Josiah and as someone moving in a monotheistic direction. The Deuteronomistic History praises only Hezekiah and Josiah as truly good kings in

37. Baly, 'Geography of Monotheism', p. 268; McKeating, *Amos*, p. 92; Smith, 'Religious Parties', pp. 42-44; Lindblom, *Prophecy*, pp. 332-35; Lang, 'Yahweh-Alone', pp. 19-20, 30-36; 'Segregation', p. 116; H.-W. Jüngling, 'Der Heilige Israels: Der erste Jesaja zum Thema "Gott"', *Gott, der Einzige* (ed. Haag), pp. 91-114; Albertz, *Israelite Religion*, I, pp. 65, 173-75; Dietrich, 'Werden und Wesen', p. 18; de Pury, 'Erwägungen', pp. 413-39; Jeremias, 'Der Begriff', pp. 441-62; O. Loretz, 'Das "Ahnen- und Götterstatuen-Verbot" im Dekalog und die Einzigkeit Jahwes. Zum Begriff der Göttlichen in altorientalischen und alttestamentlichen Quellen', *Ein Gott allein* (eds. Dietrich and Klopfenstein), pp. 494-95; E.K. Holt, *Prophesying the Past: The Use of Israel's History in the Book of Hosea* (JSOTSup, 194; Sheffield: Sheffield Academic Press, 1995), pp. 107-15.

38. Lang, 'Yahweh-Alone', p. 21; Smith, *Early History of God*, p. 149; Dietrich, 'Werden und Wesen', p. 19; *idem*, 'Der Eine Gott als Symbol politischen Widerstands: Religion und Politik im Juda des 7. Jahrhunderts', *Ein Gott allein* (eds. Dietrich and Klopfenstein), pp. 463-90.

Judah. Some critical scholars accept the significance of his role in the evolutionary process,[39] but others suspect that his reforms may have been exaggerated by the Deuteronomistic Historians to make him appear as a forerunner to Josiah. Lowell Handy, for example, suggests the destruction of the *Nehushtan* was a singular event, and the closing of the shrines outside of Jerusalem's Temple was merely done in preparation for the Assyrian military advance so as to protect the statues of gods in those shrines. Hezekiah was a polytheist in Handy's opinion.[40] Until some archaeological clues are discovered, the final verdict on the reality of Hezekiah's reform must remain undecided. If it is assumed he did contribute to the monotheistic trajectory, his activities are a logical follow-up to the prophetic critique of Hosea.[41]

Josiah's reform is perceived by scholars as a truly extensive movement which affirms exclusive devotion to Yahweh, opposition to all foreign and internal cultic abuses, and comes close to being truly monotheistic (2 Kgs 23.1-25). He is the hero of the Deuteronomistic History and portrayed as the true messianic successor to David. In 2 Kings 23 he is said to have removed from the Temple all idolatrous priests and the vessels for Baal and Asherah, closed all other shrines outside Jerusalem, destroyed the great Asherah image, removed male prostitutes, destroyed high places of sacrifice, destroyed the Topheth, removed the horses dedicated to the sun and burned their chariots, removed the altars to the sun erected by Ahaz and Manasseh, destroyed Solomon's old shrines, destroyed the shrines at Samaria and Bethel in the north, descrated bones, killed a number of opposition priests, removed the ephod, and exiled mediums and wizards. He was quite busy! This was a radical reform, and critical scholars sense the importance of his role in emerging monotheism. Bernhard Lang sees a coalition of social groups fighting for monotheism at this time: priests who wanted the Temple to be the center of religious life, merchants who would profit from pilgrimages to Jerusalem, the king who desired political centralization, and, above all, the 'Yahweh-alone' movement.[42] Josiah's reform was probably the beginning of the radical breakthrough to monotheism.

After Josiah's defeat the impetus of monotheistic development seems

39. Theissen, *Biblical Faith*, pp. 55-56; Lang, 'Segregation', p. 117; Albertz *Israelite Religion*, I, p. 181.

40. L. Handy, 'Hezekiah's Unlikely Reform', *ZAW* 100 (1988), pp. 111-15.

41. Saggs, *Encounter*, p. 23; Lang, 'Yahweh-Alone', pp. 36-38.

42. Lang, 'Yahweh-Alone', pp. 20, 38-41.

to have been reversed according to the testimony in 2 Kings and the oracles of Jeremiah and Ezekiel, but the voices of prophetic dissent still called for the exclusive devotion to Yahweh and the concomitant social justice that had been expressed in the laws of the Deuteronomic Reform movement (Deut. 12–26). Jeremiah and Ezekiel proclaimed their messages in Judah and the exile respectively, and both appear to have voiced beliefs extremely close to pure monotheism. Perhaps their contact with Babylonian thought helped to engender views of Yahweh as a universal deity, a creator of the heavens and the earth, who had a plan for all peoples, for this imagery seems to move beyond the religious values in the Israelites' faith up to that time in the opinion of some authors.[43] Their prophetic oracles paved the way for the thought of Second Isaiah later in the exile.

The Deuteronomistic History may have received its final redaction in the exile, as many suggest. Its interpretative view of Israel's religious history appears virtually monotheistic, not only in its condemnation of foreign cults, but also by its even more consistent portrayal of traditional Yahwistic religious activities as pagan. This historical-religious interpretation is the culmination of a process perhaps begun by Hosea to internally redefine Yahwism. In this worldview the golden calves are associated now with Baal and not Yahweh; Asherah becomes Baal's consort and not Yahweh's; the asherim, local shrines, and the high places are condemned routinely; and the people of Israel are portrayed as though they should have been monotheistic in their practice since the time of Moses. The Deuteronomistic History is really speaking about how religious life should have been rather than objectively as it actually was (and yet it truly admits the polytheistic nature of pre-exilic religion by its many allusions to those practices).[44] Previous oral epic traditions, like the Yahwist and the Elohist (if these traditions actually existed), were monolatrous at best, but not truly monotheistic. Perhaps, when they were merged together into one epic, a very polemical monolatry may have been evident, but that is difficult to assess.[45] As a document the Deuteronomistic History is the first radical expression of the exclusive worship of

43. Saggs, *Encounter*, pp. 43-51.
44. Schniedewind, 'History', pp. 660-61; de Pury, 'Erwägungen', pp. 414-15.
45. Hossfeld, 'Einheit', pp. 60-68; E. Zenger, 'Das jahwistische Werk—ein Wegbereiter des jahwistischen Monotheismus?', *Gott, der Einzige* (ed. Haag), pp. 26-53, who observes that the Yahwist has 'unpolemical monolatry', but when the Yahwist and Elohist were combined a very 'polemical monolatry' became evident.

Yahweh. It was also the first written 'scriptures' of the Jews, to which Genesis through Numbers would later be added (after Priestly revisions), and it would exert a powerful influence upon the development of post-exilic Judaism.

As one reads through the Deuteronomistic History there are strong monotheistic statements in both Deuteronomy and the narrative materials of Joshua through 2 Kings. Most commentators are convinced that these texts are part of the final exilic or even post-exilic redaction, thus making their thought contemporary with Second Isaiah. The pre-exilic edition generated under Josiah's rule may not have been radically monotheistic, because it was still addressing an audience with strong polytheistic assumptions.[46] However, the final exilic form of the history moves from a form of monolatry to a more monotheistic tone. Noteworthy passages reflecting monotheistic assumptions include the following,

> (Deut. 4.35, 39) '...the Lord is God; there is no other besides him...the Lord is God in heaven above and on the earth beneath; there is no other.'
> (Deut. 6.4) 'Hear, O Israel: The Lord our God is one Lord.'
> (Deut. 32.39) 'See now that I, even I, am he; there is no god besides me.'
> (2 Sam. 7.22 = 1 Chron. 17.20) 'Therefore you are great, O Lord God; for there is no one like you, and there is no god besides you.'
> (1 Kgs 8.60) 'So that all the peoples of the earth may know that the Lord is God; there is no other' (Solomon's Prayer).
> (2 Kgs 19.19) 'So now, O Lord our God, save us, I pray you, from his hand, so that all the kingdoms of the earth may know that you, O Lord, are God alone' (Hezekiah's Prayer).

Yet there is some limitation in the rhetoric of these Deuteronomistic passages; there is not quite yet a categorical denial of the existence of all other deities save Yahweh. The expressions that imply Yahweh is alone in the heavens could still be the hyperbole we find in comparable ancient Near Eastern hymns and prayers to a specific deity. The strong emphasis in Deuteronomy upon covenant allegiance to Yahweh may indicate that the people thus addressed were still polytheistic, and the covenant process leads them to reject service to those other gods. Deuteronomic rhetoric may exhibit the characteristics of 'monarchical monotheism', the praise of one deity as the greatest in the heavens.[47]

---

46. Lang, 'Yahweh-Alone', p. 45; Höffken, 'Bemerkung', pp. 88-93; Braulik, 'Deuteronomium', pp. 115-59; Vorländer, 'Popular Religion', p. 95; Dietrich, 'Werden und Wesen', p. 19; de Pury, 'Erwägungen', p. 413.

47. Wildberger, 'Deuterojesajas', p. 520; Stolz, 'Monotheismus in Israel',

Second Isaiah, however, provides us with what is the revolutionary breakthrough to monotheism, and most scholars acknowledge that his is an absolute and universalistic monotheism developed well beyond the thought of his predecessors.[48] Second Isaiah not only denies the existence of other gods, he ridicules the idol statuary and the craftspersons who make the idols (Isa. 41.21-29, 40.18-20, 44.9-20, 45.20-22, 46.1-2, 48.3-8). The extent of such criticism indicates that in this prophet we have an aggressive monotheist with strident rhetoric. In numerous places the prophet speaks of the sole existence of Yahweh, and the following are but a few good examples,

(43.10-11) '...I am he. Before me no god was formed, nor shall there be any after me. I, I am the Lord, and besides me there is no savior.'
(44.6-8) 'I am the first and I am the last; besides me there is no god... Is there any god besides me? There is no other rock; I know not one.'
(45.5-6) 'I am the Lord; and there is no other; besides me there is no god... I am the Lord, and there is no other.'
(45.18) 'I am the Lord; and there is no other.'
(45.21-22) 'Was it not I, the Lord? There is no other god besides me, a righteous God and a Savior; there is no one besides me. Turn to me and be saved, all the ends of the earth! For I am God, and there is no other.'
(46.9) 'For I am God; and there is no other; I am God, and there is no one like me.'
(47.10) 'I am, and there is no one besides me.'
(48.11-12) 'My glory I will not give to another. Listen to me, O Jacob, and Israel, whom I called: I am He; I am the first, and I am the last.'

pp. 181-82; Braulik, 'Deuteronomium', pp. 115-59; Sperling, 'Israel's Religion', p. 23; Loretz, 'Einzigkeit Jahwes', pp. 509-11, 519; Armstrong, *History of God*, p. 23. Braulik, 'Deuteronomium', pp. 138-54, however, maintains that the final exilic redaction of Deuteronomy is truly monotheistic and it antedates Second Isaiah with its consistent monotheism.

48. Lindblom, *Prophecy*, pp. 332-35, 377; A.S. Herbert, *Isaiah 40–66* (Cambridge Bible Commentary; Cambridge: Cambridge University Press, 1975), pp. 127-28; Nikiprowetsky, 'Ethical Monotheism', p. 82; Wildberger, 'Deuterojesajas', pp. 506-30, calls him the 'cornerstone' of monotheism in Israel; Saggs, *Encounter*, pp. 43-52; Stolz, 'Monotheismus in Israel', pp. 179-80; Vorländer, 'Krise des Exils', pp. 95-97; Lang, 'Yahweh-Alone', pp. 41-50; M. Lind, 'Monotheism, Power, and Justice: A Study in Isaiah 40–55', *CBQ* 46 (1984), pp. 432-46; Tremmel, *Religion*, p. 136; H. Klein, 'Der Beweis der Einzigkeit Jahwes bei Deutero-jesaja', *VT* 35 (1985), pp. 267-73; Lohfink, 'Zur Geschichte', pp. 9-25; Theissen, *Biblical Faith*, pp. 65-66; Sperling, 'Israel's Religion', pp. 6, 28; Uffenheimer, 'Ancient Israel', p. 146; Mettinger, *In Search*, pp. 204-205; Albertz, *Israelite Religion*, II, pp. 417-18; Dietrich, 'Werden und Wesen', p. 19; Loretz, 'Einzigkeit Jahwes', pp. 512-14.

This imagery is intensified by the many resounding allusions to Yahweh's primordial creation of the world, his maintenance of world order, and the direction of history, especially for the sake of his captive people. The thunderous language of creation theology carries the constant reminder that Yahweh accomplished these mighty deeds of old alone. With Second Isaiah's oracles we have arrived at true monotheism.

Critical scholars have suggested that Second Isaiah may be indebted to Babylonian thought or Persian Zoroastrian religious belief. The image of a dramatic creation of the world and the establishment of a grand plan for human history sounds as though it could have been inspired by motifs from the cult of Marduk, the creator god of Babylon, and the *Enuma Elish*, the creation account acted out in Babylon during the New Year's *akitu* festival, which Second Isaiah could have observed. This would have inspired in the prophet's imagination themes that resonated with the old El creator images from Palestine, and the result was a synthesis of traditional Yahwistic language and newly inspired ideas which are found in the majestic oracles of Isaiah 40–55.[49] However, H.W.F. Saggs provocatively suggests that maybe Nabonidus's religious reforms, which elevated the moon god Sin to prominence among the Babylonian deities, may have been inspired around 550 BCE by Jews in exile.[50] Numerous scholars suggest that Jewish contact with Persian monotheism may have sparked the intellectual breakthrough in Second Isaiah.[51]

These observations may be correct. But it is a truism in history that a people will hear and absorb from another culture that which they are ready to hear, or that which moves in an intellectual direction which they have begun to consider already. Israelites were moving toward a monotheistic breakthrough before the exile; contact with foreign thought further encouraged them in this development and perhaps offered them some language for the concepts they had been seeking to articulate. Foreign contact only would have increased the momentum of the process; it did not begin it.

---

49. Saggs, *Encounter*, pp. 43-52; Davies, *Search*, p. 116; Thompson, *Early History*, pp. 415-23.

50. Saggs, *Civilization*, p. 16.

51. M. Smith, 'II Isaiah and the Persians', *JAOS* 83 (1963), pp. 415-21; Vorländer, 'Krise des Exils', pp. 104-106; Lang, 'Yahweh-Alone', pp. 47-48; M. Boyce, 'Persian Religion in the Achemenid Age', *The Cambridge History of Judaism*. I. *Introduction; The Persian Period* (eds. W.D. Davies and L. Finkelstein; Cambridge: Cambridge University Press, 1984), pp. 282-83; Garbini, *History*, pp. 95-101; Thompson, *Early History*, pp. 415-23; Loretz, 'Einzigkeit Jahwes', pp. 514-15.

The return from exile began for Jews in the era we call the Second Temple period (539 BCE to 70 CE). It was an age in which monotheism was established among the Jews. Monotheistic values came back with the exiles upon their return to Judah; the beliefs were reinforced further with the aid of the newly generated scripture scrolls created by scribes, the Law and the Prophets. These would be promulgated in Jerusalem by Ezra (458 or 398 BCE) and exert considerable force upon the development of the Jewish ethos. True monotheism arose among the people as a Second Temple period phenomenon along with the notion of sacred scriptures. Julius Wellhausen and others viewed this period of Jewish formation as an age of sterility and legalism. Here he was most wrong. This was the truly creative period for monotheism and the Jewish religion, as it captured the masses and worked out the implications of the monotheistic revolution.

Some critical scholars, like Bernhard Lang, believe the development of the monotheistic faith still went through significant stages of development in the post-exilic age. He sees Proverbs 1–9, a post-exilic piece of literature, still fighting for monotheism in its portrayal of 'Dame Wisdom', for this was an attempt to undercut the still living and vibrant cult of Asherah by making her into personified wisdom and thereby subordinate to Yahweh.[52] The evidence that Jews in the Egyptian diaspora at Elephantine still worshipped other gods (including Anatyahu, a combination of Anat and Yahweh) provides an argument that the battle for monotheism raged somewhere in worldwide Judaism.[53] But the forces dedicated to monotheism would prevail ultimately.

In conclusion, the post-exilic era or Second Temple period should no longer be an era despised by historians as intellectually barren, legalistic and uncreative. Rather, it was an era in which Judaism, monotheism and the Bible truly arose, an era of creativity and perhaps continuing conflict and evolution in religious belief. It would be from the matrix or maelstrom of belief in this era that the great religions of Rabbinic Judaism and Christianity would be born, the twin pillars of modern European culture.

---

52. Lang, *Wisdom*, pp. 136 *et passim*. The same observations are made by Klopfenstein, 'Auferstehung', pp. 531-42; and Schroer, 'Sophia', pp. 543-58.

53. Nikiprowetsky, 'Ethical Monotheism', p. 77; Vorländer, 'Krise des Exils', p. 102; Y. Elkana, 'The Emergence of Second-order Thinking in Classical Greece', *Axial Age Civilizations* (ed. Eisenstadt), p. 59.

IV

There is even more to the story than the scenario of Israel's religious odyssey toward monotheism. We must step back and view this age from an even broader historical and cultural perspective. Israel was an important part of a dynamic intellectual advance which was occurring across the ancient world, from China to Egypt. This great intellectual movement in the civilized centers of the Old World has been called the 'Axial Age' by modern authors, who have analyzed the social, religious, philosophical and technological breakthroughs of that age. Monotheism was one of the great intellectual elements which emerged in that world-wide process. Second Isaiah was part of that advance. Heir to a great Israelite tradition, living in cosmopolitan Babylon where he was surrounded by intellectual currents flowing in from all over the world, he and other Jews were capable of a quantum leap in their religious synthesis. Thus, in that maelstrom of ideas and religious pieties Judaism was born and the breakthrough to monotheism occurred. We must learn to appreciate that their advance was part of a much wider human development also. The foundations of the intellectual and religious heritage we have today were born in that 'Axial Age' (800–400 BCE). For in that age there came the teachings of Confucius and Lao-Tzu in China, the final collections of the *Rig-Veda* and the *Atharva-Veda* from the Brahmanic priestly circles in India, the *Upanishads* from the great *sunnyasi* and other intellectuals in India, Siddharta Gautama (the Buddha), the most successful Upanishadic teacher in India and founder of Buddhism, perhaps Zoroaster in Persia (unless he lived earlier), the great intellectual tradition of Greek historians (Hecataeus, Herodotus, Thucydides, etc.), playwrights (Sophocles, Aeschylus, Euripides, Eumenides, Aristophanes, etc.), and philosophers (Socrates, Plato, Aristotle, etc.), and, of course, the Jewish faith and scriptures in the exile and early Second Temple period. It was a great age in the history of humanity.

Throughout this entire era of Israelite and Jewish existence from 1200 BCE to 70 CE these people were on an evolutionary trajectory to lay the foundation for western culture. Their accomplishments were made possible because they drew upon the ideas of civilizations far older than themselves, and they reconstructed those ideas into a new synthesis. They were able to do this, in part, because they sat 'at the edge' of those great civilizations. In particular, they were located in the trade corridor of Syria-Palestine which connected the river valley cultures of

Egypt and Mesopotamia. Not only were they heir to the traditional values of second millennium BCE Canaanite culture, but they also encountered the thought of these other two great centers of civilization. They were a simple people, new in the arena of world history, and they could appropriate cultural values from the older civilizations, use what they found of value for their social matrix, and reconfigure it slowly into their own society. This gave them a creative edge.

Social historians speak of such a people as a 'peripheral people', because they sat at the edge or the periphery of the great cultures and drew from them significant ideas and technology. The sociological implications of being such a peripheral people were discussed first by the great sociologist Max Weber.[54] He saw the cultural accomplishments of Israel and Greece to be the result of their function as peripheral societies, which could restructure creatively the values they had taken from old unchanging, complex societies of the great river valleys. Whereas the older societies feared social, intellectual, and scientific change because of the social chaos which might result, new and relatively simple societies could undertake social experiments with old ideas in a new form and thus accomplish significant social and intellectual progress. Many of the great accomplishments of the ancient world may be observed in peripheral societies of the first millennium BCE, such as Greece, Israel, Phoenicia, Persia, and perhaps to some extent in the previous millennium with the Hittites.

Using the paradigm of a peripheral society to understand the experience of Israelites and later Jews may be very helpful. As the earliest Israelites moved from the Palestinian cities in the lowlands to settle in the highlands and interact with entering pastoralists and outlaw elements, they formed early Iron Age I (1200–1050 BCE) farming villages. They were already a peripheral people in Palestine. As a new Iron Age society they began to reconstruct their social and material world out of the elements of the old Bronze Age society. Many cultures were doing this at that time. But they stayed 'peripheral', that is, they remained on the edge of the great cultural spheres of Egypt and Mesopotamia. They were not burdened by the complex social structures of the river valley cultures, they were free to implement new ideas which were drawn from those cultures. Although trade kept them in contact for years, the age of imperial warrior states—Assyria, Chaldean Babylon and Persia—brought them face to face with many new ideas. This stimulated further growth

54. Weber, *Judaism*, pp. xvii-xix, 7-8, 252-63, *et passim.*

and transformation after 750 BCE especially, including the rise of a more
organized state system in Israel and Judah and also the increased impetus
toward monotheism.

Peripheral cultures, like Israel and the later Jews, make great advances
because they can disrespect the complex social patterns of older cultures
which demand adherence. They are simple societies, often newly emergent, and they are not burdened with the social and economic needs, nor
the religious and legal agenda, of their predecessors. For example, the
Phoenicians invented the alphabet, because as merchants they required
an efficient book-keeping system. They did not respect the scribal
monopoly on complex hieroglyphs and cuneiform held by the great scribal
guilds in the river valleys. Israelites and Jews made the breakthrough to
monotheism, because they did not respect the large pantheons of deities
and the great priestly guilds, nor did they have the large number of arti-
sans devoted to the creation of sacred art and statuary and the necessary
provisioners of such great human institutions, all of which were
entrenched firmly in the societies of the river valley states. In a similar
vein, the Israelites lacked the large temple establishments, which were
nerve centers of trade, economic activity such as banking, art patronage
and other activities which are part of the healthy performance of a complex society's social matrix. Monotheism entails the rejection of many of
these things and would cause tremendous social-economic chaos in a
complex society. This is why Akhenaton failed in Egypt. A simple, new
society can create monotheism, provided it has an urban setting sufficiently large to support the religious intelligentsia capable of creating and
sustaining the movement, and only in those circumstances where the
urban setting is not too complex to be dislocated by the introduction of
the social and economic agenda of monotheistic belief. Israel was just
such a society, and even more so, the Jews in exile met those conditions,
especially because they were trying to reconstruct their society in a
foreign land. It would be socially and psychologically easier to integrate
monotheism and its concomitant values in a situation of political, religious and economic reconstruction. In exile the Jews may be seen to function quite clearly as a peripheral society even though they lived in the
middle of a great civilization. Greece and Persia, too, were peripheral
societies. Greece lay at the edge of the ancient world and produced philosophy, science, great art and the empirical method by advancing the
cultural achievements garnered from the neighboring cultures in Asia

Minor, Phoenicia, Egypt and ultimately Mesopotamia.[55] Persia lay in the highlands at the edge of the Mesopotamia cultural sphere, and they produced religion, efficient bureaucratic government, and a concept of law that contributed to world-wide civilization. Israel was one of several peripheral societies which have contributed to our modern world.

Israel arose at a crucial juncture in history, the beginning of the Iron Age. For the next five hundred years (1200–700 BCE) technological and social transformation occurred throughout the ancient Near East from India to Egypt and up into Greece and the Balkans. Israel, as a peripheral people, was on the 'cutting edge' of this advance; they were one of the new, fresh peoples in the Iron Age advance.[56] This process accelerated for them once the encounter with the great empires began, after 750 BCE, and their development then became part of the great Axial Age advance. Their proximity to high cultures and their intellectual leaders, from the pre-exilic Yahweh-alone minority to the monotheists of the exile, reshaped old values into a new system of thought. They created something new out of something very old.

Jews in exile were still a peripheral people in the middle of a great river valley civilization, for they refused to become part of the social fabric of Mesopotamia and chose instead to separate themselves by observation of Priestly laws. Basically, they rejected the values of the surrounding culture and functioned in some ways as though they were still in the highlands of Palestine. This self-imposed isolation made them distant from their neighbors, but they could draw upon the values of that great culture when they chose to do so, and they could reshape and rearticulate great ideas according to their own worldview. They were peripheral but very close to a source of inspiration; they could learn and reject ideas at the same time. They were 'culturally peripheral' now by virtue of their own created social and intellectual structures, whereas before the exile they had been 'geographically peripheral'. In this new setting their potential for intellectual development and breakthrough to new ideas was enhanced greatly. The pre-exilic religious and intellectual trajectories came to fulfillment. They now made the great leap forward to radical monotheism. Being 'geographically peripheral' in Palestine

55. H. Frankfort, 'The Emancipation of Thought from Myth', *Before Philosophy* (ed. H. Frankfort; Baltimore: Penguin Books, 1949), pp. 237-63.
56. Weber, *Judaism*, pp. xvii-xix, 7-8, 252-63; W. Davisson and J. Harper, *European Economic History*. I. *The Ancient World* (New York: Appleton, Century & Crofts, 1972), pp. 30-85; Gnuse, *Steal*, pp. 55-56.

allowed them to attain monolatry or henotheism, but being 'culturally peripheral' in Babylon enabled them to attain monotheism.

As they were surrounded by a foreign culture and as they sought the identity found in the company of fellow Jews, the common Jewish folk were inclined to accept the monotheistic values which formerly had been the property only of the intelligentsia. As a result, the pressures of exile in a foreign land caused monotheism to be the belief system of all Jews, not just the intelligentsia or the prophetic minority. Only in such unusual circumstances could a monumental evolutionary breakthrough in human culture such as monotheism become established effectively. Had the Jews remained in Palestine, they probably never would have attained pure monotheism, for they never would have experienced a crisis sufficiently great to generate such an intellectual leap.

V

The movement toward a monotheistic breakthrough in the exile experienced by the Jews was not an isolated experiment, for in the Axial Age monotheistic notions were emerging elsewhere in great centers of civilization. Scholars refer to the monotheistic ideas found in the speculative writings of India, the writings of great Greek thinkers, especially Xenophanes or Xenophon of Colophon—a pre-Socratic, and the religious teachings of Zoroaster or Zarathustra in Persia. Zoroastrianism usually receives the greatest attention in this regard, but this religion may be part of a greater Indo-Iranian religious phenomenon worthy of mention. Although a thorough discussion of Indo-Iranian religion is beyond the scope of this work, some consideration ought to be given to the monotheistic impulse found in that tradition.

Monotheism is unnatural. At best monism is all that should emerge from a reflective group of the intelligentsia. Monism finds the unity behind the diverse deities without denying them their respectful due. Monism unites religious people without rejecting their various cults and pieties. Monotheism is unnatural, for it demands people deny the gods of everyone else and then convert them. Intellectually and politically that is a big leap, not to mention that it would involve military conquest to convert other people effectively in most cultural and historical situations.

Either monism or monotheism also requires a tremendous intellectual transformation. Thinkers and religious devotees must develop a unitary view of the universe and a desire to organize the transcendent realities in a radically new way. Such an intellectual development could occur only at appropriate moments in human socio-cultural and intellectual evolution, such as the Axial Age.

Polytheism is natural. People who live surrounded by the diverse forces of nature could be expected to affirm polytheism. It expresses the natural diversity of reality quite well, and enables people to cope with the individual numinous expressions of nature by making each one a god. Polytheism makes far better moral sense, for it explains that suffering, injustice and inadequacy exist in the universe because the great cosmic forces or the gods are in conflict. Polytheism offers far more dramatic myths to explain reality and more poignant and complex rituals by which people might seek to integrate themselves into the cosmos and control it. Finally, polytheism preserves the feminine aspects of religion quite well, usually offering a female divinity who may be addressed, whereas monotheism offers only a male, and a stern father figure as well.[57] This monotheism cannot evolve by itself inherently, it needs a strong stimulus from the culture, usually a crisis, to push it into a pure and radical form.[58] For this reason, Israel's monotheism arose not in the wilderness, which could really only produce polytheism,[59] but in the crisis of the Babylonian exile. One may speak of this in two ways. Either Israel's monotheism arose in response to one great crisis, the exile, or in response to many sequential pre-exilic crises which led up to the final national catastrophe, and all these events created the final breakthrough. Either way we perceive that socio-cultural and ideational challenges of the environment pushed the monotheistic trajectory into the final breakthrough.

Movements toward a monotheistic breakthrough may be observed in other cultures of the Axial Age. What happened to them, and how were they different from Israel's religious attainment? The most significant area was that of the lands east of Mesopotamia, where the Indo-Iranian religions may be found. These religious expressions need consideration especially because of the possible interaction of thought which might have occurred between India, Iran and Mesopotamia, where the Jews

57. Baly, 'Geography of Monotheism', pp. 253-78; Sperling, 'Israel's Religion', pp. 28-29.

58. J. Finkelstein, 'Bible and Babel', pp. 431-44; Keel, 'Gedanken', pp. 20-21; Sperling, 'Israel's Religion', p. 28; Albertz, 'Der Ort', p. 93; de Pury, 'Erwägungen', p. 416; Loretz, 'Einzigkeit Jahwes', pp. 519-20.

59. Baly, 'Geography of Monotheism', p. 255, explicates this brilliantly; Albertz, 'Der Ort', p. 86.

were located, under the rule of the Persia Empire, which ruled all these areas for two centuries during the Axial Age (550–330 BCE). In reality, these areas had been connected already by trade for three thousand years before the rise of Persia, but the emergence of Achaemenid Persian unity simply increased the flow of goods and ideas to create a single cultural continuum. Historians have lamented our inability to consider the cultural inter-connectedness of this region from the Nile to the Ganges or the Nile to the Oxus in so many specialized disciplines of scholarly research, including biblical studies.[60] Throughout the Bronze and Iron Ages (3000–500 BCE) this vast geographic continuum was connected by trade routes; throughout the subsequent Persian, Hellenistic, Roman, and Byzantine periods (500 BCE–630 CE) great empires unified significant portions of this great region; and finally Islam culturally unified this area. In a study of monotheism we must acknowledge that monotheistic experiments were to be found in different regions of this great cultural region, and they may have interacted with each other. The biblical historian or theologian cannot consider the Jews in exile as though they were isolated completely from the great developments of this region. Even though they sought to create their worldview in isolation from other peoples, the Jewish intelligentsia probably encountered and considered thought that flowed throughout the lands from India to the Mediterranean.

Within this region in the first millennium BCE an intellectual breakthrough was achieved in diverse places which was,

> integrally linked to the rise of small groups of prophets, philosophers, teachers and wise men, who though they may seem to have had little effect on their immediate social, political and economic environment, yet opened the doors for future large-scale civilizational and imperial triumphs.[61]

The breakthrough was achieved especially by peoples who had been semi-nomadic in years prior to the Axial Age (Vedic warriors, Persians, and Israelites to some extent) and had settled close to great high cultural spheres (Indus Valley, Mesopotamia and Egypt) establishing an organized agricultural society out of which a class of intellectuals emerged. When those cultures underwent stress during the rise of great empires (Assyrian, Babylonian, Persian and Greek), the intellectuals articulated a new vision

---

60. M. Hodgson, *The Venture of Islam: Conscience and History in a World Civilization* (3 vols.; Chicago: University of Chicago, 1974), I, pp. 30-34, 60-62.

61. S. Tambiah, 'The Reflexive and Institutional Achievements of Early Buddhism', *Axial Age Civilizations* (ed. Eisenstadt), p. 453.

of the cosmos.[62] One of the components in each of these cultures (Vedic India, Persia and Israel) was a thrust toward monotheism.

India is as large as Europe and the religious and intellectual currents which have flowed through the large populace and varied cultures of that sub-continent have been more extensive and diverse than Europeans and Americans ever have experienced. The religious expressions of India have been more diverse than any other comparable region in the world. During the Axial Age several intellectual movements in India appear to have affirmed monotheistic ideas.

The Vedic Age, so named after the religious hymns of war, cult and meditation found in collections like the *Rig-Veda* and *Atharva-Veda* produced a number of examples of exclusive devotion to a particular deity. Within these Vedic hymns one senses 'a more unified vision of the divine' in the later texts.[63] Although the Vedas did not deny the existence of all deities save one, nonetheless, they regarded the different gods as a mask for the one divine force in the universe. Sabapathy Kulandran says it well,

> There was in the Rig Veda no attempt to dismiss as non-existent the gods other than the one worshipped for the time being. What is in evidence is the belief that the god worshipped temporarily summed up the power of the other gods and represented all that just then was of meaning to the worshipper... Worship of any particular god was dictated by the likes and dislikes, the moods and circumstances of the worshipper. This may be called polytheism; but there was another feeling constantly emerging, and undermining the practice of offering equal and indiscriminate worship to every god: the search for a unifying principle.[64]

This tendency later would manifest itself in the Classical or Epic period (200 BCE–600 CE) as the view that Brahma was the ultimate ground of being behind all the gods, a concept that began to emerge early on in the Upanishads, the great philosophical dialogues of India. This notion of Brahma would become the common assumption of the high philosophical and religious tradition of India. We would call it monism; there is one divine force behind all the gods.

---

62. H. Kulke, 'The Historical Background of India's Axial Age', *Axial Age Civilizations* (ed. Eisenstadt), pp. 390-91; Armstrong, *History of God*, p. 27.

63. E. Cornélis, 'The Imprecise Boundaries of Notions of the Ultimate' (trans. L.H. Ginn), *Monotheism* (eds. Geffré, Jossua and Lefébure), p. 4.

64. S. Kulandran, *Grace: A Comparative Study of the Doctrine in Christianity and Hinduism* (London: Lutterworth, 1964), p. 119.

Yet in the early literature, especially the Vedas, there are several divine beings and divine principles, which appear to occupy center stage, and it seems as though each one had a chance to become India's exclusively worshipped god. Varuna was portrayed as a sole, personal deity at times; but sometimes he was seen as the great lord in the pantheon of deities. His demands were ethical in some texts, which seem close to ethical monotheism. In the later Vedic writings other names appear, which are less known to students of Hinduism: Vishvakarman ('He whose work is the universe'), Purusha ('Soul of the World'), Prajapati ('Lord of Creation'), and 'That One Thing' (a causative principle rather than a god). William Tremmel sees in these texts evidence of a 'kairotic moment' in the emergence of a 'consummate religion'.[65]

In the later Upanishadic texts (700–200 BCE) several notions of divine impersonal principles, which unify the cosmos, are discussed. Brahma is the most important concept. But the authors also speak of the 'holy power of prayer' (Brahmanaspati), which ultimately is absorbed into Brahma, as a separate unifying divine force. In particular, a Brahmin priest named Yajñavalkya produced the *Brihadaranyaka Upanishad*, which is the best expression of those monistic tendencies.[66]

In the Classical or Epic period (200 BCE–600 CE) with the rise of personal deities like Vishnu and Sheva (or Shiva), there again appeared monotheistic tendencies. Vishnu devotees spoke monotheistically, particularly in their devotion to the incarnation, or *avatar*, of Vishnu as the hero Krishna. One of the manifestations of Krishna is the person, Vasudeva, who may have been historically a religious thinker, but who was merged into the Krishna traditions. Other manifestations of Vishnu which received exclusivistic devotion were Narayana and Bhagavat. Vaisnavite piety focused upon a number of divine incarnations, or *avatars*, with almost monotheistic piety. In the Mediaeval Age (600–1600 CE) the followers of Ramanuja (c. 1150 CE), who were Vaisnavites, also tended to direct their devotion aggressively to particular incarnations of Vishnu.[67]

---

65. N. Macnicol, *Indian Theism: From the Vedic to the Muhammadan Period* (Delhi: Munshiram Manoharlal, 1915), pp. 10-16; Tremmel, *Religion*, p. 138; and Cornélis, 'Boundaries', p. 6.

66. Tremmel, *Religion*, pp. 138-39; Cornélis, 'Boundaries', pp. 4-5.

67. Macnicol, *Indian Theism*, pp. 35-41, 102; E. Carpenter, *Theism in Medieval India* (The Hibbert Lectures, NS; London: Williams & Norgate, 1921), pp. 220-27, 244-45.

In conclusion, Indian Hinduism provides us with several good examples of monistic or somewhat monotheistic thought. However, historians of Hindu religious development are quick to point out that these are not really examples of monotheism. Nicol Macnicol observes that the true monotheistic spirit was alien to India, because India could not accept the intolerance for the other gods that true monotheistic devotion to one deity would bring. He believes that the early Aryans came into India bringing the best potential for monotheism with their devotion to Varuna, but the failure of Varuna spelled the ultimate defeat for any later attempt. There are several reasons for this: 1) The need to avoid strife on a large scale among the many groups in India made anyone reticent to assume the 'monotheistic arrogance of the Hebrew prophets'. 2) The harshness of the environment in the natural and social order in India created pessimism toward life and made it difficult to adore a personal deity who could permit so much suffering in the world. 3) Instead of a personal deity a pantheistic perception of the divine realm was preferred; the gods were in the total world environment rather than separate from it. 4) 'A decided pantheistic bias' led the populace to 'amalgamate and then blend its gods—to encourage one as the "All-god" to swallow the others.' But any one particular deity did not have a personality suffici-ently distinct to dissolve the others, so they all remained absorbed in an impersonal divine ground of being. 5) 'Nothing has cramped Indian theism more than the imperfectly ethical character of the karma doctrine.' The notion of karma hindered the development of theism and especially monotheism. It was easier to accept that an impersonal, mechanical universe rather than a personal being could bring about suffering (*maya*), justice, retribution (*karma*), and reincarnation (*samsara*). Essentially, when we observe those later attempts to elevate one particular deity, often the deity is merely an extension or an abstraction of the greater ground of divine being or the monistic principle, which permeates the universe. In Hinduism it is difficult to distinguish monotheism from monism, but invariably what we observe is monism.[68] It is for this reason that the biblical scholar, Denis Baly, preferred to characterize Vedic thought and the Upanishads as 'proto-monotheism'.[69] Indian thought portrays the divine in speculative and pessimistic fashion as ontologically one, non-personal, all-pervading and pantheistic.[70] This is not Jewish monotheism.

68. Macnicol, *Indian Theism*, pp. 10-19, 88, 102, 192-93.
69. Baly, 'Geography of Monotheism', pp. 258-59.
70. Macnicol, *Indian Theism*, p. 16; Tremmel, *Religion*, pp. 138-39.

To the modern reader of the west the Indian perceptions might describe more what we would call the great natural order. The bottom line is that in India no one deity ever emerged to win the devotion of great numbers of people for any length of time.

When we turn to the consideration of Zoroastrianism, however, we appear to have a better candidate for monotheism. Whereas in Hinduism the ultimate is non-personal, pantheistic and monistic, in Zoroastrianism the divine is personal, transcendent and monotheistic. However, sometimes the monotheistic spirit seems to be swallowed up by a dualistic emphasis, as both a principle of light and a principle of darkness receive equal attribution of power in the cosmology of the universe.[71]

The origins of the religion are attributed to a prophet named Zoroaster or Zarathustra, who traditionally is assigned to the early sixth century BCE by Zoroastrian sources ('258 years before Alexander', or 588 BCE according to *Bundahishn* 36.8). However, much earlier dates have been attributed to Zoroaster by some recent scholars, Mary Boyce (1700–1200 BCE) and Gherardo Gnoli (1000 BCE), on the basis of linguistic relationships between the Persian Gathas of the *Zend-Avesta* and the early Vedic hymns, but their ideas have not met with complete acceptance yet.[72] The traditional date would make Zoroaster contemporary with Second Isaiah in the Axial Age. If Zoroaster is dated to a much earlier age, scholars correspondingly suspect that his direct contribution to the emergence of monotheistic belief was less significant.

The sacred literature of Zoroastrianism is the *Zend-Avesta*, which is dated to the fifth century CE or later by scholars. It is composed of the Yasna (liturgy), Yashts (sacrificial hymns), and the Videvdat (purification guidelines). This literature, especially the old portions, shows great similarity with Hindu texts, and this leads scholars to speak of the continuity in Indo-Iranian religion. Part of the Yasna contains the most ancient hymns, the Gathas, some of which may go back to Zoroaster. The Gathas

71. Tremmel, *Religion*, p. 129.

72. M. Boyce, *A History of Zoroastrianism* (3 vols.; Leiden: Brill, 1975, 1981, 1991), II, pp. 1-3; *idem*, 'Persian Religion', pp. 279-81; G. Gnoli, *Zoroaster's Time and Homeland* (Naples: Institutio Universitario Orientale, 1979), pp. 77, 227; Cohn, *Cosmos*, pp. 77-79. Their views are sternly critiqued by E. Yamauchi, *Persia and the Bible* (Grand Rapids: Baker, 1990), pp. 413-15, who favors the traditional date around 600 BCE. R.C. Zaehner, 'Zoroastrianism', *The Concise Encyclopedia of Living Faiths* (ed. C. Zaehner; Boston: Beacon, 1959), p. 209; and J. Noss and D. Noss, *Man's Religions* (New York: Macmillan, 7th edn, 1984 [1949]), p. 334, also endorse the traditional date.

are used tentatively to reconstruct his teachings, but because the transmission time is more than a thousand years, there is controversy over whether Zoroaster taught all that is found within the Gathas, or whether he was a monotheist, a dualist or a henotheist. There is particular uncertainty on these issues for those scholars who date Zoroaster much earlier than the tradition maintained.[73]

Supposedly Zoroaster proclaimed a message of devotion to Ahura-Mazda, the god of light, who demanded a highly ethical lifestyle from followers. He begat two spirits, Spenta Mainyu, the 'Beneficent Spirit of the Truth' (*asha*), and Angra Mainyu or Ahriman, the 'Hostile Spirit of the Lie' (*druj*). Between these two beings there will be a struggle until the end of time, and then the Spirit of Truth will win completely with the coming of the savior figure, the *saoshyant*. In the meantime, all people have the free will to choose between the two spirits and to be part of either the good 'Kingdom of Light' or the evil 'Kingdom of Darkness'. The 'Kingdom of Light' or 'Kingdom of Righteousness' is established upon the earth and struggles with evil until the end of time. The moral imperatives to believers issued by Zoroaster has led scholars to call this a religion of 'ethical dualism'. Initially, it is difficult for us to decide whether Zoroastrianism is primarily monotheistic or dualistic, and scholars are not sure which nuance goes back to the teachings of Zoroaster himself. In some later portrayals it is Ahura Mazda or Ohrmazd who is put in opposition to Ahriman, as if they were twin brothers, both descended from Zurvan, whose name means 'Infinite Time' or 'Divine Time'. This later portrayal sounds even more dualistic. Dualism was predominant in the later Zoroastrian state religion of the Sassanian Empire (226–652 CE), so scholars doubt whether it should be attributed to Zoroaster.[74] Everyone concedes it is difficult to ascertain the precise views of the prophet.

Discussion of the interaction between Zoroaster's teachings and Judaism in the sixth century BCE during the Babylonian exile and in later years is rendered difficult not only by our inability to determine what

73. Zaehner, 'Zoroastrianism', pp. 209-10; Noss and Noss, *Religions*, pp. 334-36; Yamauchi, *Persia*, pp. 436-42.

74. Zaehner, 'Zoroastrianism', pp. 210-20; J. Duchesne-Guillemin, *Symbols and Values in Zoroastrianism: Their Survival and Renewal* (Religious Perspectives, 15; New York: Harper & Row, 1966), pp. 35-49; Noss and Noss, *Religions*, pp. 336-39; Tremmel, *Religion*, pp. 131-32; N. Smart, *The World's Religions* (Englewood Cliffs, NJ: Prentice-Hall, 1989), pp. 215-22; Yamauchi, *Persia*, pp. 433-42; Cohn, *Cosmos*, pp. 77-104.

Zoroaster taught and the question of monotheism and dualism in his teachings, but also by the time of the appearance of Zoroastrianism in the Persian Empire. Although many people, especially those in biblical studies, assume that Cyrus the Great (ruled 559–530 BCE) was Zoroastrian, he probably was not. Darius I (ruled 522–486 BCE) was probably the first Zoroastrian Persian king, and if so, the possible contact between exilic prophets, like Second Isaiah, and Zoroastrianism is minimized greatly.[75] Therefore, biblical scholars who facilely speak of Persian influence upon Jewish thought ought to be more cautious in view of these reservations about the nature and extent of Zoroastrianism. Perhaps, there was some general interaction between exilic Jewish thinkers and greater worldwide religious thought, but Zoroastrianism would be only one component of that influence.

The important question for this study is the nature of Zoroaster's monotheism, which is difficult to reconstruct. There is a wide range of agreement among scholars, both in biblical and Zoroastrian studies, that Zoroaster was probably not a true monotheist.[76] Denis Baly describes Zoroastrianism as 'pseudo-monotheism' (like Atonism in Egypt) because of its dualistic rhetoric.[77] Jeffrey Burton Russell prefers to describe it as monolatry, because it appears to be mid-way between monotheism and dualism or between monism and dualism. It flirts with monotheism because Ahriman is said to exist only contingently in some texts.[78] So, Zoroastrianism falls short of the absolute monotheism of the Jews, although it comes much closer than the monism and occasional monotheistic speculations in India. Zoroastrianism should not be belittled, however, for it still was a very significant intellectual breakthrough of the Axial Age.[79]

What makes it different from the Jewish experience? Jacob Finkelstein observed that a monotheistic movement will not arrive at a pure monotheistic portrayal of God inherently and inevitably; only if the environment

75. Yamauchi, *Persia*, pp. 419-33.

76. Yamauchi, *Persia*, pp. 437-42, lists a great number of scholars who concur on this conclusion.

77. Baly, 'Geography of Monotheism', pp. 259-60.

78. J.B. Russell, *The Devil: Perceptions of Evil from Antiquity to Primitive Christianity* (Ithaca, NY: Cornell University Press, 1977), pp. 98, 107-108, who also believes that the idea of Ahriman's contingent existence influenced later Christian thought.

79. Lohfink, 'Gott und die Götter', pp. 50-71.

provides the correct stimulus will true monotheism emerge.[80] For Jews this stimulus was the crisis of the Babylonian exile. With their homeland and Temple destroyed, Jews found themselves exiled and ruled by foreign powers, theoretically forced to admit the religious, national and political supremacy of the Babylonian gods. But some of them refused to do this. In spite of their experiences they proclaimed their belief in Yahweh, and to do so in a foreign land meant the hard denial of the existence of other gods. Zoroastrianism was never the religion of any exiled peoples in its early years, so it never had to deny the existence of other national deities. Instead, the Zoroastrian religion was the belief system of the victors, the Persian Empire. It was an imperial religion, perhaps used to consolidate portions of the eastern half of the empire. Persians never proselytized in the western half of the empire. It seems as though Persians considered it their religion, but saw no need to share it with others or impose it upon them. The gods of other conquered peoples could be ignored blandly by the political winners, who might even give token acknowledgment to the gods of those other peoples for political reasons, as they seem to have done with the Jews according to the testimonies of the books of Ezra and Nehemiah. In actuality, it was a national religion of the state, what Baly considers a form of 'pseudo-monotheism'.[81] The most it could do was flirt with consistent monotheistic or monistic thought.[82]

It has been suggested that if Second Isaiah were influenced by Zoroastrianism, he may have been making counter claims against that religion rather than accepting its thought.[83] This suggestion makes more sense than those of scholars who speak of direct influence in rather simplistic terms. Rainer Albertz points out what may be more than just a coincidence: Zoroaster's god is grounded in the order of creation, whereas Yahweh of the Jews may have been portrayed as a creator of the world at this time, but the primary focus in exilic epic literature was upon Yahweh as liberator of slaves, a great act in history.[84] The emphasis upon Yahweh as liberator in the exodus implies that the Jewish portrayal of God sprang more from the despair of an oppressed people. By

80. J. Finkelstein, 'Bible and Babel', pp. 431-44.
81. Baly, 'Geography of Monotheism', pp. 260-61.
82. Cornélis, 'Boundaries', pp. 4-5.
83. Baly, 'Geography of Monotheism', p. 275.
84. Albertz, *Israelite Religion*, II, pp. 418. Cf. Moltmann, 'Inviting Unity', pp. 51-52; Sperling, 'Israel's Religion', p. 22; Uffenheimer, 'Ancient Israel', p. 144.

contrast, Marduk and Ahuda-Mazda, both creators and sustainers of the world order, were worshipped by the victors of war and the builders of empires. A god who liberates slaves overturns the world order, the opposite of one who sustains it. Those who worshipped Marduk or Ahura-Mazda as the great world creator deities also aspired to rule that very world in the name of the deity. By contrast the people of Yahweh did not aspire to world dominion, their religion was a 'monotheism from below'. Perhaps, this is why Second Isaiah's early portrayal of Cyrus as the Servant of Yahweh later gave way to the images of the Suffering Servant in the so-called servant hymns.

This contrast also appears in the respective eschatology of the Jews and the Zoroastrians. In Jewish apocalyptic the world becomes increasingly corrupt and evil until God intervenes to create a new world order, 'a new heavens and earth'. However, in Zoroastrian eschatology there is indeed an increase of evil in the ages of gold, silver, bronze and iron, but in the final age of iron just before the coming of the messianic *saoshyant*, the human condition suddenly improves and morality abounds, so that the *saoshyant* serves to perfect the improving world order with judgment day. Again, this is a contrast between the view of the world from the vantage point of the oppressed versus the view of the victors. The monotheism of Judaism comes 'from below', whereas Zoroastrian monotheism comes 'from above' and never becomes truly absolute monotheism.

In other ways there are interesting similarities. Although Zoroaster's preaching context, as implied by the Gathas, may have been the pastoral steppe land of northeastern Persia, southwestern Siberia and western Afghanistan, nonetheless, the religion flourished and spread (and perhaps transformed itself radically) as it spread through the agricultural regions of Persia from the sixth century BCE onward. It was a religion of farmlands and small urban centers during the great social and intellectual development which occurred in Achaemenid Persia, which in turn was part of the Axial Age.[85] Later Islam also would be an urban or small town phenomenon in Mecca and Medina.[86]

This returns us to our central focus: the emergence of Jewish monotheism was part of a great intellectual advance occurring in many parts of the world during the Axial Age. Monotheism and monism were

---

85. Pettazzoni, *All-Knowing God*, p. 137; Baly, 'Geography of Monotheism', p. 260; J.C. Heesterman, 'Ritual, Revelation, and Axial Age', *Axial Age Civilizations* (ed. Eisenstadt), p. 405.

86. Baly, 'Geography of Monotheism', pp. 276-78.

concepts that received speculative consideration in several places of the world, but only the Jews in exile appear to have arrived at consistent monotheism. In China thinkers simply chose not to deal with issues such as a 'self-existent and perfect God and an imperfect and transient Creation, Good and Evil as all-pervading aspects of the universe', choosing rather to view the cosmos as 'a single interacting system, in which no internal cleavages of an ultimate nature could exist'.[87] In other words, the issues of monotheism in religion did not appeal to Chinese intellectuals or religionists. Among the pre-Socratic philosophers certain individuals, such as Xenophon and Antisthenes, articulated a sophisticated monism. While Xenophon of Colophon may have criticized anthropomorphic imagery for the gods and uttered monotheistic ideas, he still fell short. The best that can be said is that he came close to monotheism.[88] The thoughts of the pre-Socratic thinkers never captured the imagination of the masses to produce monotheism, at best the Hellenistic world merged all gods into one divine principle. Their views remained 'monotheistic intuitions'.[89] In the many Hindu texts there are intimations of monotheistic thought, but they likewise fell short of pure monotheism. Devotion to specific deities never became radical enough to deny other deities, and invariably an impersonal monism arose which stood in the distance behind the existing multiplicity of the gods. Zoroastrianism came the closest to monotheism, but it kept flirting with dualism, and the difficulty of historical reconstruction makes it problematic for us to say what Zoroaster may have taught in reality or what may have been the real shape of Achaemenid Zoroastrian belief. Essentially, Jewish monotheism stands between Hindu monism and Persian dualism. Hindu thought is monistic and non-personal, Zoroastrian thought is dualistic and personal, while Jewish beliefs are monotheistic and personal.[90]

Most important of all, Jewish monotheism survived. It alone gave birth to the dynamic three monotheistic faiths of the west, Rabbinic Judaism, Christianity and Islam. It alone is the monotheistic faith which can be

---

87. M. Elvin, 'Was There a Transcendental Breakthrough in China?', *Axial Age Civilizations* (ed. Eisenstadt), p. 326.

88. M. Meslin, 'The Anthropological Function of Monotheism' (trans. R. Murphy), *Monotheism* (eds. Geffré, Jossua and Lefébure), p. 29; Elkana, 'Classical Greece', p. 52.

89. Pettazzoni, 'Formation of Monotheism', p. 46; Meslin, 'Anthropological', p. 30.

90. Russell, *Devil*, p. 220; Tremmel, *Religion*, pp. 129-30.

said to have shaped the destiny of human religious development. More than that, Judaism gave birth to a social and intellectual worldview which has shaped our reality. It developed a view of the world which began to stand in dialectical tension with the reigning world view. This development was exilic and post-exilic in origin and ought not to be projected back into the days of the early settlement, as scholars were wont to do in a former generation. Nor was it as radically new, as scholars too often had supposed. But it was a new reconfiguration of many elements which had been in the minds of the religious intelligentsia for centuries. A reconfiguration of old elements in either a genetic or cultural sphere is to be considered an evolutionary breakthrough. The nature of this evolutionary breakthrough, this 'old wine' in 'new wineskins', is the topic of consideration in the next chapter.

VI

Perceptions of emergent monotheism among Israelites and the Jews are changing, and perhaps with these changes modern intellectual horizons will broaden. Biblical theologians now sense that monotheism evolved in a revolutionary process, that it came much later in Israel's history than previously suggested, and that it was part of a greater worldwide intellectual advance.

Consideration of the biblical text leads students of the Bible to read more closely the testimonies and memories which are embedded within the text, especially the Deuteronomistic History. Here there is evidence of the multi-faceted religious piety of pre-exilic Israelites, even though it is the object of Deuteronomic diatribe and fulminations. Indeed, there is evidence within the biblical text that monotheism emerged only after a long and hard struggle with the diverse religious currents in Palestine.

Yahweh devotion originally was part of the matrix of Canaanite religion, and only slowly did Yahweh arise to defeat and destroy the other gods. Yahweh advanced from being the deity of a very small tribal group in the highlands of Palestine, to be the national high god of two small Palestinian states, and finally to emerge as the sole god in the heavens. The process of emergence may be described best with the model of 'convergence' and 'differentiation'. Yahweh absorbed several deities and their aspects while rejecting particular divine attributes and cultic activities. Perhaps, it is this process of differentiation which is the surest sign of an emergent monotheistic process. Had Yahweh merely absorbed all the gods and their cultic practices, the result would have been an undifferentiated 'over-God' or monistic principle, which merely accepted and tolerated all pieties, such as Brahma became in India. This nebulous form of divinity could never obtain deep commitment from believers or create an identity for exiled Jews. Rather, the process of differentiation, the rejection of certain practices as intolerable, assured that this deity would have a clear identity and provide definite direction for believers in matters of worship and morality. Only a religion with such a clear sense of purpose and direction could provide support for later Judaism and Christianity, so as to bequeath a lasting heritage to western culture.

The point of crystalization was the exile, a moment of trauma and rebirth for a people who would become the Jews. The stages or crises which led up to the exilic break (Elijah, Hosea, Hezekiah, Josiah and Jeremiah) were necessary and crucial to the final victory of monotheism. They were, however, prolegomena! With the Deuteronomistic History, Second Isaiah and the Priestly theologians, the monotheistic victory was complete. In exile certain social factors mitigated in favor of such a monotheistic worldview: 1) The people were forced to define themselves in the face of an alien world. 2) That alien world provided new ideas which furthered the intellectual trajectories which had begun already before the exile. 3) An ethos and a culture were reconstructed out of the complete collapse of the old society and its values, so that new creative ideas could be articulated. 4) The oppressed losers of war envisioned a worldview that rejected the old values of empire, class and religious stasis. A 'religion from below' emerged to move beyond the establishment values of a 'religion from above'. Only in this context could a truly lasting monotheistic faith be born; the contemporary religious movements in India and Persia fall short because they were not 'religions from below'.

This religion of the Jews which emerged in the exile and post-exilic era was the most radical religious expression of that age in terms of monotheistic expression. A brief review of comparable monistic and monotheistic movements seems to indicate that Jewish monotheism was more radical in its self-definition. It was more ready to deny the other gods, to proclaim a unique message, or to affirm a chosen people. In effect, it was ready to endure for a longer time and make great social and religious impact.

Biblical scholars and theologians must now develop new attitudes and insights about emergent monotheism in its great social and intellectual milieu. 1) Jewish monotheism emerged late, in the exile and beyond. Previously the Jewish post-exilic period was spoken of as a dull, legalistic and non-creative age. Biblical theologians must change their rhetoric and recognize this era to be the most formative in shaping the biblical text and faith as we know it. 2) Israel was a peripheral people in the ancient world, both as residents in Palestine and exiles in Babylon. As such they took the best thought of the high cultures and reshaped it in a new fashion in their simpler social setting of Palestine or the social and intellectual disintegration and despair of the exile. This tension of being in contact with the great cultures yet being simple enough to construct a new worldview is what made the great evolutionary/revolutionary breakthrough possible. Those of faith today, who view the action of God in the human process, will affirm that this is how God chose to work through the human experience—through just such a people as the Jews. 3) Finally, we shall see that Israel and the Jews were part of a greater human advance in the first millennium BCE Axial Age. We can understand them better if we view them in terms of continuities and discontinuities they shared with other great and creative cultures around them. In the past we compared the values of the biblical text with the cultures of Egypt, Mesopotamia and Canaan, but in the future we ought to make our comparative observations between the biblical values and the literature and culture of India, Persia and Greece, who were truly more contemporary with the formation of the biblical texts and canon. (John Van Seters has made just such a case for the comparison of Pentateuchal and Deuteronomistic texts with Greek literature of the sixth and fifth centuries BCE, especially the historiographical tradition.[91]) This arena of study may provide much useful research in the future.

Jewish monotheism ultimately emerged as a breakthrough after six centuries of struggle in preparation for its ultimate crystalization in the exile. In the post-exilic age Jews worked out the religious and intellectual implications of this new concept. Jewish monotheism was a reconfiguration of old elements of belief in the ancient world which produced a new breakthrough—a new revolutionary movement of thought which not only has created the modern religious world today, but will continue to shape the future as the implications of monotheism continue to unfold.

---

91. Van Seters, *In Search of History: Historiography in the Ancient World and the Origins of Biblical History* (New Haven: Yale University Press, 1983), pp. 8-54 *et passim*; *Prologue to History*, pp. 78-103 *et passim*.

Chapter 5

THE WORLDVIEW OF EMERGENT MONOTHEISM AMONG THE JEWS

> The world of Israelite religion is neither wholly discontinuous nor is it a
> random collection of features from older versions. It is a world made from
> previous worlds.[1]

Ronald Hendel's observation concerning the Israelite or Jewish ability to
create a new worldview nicely summarizes my image of the relationship
between biblical thought and the antecedent worldviews of the ancient
Near East. Israelite thought was not in diametric opposition to the ancient
Near East; rather, it drew heavily upon existing thought forms to create
a new synthesis. While almost any aspect of Israelite or Jewish faith may
be found in the ancient world, it is the overall synthesis of these elements
and the particular emphases given to certain aspects of thought that
makes the biblical worldview an evolutionary advance over the beliefs
found in its contemporary world.

I

In the scholarship of a past generation scholars were tempted to make
sweeping generalizations to contrast Israelite and ancient Near Eastern
thought. The following grand statements were made: 1) Israelites
developed a sense of history and created historiography in their epic
literature, while the ancient Near Easterners thought in cyclic terms,
influenced by the recurrent patterns in nature, and expressed their beliefs
in myths or stories about the gods. 2) Yahweh was a god of history and
the social arena, while the gods of the nations were tied to their specific
natural phenomena and unable to transcend those limitations. 3) Israelites,
especially after the message of the classical prophets, expressed their
religiosity in terms of moral behavior, thus producing ethics, whereas the
ancient Near Eastern belief systems expressed piety primarily through

1.   Hendel, 'Worldmaking', p. 17.

sacrifice, cult and ritual in an attempt to contact the divine realm. 4) With the open-ended view of reality which resulted from a historical or linear perspective, the Israelites assumed that both Yahweh and human beings were existentially free to make decisions. On the other hand, the cultic view of the ancient Near Eastern world led the ancients to see great cyclic patterns, as in nature, which led them to stress cosmic destiny and fate, which in turn meant that the actions of people were pre-determined. The linear perception was reinforced by the mono-theistic view of one god who transcended the diverse forces of nature for Israelites, while the ancient Near Easterners saw many deities, each one associated with a particular force in nature, which was repetitive and predictable. 5) If people and the divine realm were free, then any attempt to manipuate Yahweh by cult or magic was blasphemous, but in the ancient Near East such cultic manipulation was standard religious activity. Divination was considered acceptable in a world where all the great cosmic and natural forces were predictable; divination sought to discern the direction of the great cosmic forces, or perhaps to bend their direction a little bit for the benefit of human suppliants. 6) A sense of social justice arose in Israelite thought, especially with the prophets and the Deuteronomic Reform movement, but in the ancient Near East no such phenomenon occurred on a wide scale. 7) The imperative for social justice and reform combined with the sense of human freedom produced a radical ideal of equality and egalitarianism in Israel, while the same was lacking in the class conscious and oppressive societies of the ancient Near East. This was reinforced by the difference between monotheism and polytheism. As people worshipped one and the same deity, it gave them a sense of equality; but when they believed in a great pantheon of deities ranked into greater and lesser gods, this tended to reinforce the existence of classes upon the earth. 8) Finally, the monotheism of the Israelites enabled them to envision a universal deity with dominion over the whole world and all its people, thus leading them to transcend religio-national politics and affirm a worldwide common humanity. This would lead eventually to a sense of mission endeavor, as expressed in a book like Jonah, and best epitomized in that most successful of all Jewish heresies, Christianity. By contrast the ancient Near East had many national deities with their own national and territorial states, all at war with each other. Any particular god sought to rule the other gods, and when successful, his or her patron state on earth would be victorious over other countries and city states.

In the past generation these sweeping stereotypes were critiqued by biblical theologians.[2] Ancient Near Eastern historians pointed out that the ancient world had a concept of history, generated historiographical literature and envisioned deities who acted in the social or historical arena.[3] The portrayal of ancient Near Eastern deities as gods of nature was overgeneralized, for they also had significant social and existential roles, as can be observed in prayers, hymns and royal inscriptions of the second and first millennium BCE. The portrayal of the evolution in Mesopotamian religion by Thorkild Jacobsen was most enlightening in this regard to show the personal and social dimension of the gods.[4] The same is true for Canaanite deities, who likewise had social concerns, such as justice, the security of the king, and the stability of human society.[5] Egyptians and Mesopotamians, in particular, had a sense of morality and ethics, as well as social justice imperatives, which had been clearly articulated by scholars as early as James Henry Breasted's classic work, *The Dawn of Conscience* (1933), and his earlier *Development of Religion and Thought in Ancient Egypt* (1912).[6] The same was pointed out by subsequent authors to critique the easy generalizations which biblical theologians too often had made. Ethical concepts were observed in the wisdom literatures of Egypt and Mesopotamia, and moral values were observed even in the lawcode of Hammurabi. One can find many allusions to the demand for social justice which is expected to be brought about by kings; such texts exist from the time of the Sumerians onward. One may find proclamations by royal figures who liberate poor people from debts and slavery issued in both the ancient Near East and the Hellenistic world, and such texts underlay the biblical concepts of Sabbath Year and Jubilee Year.[7] The stark contrast between Israelite notions of free will

2. Childs, *Biblical Theology*, pp. 13-87, critiqued the entire Biblical Thelogy Movement which articulated these observations.

3. Albrektson, *History*; Gnuse, *Heilsgeschichte*.

4. Jacobsen, *Treasures*, pp. 145-219.

5. Schmidt, *Faith*, pp. 138-40; Simkins, *Creator*, pp. 82-89.

6. Breasted, *Development*, pp. 165-256 *et passim*; *idem*, *Dawn*, pp. 182-222 *et passim*.

7. E. Hammershaimb, 'On the Ethics of the Old Testament Prophets', *Congress Volume (Oxford, 1959)* (VTSup, 7; Leiden: Brill, 1960), pp. 75-101; C. Fensham, 'Widow, Orphan, and the Poor in Ancient Near Eastern Legal Literature', *JNES* 21 (1962), pp. 161-71; Sperling, 'Israel's Religion', pp. 14-16; E. Otto, *Theologische Ethik des Alten Testaments* (Theologische Wissenschaft, 3.2; Stuttgart: Kohlhammer, 1994), pp. 143-44; M. Weinfeld, *Social Justice in Ancient Israel and in the Ancient*

and ancient Near Eastern determinism, cultic divination and manipulation of the gods has been criticized also. There is equal evidence of ideas of freedom and also attempts at divine manipulation in both Israel and the ancient world.[8] Warnings have been issued about facilely declaring ancient Israel an egalitarian society in contrast to the ancient Near East, for the prophetic critique acknowledged that social classes and oppression did exist and were the norm for society in pre-exilic Israel, and these problems may have continued well into the post-exilic era.[9] Finally, the concept of a universal deity holding sway over all peoples is found in the ancient Near East, even if the texts are not radically monotheistic. Most certainly the hymns to Aton proclaim some form of divine universal rule.[10] In a past volume I tried to summarize briefly these diverse critiques of the *Heilsgeschichte* approach to interpreting the biblical text.[11]

The generalizations made concerning the contrast between Israel and the ancient Near East appear to have been influenced by the anthropological paradigms of great scholars from previous generations. In an excellent monograph Gary Anderson focuses upon the influence of the writings of James Frazer (*The Golden Bough: A Study in Magic and Religion*, 1913), who contrasted the 'primitive mind' with its emphasis upon magic with the modern rational mind. Anderson believes that Frazer's model enabled biblical scholars to portray the ancient Near East as primitive and Israel's religion as modern in a contrast designed for an 'apologetic goal' for biblical theology. In reality, behind the so-called primitive ancient mind there really was a simple scientific view of reality, and Israel's thought, even in the Second Temple period, still displayed

Near East (Minneapolis: Augsburg–Fortress, 1995), especially pp. 45-74, which stress the role of kings in bringing justice to the land, and pp. 152-78, which discuss the ancient origins of Sabbath Year and Jubilee Year.

8.   J.J.M. Roberts, 'Divine Freedom and Cultic Manipulation in Israel and Mesopotamia', *Unity and Diversity* (eds. H. Goedicke and J.J.M. Roberts), pp. 181-90; Saggs, *Encounter*, pp. 93-152; Gnuse, *Heilsgeschichte*, pp. 73-83.

9.   A. Dearman, *Property Rights in the Eighth-Century Prophets* (SBLDS, 106; Atlanta: Scholars Press, 1988); D. Snell, 'Ancient Israelite and Neo-Assyrian Societies and Economies: A Comparative Approach', *Tablet and the Scroll* (eds. Cohen *et al.*), p. 224.

10. Breasted, *Dawn*, pp. 272-302; who felt that Aton's universalism was the most developed expression in the ancient Near East; Sperling, 'Israel's Religion', pp. 14-16.

11. Gnuse, *Heilsgeschichte*, pp. 1-151.

some primitive aspects. Both the ancient Near East and Israel moved from a more primitive to a more sophisticated worldview in the Bronze Age and Iron Age (3000–300 BCE). Smith highlights such an intellectual transformation in Mesopotamia with a comparison of the earlier *Atrahasis Epic* and the later *Gilgamesh Epic*. Israelites and Canaanites, or ancient Near Easterners in general, were all similar in their religious assumptions, except that Israel's limitation of the cult to serve only one national high god created some differences in the nature of sacrificial service. Anderson's critique is excellent, and I concur with its conclusions.[12]

However, I would suggest that another scholar also may have influenced the stark portrayal of Israel and the ancient world. In his classic work, *The Myth of the Eternal Return or, Cosmos and History* (1954, French edn, 1949), Mircea Eliade advanced a brilliant comparison between the cyclic or nature oriented worldview of primitive peoples and the linear or historical worldview of contemporary Western European society.[13] Although many have critiqued aspects of his paradigm, it still has much to recommend it. This author believes that many of Eliade's ideas were used, either directly or subconsciously, by the *Heilsgeschichte* biblical theologians, for their stark contrasts of Israel and the ancient Near East are quite similar to his portrayal of primitive and modern world-views. There, however, is the irony. Eliade contrasted primitive thought and modern thought. The worldviews of the ancient Near East and the bible are neither, but instead they lie on an evolutionary spectrum somewhere between primitive and modern thought. This is the chief point made by Gary Anderson: ancient Near Eastern and biblical thought are not primitive but both contain primitive elements. There is a spectrum of intellectual development, and the thought reflected in the texts from ancient Egypt, Mesopotamia, and Israel lie between the great archetypes used by Eliade and also by the *Heilsgeschichte* biblical theologians.

I propose the following paradigm (which is still somewhat over-generalized): there are at least four stages of evolution in human thought using the Eliade paradigm. The first stage is the primitive or cyclic thought described by Eliade. (However, some anthropologists warn us that primitive people are still far more sophisticated than we have

---

12. G. Anderson, *Sacrifices*, pp. 7, 13-23; van der Spek, 'Assyriology', p. 123.

13. M. Eliade, *The Myth of the Eternal Return or, Cosmos and History* (trans. W. Trask; Bollingen Series, 46; repr.; Princeton, NJ: Princeton University Press, 1974 [1949]).

acknowledged.) This model prevails among the very primitive and isolated societies in our world today and may have typified the thought of the ancient Near East prior to 3000 BCE. Thorkild Jacobsen attributes a very animistic form of thought to Mesopotamia in this era, for example.[14] His categories dovetail nicely with the portrayal by Eliade.

The second stage begins with the emergence of the state and the development of writing in the Bronze Age after 3000 BCE. Historians have affirmed that the emergence of literacy brings a new complexity and abstraction to human philosophical and religious reflection.[15] Most likely, ancient Near Eastern cyclic thought began to break down over two thousand years before Israel appeared on the scene. Biblical scholars who sought to create a radical contrast often compared biblical thought with third millennium BCE Mesopotamian texts to harden the dichotomy, while a more legitimate first millennium BCE collection of texts would have indicated the tremendous similarity between Israel and the contemporary cultures.[16] Israel really grew out of a trajectory begun around 3000 BCE in the ancient world, and perhaps with some other cultures on the periphery of the great river valley civilizations Israel provided an avant-garde cutting edge in intellectual development.

The third stage began with the cultures that made intellectual breakthroughs in the Axial Age, including Greece, Israel, Persia, India and China. All these cultures drew upon the values of earlier civilizations, all took ideas latent or subordinate in those older cultures and made them into core ideas for social, religious and ideational values of their new societies. All were peripheral societies who were able to develop new ideas because they were new on the scene of world history with their simpler social structures. They reconfigured the older values of their age, achieved breakthroughs in intellectual, religious, social and technological areas, and laid the foundation for the cultures of our modern world.

The fourth stage is our modern intellectual world. Historians of ideas might quibble over when the modern age began, but that is really irrelevant for this discussion. The modern intellectual world, Eliade's linear society, might be said to have developed with the Renaissance in Europe, which occurred during the years 1200–1350 and 1450–1600 (with an

---

14. Jacobsen, *Treasures*, pp. 23-73.

15. Graham, *Written Word*, pp. 11-20; Shanks, 'Frank Cross', p. 25; Lewis, 'Persepolis Tablets', pp. 17-32.

16. Saggs, *Encounter*; Gnuse, *Heilsgeschichte*, pp. 33-83.

interlude created by the Black Plagues), or with the Enlightenment in the years 1650–1800.

This four-stage process of intellectual evolution is proposed to highlight a broader perception of Israel's relationship to the ancient world. In the past biblical theologians took the imagery of a Frazer, or Eliade, or of *Heilsgeschichte* theologians and compared the ancient Near East to Israel like the contrast of stage one to stage four in the preceding paradigm. In actuality, the comparison should be far more subtle. The ancient world and Israel are between these two stark contrasts of the cyclic and linear worldviews. By my simple analogy the ancient Near East ought to be viewed as stage two and the Israelites or the Jews as stage three. It should be recognized also that the comparison is between the ancient Near East of 3000 to 500 BCE and the biblical texts and their thought which really emerged from the time of the exile onward (after 500 BCE), so the comparisons are still a little unfair. But the point is that Israelite or Jewish thought grew out of ancient Near Eastern thought, and indeed did develop beyond it. It is wrong to make dialectical comparisons, but it is also wrong to deny that there were any differences in the two intellectual worldviews.

Pedagogically this new paradigm has several strengths: 1) This more complex paradigm tries to view the process from *le longue duree*, in the words of Fernand Braudel, the great world historian, for it sees Israel and the ancient Near East in the broader context of human intellectual development. 2) This model recognizes more clearly that Israelite thought flows out of ancient Near Eastern thought in an evolutionary process, in which Israel draws forth and reconstructs older thought in a new creative fashion. 3) It also acknowledges that Israel's synthesis is something new and different, though not as radical as the old dichotomies implied. 4) The model envisions Israel and the Jews not in isolation, but as part of an Axial Age process, obtaining an intellectual breakthrough along with other intelligentsia in Greece, Persia and India. 5) Finally, the model admits that Israelite or Jewish thought is not as modern as we are, but that their perceptions retain what we might call primitive elements, and they are removed from us by at least one foundational level of human intellectual development. We may be built upon biblical thought, but we have moved beyond it, too. When speaking of Israel's worldview and contemporary ancient Near Eastern thought, we can no longer compare them diametrically as 'cyclic' and 'linear', but now we recognize that they are evolving points on a spectrum of human intellectual development.

If we wish to retain the catchy phrases, we should speak of the thought of the ancient Near East as 'post-cyclic' or 'post-mythic' and the thought of Israel as 'pre-linear' and 'pre-historical'. It would capture at least a more subtle nuance in our pedagogical portrayals.

II

If we return to the stereotypical comparisons of Israel and the ancient Near East, perhaps we can begin anew with them. In their stark diametrical presentation they were in error. But there was a kernel of truth in some of the old statements which may be articulated in a more nuanced fashion. When monotheism does emerge, it brings new social and religious insights. We should be able to say something about these new intellectual assumptions without denigrating the predecessor worldviews out of which monotheism evolved.

As the monotheistic worldview arose, it created a new synthesis out of old ideas, which often involved elevating to a higher level of importance certain concepts and values which previously had been subordinate. This is comparable to how latent genes manifest themselves in the emergence of a new species. In the religious worldview that existed prior to the monotheistic revolution there are images of deities who act in history, notions of universalism, ethics and a demand for social justice in the literatures of Egypt and Mesopotamia, but biblical thought brought them to the fore and made them central themes in the new monotheistic ideology. Essentially, biblical thought is not unique in expressing those concepts; rather, the biblical authors go beyond their predecessors in the reconfiguration of new ideas. This synthesis creates something new, even though specific elements of the worldview are old.[17] This accords well with evolutionary theory, for the genetic breakthrough to a new species involves the recombination of genetic material in a new form to create latent or recessive genes, which become dominant genes as the evolutionary breakthrough occurs. Certain themes found in the ancient Near Eastern texts move from a recessive role to become dominant factors in the new ideology.

The experience of exile and the total destruction of the nation, the cult and their own worldview turned the Israelites and the Judahites into Jews, a significant sign of their transformation. The collapse of their ideological world meant that in the reconstruction of their new worldview they had

17. Miller, 'Israelite Religion', pp. 207-208.

less reverence for old traditions of the greater ancient Near East, they were more prone to reject aspects of the 'common theology' or 'common worldview' of the ancient world. There may have been a propensity in this direction already among the intelligentsia before the exile. Since they were a peripheral society already in Palestine, they were naturally selective concerning the language, ideas and customs they encountered from the high cultures of Egypt and Mesopotamia. Also, their self-styled rhetoric of being freed slaves and newcomers to the world scene made them less respectful of inherited ancient Near Eastern values. H.W.F. Saggs speaks of Israel's unique views in terms of what they did not say, for actually everything they said was previously articulated in the ancient world. Their creativity in the new synthesis of thought was their deliberate omission of certain ideas, a high degree of selectivity, and a particularly strong focus on certain things, such as the de-emphasis upon nature, the aniconic portrayal of the divine without human or animal figures, the removal of multiple wills in the cosmos, and the overall reduction of a multiplicity of forms in understanding the divine. As they omitted these aspects, says Saggs, they also became gradually intolerant of them and all foreign religions, and this slide toward intolerance accelerated under the pressure of foreign political oppression.[18]

As we proceed with this perspective, however, some cautious reservations should be made: 1) With the extremely limited and selective number of ancient Near Eastern texts we possess from three thousand years of literacy, we cannot be sure absolutely of what was a significant or what was a minor theme in the worldview of Egypt and Mesopotamia.[19]

2) Sometimes it is tempting to find the evidence of moral superiority or new and unique values in a biblical text, and we may be reading our own beliefs into those passages. The same expressions may be read differently in both Mesopotamian and biblical texts, because we know to view one as coming from a polytheistic author and the other from a monotheistic author, and we may not wish to see how both texts might be expressing similar beliefs. Sometimes we find moral superiority in the biblical text, when in reality the narrative merely expressed things differently because the plot was slightly different, as is the case with the biblical flood narrative's divergence from Mesopotamian counterparts.[20]

18. Saggs, *Encounter*, pp. 92, 116, 185-86; *idem, Civilization*, pp. 15-16.
19. Machinist, 'Distinctiveness', pp. 425-26.
20. J. Finkelstein, 'Bible and Babel', pp. 436-38; Machinist, 'Distinctiveness', p. 423.

3) Simply because particular beliefs and customs found in the ancient world are not mentioned in the biblical texts does not mean that they were rejected by the Jews. There may be beliefs or customs accepted in such a matter of fact fashion so as not to necessitate their recording, and we might mistakenly assume that such things were rejected.[21] Although the principle of observing what the bible does not say is a good working assumption, we still must be cautious with it.

4) A more nuanced use of the concept 'cultural borrowing' must be adopted. Too often we speak of borrowing as though a superior culture imposes certain values upon the less developed culture. This is not so. Sociologists and anthropologists have observed frequently that when a primitive culture encounters a superior culture, they often take elements from that culture as they have need or desire and ignore the other elements. Furthermore, these cultures often radically reinterpret those elements to fit into their own worldview. Thus, they do not throw away their old values completely and adopt the new worldview. Anthropologists say it is better to speak of 'cultural appropriation' rather than 'borrowing'. For people take the ideas from other cultures and make them their own by reformulating them to fit into their social and intellectual categories. I even prefer to speak of 'cultural cannibalization' to stress how truly ideas are appropriated, reformulated and sometimes used in a radically different way to express new concepts.

Israelites and Jews engaged in 'cultural appropriation' and sometimes 'cultural cannibalization'. They took ideas and made them their own, and sometimes used the ideas or motifs to reject the system of thought out of which those ideas came. Biblical themes in the creation and flood stories are taken from Mesopotamian narratives, but in turn reject the polytheism, moral values and political legitimations expressed in those older narratives. In particular, one thinks of the differences between the biblical story of creation and the Babylonian *Enuma Elish* with its attendant assumptions and values. Israelites and Jews were not passive recipients of ideas, they did not simply borrow, they sometimes stole ideas with a vengeance. It is likely that in the pre-exilic era the adoption of themes from the 'common theology' of the ancient Near East and especially the West Semitic religious realm may have been more unconscious and passive, but with the monotheistic breakthrough in the exile this process became increasingly aggressive as Jewish thinkers used new ideas and turned them polemically against their originators. This

21. Miller, 'Israelite Religion', p. 211.

aggressive appropriation may characterize the narratives of the primaeval history in Genesis 1–11 in general, and may indicate the post-exilic origin of these passages.

Werner Schmidt introduces some apt perceptions into this discussion. He disdains terms such as 'borrowed' and 'syncretism', and prefers a metaphor like the 'core and the husk'. Ideas were adapted and transformed by Israelite and Jewish thinkers, but these themes would constitute the 'husk'. The 'core' would be the heart of the Israelite or Jewish faith which used these new ideas for its own purposes. To this 'core' belong the integrating principles which organize all of the motifs in a coherent way. For Schmidt the 'core', which he believes characterizes biblical thought, came from the pre-settlement era and spoke of the exclusiveness of Yahweh and his aniconic portrayal. A double process of 'recognition' and 'rejection' describes how biblical thinkers 'took' motifs from foreign cults (among which he includes the cults of Baal and El, though we would consider them indigenous to early Yahwism). Using the criteria of the exclusivity and imageless portrayal of Yahweh, Israelites and Jews appropriated or 'recognized' some ideas as compatible and 'rejected' others as incompatible. He dates the bulk of the process early, to the time of the united monarchy, when perhaps most of it really occurred right before, during and after the Babylonian exile. For Schmidt 'borrowing' means 'reinterpretation', and thus the biblical texts have both a commonality with the ancient world and a peculiar distinctiveness at the same time.[22]

Schmidt's categories are excellent for future discussion, except for his propensity to date the process too early and to articulate the 'core' too concretely. The exclusivity of Yahweh and the aniconic portrayal were probably not important factors in the pre-exilic religion of Israel, as archaeology and the newer critical understanding of the biblical texts indicate, but perhaps they arose as important categories prior to the monotheistic breakthrough with the preaching of the classical prophets and Deuteronomic reform. They were part of the latent genetic mutations which led up to the monotheistic revolution. The so-called 'core' of Yahwistic faith was probably more nebulous and would be difficult to define. Schmidt's concepts of 'recognition' and 'rejection' dovetail nicely with the language of Mark Smith, who speaks of convergence and differentiation of religious imagery. Both scholars describe the complex process nicely.

This leads to another significant nuance in our new understanding of

22. Schmidt, *Faith*, pp. 1-3, 177-84.

the biblical worldview. The ideological implications of the monotheistic revolution unfold later than authors assumed previously. In a previous generation the new worldview of Israel was discussed by the textbooks in conjunction with the settlement process, the united monarchy, or at the latest with the classical prophets. Since I suggest that true monotheism comes only with the exile, the corresponding values of the 'linear worldview' must be attributed to that later date, also. Although certain characteristics of the new worldview may be seen in the oracles of classical prophets, I admit quickly that those oracles were not written down and organized until the exile and post-exilic era, so that some of that sophistication may be attributed to the later redactors. Likewise, the Deuteronomistic History may have pulled together many diverse pre-exilic oral traditions and fragmentary memories, but the final edition of that history is an exilic creation at the earliest, and in those final editorial activities can be seen great theological sophistication. Further, the strident monotheism of Second Isaiah and the later Priestly editorial work in the Pentateuch comes from the exile and post-exilic era, and here can be seen some of the most advanced insights and expressions of the monotheistic worldview. The new worldview is a late product and should be seen as such; pre-exilic religion in Israel and Judah should be viewed as much more closely knit to the greater West-Semitic religious continuum of Syria and Palestine, and it contained only the seedlings which would come to maturity in the exile and beyond.

This new perspective has significant pedagogical implications, most important of which is the recognition that Second Temple period Judaism is the arena in which monotheism came to rich fruition. Julius Wellhausen denigrated the period as one of scribalism and priestly legalism. Not only was he wrong, but the Priestly editors may have been the most brilliant and creative theologians on the monotheistic trajectory. How we envision the pre-exilic and post-exilic eras should change, and how we write the textbooks most definitely must change.

What emerges as a monotheistic belief system in the post-exilic period may be placed in contrast with the ancient Near Eastern thought. Biblical theologians are, of course, viewing the product of an Axial Age revolution with the worldview out of which it arose. They are comparing Jewish thought after 500 BCE with ancient thought from 3000 to 500 BCE, and that is a little unfair. Therefore, comparisons must be nuanced and sensitive to the fact that we are comparing two worldviews from across the ages.

III

Let us return to the sweeping generalizations of the *Heilsgeschichte* theologians to observe how we might redefine them for contemporary understanding.

1) Yahweh was portrayed as the Lord of history and the social arena, and his actions were described in epic form; while the gods of the nations were connected to the forces of nature, and their actions were described in myth.

We now appreciate more how historical and epic thought evolves slowly out of mythic modes of thought. Frank Cross was one of the first to focus closely on this as an important process.[23] We also recognize that historical modes of perception were emerging in the first millennium BCE, especially among the Assyrians and the Chaldean Babylonians. Assyrians saw Ashur and Ninurta as deities who proclaimed a manifest destiny for Assyrians to rule the world; the old static worldview was replaced with one which said that, 'the gods had a plan in history, and that Assyria was the primordial agent in the plan'.[24] To a slightly lesser extent the Chaldeans had the same vision of Marduk. Most likely the Achaemenid Persian portrayal of Ahura-Mazda was as developed, or more so, than either Assyrian or Babylonian beliefs. These views are quite comparable to the biblical views, as ancient Near Eastern historians have pointed out quite adamantly in the past generation. Just as the old storm god Yahweh became a deity of history and social events, so also the storm gods Ashur and Marduk underwent a parallel transformation. Israel was part of the intellectual scene, and one can no longer contrast Israel with the ancient Near East on this issue.

However, the Israelite or Jewish portrayal of a deity active in history did develop more than in those other societies. The biblical view would declare Yahweh to be totally a god of historical and social action, and the nature imagery would fall into oblivion. The portrayal of Yahweh as a social deity was indeed comparable to what we see in Assyrian and Babylonian texts, but Israelite and Jewish thinkers took this imagery to a new level by making Yahweh radically transcendent over the diverse forces of the world. Ultimately, it became the central theme in the

---

23. Cross, *Canaanite Myth*.
24. Saggs, *Assyria*, p. 265.

Pentateuchal and Deuteronomistic narratives.[25] In this literature one finds a well-defined image of Yahweh's plan in history over a long period of time. Although Mesopotamia produced great histories which likewise covered long periods of time and saw history governed by cultic agenda, such as devotion to Marduk's temple in Babylon (including the *Curse of Akkad, Chronicles of Early Kings, Weidner Chronicle, Neo-Babylonian Chronicle, Assyrian Synchronistic History, Ecclectic Chronicle* and the *Chronicle of the Early Kings*, among others),[26] the biblical narratives have a somewhat more sophisticated moral agenda in their review of human events. The biblical texts see a grand promise and fulfillment pattern in history, they proclaim retribution not only for cultic infidelity and polytheism but also for ethical offenses (e.g., Naboth's vineyard), and they have a vague sense that Yahweh leads people into the future.[27] Although these elements might be found in the great Mesopotamian literary works in some primitive form, biblical historiography developed them much more.

2) In the past Yahweh was portrayed as a social deity who transcended nature, while the ancient Near Eastern deities were equated with the various phenomena of nature, and thereby were limited to categories such as the sun, moon, wind or water, and unable to become personal

25. J. Barr, 'The Interpretation of Scripture. II. Revelation through History in the Old Testament and in Modern Theology', *Int* 17 (1963), p. 201; P. Hanson, 'Jewish Apocalyptic Against Its Near Eastern Environment', *RB* 78 (1971), pp. 31-38; Fohrer, *Religion*, p. 79; Saggs, *Encounter*, p. 92; H. Butterfield, *The Origins of History* (New York: Basic Books, 1981), pp. 86, 116, 159; O. Eckart, *Ethik*, pp. 47-218.

26. These texts were discussed in this regard by Gnuse, *Heilsgeschichte*, pp. 33-51.

27. H. Gese, 'The Idea of History in the Ancient Near East and the Old Testament', *The Bultmann School of Biblical Interpretation: New Directions?* (ed. R. Funk; New York: Harper & Row, 1965), pp. 62-64; Lindblom, *Prophecy*, p. 325; J.R. Porter, 'Old Testament Historiography', *Tradition and Interpetation: Essays by Members of the Society for Old Testament Study* (ed. G. Anderson; Oxford: Clarendon Press, 1979), p. 131; Butterfield, *History*, pp. 89, 98, 159; C. Evans, 'Naram-Sin and Jeroboam: The Archetypal Unheilsherrscher in Mesopotamian and Biblical Historiography', *Scripture in Context. II. More Essays on the Comparative Method* (eds. W. Hallo, J. Moyer and L. Perdue; Winona Lake, IN: Eisenbrauns, 1983), p. 110; Van Seters, *Abraham*, pp. 359-61; J. Licht, 'Biblical Historicism', *History, Historiography and Interpretation: Studies in Biblical and Cuneiform Literatures* (eds. H. Tadmor and M. Weinfeld; Jerusalem: Magnes, 1984), pp. 109-111.

deities who could demand social responsibilities from their devotees.

Although scholars often overemphasized the difference between Yahweh as a social deity and the nature orientation of the other gods, there is some truth to the generalization. To be sure, Yahweh had a long standing tradition as a storm god, and indeed Mesopotamian and Egyptian deities were active in the personal and social arenas, especially Ninurta, Ashur and Marduk. Nevertheless, critical scholars recognize that the ancient Near Easterners never entirely cut the gods free from their specific nature connections. Even in the later first millennium BCE portrayals the gods retain aspects of their original nature metaphors, whereas ultimately Yahweh made the separation completely. Yahweh's character thus developed more in biblical literature.[28]

There is more to this discussion, especially in regard to the contrast between monotheism and polytheism in any culture. In polytheism or even henotheis diverse deities in the divine realm always will have specific numina and attributes credited to them, but in radical monotheism all the attributes have to be given to one deity, until finally that deity transcends them all. One might notice that whereas the ancient Near Eastern deities could be seen as 'inside as well as outside the phenomena they represented', Yahweh was always outside or above those phenomena.[29] Even in the Aton cult, the closest the ancient Near East came to monotheism, the deity did not escape association with the sun, a phenomenon 'inside' nature.

Michael Fishbane observes that the cosmos for polytheists is an interlocked and interconnected 'plenum' or unity 'pulsating with divine life'. The gods, in effect, are the natural order in a holistic sense: each emerges from the organic oneness of the natural order to exemplify part of it. The gods are 'immanent and near, and there is a deep harmony linking man and god and world'. There is a 'cosmic organum' with resonant sympathies that people and deities merge into in order to obtain harmony, whether it is *Ma'at* in Egypt or *Me* in Mesopotamia. Cultic activities enable people to enter that terrifying yet nurturing organic oneness of reality.[30] Polytheism, says A. Brelich, then differentiates that great divine unity into manifold gods, and they become immanent and

---

28. Moriarity, 'Word', pp. 359-361; Reventlow, 'Eigenart', pp. 199-217; Dietrich, 'Werden und Wesen', p. 23.

29. Machinist, 'Distinctiveness', p. 424.

30. Fishbane, *Garments*, pp. 50-52.

accessible to the devotees.[31] Because divinity is 'experienced as an ingredient immanent in a restless cosmos', religious observances are the petitioners' attempts at 'subservience, negotiation, and even...control', according to Frans Jozef van Beeck.[32]

Radical monotheism destroys that 'oneness'. In radical monotheism the god cannot be immanent in any of the diverse phenomena of nature individually; he or she must be present in all equally, and that inevitably becomes presence in none. There is then only the 'God' above and the inanimate realm below. Monotheism loses the particularities of the divine as it combines them into one deity. The world below will have only creatures in it. That 'God' then is a transcendent deity high in the heavens. Yet that singular deity must still relate personally to people, he cannot exist as a *deus otiosus*, as can happen to the high, creator deity in polytheism (like El in the Ugaritic literature). If the manifold expressions of nature are inadequate vehicles for the divine manifestations on the personal level, then the social arena becomes the sole mode of revelation and divine immanence. Therefore, polytheism or henotheism can never create the radical stress upon the social dimension and the concomitant rejection of the natural dimension for revelation. Nor could polytheism ever assault the organic unity of the world in which the gods are manifest. But when the world is emptied of gods, the one 'God' who is distant must become present to people socially and existentially. So, the Jews split the divine–human nature continuum by casting 'God' into the heavens. Yahweh then was no longer in nature, but Yahweh was still lord over nature, and it was responsive to the divine will.[33] The Jewish 'religious intuitions...theoretically drove an impossible wedge between the God of Sinai and the gods of nature'.[34] This has implications for the religious response, or ethics. Again, this is not to say that the Jewish understanding of Yahweh as a deity who transcends the natural realm is the opposite of ancient Near Eastern belief, it rather stresses how the Jewish views moved beyond the ancient Near East on that trajectory of socializing the high god because of the ideological factors which monotheism provides.

An important corollary to this is the treatment of the old gods. When

31. A. Brelich, 'Polytheismus', *Numen* 7 (1960), pp. 123-36.

32. van Beeck, 'Israel's God', p. 225.

33. Moriarity, 'Word', pp. 360-61; Stolz, 'Monotheismus in Israel', pp. 182-84; Nicholson, *God*, pp. 207-208; Fishbane, *Garments*, pp. 53-60; Dietrich, 'Werden und Wesen', pp. 21; Albertz, 'Der Ort', p. 81.

34. Fishbane, *Garments*, p. 58.

only one being is allowed the title of 'God', then the other beings must be redefined as angels or demons. Henotheism or monolatry does not need to do this; it can allow the lesser gods to be ignored or sink into inferiority or become part of a nameless lump, like the 'heavenly host'. The use of this expression in pre-exilic texts at times may refer to a collective aggregate of divine beings who are lesser gods, and this would be a good indication that monolatry rather than monotheism characterizes the perception of those speakers. It is also indicative of the process of movement toward monotheism, for these other deities are in the early stages of being phased out. In this regard, Theodore Mullen has a good point when he stresses how the 'heavenly host' of Yahweh seem to have no individual names. They have lost their status as real gods and are being turned into a nameless collective.[35] This divine 'lump' of the gods was depersonalized late in the pre-exilic era; in the post-exilic era the 'heavenly host' evolved into angels and demons.

Sometimes a particular deity seems to gradually transform into an angel or a demon most directly, such as is the case with the Christian conversion of pagan peoples. Then specific gods, like Pan and Loki, simply became demons; or good gods were absorbed into the personalities of saints. Sometimes an old god might become an entirely new figure, so that Baal imagery became part of the portrayal of the 'Son of Man' figure in Daniel 7 or St Michael in the book of Revelation. At any rate, radical monotheism undertakes a drastic demotion of the gods by turning them into something lower in status than even the old 'heavenly host'. Yahweh absorbs the characteristics of the other gods and then excludes them from the universe, so that there is a great 'decline of the gods'.[36]

This has tremendous implications for popular familial piety, an area that biblical scholars have often overlooked. In the pre-exilic era the henotheistic Israelites thought it perfectly natural to worship the high god Yahweh in a corporate assembly, but in their homes they had fertility figures, and probably revered asherim and local baalim extensively. Women especially were attracted to the cult of Asherah and the Queen of Heaven, for she was a feminine being in the divine realm and Yahweh was very masculine. But in the post-exilic era Yahweh replaced the asherim and the baalim in familial piety. This did not happen without a psychological struggle, as indicated by the staunch retention of Asherah

35. Mullen, *Assembly*, pp. 279-82 *et passim*.
36. Russell, *Devil*, pp. 184-85; Dietrich, 'Werden und Wesen', pp. 19-21.

among the diaspora Jews at Elephantine in Egypt in the sixth and fifth centuries BCE. Rainer Albertz has attempted to trace the evolution of such familial piety, and he observes this aspect of post-exilic change was significant—the transcendent Yahweh had to become the focus of family piety.[37]

Strangely enough monotheism does create problems for itself in this process. When the heavens are emptied of the gods, the need for a culprit for evil emerges. When there are other deities one can blame a particular god or all the other gods for the evil that occurs. In the polytheistic assumptions it is even acceptable to attribute bad things to the good god, because with so many deities there is a conflict of wills in the divine realm, and such conflict and tension can lead even a good god to will evil things on the earth. But in radical monotheism the one transcendent deity rises above willing evil things upon people such as suffering and death. These evil things must result either from human free will and sin, as Genesis 3 implies, or they come from an evil principle which becomes personified as the devil. Radical monotheism eventually creates a devil, as Judaism did after 200 BCE. Christianity and Islam both followed suit by retaining the nasty fellow, and then monotheists have argued ever since as to whether the devil is a personified being (as revivalist preachers would have it), or merely the abstract principle of evil, a negative level of being (as Augustine would have it), or the dark side of human nature (as liberal Christian theology would have it). Ultimately imagery attributed to satan or the devil is the personification of the dark side of God or the old gods into one being. Such personification always runs the risk of creating a counter deity and thus subverting monotheism into dualism.[38] Zoroastrianism, Qumran sectarians and perhaps revivalistic preachers today, all have become dualists to varying degrees.

Needless to say, radical monotheism creates another problem for itself, the question of theodicy, or the origin of evil and suffering in the world. In general, we see this question emerge in the post-exilic literature, especially in the wisdom literature of Job, Sirach and the Wisdom of Solomon. The question of suffering also underlies the creation and use of lament hymns in the Psalter. Monotheism did not create the debate over the origin of evil, for we may observe it already in Mesopotamian myths,

---

37. Albertz, *Israelite Religion*, II, p. 401.

38. Russell, *Devil*, pp. 176-220, provides an excellent analysis of this phenomenon; Dietrich, 'Werden und Wesen', p. 20; K. Koch, 'Monotheismus und Angelogie', *Ein Gott allein* (eds. Dietrich and Klopfenstein), pp. 565-81.

such as the story of Adapa and the loss of immortality and the story of Enki's creation of deformities. But monotheism does intensify the discussion, for when there is one divine will in the heavens, believers will inquire more ardently why that singular deity wills evil. When there were many gods, with many wills in conflict in the divine realm, it was easier to accept that evil could happen upon the earth. When only one god remains in the heavens, evil seems very unfair. Monotheism with its deity who transcends the phenomena of this world radically intensifies the theodicy debate, and monotheistic philosophers have struggled with the question ever since.[39]

Finally, monotheism creates the need or the problem to reconcile great tensions in the divine nature. The one deity must become transcendent yet immanent, source of judgment and blessing, wrathful yet loving, author of good and either author or permitter of evil. Radical monotheism brought contradictory roles for Yahweh. Thus, in Genesis 1 Yahweh creates the cosmos like the high god El or Marduk, but in Genesis 2 Yahweh forms people like Belet-ili in the Mesopotamian *Atrahasis Epic*. In Genesis 7–9 Yahweh brings the flood like the high god of the storm, Enlil, but he compassionately saves people, like Enki, the antagonist of Enlil in the Mesopotamian flood stories.[40] Walter Dietrich speaks of how religious discourse with only one deity is more intellectually difficult than having to work with a pantheon of gods, and David Petersen notes that, '...one senses that the deity in Jewish, Christian, and Muslim traditions is equally, if not more, complex, having to perform as an agent of both judgment and salvation'.[41]

This demands sophisticated thinking, or what historians call the 'second level' or the 'second order' of intellectual reflection found in the Axial Age.[42] It involves the intellectual courage to use paradox extensively in

39. J. Finkelstein, 'Bible and Babel', pp. 437-39; Moriarity, 'Word', p. 360; Reventlow, 'Eigenart', pp. 213-15; R. Knierim, 'The Task of Old Testament Theology', *HBT* 6 (1984), pp. 25-57; W. Brueggemann, 'Theodicy in a Social Dimension', *JSOT* 33 (1985), pp. 3-25; K. van der Toorn, *Sin and Sanction in Israel and Mesopotamia: A Comparative Study* (Studia semitica neerlandica, 22; Assen: Van Gorcum, 1985), pp. 1-115; Halpern, 'Brisker Pipes', p. 106; Petersen, 'Israel and Monotheism', pp. 101-103.

40. Petersen, 'Israel and Monotheism', pp. 101-102.

41. Dietrich, 'Werden und Wesen', p. 20; Petersen, 'Israel and Monotheism', p. 103.

42. Eisenstadt, 'Characteristics', pp. 1-25; *idem*, 'Ancient Israel', pp. 127-34; Elkana, 'Classical Greece', pp. 40-64.

the description of the divine, and it admits the deeper mystery of understanding the divine which transcends human knowledge. This appears in China as talk about the inability to understand the Tao, and in India as the attribution of total transcendence and yet total immanence to Brahma, who is beyond the universe and all existence (*Para Brahma* or *Niguna Brahma*) and yet is 'enfleshed out' as the world or *Maya* (*Apara Brahma* or *Seguna Brahma*). So also in theistic Judaism the attribution of characteristics to the divine nature, which stand in tension, is a sophisticated form of speculation. It begins with a classical prophet like Hosea, who can imagine God as the loving yet angry husband or parent. It comes to fruition with the radical monotheism of the post-exilic period portrayal of a God who has transcended nature but absorbed all the divine characteristics of the old gods (except for evil, which is subcontracted eventually to the devil). Radical monotheism has the courage to work with paradox in describing the divine nature.

Israel's monotheism has the distinctive ability to declare that the national god of a particular people may express wrath against that people. Whereas the ancient Near Easterners might speak of how their gods deserted them in order to cause their military downfall, Israelite prophets already before the exile would declare that their God actually used the foreign nations directly to punish the chosen people. This moves significantly beyond prior expressions in the ancient world.[43] Furthermore, the rationale for that divine punishment has changed. There are examples of ancient Near Eastern deities expressing displeasure against their people for cultic offenses. But the frequent portrayal of Yahweh as potentially being wrathful because of ethical violations seems to be more developed in biblical literature, for Yahweh has enduring standards which people must meet for all time. Again, biblical faith is not the opposite of ancient Near Eastern beliefs; rather, it has developed the idea of a morally indignant deity more consistently. The image of wrath in one's own god is the tip of the iceberg in monotheistic speculation. One god is the source of wrath and compassion, and if you are beginning to think in monotheistic terms, the portrayal of divine wrath will become a leitmotif.[44]

This discussion began with the observation that formerly biblical theologians portrayed Yahweh as a social deity in opposition to the nature deities of the ancient Near East and Canaan, and this was an

43. Lohfink, 'Das Alte Testament', pp. 28-47; Dietrich, 'Werden und Wesen', p. 21.
44. Jacobsen, *Treasures*, p. 164.

overgeneralization. Indeed it was, but there remains an aspect of truth to the caricature. Belief in one deity entails several radical intellectual assumptions, which begin to appear very early in the monotheistic trajectory of Israel, most notably with the classical prophets, and these notions then come to fruition in the post-exilic era. Belief in one god causes the reflective believers to move the deity beyond the diverse numina of the natural order, turn nature into a physical 'godless' realm, speak radically of the social and historical arenas as avenues for the divine, destroy the old gods by transformation, and face difficult philosophical questions, such as the origin of evil, the justice of god, and paradox in the divine nature. Scholars now acknowledge that we ought not place Israelites and Jews in opposition to the ancient Near Eastern worldview, but must sense that their role in the great Axial Age intellectual revolution went beyond the values of polytheistic or even henotheistic religions. As Michael Fishbane concludes, there still is truth in the old 'cosmos' versus 'history' dichotomy.[45]

3) In past years biblical scholars said that Israelite Yahwism developed morality and ethics, while ancient Near Eastern religious expressions manifested degenerate cultic activity and manipulative sacrifice, which offered no true moral guidance to people.

This was expressed too starkly, for it overlooked a long literary tradition in the ancient world which articulated moral social norms for human behavior. One may find this tradition best represented in the wisdom tradition of ancient Egypt, as in the proverbial collections of *Ptah-hotep* (2500 BCE), *Amen-em-het* (1900 BCE), *Amen-em-ope* (1100 BCE), and stories like the *Tale of the Eloquent Peasant* (2100 BCE). It is found in texts which oblige the Mesopotamian kings to proper behavior and the maintenance of justice in the land. So, it was improper for scholars to speak of the ancient Near East as lacking morality and ethical standards.

However, here again the question may be raised concerning the degree of difference between Israel and the predecessor cultures, especially recognizing that biblical texts in the legal and prophetic collections were shaped by a monotheistic intelligentsia during and after the exile in the Axial Age revolution. One can ask the question concerning the impact of such socially and ethically minded literature in Egypt and Mesopotamia. Was it not confined to the intellectuals and the scribal elite, so that it may have had little impact upon the social and political realia of that age? Such a question may be answered in the affirmative, but we must

45. Fishbane, *Garments*, p. 55.

admit it is truly difficult to gauge the impact of these ideas in Egypt and Mesopotamia from the distance of several thousand years and with the few texts that we possess. But from our limited vantage point it does appear that some Israelites, the Deuteronomic reformers, and the post-exilic Jews saw ethical guidelines as more important and used them more extensively in shaping their society than can be observed elsewhere in that age. In part, this was possible because Israelites and Jews lived in a simpler society than the river cultures of Egypt and Mesopotamia. Especially after the exile, as Jews reconstructed their society, it was possible to elevate moral and ethical norms in the recreation of their worldviews and social structures. Also, Israel and post-exilic Judaism were really peripheral cultures. They stood at the edge of the great high cultures where they could 'appropriate' (not just 'borrow') ideas, reconstruct and use them, and then ignore what they did not need or appreciate. In a similar way, Phoenicians invented the alphabet when powerful and cautious scribal guilds in Mesopotamia would not dare to simplify their complex cuneiform script, lest they lose their professional monopoly on writing documents for palaces, temples and businesses (like lawyers and law today). Likewise, Greece made advances in law, government and philosophy. Israelites and Jews made their contribution in religion and ethics. Again, we feel constrained to say that the biblical tradition did not contradict prior values of the ancient world, but further developed the ethical tradition in human culture. What values might have received less emphasis in shaping human culture in the older cultures became the dominant mode of discourse among the Jews.

While we cannot prove that ethics moved from being a minor factor in ancient Near Eastern culture to becoming a dominant force in Jewish culture, there are some subtle indications that this is so. In a polytheistic system of belief there are many gods, and so many divine wills in the heavens, which may conflict with each other.[46] Even in henotheism the other gods are subordinate, but their wills do not disappear. In Mesopotamian myths, especially, we see the conflict among the gods in creation accounts like the *Atrahasis Epic* and the *Enuma Elish*. By contrast, in Genesis 1 the world is created by the will and word of one deity.

Critical scholars have regarded the conflict of divine wills in a polytheistic worldview as being significant for moral values. The mythological world is jealously divided among the various powers and is very particular, in contrast with a transcendent deity who is non-particular, non-ethnic,

46. Von Soden, 'Das Fragen', p. 46; Saggs, *Encounter*, p. 116.

non-seasonal and non-local, a view produced by the diaspora experience.[47] The best the mythological mind can create is a 'bland drift towards the idea that all gods were but aspects of the One'.[48] Polytheism scatters people's attention among many gods, but monotheism focuses it upon one god.[49] Polytheism presents believers with a 'plurality of superhuman wills' which means the 'gods cannot act consistently' to give a single moral imperative to people. Different deities require different cultic and ethical responses. Yes, the polytheists have ethical imperatives inherent in their religions, but they can never be sure that a particular ethical mandate will survive in the long-term conflict of the divine realm. There is 'no assurance or hope that right conduct would assure their well-being'. Ancient Near Easterners were moral, perhaps more so than their rustic pre-exilic Israelite counterparts, but they ultimately could experience neither religious certitude nor satisfaction from their moral behavior. Monotheism provides one divine will and one clear ethical imperative, which will suffer no rival or challenge from the divine realm. In effect, biblical ethics can be developed more, speak with greater authority, and above all, provide better security for faithful believers seeking moral directives.[50] Once more a degree of difference can be seen between biblical thought and the predecessor worldviews, and it is due to the monotheistic ability to proclaim morality and ethics in sterner fashion with uniform authority.

There are further ideational implications which flow from this. In a more directly proclaimed revelation of ethical imperatives, the addressed humanity feels inadequacy more deeply. This 'profound sense of human inadequacy' leads the religious adherents to speak more of guilt rather than impurity and of forgiveness more than purification.[51] In addition, the address is a verbal moral imperative. The 'Word' which confronts people takes the place of visual images, or icons of the gods. One may see this notion begin to emerge in the oral proclamations of the prophets and come to fruition in the post-exilic period when the oral words were converted into a 'Written Word' and eventually into a canon. This is furthered by the sole deity's transcendence over the forces of nature. A great abyss opens between God and people, nature, or the world below.

---

47. van Beeck, 'Israel's God', pp. 225-26; Albertz, 'Der Ort', p. 81.
48. Saggs, *Civilization*, p. 15.
49. Moltmann, 'Inviting Unity', pp. 51-52; Albertz, 'Der Ort', p. 81.
50. J. Finkelstein, 'Bible and Babel', pp. 438-42.
51. J. Finkelstein, 'Bible and Babel', pp. 439-41.

Revelation cannot be found in nature, but only in the spoken word in the arena of history. 'Word' thus replaces 'image' and the imperative is now more clear, and it directs people more to social behavior than to cultic activity.[52]

Several authors have been led to affirm that Jewish ethics may not be different in content from the ancient Near Eastern texts, but there is a certain superiority in the intellectual context in which it is expressed.[53] This perception ought to affect the way in which we read biblical narratives. Formerly scholars made point by point comparisons to find evidence of biblical moral superiority. Sometimes we forced the argument on specific issues. Now we should realize that the entire narrative speaks a moral message from a greater monotheistic context. Jacob Finkelstein points out how often monotheistic and polytheistic texts are really similar, and the trivial differences are overplayed by us. Morality is not found in the details of a narrative, but in the greater message of the total context. He demonstrates this with the Mesopotamian and biblical flood accounts, wherein the real difference is in the self-understood monotheism of the biblical narrative, which lends the image of greater divine control and moral purpose to the whole story, and not in any individual phrase or motif which differentiates the stories.[54]

The Jewish distinction is not found in the content of ethical imperatives, but rather in their powerful and uniform address to human existence. This direct address of the word from the distant deity gradually impresses upon the listener the great human responsibility to respond and obey. This, in turn, leads to a greater awareness of human freedom and responsibility.

4) In past generalizations scholars spoke of human freedom found in Israelite religion and the idea of cosmic pre-destination and determination found in the ancient Near Eastern texts. Critical scholars were able to point out examples of texts in the ancient Near East to show that we had overemphasized ideas of cosmic repetition and that notions of determinism were breaking down among the intelligentsia. In turn, they

52. J. Finkelstein, 'Bible and Babel', pp. 439-41; Lambert, 'History and the Gods: A Review Article', *Or* 39 (1970), p. 172; Moriarity, 'Word', pp. 345-62; Theissen, *Biblical Faith*, p. 75; Elkana, 'Classical Greece', p. 53.

53. Butterfield, *History*, pp. 64-69; J. Moyer, 'Hittite and Israelite Cultic Practices: A Selected Comparison', *Scripture in Context II* (eds. Hallo, Moyer and Perdue), pp. 19-38; Otto, *Ethik*, pp. 215-19.

54. J. Finkelstein, 'Bible and Babel', pp. 440-43.

also pointed to texts in the Bible which implied pre-determined forces in the world, which had been overlooked in exegesis and theologizing.

Here again the proper characterization may be to stress the degree to which cultures may have spoken of cosmic determination and human freedom. There may have been a progression toward stressing human free will after the advent of literacy in 3000 BCE, and Israel was part of this evolving process. Historians speak of how the ability to write and record gives people, especially the intelligentsia, the insight into the power they have over the world around them. They can capture the oral word and preserve it, they can create records to shape the affairs of priests and kings, and they can record sacred liturgies—thereby capturing their power in a written expression over which they have control.[55]

Perhaps the invention of the alphabet furthered this process of intellectual evolution. Frank Cross speaks of how the alphabet created both 'logic' and 'skepticism', because a person may organize and observe reality in a simple, linear and written form. Writing makes possible 'the examination and re-examination of an easily visualized record of a legal argument, a classification of scientific items, a philosophical discourse, a historical narrative or a piece of royal propaganda'.[56] The alphabet made possible the emergence of philosophy and science in Greece and monotheism, ethics and social justice in Israel. Writing made possible the prophetic critique of the sacred claims of 'deified kings and hierarchical class structure assumed to be part of the order of creation'. It helped Greece and Israel to become radical new societies which experienced a 'profound break from the older conservative and hierarchical societies of the ancient Near East'.[57]

Therefore, writing may have helped begin the process of developing a sense of human freedom and power over the cosmos, and maybe the alphabet accelerated this process. If so, Israel stood to profit from the culmination of this on-going process in the middle of the first millennium BCE, after the apparent increase in literacy indicated by the archaeological record after 700 BCE.[58] (This date is later than the time implied by Cross in the previous quotes, for the most recent scholarly perception of when literacy emerged in Israel is being revised downward.)

55. Graham, *Written Word*, p. 16; Shanks, 'Frank Cross', p. 25; Lewis, 'Persepolis Tablets', pp. 17-32.
56. Shanks, 'Frank Cross', p. 25.
57. Shanks, 'Frank Cross', pp. 25-26.
58. Jamieson-Drake, *Scribes*, pp. 48-80 *et passim*.

Regardless of the discussion over whether literacy creates the concept of freedom, many authors sense that biblical literature stresses human freedom more than ancient Near Eastern literature. To be sure, the notions of human freedom and responsibility existed before the first millennium BCE, but the Israelites and Jews seem to have stressed them to a higher degree. One may still find strong evidence of determinism in ancient Near Eastern texts proportionately greater than in biblical texts.[59]

Furthermore, if Yahwism and Judaism stressed human freedom more, then any use of magic or divination to manipulate God would be lessened appropriately. One may find evidence of magical and divinatory concepts in the biblical text, which certainly reflects the popular piety of Israelites in the pre-exilic period. Nevertheless, a comparison of biblical texts with ancient Near Eastern texts reveals far less concern with manipulating the divine realm among Yahweh devotees. Ancient Near Eastern texts have extensive references to many different forms of divination, while the biblical texts have only vague allusions to a few practices, and zealous condemnation of such practices abounds in many passages. By the exile and post-exilic period Jews rather consciously condemned divination because of its attempt to manipulate Yahweh. Israelites and later Jews had begun the process of breaking out of the 'tight ring of magic'.[60] The ultimate result was a view of the world in which people no longer feared the forces of nature or the unknown future. The world became rationalized, it was a place emptied of the gods, and people 'ruled' over the natural order (Gen. 1.28), for they were only a little less than the angels or 'gods' (Ps. 8).[61] The universe was seen no longer as predictable, as a throbbing and dynamic nexus of powers to be feared or manipulated, as a place where mysterious wills abounded; rather, it was the arena for human life.

This view comes to fruition in the post-exilic era, as the later Priestly texts of Genesis 1 and Psalm 8 imply. The affirmation of human freedom, rejection of divine manipulation, and the liberation from a mysterious

59. W. Lambert, 'Destiny and Divine Intervention in Babylon and Israel', *OTS* 17 (1972), pp. 65-72; Jacobsen, *Treasures*, p. 81; Saggs, *Encounter*, pp. 71-72; van der Toorn, *Sin*, pp. 1-115; Nicholson, *God*, p. 216; Dietrich, 'Werden und Wesen', p. 22.

60. Moriarity, 'Word', p. 360; Eisenstadt, 'Ancient Israel', p. 128; Nicholson, *God*, pp. 208-10; Uffenheimer, 'Ancient Israel', pp. 156-62.

61. Moriarity, 'Word', p. 160; Schmidt, *Faith*, p. 173; Nicholson, *God*, pp. 209-15; Dietrich, 'Werden und Wesen', pp. 21-23.

natural order emerged slowly in Israelite thought, much later than biblical theologians assumed a generation ago. The first glimmerings may be observed in the classical prophets, but some primitive notions may be located in their oracles and even in a book as late as Deuteronomy. Deut. 21.1-9 states that the blood of a murder victim will pollute the ground and deter crop growth, and Deut. 23.9-14 observes that human excrement in the military camp will cause Yahweh to leave the camp. The old notions did not die easily, even late biblical texts accept some rather primitive ideas, and, of course, superstitious customs which betray the assumptions of a mythic worldview would continue among the people for centuries—even until today. With the emergence of radical mono-theism in the exile and beyond, the old worldview began to crumble quickly in the minds of the Jews, and the biblical text reflects that experience. Biblical thought is part of a greater evolutionary development in the ancient world beginning around 3000 BCE, which is still occurring today—for some people still have horoscopes, palm readers and other forms of superstition, all of which betray fearful anxieties and a flight from freedom and responsibility. The biblical tradition is not unique in its perceptions in the ancient world, but its contribution to the evolutionary advance and the affirmation of human freedom in the cosmos is truly significant in the course of human history.

5) Biblical theologians of a former age especially relished speaking of Israel's sense of social justice and egalitarianism in contrast to the class-oriented and oppressive societies in the ancient Near East and the Canaanite city states. This contrast has been an important rhetorical device for advocates of an Israelite internal revolution in early Iron Age I (1200–1050 BCE), including George Mendenhall, Norman Gottwald and liberation theologians in general. As biblical theologians they proclaimed a message that needed to be heard most by twentieth-century Christian audiences, but their caricatures may have been overdrawn.

Critics have pointed out that ancient Near Eastern texts had an old venerable tradition of speaking out on behalf of the poor and oppressed. James Henry Breasted, in particular, lauded the accomplishments of Egyptian thinkers in the third millennium BCE wisdom texts, and referred to the emergence of Osiran religion in the First Intermediate Period (2400–2100 BCE) as the world's first democratic revolution.[62] Other authors, too, stressed the presence of social values and ideas of justice

---

62. Breasted, *Development*, pp. 142-98; *idem, Dawn*, pp. 94-151.

for the poor in ancient Near Eastern documents.[63]

On the other hand, biblical theologians who argue for the significance of Israelite and Jewish contributions to the concept of social justice for the poor ought not to concede too much. Here the biblical tradition may have provided an even more significant advance over the values of its contemporary culture. Rhetoric in texts of ancient Egypt and Mesopotamia spoken on behalf of the poor was often articulated by middle class scribes, or members of the intelligentsia, who did not hold the reins of power. Texts which spoke of how the king or pharaoh brings justice to the land were probably designed more for political propaganda. River valley states were by necessity tightly ruled, class-oriented societies.[64] The laws in the codes, such as that of Hammurabi, clearly acknowledged class identity in the process of administering justice, and the laws clearly were designed to protect people of power and wealth against the poor. To be sure, the kings of Israel and Judah were probably tyrants of the same ilk as all the kings around them—critical texts like 1 Samuel 8 and 12 certainly say as much. But in this one corner of the world the dissident words of prophets were remembered, for a brief time some social reform may have occurred under Deuteronomic reformers (622–609 BCE), and most important of all, this literature of social reform was written down, collected and proclaimed as an authoritative religious and social guide for the reconstruction of the post-exilic community of Judaism. No other society took the literature of dissent and placed so much of it into a sacred text, which in turn provided the blueprint for religious and social life. Here biblical theologians should continue to stress the great contribution of the biblical traditions to human history.

The ancient Near East provided ideas to the Jews. Perhaps institutions such as the Sabbath Year (Deut. 15) and Jubilee Year (Lev. 25), for example, were inspired by Babylonian Amorite edicts (*Mishnarum* and *Andararu* proclamations of the kings) from the early second millennium BCE. But the Jews attempted to make these institutions more extensive and regular mechanisms in the economic life of a society; they even kept the Sabbath Year for many centuries. The implementation of these two institutions certainly reflects a new mentality in the ancient world.[65]

63. Hammershaimb, 'Ethics', pp. 75-101; Fensham, 'Widow', pp. 161-71.

64. K. Wittfogel, *Oriental Despotism* (New Haven: Yale University Press, 1957).

65. Gnuse, *Steal*, pp. 32-45; *idem*, 'Jubilee Legislation in Leviticus 25: Ancient Israel's Social Reform', *BTB* 15 (1985), pp. 43-48; Uffenheimer, 'Ancient Israel', pp. 153-54.

Perhaps, rhetoric to care for the poor, the widow and the orphan may be found in ancient Near Eastern texts, but the Jews tried to make this message more central in the values of their society. The imperative to care for the marginal was strengthened greatly by its connection to the central message of Jewish faith, the deliverance from Egypt by Yahweh through the exodus—'you shall take care of the poor, the widow, the orphan, for I, the Lord, delivered you from the land of slavery'.

The call for justice in the Hebrew Bible is connected to the image of Yahweh as the liberator of slaves. While other countries emphasized their high gods (Re, Atum, El, Marduk, Ninurta, Ashur, etc.) as creators of the world, the biblical texts stressed how Yahweh freed slaves. This also means that the historical and social dimension are stressed more than the cosmic dimension, and this provides a more consistent portrayal of Yahweh's actions in the historical arena. This image of Yahweh as the liberator of slaves gives tremendous impetus to social justice imperatives. The proclamation of Yahweh's liberation of slaves in the exodus restores the image of immanence to the portrayal of the deity, and this balances the image of transcendence caused by being the only god in the heavens.[66] Contemporary biblical theologians correctly speak of how the emergent monotheistic process was connected deeply to the struggle for justice and social equality.[67] Rainer Albertz asserts that monotheism and social justice can emerge only as significant ideological agendas in the wake of the destruction of city, palace and Temple in 586 BCE, for then the theologians became free to articulate these values for the creation of a new society.[68] The portrayal of Yahweh as the liberator deity and the demand for a just society may set the Jewish world view apart from other predecessor cultures in the ancient world to the greatest degree.

Monotheistic religions in general arise with social agendas and an imperative to change people's attitudes and values. Zoroaster, Jesus and Muhammed all had a radical reform agenda which included social values, or at least they had these values later attributed to them by the

---

66. Moltmann, 'Inviting Unity', pp. 51-52; Sperling, 'Israel's Religion', p. 22; Uffenheimer, 'Ancient Israel', p. 144; Luckert, *Egyptian Light*, p. 128, colorfully speaks of how this religion 'toppled many a grand domesticator and pretender to divine authority'.

67. Stolz, 'Monotheismus in Israel', p. 184; Lohfink, 'Das Alte Testament', pp. 28-47; *idem*, 'Zur Geschichte', p. 25; Hendel, 'Worldmaking', pp. 13-15, though he dates the process very early in Israel's history.

68. Albertz, *Israelite Religion*, I, pp. 63-65.

tradition. They elevated an old deity, reconfigured the message about this deity, and the result was a vision to reorganize the entire world order.[69] Monotheistic movements break through the established order with religious and social agenda, and sometimes they try to use a government apparatus to carry out their reforms.[70] In this latter attempt they can become tyrannical rather than liberating, they become 'monotheisms from above'. At any rate, all monotheistic movements have political patrons at some point who seek to implement the social and religious values: Josiah, Ezra, Nehemiah, Prince Vishtaspa (patron of Zoroaster) and the caliphs of Mecca (Abu Bakr, Umar, Uthman and Ali).

Judaism may have been the first true monotheism, and it certainly underlay the later monotheisms of Christianity and Islam. It is of the highest significance that the core event was the proclamation of Yahweh as the liberator of slaves. For this raised to supreme importance not only the historical dimension, but a sympathy for the oppressed and lowly, an imperative for a just society, and the implication that all people were radically equal before God.

One might sense in the piety of ancient Near Eastern laments and prayers the notion of how all penitent devotees stand equally before the deity, and such language may have planted the seeds that would germinate in later Jewish thought. But any further comparison reveals the passion of rhetoric in the biblical text, the many laws and the prophetic cry for reform, all of which indicate that the biblical tradition has moved well beyond the ancient world in its cry for justice and egalitarianism.

The only new perception that recent critical study brings to this exposition of the biblical texts is that the emergence of this grand biblical proclamation came later in Israel's history than was previously assumed. The earliest sense of egalitarian reform may be found in the Book of the Covenant (Exod. 21–23) which is variously dated between 1050 and 700 BCE, and most recent scholarly suggestions favor the later date. The classical prophets assume a sense of egalitarianism in their call for justice, although much of the language in the prophetic books may be the product of the exilic and post-exilic redactors who created the books in their final written form. The Deuteronomic Laws in Deuteronomy 12–26 may be considered the first real declaration for social justice and human dignity, and they may originate in their present form in the reforms of Josiah (622–609 BCE) and subsequent exilic redaction (550 BCE). Further

---

69. Stolz, 'Monotheismus in Israel', pp. 151-54.
70. Stolz, 'Monotheismus in Israel', p. 184.

reform legislation is found in the Priestly Laws organized between the years 550 and 400 BCE, though some specific laws may date back to the eighth century BCE. The best example of Priestly social legislation is the ideal vision of land redistribution in the Jubilee Year, despite the fact that it may never have been implemented in history.[71] The full vision of social justice and equality thus falls into place in the exile and post-exilic era with the emergence of the biblical texts in written and authoritative form. In the future when biblical theologians speak of the egalitarian message in the biblical text, we must acknowledge its truly significant emergence with the later eras of Israelite and Jewish history.

Nor should the historical reality be forgotten, as recalled by the classical prophets, that in the time of the monarchy peasants were treated no better than they were anywhere else in the ancient world. Biblical theologians must be careful not to attribute too much egalitarianism to the early periods. To be sure, the heuristic paradigm of 'mono-Yahwism' advanced by Norman Gottwald has value in describing the early settlement process of Iron Age I (1200–1050 BCE). As peasants reconfigured themselves in highland villages, they probably had a simple lifestyle that entailed a high degree of equality. They also connected the new lifestyle with devotion to the tribal god, Yahweh, to whom they paid their primary devotion. However, this equality and religious piety was more unconscious than deliberate; it was a result of the socio-economic conditions in which they lived. These egalitarian values would not be articulated in clear fashion until after the many years of state formation and economic development, which victimized many people. Then, the religious intelligentsia, upon reflection on their past, would express their views in the written biblical literature. Early highlanders lacked the sophisticated worldview essential to undergirding any expressions of social equality. That articulation would come later, in the exile and beyond. Perhaps, the image of those early highland communities inspired the later exilic theologians, but those highlanders did not have the beliefs of the later theologians. Furthermore, the narratives which describe the beliefs of the early highland villages were crafted by the later Deuteronomistic Historians and Priestly editors. One cannot imagine the later theologians portraying their spiritual ancestors without casting them in their own image to legitimate their own religious and social agenda. Therefore, we must admit the lateness of the rhetoric devoted to the proclamation of justice, equality, and reform.

71. Gnuse, *Steal*, pp. 32-45; *idem*, 'Jubilee', pp. 43-48.

6) Older portrayals of Yahwism envisioned Yahweh as a universal lord transcending the forces of nature and political entities, while the gods of the nations remained mired in their nature phenomena and local politics of city-states and regional empires.

In response to this image one immediately thinks of the universal dominion of Aton as beautifully expressed in the Amarna hymns, or the Assyrian and Babylonian beliefs concerning the manifest destinies of Ashur and Marduk to rule the world through the agencies of the respective chosen peoples of Assyria and Chaldean Babylon. One cannot deny that the ancient Near East knew how to attribute universalism to a high god.

But the question that must be presented immediately is what kind of universal rule was expressed in those older ideologies. The universal rule of Aton, Amun-Re or Seth from Egypt; Ninurta and Ashur from Assyria; and Marduk from Babylon were really expressions of expansionistic military empires. To a certain degree this is true also of Ahura-Mazda in the Zoroastrianism of Achaemenid Persia. Yes, indeed, the concept of universalism existed in the ancient world, but it was a nationalistic, militaristic, and hence limited, vision of universal rule by one god.

Again, the Jewish vision moved beyond that of predecessor cultures in the portrayal of divine universal dominion, and most likely its theologians were inspired by those previous images. The most articulate expression of Yahweh's universal rule comes from Second Isaiah in the exile. Here the universal rule of one deity is predicated upon different values than had been expressed previously in the ancient world. Yahweh's universal dominion over all peoples is connected to a sense of moral justice. It dissolves the link between religion and politics, where a high god's rule is determined by the extent of the devotees' empire. For Second Isaiah, Yahweh was so truly universal in divine rule that a foreigner, Cyrus the Persian, could be a tool of divine action. No one had made claims so radical for the deity to hold such universal dominion over all by ruling through a foreign power. Yahweh indeed was portrayed as the first truly universal deity, capable of transcending national and ethnic politics.[72] In addition, Yahweh was proclaimed lord over other nations not by virtue of a combat myth, as was the case with Marduk. Although Second Isaiah alludes to creation images, some of which imply conflict, Yahweh

---

72. Lind, 'Monotheism', pp. 432-46; Redford, *Egypt*, p. 262; G. Janzen, 'On the Moral Nature of God's Power: Yahweh and the Sea in Job and Deutero-Isaiah', *CBQ* 56 (1994), pp. 458-78; Dietrich, 'Werden und Wesen', p. 19.

really rules more by the proclamation of divine justice and salvation. 'Word' has now replaced combat as the rationale for the high god's universal dominion.[73]

The mode of expressing universal dominion has implications that other religious statements concerning Aton, Amun-Re, Ashur and Marduk all lacked. This universal deity cares for all those other people outside the 'chosen elect'. The chosen people now must 'represent a channel through which God mediates his care for all mankind'.[74] The lands outside of Palestine all belong to Yahweh, they are no longer unclean, their people belong to Yahweh, and the Jews must bear witness to them.[75] The other deities with their grandiose claims to universal sway only encouraged imperial conquest, war and oppression. This universalism of Yahweh, predicated upon the proclamation of justice and salvation, instead affirms peace and ultimately a universal brotherhood and sisterhood. This universalism leads eventually to the Christian mission.

Jewish monotheism, as noted in Chapter 4 of this book, is monotheism 'from below', the religion of an oppressed people. It does not undergird imperial conquest as other 'proto-monotheisms', 'pseudo-monotheisms' or even true monotheisms have done in human history. It will not predicate the universal dominion of Yahweh upon imperial conquest, but rather upon justice, righteousness and love. The people who saw their beginnings in slavery and made their breakthrough to monotheism in diaspora never could have affirmed imperialism in their universalism. Without those experiences the monotheistic trajectory among Israelites and Jews could not have come to the full expression of compassion and justice that it did. It is fortunate for us that it did so evolve. The universal dominion of Yahweh predicated upon justice and morality only then could become the religion of the Judaeo-Christian heritage, which proclaims unto this day the brotherhood and sisterhood of all people.

Once more, we observe that the Jews did not invent the concept of a universal deity. But they were the only people who could express it 'from below', strip it of political pretensions, and thus create the potential for a truly worldwide religion. The Jews did not invent, but they further developed universal monotheism.

The consideration of all these motifs has a common purpose to it. Contemporary critical scholars have viewed the old stereotypes that were

---

73. Janzen, 'Moral Nature', pp. 458-78.
74. Saggs, *Encounter*, p. 176.
75. Sperling, 'Israel's Religion', p. 7.

used by biblical theologians in a former age, especially those theologians associated with *Heilsgeschichte* theology or the Biblical Theology Movement. Their portrayals were grand, but stark and overgeneralized. Most critical research has attacked their dichotomies of the cyclic fertility religions of the ancient Near East and the linear historical religion of Israel. But if those critiques force us to discard all our paradigms, they do us a disservice.

Biblical literature is an intellectual step beyond ancient Near Eastern thought, as is Greek thought also. Israelite and especially Jewish theologians developed the thought of their predecessors in the ancient Near East. They did not utter things which were radically unique, nor did they articulate a worldview in dialectical opposition to previous beliefs. Their ideas flowed out of the ancient world, perhaps no single idea was new. But they enriched the thought they inherited, they reconfigured themes, and they stressed certain ideas more than had been done previously. They were an evolutionary breakthrough as they reconstructed a new matrix out of old ideas. This conforms to the modern understanding of how evolution, a new reconfiguration of the old genetic material, produces an evolutionary breakthrough, a new species, and gradually that species unfolds the implications of the transformation. We still are unfolding the implications of the Jewish monotheistic breakthrough over two millennia past.

The motifs discussed typify this evolutionary process. Descriptions of the gods acting in the social arena or history existed before the Jewish breakthrough, but the Jews elevated the discourse to a new level with the monotheistic thrust which propels the portrayal of the deity beyond nature phenomena, casts the other gods from the heavens, and raises deep philosophical questions. The Jews were not the first to create ethical discourse, but they used such language more extensively, making it the center of their theologizing and changing the way both people and the world were viewed. The Jews accelerated the trajectory of reflection upon human freedom, which may have emerged embryonically with the appearance of writing. They, more than others, saw the implication that true freedom of people coincides with freedom in the divine realm, and thus magic and divination, or any manipulation of God no longer could be accepted. The tradition among the intelligentsia in the ancient world of calling for justice in society was elevated by them from a recessive mode to a dominant mode, and it became a central element in conjunction with the exodus theme in professing their religious and social values.

Finally, their understanding of Yahweh's universal domain was not imperialistic but compassionate, it alone could proclaim a true unity of all peoples. In all of these issues Israelites and Jews were not unique, they did not invent. They furthered and developed ideas, they reconfigured ideas, they selected and expanded ideas, in short, they were a new synthesis as well as a culmination of the ancient world. Their age of intellectual ascendancy would be in exile and thereafter, when they were a conquered people. For from the weak shall come the true victors.

> Israel arose as the ancient, brilliant cultures of Mesopotamia and of Egypt had become decadent or moribund... They had their season and the ancient world was ripe for change.[76]

IV

In the last three chapters I have struggled to envision a new way of understanding the emergence of monotheism in the biblical tradition. Central to this entire endeavor is the portrayal of emergent monotheism as a process. Monotheism emerged in a developmental trajectory which began in the beliefs and intellectual articulations of the ancient Near East. The seedbed for the ideas among Israelites and Jews was a village society in highland Palestine reconstructed out of the elements of the old deteriorated Late Bronze Age society, and here retreating farmers, highland pastoralists and outlaw elements merged to begin a new life. This simple society was ready in an unconscious way to develop the new social and religious ideas of the Iron Age. With them the seeds of a future monotheistic development were planted in the occasional tendency of some of their members to devote themselves to the new deity from the southern wilderness, Yahweh.

The emergence of true monotheism would take six centuries and come to fruition only with the crisis of the exile. In this process it would take social and religious crises to move the process toward its final culmination. But only the ultimate dislocation of national destruction that would create a landless people in exile could lead this people to the ultimate conclusion that their god alone existed and all other deities did not. Without this final crisis radical monotheism could not have arisen, for only an extreme crisis could produce such a radical form of belief as monotheism. Otherwise this people might have wallowed in henotheism or monolatry or some weak form of intellectual monism for an indefinite period of

76. Shanks, 'Frank Cross', p. 26.

time. As such their intellectual expression would have been frozen until they would have been absorbed into the greater Hellenistic culture of a later age—as happened with so many cultures and peoples.

Biblical theologians have spoken of the emergence of monotheism in the past as though it came with Moses (Albright) or the classical prophets (Wellhausen). This new perception stresses that we ought to look more to the exile as the age of the final breakthrough, and yet consider the entire six century span from Moses to the exile as the trajectory of monotheistic evolution. Monotheism is a process which takes centuries to come to its culminating breakthrough.

In addition, I have sought to express the conceptualization of this mono-theistic process as an intellectual endeavor which is both evolutionary and revolutionary. Historians and anthroplologists of religion have argued for years whether monotheism arises primarily through a gradual process or by a great prophet in a singular period of history expressing radical new ideas. I have uttered a resounding affirmative to both viewpoints.

Emergent monotheism is both evolutionary and revolutionary in the biblical tradition. The pre-exilic era was one in which the preliminary religious steps were made in creating a form of Yahwistic monolatry in a series of socio-religious crises. This evolutionary period of preparation culminated in the revolution of the exile when radical monotheism broke through into the hearts and minds of Jewish intellectuals and later the Jewish people as a whole. This final stage was not inevitable, even though it had preparation in the six previous centuries. Only the radical crisis produced radical monotheism. Other comparable movements in the ancient Near East, India and Persia fell short for lack of such a final crisis and an intellectual and religious leap of faith.

I have sought to undergird this understanding of emergent monotheism with a heuristic paradigm, an understanding of evolutionary advance which likewise sees evolutionary development both as a gradual process and a revolution. True evolutionary advances on the genetic and biological level occur when slow gradual genetic mutations set the stage for a rather sudden transformation which produces a new species in macro-evolutionary fashion. Although many other authors have described the emergence of biblical monotheism as an evolutionary process culmi-nating in the exile, and I have cited them copiously, this newer under-standing of evolution may bring diverse perceptions of contemporary scholars into a meaningful heuristic paradigm. That paradigm affirms that human advance occurs in an evolutionary mode which is both gradual and abrupt—what scientists would call 'punctuational advance'.

To this end I have tried to approach the questions of emergent monotheism from a broader perspective, especially following guidelines laid down by the questions put forth by David Petersen.[77] Although this volume could not address all the questions he raised, it attempted to speak to those most germane to a new understanding of the monotheistic process.

Thomas Kuhn speaks of scientific revolutions occurring when the scholarly community looks at the same data but then reconfigures it according to the parameters of a new theory. Usually no one person discovers all the data and creates a new hypothesis; rather, the scholarly guild becomes gradually dissatisfied with the old theory, and when a new one is finally hypothesized, scholars are ready to seize upon the new construal.[78] This is perhaps the same phenomenon which has occurred in biblical studies in the past generation. New archaeological discoveries combined with a critical reconsideration of the biblical texts have made biblical theologians ready for a re-articulation of our understandings of biblical religion. This new model sees monotheism emerge late, in the exile, and arise only slowly throughout Israel's history.

I wish to add to that arising consensus a few additional conceptualizations. The whole process of emergent monotheism may be seen as both evolutionary and revolutionary using contemporary scientific paradigms. The process also unfolds many intellectual implications after its primary breakthrough, and this will take millennia in human culture. Indeed, we are still part of the on-going monotheistic revolution. Other insights deemed worthy of use in future theological and pedagogical discourse have been drawn together from a number of authors. Not all of the paradigms will appeal to every reader, but hopefully some will inspire and merit further consideration.

There are dramatic ways of speaking of the exilic emergence of monotheism. The moment of evolutionary breakthrough to radical monotheism may be called a 'kairotic episode' or a 'kairotic moment', and the resulting monotheistic faith may be deemed a 'consummate religion' according to William Tremmel.[79] A similar description of the moment of breakthrough is 'punctuational advance', a term borrowed from biology, which stresses that the era of the exile punctuates the otherwise gradual

---

77. Petersen, 'Israel and Monotheism', pp. 92-107.
78. Kuhn, *Revolutions*.
79. Tremmel, *Religion*, p. 133.

process of development with quick and significant intellectual articulations which 'advance' the evolutionary process to a level of significant fulfillment. Subsequent intellectual developments then unfold the implications of the breakthrough. Such a time of advance is made possible by a 'crisis', which creates the social and intellectual challenges which demand a reconstruction of values.

This advance is both traditional and avant-garde, for it takes old ideas and puts them together in a new synthesis. In biology we likewise observe how speciation is accomplished by the reconfiguration of old genetic materials. Biblical monotheism drew upon many elements and ideas which had been in existence for years and put them forward in a new ideological form. Scholars' language should favor words like 'reconstruction', 'reconfiguration' and 'reconstrual' when talking about the biblical worldview. Other terms, often used by scholars, to describe the development of biblical thought have included 'transmutation' and 'transformation'. Above all, contemporary authors need to relinquish the use of the word 'unique' when describing biblical thought, for that was the term truly overused by the past generation of biblical theologians.

Some excellent scholarly works have proposed language to describe aspects of this emerging process. Mark Smith describes the emergence of the divine figure in the trajectory of monolatry and monotheism as a complex intellectual evolution involving 'convergence' and 'differentiation'. Convergence occurs as images of the different gods are drawn into the persona of Yahweh, and differentiation refers to the process by which unacceptable characteristics and cultic activity are rejected.[80] Werner Schmidt expresses similar ideas with his less catchy expressions of 'recognition' and 'rejection'. He also believes that this process was directed by the conscious use of beliefs such as the exclusive worship and aniconic portrayal of Yahweh.[81] Their categories are extremely useful in the discussion of pre-exilic religion.

Various authors have provided terms to describe Israel's religion before radical monotheism was attained. The old expressions, quite comparable in meaning, were monolatry and henotheism, but both are too vague to describe the nuances in the evolutionary process. More helpful terms include 'radical monolatry', 'intolerant henotheism', 'incipient monotheism', 'radical henolatry', 'national monolatry' and others proposed by authors discussed in this volume. Although some might be

80. Smith, *Early History of God.*
81. Schmidt, *Faith*, pp. 1-4, 136-81.

dismayed by the diversity of expressions, I believe it to be a positive sign that scholars have attempted to nuance more carefully their designations of Israelite religion. Perhaps, the best attempt to refer to the early stages of monotheistic evolution is the phrase, the 'Yahweh alone movement' or the 'Yahweh aloneists'.

Also valuable are categories which attempt to delineate the various forms of monotheistic belief, even though they may be subject to debate. Denis Baly utilizes theconcepts of 'pseudo-monotheism', 'proto-monotheism', and 'imperial monotheism' to describe the spectrum of religious movements which appear monotheistic.[82] Perhaps, he is too strict to limit true monotheism only to Judaism, Christianity and Islam, but many, including Raffaele Pettazzoni,[83] would agree with him. Norman Gottwald's use of the term 'mono-Yahwism' to describe highland Israelites is valuable,[84] for even though this people was not yet mono-theistic, they had the proclivity to venerate Yahweh highly and they laid the foundations for some of the later social developments in Judaism. Gottwald probably attributed too many of the later Israelite and Jewish values to those early 'seedling communities' of the highlands, but he did capture the spirit of the greater biblical tradition.

Of central importance is the understanding of the Axial Age, an era when great intellectual advances occurred across Asia and the Mediterranean. Historians, sociologists, philosophers and scholars of reli-gious history use the term to describe the worldwide intellectual advance from 800 to 400 BCE. Many cultures undertook a movement toward monotheism, but the Jews appear to have been the most successful. Use of this term strongly reminds us that the Jewish religious breakthrough was part of a greater process in the world.

Modern theorists have provided us with an abundant blessing of new images and terminology by which to express our understanding of Israelite and Jewish religious development. Hopefully, readers increasingly will find these concepts useful in pedagogy, biblical theology, and even scholarly discussions.

These wide-ranging observations have included consideration of monotheistic-like religious expressions in the ancient world to discern their relationship to Jewish monotheism. The general conclusions of scholars are that these other movements fell short of the Jewish

---

82. Baly, 'Geography of Monotheism', pp. 253-78.
83. Pettazzoni, 'Formation of Monotheism', pp. 40-46.
84. Gottwald, *Tribes of Yahweh*, pp. 592-621 *et passim*.

accomplishment. In the ancient Near East devotion to deities could appear rather exclusive at times. In Egypt deities such as Ptah at Heracleopolis, Amun-Re and Seth in the New Kingdom era, and especially Aton at Amarna were recipients of exclusive devotion for a time. Of these, the Aton cult was the closest to monotheism prior to the Jewish breakthrough, but it was the cult of one man, Akhenaton, who made no effort to spread it. It was a sterile movement with no effective message, and so it died. Egypt was not the place and the second millennium BCE was not the time for monotheism to emerge successfully. The other deities mentioned above seem to have been merely consummate reflections of the totality of the gods—hardly true monotheism. Mesopotamia produced several deities who received apparently exclusive veneration, most notably Marduk and Sin in Babylon and Ninurta and Ashur in Assyria. However, our texts always reflect something less than monotheism, because the existence of other gods is not denied, thus suggesting that each deity, when worshipped exclusively, merely absorbed the other gods temporarily and with respect for their continued existence. In some texts the elevation of one god was connected to the rhetoric of imperial aspirations of a conquering empire, in others the deity was symbolically representative of all the gods, and in prayers and laments the petitioner addressed the deity with exaggerated language of exclusivity in order to motivate the god to act. In all instances, the texts fall short of monotheism.

In India and Persia are movements which come much closer to monotheism. In India in the late Vedic texts and the Upanishads we can find many examples of gods or abstract principles elevated to a supreme position of importance in the universe. But either the expression is short-lived in the religious history of India, or the language evolves into monism rather than monotheism. Monism allows someone the philosophical abstraction of affirming a singular will in the universe with the comfort of retaining polytheism, or better said, without the discomfort of having to jettison all the other gods.

In Persia the prophet Zoroaster affirmed belief in Ahura-Mazda and founded what would become or later evolve into the Zoroastrian religion, which is traditionally defined as monotheistic. But all Zoroastrian scholars admit problems in determining the nature of Zoroaster's original teachings and the nature of early Zoroastrian belief, since the sacred scriptures, the *Zend-Avesta*, arose much later in the fifth to eighth centuries CE. Within the Zoroastrian tradition there has long been a prevalent dualism, which leads me to wonder whether Zoroastrianism was true monotheism in its early years. In addition, as the religion of the Persian Empire (550–330 BCE), it was an imperial monotheism with no need to seriously deny the existence of other gods. Although Zoroastrianism should lay claim to being the most significant monotheistic expression next to Judaism, its monotheism may not be as radically absolute as the Jewish expression in the exile.

Monotheism emerges clearly in the trajectories of Israelite and Jewish thought. I wish to stress the Jewish dimension, because the truly significant breakthrough came in the exile and the intellectual implications of radical monotheism were unfolded most effectively in the Second Temple period (539 BCE–70 CE). I might create the stages hypothetically by which monolatry arose and later became the monotheism expressed in the Bible, but it is a most speculative and subjective task. Many scholars have done this, and Chapter 2 summarized their speculations. Generally authors fall into two groups. Some maintain there were significant stages of development in the pre-exilic era leading up to the exilic breakthrough. Others believe that the religious evolution came completely during and after the exile. I have followed the model proposed by the former scholars, but even if the latter scholars are more correct in their assessment, the overall paradigms suggested in this volume would describe the process of monotheistic emergence adequately. Monotheism still would be viewed as an evolutionary process leading to some point of revolutionary breakthrough, the date would simply be later. Furthermore, the greater heuristic paradigm of 'punctuated advance' would continue to have value, and biblical theologians still would view the Judaeo-Christian heritage as undergoing the continued development of implications which flow from the revolutionary breakthrough.

Those scholars who propose significant stages of development in the pre-exilic period generally concur on a model which may be useful as a pedagogical paradigm. Basically, they see the following persons and their supporters as significant in the development of monotheism: 1) Elijah, who may not have rejected the existence of all the other gods, nonetheless argued for an exclusive devotion to Yahweh by Israelites, and he may have equated Yahweh and El. 2) Hosea, who likewise may not have denied the existence of other gods, certainly attacked internal Yahwistic cultic activity as unacceptable, including the golden calves and the baalim. 3) Hezekiah may have instigated certain reforms in the direction of Hosea's suggestions, including the removal of the *Nehushtan*. 4) Josiah set in motion a reform movement which looks almost monotheistic (and may have been in the minds of many) by virtue of its extensive removal of cultic objects and the attempt to shape the piety of the masses. 5) Jeremiah and Ezekiel uttered oracles which appear virtually monotheistic in content and whose images of God begin to take on the appearance of an international deity with universal concerns. 6) Finally, Second Isaiah and the Priestly editors have very clear monotheistic statements and expressly deny the existence of other gods. With minor variations virtually all the scholars affirm some model which takes these persons into account as serious forces in the development of the monotheistic trajectory.

Additionally, contemporary critical scholars are leading us to view the pre-exilic religion of Israel as a much more polyglot agglomeration of beliefs and practices. The diverse devotions to El, Baal, Asherah and the heavenly host were all part of common Israelite religion, perhaps accepted as normal by the vast number of good Yahweh devotees. Cultic activity included, as a matter of course, sacred prostitution, sun veneration and even human sacrifice. Yahwism differed in the various regions of Palestine, and people may have revered different Yahwehs at local shrines. Yahwism in the pre-exilic period was simply another expression of West-Semitic religion. Essentially, we are being led to reconstruct our perception of Yahwism. Yahwism was not in conflict with the Canaanite religion; rather, it was 'the religion of Canaan' and later monotheistic Yahwism grew out of it.

We can no longer speak of the many ways in which Yahwism was unique, it probably was not unique in any specific expression, even in later monotheistic Yahwism. Monotheistic Yahwism was special in the emphasis it gave to certain themes and how it reconfigured them. In our biblical theology we must now more carefully nuance how Israelite and Jewish faith articulated its worldview in relationship to the rest of the ancient world. For this reason I attempted to explain the ways in which the old *Heilsgeschichte* theologians expressed Israel's differences from the ancient Near East, then I tried to articulate the same ideas in nuanced fashion for the contemporary biblical theological task. In each instance biblical faith did not contradict earlier ideas but developed them more and went beyond previous understandings.

Israelites and Jews did not invent the linear view of reality, but did give it greater emphasis in their intellectual articulations. The Deuteronomistic History, for example, is more thoroughly permeated with ideas of divine action in human events and a wide range of religious and ethical criteria by which to adjudge humanity than comparable ancient Near

Eastern historiography. The early monolatry of epic literature and the prophets and the later emergent monotheism of the Deuteronomistic History and the Priestly editors portrayed Yahweh as increasingly trans-cendent over the forces of nature, and they moved even further in this direction of envisioning a social deity than their Assyrian and Babylonian predecessors of the early first millennium BCE. Ethics and morality were more central in their reconstruction of social values, perhaps because monotheism with its social deity would make an ethical imperative more direct and demanding. Likewise, the cry for social justice and egalita-rianism, which was not new to the ancient Near East, could become the dominant mode of discourse in the simpler, peripheral societies of Israel and Judaism, especially in the age of social and intellectual reconstruction during and after the exile. A monotheism affirmed by the oppressed will cry more loudly for justice than the monotheisms of the victors, and the universalism connected with the belief in one God will be more generous to the masses of humanity.

Israel's form of intellectual contribution might be best described as a reconstruction, reconfiguration or reconstrual of previous thought. The quest to find something unique in biblical thought, that was so much in fashion, produced forced generalizations. We should not search for the unique, but rather for how old ideas were transformed. All of the biblical themes were already in place in contemporary ancient Near Eastern thought: divine intervention in history, divine purpose or a plan for people, social deities, a call for justice for the poor, and an impetus for the exclusive veneration of one deity. Whereas such ideas were minor themes in the ancient world, the Jews developed them and made them central to their worldview.

Biblical scholars in the past have suggested the image of reconstruction as a model by which to understand the worldview of the biblical text.[85] In particular, Walter Brueggemann speaks of the 'mutation' or

85. A. Malamat, 'Doctrines of Causality in Hittite and Biblical Historiography', *VT* 5 (1955), p. 1; K. Koch, 'Der Tod der Religions-stifters', *KD* 8 (1962), pp. 112-14; R. Rendtorff, 'Die Entstehung der israelitischen Religion als religionsgeschicht-liches und theologisches Problem', *TLZ* 88 (1963), pp. 735-46; J. Hayes, *Introduction to the Bible* (Philadelphia: Westminster Press, 1971), p. 136; Cross, *Canaanite Myth*, p. 143; J. Krecher and H.P. Müller, 'Vergangenheitsinteresse in Mesopotamien und Israel', *Saeculum* 26 (1975), pp. 13-44; J.R. Porter, 'Old Testament Historiography', *Tradition and Interpretation: Essays by Members of the Society for Old Testament Study* (ed. G. Anderson; Oxford: Clarendon Press, 1979), p. 131; Stolz, 'Monothe-ismus in Israel', pp. 144-89; N. Gottwald, 'Early Israel and the Canaanite Socio-

'transmutation' of those values inherited by biblical thought which
reflects a struggle to break free of the 'common theology of the ancient
Near East'.[86] Use of this model may reconcile the various perspectives
of biblical scholars. Some historians of religion stress the slow, evolutionary development of Israel's faith, while others stress the radical
departure from previous values. The process of reconstruction absorbs
old values, thus reflecting the image of gradual metamorphosis, yet the
process places these values in conjunction with other ideas to produce a
new synthesis, and that gives the impression of a radical breakthrough.
For example, the portrayal of Yahweh with El characteristics to cast him
as a creator deity reflects great continuity with the past—especially with
the old second millennium BCE religion of Palestine. But when Second
Isaiah culminates the process of Yahweh's absorption of El characteristics
and elevates Yahweh as creator and universal lord of the cosmos, one
senses this to be an intellectual breakthrough. We observe this phenomenon in the text and sense that it is both an evolutionary process and a
revolution. Biblical authors were unique in the way they reconstructed
ideas, not in generating any one particular image or idea. Even a scholar
as critical of the old *Heilsgeschichte* comparisons as Niels Peter Lemche
can praise the intellectual quality of this new synthesis, despite the fact
that no one component within the intellectual system is unique in the
ancient world,

> Without doubt, the description of the Yahwistic faith which is provided
> by the Old Testament presents this religion as being unique in its Near
> Eastern setting. None of the religious manifestations from other parts of
> the ancient Near East can be compared to the synthesis which was the
> Israelite religion according to the Old Testament. It does not detract from
> this evaluation that almost any single component of the synthesis can be
> paired with corresponding elements belonging to other parts of the Near
> East.[87]

In conclusion, I postulate that Israel and the later Jews did not invent
a worldview in contrast to ancient Near Eastern thought, but drew
upon existing ideas and reconfigured them to make a great Axial Age

---

Economic System', *Palestine in Transition* (eds. Freedman and Graf), pp. 32-33;
idem, 'Two Models', p. 7; Frick, *Formation*, pp. 193-94; Eisenstadt, 'Ancient Israel',
pp. 127-34. These views were evaluated by Gnuse, *Heilsgeschichte*, pp. 135-51.

86. W. Brueggemann, 'A Shape for Old Testament Theology. I. Structure
Legitimation', *CBQ* 47 (1985), pp. 28-46.

87. Lemche, 'Israelite Religion', p. 102.

breakthrough. Old ideas, perhaps recessive in the social and intellectual matrix of the ancient world, were turned into dominant themes and core assumptions in the biblical worldview. Israelites and Jews were a new society not bounded by tradition and the beliefs of societies millennia old. When in the exile the 'kairotic moment' was experienced and 'consummate religion' attained, these peripheral people were ready to draw conclusions that moved well beyond the confines of the thought which preceded them. The parallel with Greek thought in other areas of speculation may be drawn, for here too a 'kairotic moment' was occurring also. Israel and the Jews were part of an evolving trajectory wherein gradual but significant evolution occurred with implications for all of human history. This gradual but significant evolution, this trajectory which comes to a point of breakthrough, is like the macro-evolutionary experience that occurs when a new species is born. The Jews after the exile were such a 'new species'.

The evolution which culminated in the revolution of the exile was in one sense a conclusion to a process. But in another sense, from a truly evolutionary perspective, a significant breakthrough is really the beginning of another process. The monotheistic breakthrough began the movement which would become the Judaeo-Christian tradition. The period of time since that breakthrough is one in which the implications of radical monotheism are being worked out in terms of their social and religious imperatives, and Judaism and Christianity both testify to the rich expressions that have flowed from the monotheistic revolution for over two thousand years. What we must perceive is that the revolution begun so long ago is still occurring today, and Jews and Christians are still working out implications and unfolding the latent message of that radical breakthrough.

Chapter 6

THE ONGOING TRADITION OF EMERGENT MONOTHEISM

Scholarship has begun to stress the gradual nature of Israel's religious and socio-political development. The final crystalization now is dated to the exile and beyond for the emergence of monotheism and biblical literature. The result is that scholars are now more prone to stress Israel's continuity with the ancient Near Eastern cultural sphere and the surrounding ancient Near East rather than speaking of an early break-through in the Mosaic or settlement era, as they did in a previous gene-ration. Israel arose out of a matrix which was part of a spectrum in the ancient world, and its crystalization occurred in the Babylonian exile and Second Temple or post-exilic era.

Now that scholars speak of gradual process and evolution in Israel's history rather than an initial emergence in the early pre-exilic period with a strong religious and socio-political opposition to the existing values of the ancient world, what will be the impact upon biblical theo-logy and biblically inspired ethics? Here, I offer some speculative sug-gestions as to themes engendered for biblical theologians, some creative ideas for discussion rather than a systematically defended position. The new paradigms may lead to nuanced understandings about social reform, intellectual change, religious tradition, and the philosophy of history.

I have spoken of the monotheistic experience as both revolution and evolution. Monotheism emerged over the six hundred year period of pre-exilic history, but in reality this is such a short period of time, that emergent monotheism is worthy of being called revolutionary. Six hundred years is short in relation to the vast amounts of time involved in biological evolution or even human cultural evolution. Monotheism is also revolutionary in that it was not an inevitable process, but for the Babylonian exile, it would not have emerged among the Jews at all. Perhaps, we might be heirs instead to some form of Hellenistic monism, for certainly philosophical monism was the path chosen by India. My views are stated superbly in an excellent essay by V. Nikiprowetsky:

It must be realized that ethical monotheism was not a 'natural' and universal *fait accompli*, destined for all mankind from the very beginning... It simply represents the culmination of a historical process belonging to Israel and to Israel alone... If, then, monotheism required centuries to reach maturity, we may state with some confidence that the Mosaic religion had sown its seeds. But we cannot stress too much how slowly this process evolved in practice... it does represent a true spiritual revolution and it continues to deserve being considered as one of the moral and intellectual bases of modern society.[1]

It is also a particular thesis of mine that the monotheistic revolution is unfinished, it is still occurring, and the implications of monotheistic religion are unfolding still in our own age. Perhaps, this is the cardinal conclusion to be drawn from contemporary critical studies for the theological task before us. Monotheism has been emerging for three thousand years; we are still part of the grand unfolding of that initial mutation which occurred between the Israelite settlement and its culmination in the Babylonian exile.

I

Heilsgeschichte models of the previous generation inspired a concomitant social ethos. The emphasis upon a God who acts in history to save people translated into religious imperatives which called for a just and fair society today. Theologians and preachers used this imagery to inspire people to recreate the egalitarian society in the modern world which painfully emerged in ancient Israel. Nowhere is this more evident than in the writings of both George Mendenhall and Norman Gottwald, whose work came very late in the movement and also functions as a bridge to contemporary understandings.[2] In particular, liberation theology tapped its roots deeply into the scholarship of these men and many other authors resonating the same ideas.[3]

The common theme in these works was the extreme contrast between Israel and the surrounding environment in both socio-political and

1.   Nikiprowetsky, 'Ethical Monotheism', pp. 69, 80, 86.
2.   Mendenhall, *Tenth Generation*; Gottwald, *Tribes of Yahweh*, pp. 3-802.
3.   J. Miranda, *Marx and the Bible: A Critique of the Philosophy of Oppression* (trans. J. Eagleson; Maryknoll: Orbis Books, 1974); S. Croatto, *Exodus: A Hermeneutics of Freedom* (trans. S. Attanasio; Maryknoll: Orbis Books, 1981); Pixley, *God's Kingdom*; *idem*, *On Exodus*; essays in Gottwald, *Bible and Liberation*; essays in Schottroff and Stegemann, *God of the Lowly*, pp. 3-168.

religious values. Israelites stood in dialectical opposition to the values of
their age, the assumptions of class, oppression and power. Israelites
created a worldview with a sense of equality and justice which has been
bequeathed to us in the Judaeo-Christian ethos. The implication for
modern readers was that we, too, must become a counter-cultural movement in the modern world. By affirming traditional Jewish and Christian
values modern believers could stand in bold opposition to the values of
consumption, greed and disregard for marginal people in the world,
attitudes which seem to predominate in our contemporary narcissistic
society. Many biblical theologians used the paradigm of contrast in the
biblical world to point analogously to the flaws in our own society. The
modern parallel paradigm was the imperative of the Judaeo-Christian
message for social reform over against the state of affairs in the modern,
industrial world.

   Biblical theologians produced grand portrayals of the ancient Near
Eastern worldview, the Canaanite worldview and Solomon's repristina-
tion to the old city state system, which made them sound strikingly similar to modern capitalistic society. Likewise, the image of Israelite values,
or the prophetic and Deuteronomic reform movements, appeared to
contain the elements that liberal social reformers and Judaeo-Christian
theologians prized. When the reader saw the contrast between Israel and
the ancient world, or the contrast between the 'statism' of the Israelite
monarchy and the egalitarianism of the prophetic reformers, he or she
was drawn to see the modern implications in the biblical text. Many
excellent theological and pedagogical works were produced in that age
in my opinion.[4] Those works undertook the task which is paramount for
biblical theologians—they made the text relevant for the modern age.
The particular message of those theologians still remains most meaningful for our age. But now with the appearance of new models concerning
the Israelite conquest or settlement process and the emergence of monotheism among the Israelites and later Jews, the task to weave a meaningful
theological interpretation has not disappeared. We are called upon to
sing a new theological song, working from the insights provided by our

---

   4.   Most notable are the efforts of W. Brueggemann, *The Prophetic Imagination*
(Philadelphia: Fortress Press, 1978); *idem*, *Old Testament Theology: Essays on
Structure, Theme, and Text* (Minneapolis: Fortress Press, 1992); and especially a
recent essay, *idem*, 'Pharaoh as Vassal: A Study of a Political Metaphor', *CBQ* 57
(1995), pp. 27-51.

new paradigms. That new theological song must not lack the conviction and the sting found in the theological expressions of a previous generation.

II

Has the ground been pulled out from under the biblical theological endeavor by the new critical theories? May we still speak of a theologically inspired social reform ethos with these new models of Israel's social and religious origins? Now that critical scholars speak of gradual process and evolution rather than Mosaic or early Iron Age I religious revolution and dialectical opposition to the ancient world, what will be the impact upon biblical theology, ethics and preaching?

Whereas a former generation saw the Church's cry on behalf of the poor rooted in a biblical imperative of dialectical opposition to the world, the next generation of biblical theologians may ground their social reform ethos in the gradual processes observed in the Judaeo-Christian tradition and human culture in general, which bring about justice and equality. Monotheism with its concomitant social values may not have arisen dramatically early in Israel's history, but it did emerge gradually and decisively in the exile. The religious beliefs which accompany emergent monotheistic faith and its social implications are still valid for modern believers. Jews and Christians are still heirs of this faith, regardless of the era of its emergence or the length of time necessary for the ideas to mature. The contrast between Israelite or Jewish monotheism and the thought of the ancient world may not be as great as believers were wont to portray in the past, but some valid distinctions are still there and worthy of recognition. We who belong to the Judaeo-Christian tradition are still part of an intellectual movement with significant religious and social beliefs, and we are called upon to commit ourselves to those values and their implementation.

In the past Israel was described as a nomadic people who entered the land either peacefully (Albrecht Alt, Martin Noth) or violently (William Albright, George Ernest Wright, John Bright), and as a result, it was believed, Israelites thought differently than the sedentary Canaanites already resident in the land. The paradigm of contrast was a natural pedagogical tool. We contrasted the nomadic, monotheistic, linear-thinking Israelites with polytheistic, sedentary, cyclic-thinking Canaanites, with our affirmation going to the former. Now that we perceive that Israelites gradually evolved out of Canaanites in the land in an unconscious fashion, we recognize that the differences in worldview arose much later in the exile.

In our current pedagogy we can no longer emphasize the dramatic nature of the Israelite worldview; rather, we must stress the theme of organic growth and transformation in response to many crises. We must appreciate more sensitively the common values and connections the biblical values had with contemporary worldviews. The 'eye of faith' may perceive now that God was active in the socio-historical dynamics of Israel's gradual evolution. The new implication for contemporary biblical theologians may be to sense the presence of God correspondingly in the broader, worldwide human cultural processes today.

This may be an even more effective way to call for religious, social and economic reform in today's world than the old model of dialectical opposition and the rhetorical contrast of paradigms. By recognizing that monotheism arose in an evolutionary process over many centuries, we may be led to perceive that we are still on the trajectory of an evolutionary process which continues to unfold the social and religious implications of monotheism. We are part of an unfinished process—the development of total monotheism. In the past our call to reform was like a clarion call to return to the values of the biblical era. This gave the impression that those values had somehow been lost and now we were recovering them. There may have been some truth to this, for often the hallmark beliefs of Judaism and Christianity become encumbered with the concerns of institutional needs and the preservation of stability in the Church and society, and subsequently the voices of reform must remind us of what is truly important in our belief system. In the history of the Church there are sometimes swings between eras of institutional concerns and brief times of reform.[5] However, to use the rhetoric of returning to the old biblical social values creates the impression among the Christian audience that their forefathers somehow betrayed the biblical faith at some point, This, of course, can create much of the resistance to the message of social reform in the Church. Theologians and preachers might unconsciously portray themselves as the restorers of a 'lost faith', and that will not 'sell' too well in the pews, especially among those faithful believers who recognize and respect the significant contributions

---

5. E. Käsemann, 'Ministry and Community in the New Testament', *Essays on New Testament Themes* (trans. W.J. Montague; SBT, 41; London: SCM Press, 1964), pp. 63-94.

of past theologians and religious movements. Even more so, the appeal to a past biblical faith loses sight of the most important realization to be made: that there is an on-going religious and intellectual tradition of monotheism that is rooted in the Bible, which we must continue, as have our predecessors before us. We are not returning to some fixed and pristine past, we are continuing the process of development, which in some eras did not evolve as quickly as it should have. We also recognize that the past was not so pristine either, and that some of the values of the biblical tradition are less moral than those we require today. If we sense that we continue the trajectory of evolution in faith and ethics begun by the biblical tradition, we can admit that there are points at which the biblical tradition is primitive (holy war, slavery, subordination of women, etc.), even in the New Testament. Yet the biblical tradition calls upon us to keep the spirit begun by the biblical tradition and move beyond those primitive points of belief at which the trajectory began. We will be faithful to the spirit, not the letter, of the religious and social message in the biblical text.

Contemporary scholarship will give us a new way of speaking. Our modern call to reform is not really an overturning of present values in an attempt to return to the authentic biblical worldview; rather, it is the imperative to continue the natural, God-given process of unfolding the implications of the monotheistic evolutionary revolution. In effect, we may speak of the imperfections of the past as being such because they were 'on the way' to becoming the fuller manifestation of monotheism. Likewise, we then must admit that we, too, are imperfect, for we also are on the way to the fuller monotheistic faith of the future. Our imperative is to continue the process of change and reform, to continue to unfold the centuries-long development of monotheism. It would be akin to saying that just as monotheism did not emerge until late in Israel's history, perhaps the fuller social implications of monotheism have not yet been unfolded completely even today. It is our duty to keep the process moving. We do not 'return' to the past biblical values, we still continue the 'develop' or 'unfold' them in the world today.

Such a perspective would help us address some of the anomalies or problems we face in social issues articulated in the biblical text. The values found in the Hebrew Bible affirm the equality of all believers before God, but yet theirs was a patriarchal society which subordinated women and children, and legitimated at least a limited form of slavery. So also in the New Testament, Paul can state that in Christ there is neither male nor female, slave nor free, yet in his letters he appears to acknowledge the existence of slavery and the lower status of women in the everyday Graeco-Roman world. We must perceive that Paul is the beginning of a trajectory, and not all the implications could be unfolded in his own age. Richard Bauckham observes that although both the Hebrew Bible and the New Testament accepted slavery, this is no indication that we should also, and thereby freeze ourselves at the same level of ethical development as our spiritual forebearers were two thousand years ago. He states, 'and it is perfectly proper that we should follow the direction of these Old Testament principles as far as they point, even beyond Old Testament practice, and, for that matter, even beyond New Testament practice'.[6] Eventually slavery would be abolished and women would obtain equality in Christendom, but it would take centuries—much longer than it should have! All the implications of the biblical message could not be worked out in terms of their social imperative in one generation, especially since those early Christians were socially marginal and few in numbers. But the process was begun and has been coming to fulfillment ever since. We must come to understand that we are still part of an evolving process of social reform implied by the religious message of the Hebrew Bible and the teachings of Jesus and Paul.

The biblical tradition was a breakthrough for its age in terms of certain human values. But in light of modern understanding, many of its values are primitive, as was clearly and painfully demonstrated by a recent series of essays on the ethical teachings of the biblical traditions in a book entitled, *What the Bible Really Says*.[7] What this book reveals is the primitive state of ethical beliefs and practices endorsed by biblical texts on many issues, including war, women and slavery. What we must realize is that these writings are two to three thousand years old. Our ethical sensitivities are advanced because they have been inspired and schooled by the biblical texts. We must acknowledge that the biblical tradition began a process which would transcend its own position on so many issues. For its age it was an intellectual breakthrough, but it does not create an ethical value system to which we should wish to return. That would deny the very spirit of the biblical message which set the process of human reform in motion. We may observe inadequacies in the biblical tradition, but that is because we are observing the beginning

6. R. Bauckham, *The Bible in Politics: How to Read the Bible Politically* (Louisville, KY: Westminster/John Knox, 1987), p. 109.

7. Essays in Smith and Hoffmann, *Bible Really Says*, pp. 11-237.

of an evolutionary process, which was set in the first millennium BCE. Bauckham again affirms,

> Hence, in Israel, freedom entailed not inequality, but equality. That this principle of freedom was not carried through with complete consistency— in relation, for example, to the status of women, or to the institution of slavery...should not obscure the enormous significance of the breakthrough in principle.[8]

Our duty is not to duplicate the ethical teachings of the Bible, but to move in the direction in which they have attempted to send us for the past two millennia.

In a certain sense Christians have had that understanding in regard to certain social and ethical issues in the Hebrew Bible. The Deuteronomistic History enjoins its audience to affirm the institution of Holy War. It is true that the authors of the Deuteronomistic History may have intended for the audience of the late seventh century BCE to implement this more in spiritual categories or in religious reform than on the actual battlefield. However, Josiah certainly took the imperatives literally when he killed the priests at heterodox shrines, such as Bethel (2 Kgs 23.20). At any rate, modern Jews and Christians stand back from the passages of Holy War in the Deuteronomistic History and recognize these passages do not literally apply to us. There is a difference between these rough-hewn men and women in their age and our own. We have evolved or moved beyond their religious piety. Yet the roots of our beliefs lie in those very same texts.

The same might be said for the corpus of Israelite laws. Christians recognize that by virtue of the new covenant the 'old Law' has passed away. Yet for centuries Christians have used some of those laws and have been inspired by the values which undergird them. Modern preachers have found within these laws a sense of human dignity and equality which can inspire our preaching and social message today.[9] Here again we do not seek to apply the laws literally, but rather inquire after the spirit of their content. For we know our social context is radically removed from that of the first millennium BCE. 'Old Testament law can be a model for us not as a static blueprint, but as a dynamic process whose direction we can follow, in some cases, beyond the point at which the law itself had to stop.'[10] These Hebrew laws created the assumptions by which Jews and

---

8. Bauckham, *Bible in Politics*, p. 106.
9. Otto, *Ethik*, pp. 18-116, 175-219.
10. Bauckham, *Bible in Politics*, p. 37.

Christians think today; they are foundational for our values. Yet we have
moved beyond them in the evolutionary process.

Here is the core insight. There is an evolutionary process. Those texts,
religious beliefs and values have set a process in motion. We can never
return to the belief system of the seventh-century BCE Israelites or the
first-century CE Christians, even though we have grown from those
experiences and use those very texts as the ultimate norm of religious
authority in the Judaeo-Christian tradition. We can look at biblical texts
and intuitively feel which messages have abiding relevance for us, and
which ones do not. Down deep we know we have moved beyond their
social situation and cannot apply their ideas and moral imperatives with
heavy-handed literalness.

This perception must be brought into focus for the purpose of understanding the nature of religious development in the Hebrew Bible. It is
an on-going evolutionary process and Jews and Christians are still part
of that dynamic process. When we work with stark contrasts in our
pedagogy, such as comparing egalitarian Israel diametrically to the tyrannical ancient Near East or Canaan, in order to appeal to the modern
audiences, we tend to absolutize the biblical value system and make it
appear unchanging. In reality, the great monotheistic value system of
Israel was ever-changing, it evolved for a thousand years, and it still is
undergoing transformation today.

The appeal for justice and equality in today's society, the clarion cry
on behalf of the oppressed, must still be inspired by the traditions of the
Hebrew Bible. The rationale behind the rhetoric will be different. We
shall not appeal to the value system of early Israel, or the prophets, or
whatever. We shall appeal to the evolving process, the great trajectory,
begun by the biblical authors, of which we are still a part.

III

This process of unfolding the implications of monotheism has not always
been smooth in the history of Christendom. It took Christians nineteen
centuries to realize that faith entailed the abolition of slavery, and twenty
centuries passed before the equality of men and women began to be
actualized in society and in the Church. Yet those values were latent in
the biblical text waiting to be read and heard.

The process of religious development in Israel likewise was uneven,
and often involved a struggle. If our new understanding about the late

emergence of monotheism is correct, it only serves to demonstrate to us the long and arduous journey that an intellectual breakthrough will undertake. The word 'breakthrough' implies a much shorter period of time than six centuries, but this is a misconception. An intellectual insight or set of beliefs will take time to unfold in the human socio-historical context, even centuries.

This new perception implies that the monotheistic evolutionary revolution was comparable to planting a seed, which contains within itself the genetic pattern for the developing plant, but that final growth takes time. From its early inception in Israel and Judaism the implications for a new humanity were present in embryonic fashion, even though the people in those highland villages down through the time of exiled Jews could not conceive of the later and greater process that would come from their actions and beliefs. Over the years social, political and religious values have evolved. Advanced ideas may have surfaced with certain creative thinkers along the way, but in general the full system of thought had to move slowly as the values took root in the hearts and minds of the people, their culture and their ethos.

This advance was made possible by the exigencies of human experience. Political and religious conflict often provided the greatest stimulus for advance. As has been hypothesized by some authors the significant developments in the monotheistic process may have accompanied social and political challenges, crises and upheavals for the people. The entrance of Tyrian Baalism in the ninth century BCE may have sparked the efforts of Elijah and Elisha. The changing economic conditions and oppression of the eighth century BCE inspired the beginning of the classical prophetic movement. The collapse of the Assyrian Empire in the seventh century BCE set the social and religious reforms of Josiah in motion. Finally, the destruction of Jerusalem in 586 BCE assured the eventual triumph of monotheism among the common people as they searched for a new ethos in exile by which they might survive intellectually and physically. All of these were traumatic social experiences for these people called Israelites, and all of them have been perceived by scholars as benchmarks in the development of the religion. It appears that religious change accompanies social upheaval. Most notably the most traumatic experience may have been the event which assured the ultimate success for monotheism. What can be observed is that religious advance is not a smooth and gradual process, but one fraught with struggle and irregular development. As Rainer Albertz concludes,

> the development to monotheism was by no means 'pre-programmed'
> from the beginning, so that to some degree it took place 'automatically',
> but had to be fought out in an open process which at first involved many
> social conflicts.[11]

Such is the nature of any viable and valuable intellectual development.

My conceptualization of the development of monotheism is rather hypothetical. But there are several examples from the biblical text which may elucidate the nature of this religious and social development in Israel and Judaism. In the lawcodes we may observe the development of a greater sense of justice, equality and protection of the oppressed. This developmental process may parallel the emergence of monotheism to some degree. It can be seen in the corpus of laws known as the Book of the Covenant (Exod. 20.23–23.19) and the Deuteronomic Laws (Deut. 12–26). We may observe an initial breakthrough in human rights with some of the early laws in the Book of the Covenant, which scholars have dated anywhere from 1050 to 750 BCE. But a fuller explication and application of these laws appears in the Deuteronomic legislation, which was produced by a prophetically inspired reform movement in Judah that came to some position of authority around 622 BCE. A comparison of the two lawcodes indicates that Deuteronomy 12–26 shares so many parallels with Exod. 20.23–23.19 that it must have been a revised and expanded version.[12] Among the diverse agendas behind this revision there is a clear attempt to provide more rights for poor and marginal people. A continual refrain found in Deuteronomy 12–26 is the imperative to care for the poor, the widow, the orphan and the sojourner in the land. It is worth noting that Deuteronomy also has a much stronger emphasis upon monotheism. The call for social justice and monotheism here appear to have shared interests.

Deuteronomy's reform oriented message which seeks greater protection for the poor and marginal expands upon the old legislation from Exodus in many ways, but the best illustrations may be drawn from laws concerning slaves and women. Exod. 21.1-6 nobly provides for the release of a debt slave after six years of personal service—a great blow in alleviating the gap that so often develops between rich and poor. However, Deut. 15.12-18 expands upon this legislation, perhaps in response to abusive actions of the rich and powerful in the eighth century

11. Albertz, *Israelite Religion*, I, p. 62.

12. D. Patrick, *Old Testament Law* (Atlanta: John Knox, 1985), pp. 97-98, provides a good summary chart for comparison of the lawcodes.

BCE who were able to find loopholes in the earlier laws. The laws in Deut. 15.12-18 extend the release of debt slaves also to women, demand that the released slave must be provisioned by the owner lest the freed slave fall quickly back into debt, and call for the release of slaves to occur universally throughout the land every seven years (as implied by placing the slave release legislation after the Sabbatical debt release laws in Deut. 15.1-11). These reformed laws sought to undo the social damage caused by unscrupulous masters who would keep slaves in debt by deliberately miscalculating the debt slave's six years of service and by quickly getting a newly released debt slave back into deep debt. We see a legal trajectory here from Exodus to Deuteronomy, in which the spirit of the law is designed to protect slaves, so that the letter of the law must change according to new social circumstances. To appeal to these laws to justify the institution of slavery, as was done by some pious Christians in the early nineteenth century, would miss the point of the evolutionary trajectory. The laws are designed to alleviate the suffering of the debt slaves, provide them greater rights, and make their access to freedom more certain. In modern terms these laws would imply that slavery ought to be abolished in all forms, for such abolition would be the culmination of the two thousand year trajectory set in motion by these laws.

Likewise, the laws designed to provide rights for women reflect the same trajectory of development. In the Book of the Covenant women are provided with dignity and rights by legislation which attempts to protect female slaves (Exod. 21.7-11, 20, 26-27) and widows (Exod. 22.21-24). The legislation in Deuteronomy provides even more protection: by instituting the practice of divorce papers which enable a divorced woman to remarry legally without the accusation of bigamy or adultery (Deut. 24.1-4); by articulating guidelines to protect women prisoners of war (Deut. 21.10-14); by expanding the guidelines to protect widows (Deut. 24.17-22); and by enacting the Levirate Law which ensures a widow the support of a future son someday (who also can inherit the family land legally) through the agency of her deceased husband's brother (Deut. 25.5-10).

In many ways the laws of Deuteronomy expanded upon the legislation of the old Book of the Covenant. They sought to plug the loopholes in the old laws, which originated in a much simpler society. These loopholes became evident in Israel and Judah during the economic and political development of the eighth-century BCE when the rapacious greed of the rich and powerful victimized many poor highland peasants. Inspired by the critique of the eighth-century classical prophets, the Deuteronomic reformers elaborated upon the older laws. The common themes in their new legal formulations were the exclusive worship of one God and the defense of the poor and marginal elements of society.

For our purposes what we observe here is an evolutionary development in the legal traditions stimulated by the social, political and economic forces of that age. The evolutionary development is an unfolding of latent ideas found already in the earlier laws, but their fuller manifestation would come only in the crucible of human cultural experience. The cultural experience of Israel served to develop the concepts of monotheism and social reform over the years.[13] Like a seed planted early in the Palestinian highlands these values would mature slowly until they took their fuller form in the exile and beyond. But even then the 'monotheistic revolution' was not complete.

Christians believe that Jesus took the religious and social teachings of the Hebrew Bible and developed them even more in his radical ethic of love and total obedience to God. His message was not totally new, but it built upon and further developed the Israelite and Jewish intellectual values he had inherited. He kept the 'monotheistic revolution' or the evolutionary process going. His imperative to go beyond the requirements of the law was certainly in accord with the spirit of the classical prophets and the Deuteronomic reformers, but he expressed these insights with a pungent clarity that would assure that his sayings would continue to inspire millions of people for thousands of years. He was the 'one through whom the insights and vision of Jewish prophetism transformed the West and the East as well'.[14] His radical call to love one's enemies and to embrace a common humanity in its pain and suffering[15] was an evolutionary breakthrough in the human cultural experience. It was a significant early move toward a common humanity which transcends the particularity of families, groups, tribes and nations. It is an imperative to seek a goal toward which we still painfully aspire today.

Jesus' Sermon on the Mount contains insights which still await a fuller application in the arena of human culture. Jesus proclaimed a message of the love of enemies and non-violence, or perhaps an ethic of passive

13. Albertz, *Israelite Religion*, I, pp. 1-242.

14. J. Cobb, Jr, *Christ in a Pluralistic Age* (Philadelphia: Westminster Press, 1975), p. 98.

15. Brueggemann, *Prophetic Imagination*, pp. 80-108; Theissen, *Biblical Faith*, pp. 82-128.

non-violent resistance to evil. For generations the vast majority of Christian theologians and ethicists believed this imperative could be fulfilled only on an individual level between persons, but that it was not applicable on a corporate level as a guideline for interactions between peoples and nations. Then in this century Mahatma Gandhi and Martin Luther King, Jr, first seriously applied the principle of non-violent resistance on a large social scale, and the results were the independence of a large Asian country and greater rights for a minority within the larger society of America. This was accomplished without revolution and bloodshed, which so often accompany such significant social change in too much of human history. Those Christians who previously considered the sayings of Jesus too ideal for the 'real world' were put to shame by those dramatic accomplishments in the twentieth century.

The 'monotheistic revolution' still continues to unfold its implications even today. The seeds were planted three thousand years ago, but it took more than half a millennium for monotheism to emerge among a people, and the fuller intellectual implications of the movement are still unfolding today. The blossoming of a system of thought requires a long social process as it effects change in the lives of many people. Religious and social values unfold together in the long process of the monotheistic revolution. Israel arose out of Canaan, post-exilic Judaism arose out of Judah and Israel, and both Christianity and modern Judaism arose out of Second Temple Judaism. Christianity and modern Judaism have continued the great evolutionary thrust and will continue to do so, hopefully for millennia to come.

For two millennia now the Church has carried the messages of Jesus, Paul, and the other New Testament authors to the ends of the world. Although the spiritual or psychological dimension of that message, the proclamation of forgiveness and salvation, has been preached with varying degrees of clarity over the centuries, too often the Church has not impressed the social dimension of the Judaeo-Christian tradition upon the masses. This has been due primarily to the socio-historical exigencies of the Christian experience; for many centuries the Church was the political, as well as religious, custodian of barbarian Europe. These custodial responsibilities created a mentality of order and stability rather than reform and egalitarianism in the corporate soul of the Church. To be sure, there were exceptions: religious orders and dissident movements often arose in the life of the church to capture the spirit of reform, justice, and equality. But essentially it was not until the modern era, and even the post-

Enlightenment age, when the Church became sufficiently disenfranchised from political power, Catholic and Protestant alike, that Christians could awaken to the fuller message of the Christian gospel and the responsibilities it entailed, especially in the social arena.

The modern era has seen the awakening of a Christian social message in the popular theology and proclamation of the Church: attempts to aid the poor, the call to abolish slavery, well-intentioned though misdirected efforts on behalf of temperance, campaigns for racial equality, the drive for women's rights, the call to end world hunger and eradicate certain diseases around the world, and many other movements inspired by Judaeo-Christian values. It took us centuries to implement some of these campaigns, yet Jesus clearly directed his listeners to undertake these activities two millennia ago. It does take time for the fuller implications of an intellectual breakthrough to manifest themselves, because the socio-historical conditions have to be right for people to undertake such actions in their society. In the future, new movements may arise, such as the recognition of diverse sexual identities and the rights of artificial and hybrid life forms, and they, too, may draw their inspiration and their strength from biblical imperatives, even though such specific issues could not have been envisioned in the first millennium BCE. It will be yet another example of how the biblical message will continue to unfold for future generations.

IV

The study of biblical texts has impressed upon biblical theologians for many years what is the nature of that phenomenon called 'tradition' by theologians and church historians. What we perceive in the so-called biblical 'tradition' or 'traditions' is an intellectual process which develops over many centuries in a socio-historical and religious matrix. The traditio-historical evaluations of biblical texts are attempts to study the process of how texts change and grow, under the influence of oral bards and scribal editors, in that centuries-long process of development of Israelite and Jewish thought. What has been impressed upon us is how the pattern of development often includes a critical response by one generation of ancient biblical theologians to a previous generation.

In our standard introductions to the Hebrew Bible or Old Testament the tensions of diverse theological traditions often are stressed. For example, Deuteronomy and Proverbs espoused the principle of retribution in this life for human actions. The book of Job rejected the notion of individual retribution and affirmed our inability to understand the pattern of good and evil in the world. Sirach and Wisdom of Solomon responded tentatively to Job by attempting to rebuild the principle of retribution in a limited fashion and so preserved the integrity of God (theodicy). Or again, Isaiah promised that the city of Jerusalem, the Temple and the Judahite king would not fall. But Jeremiah flew in the face of a false confidence rooted in Isaiah's oracles a century later and declared God's willingness to destroy city, Temple and king because of the people's sin. Then Second Isaiah arose after the debacle of destruction which removed all three institutions in 586 BCE, and the prophet promised a restoration of city and Temple. Still again, in the old Pentateuchal theory of development the Yahwist preceded the Elohist, and both antedated the Deuteronomistic Historians and Priestly editors. Here we observed in our older textbooks that the Yahwist spoke of God in intimate and direct fashion, while the Elohist was far more reserved in describing the presence of God. For the Yahwist God was unconditionally gracious, but in the Deuteronomistic History salvation was conditioned upon human repentance, and in the exile and beyond the Priestly editors once more stressed God's unconditional gracious presence through a series of covenants. For Deuteronomistic Historians the Sinai covenant was the ultimate act of divine election, but the Priestly editors spoke of covenants with Adam, Noah, Abraham and Jacob, in addition to the covenant mediated by Moses. In the New Testament the four different gospels originated in separate first-century CE Christian communities, and each one reflected a different theological image of the teachings and actions of Jesus, so that ultimately each one was a creative interpretation of the received oral tradition. The anti-nomian spirit of Paul contrasted with the later moralizing found in the general epistles, which were addressed to churches in a period of growth and institutionalization. Paul's emphasis upon grace without the law contrasted with the emphasis in Matthew and James upon doing the works encouraged by a new spiritual law. In both testaments there are tensions between the various writings, because they spoke to different communities at different times, and the theological needs of each of those communities were unique to their own situations. Together all these nuanced theological positions combine to make a full, balanced theological exposition. Often the full theological position that is best for the modern community of faith to assume must be found in the tension or compromise between these various segments of the biblical text. The component parts, though in tension, came together like the various instruments in a symphony to produce a unified sound. Too often people have tried to smooth these tensions into one bland harmony in an effort to take the bible 'literally', when in reality that is precisely what they have not done with their forced harmonizing. Others have critically said that the Bible contradicts itself. This, too, is an overstatement. Different texts and theological traditions in the Bible spoke differently to the various ages and communities of faith, because diversity is the nature of the human condition, and the message of the biblical text reflects the need to address that diversity in serious fashion. The diverse messages must be held in tension in order to hear the full effect of the theological 'symphony'.

Biblical theologians were impressed by the 'tradition' process evidenced in the Bible as one in which there were dialectical theological tensions emerging over centuries of socio-historical and intellectual development. These theological tensions were not meant to be diluted or ignored, but rather they were discerned by biblical theologians as testimonies to the nature of the human intellectual endeavor. Different answers may be given to the great and difficult questions of human existence and the divine–human relationship at different times and places. There are no simple religious answers; the ambiguity of two statements in tension sometimes is the best answer to complex existential questions. For example, Isaiah spoke of hope while Micah spoke of judgment and doom for Judah in the late eighth century BCE. Both were adjudged to have spoken faithfully by a later generation who saw in the complexity of historical events that both punishment and deliverance were visited upon Judah— Jerusalem survived amid great destruction in the province. Two contradictory messages together intuited and described the nature of the experience.

'Tradition' is a process of intellectual development, often containing what appear to be contradictions. In reality, tradition contains the diverse viewpoints and experiences which must all be taken together to apprehend the fuller picture of human religious experience. In the biblical text such diverse traditions must be drawn together in theologizing in dialectical tension in order to address the great religious questions. Biblical theologians sensed this deeply after considering the millennium of intellectual evolution which lies within the Hebrew Bible and the New Testament.

This view of 'tradition' departs radically from a more popular view of tradition, sometimes held by some church theologians and ecclesiastical authorities, who see tradition as a repository of long-held and cherished beliefs, each layer of theological contribution building harmoniously upon the ideas which preceded it. Such a dogmatic view of tradition tends to flatten it in unilinear fashion, turning the great 'Tradition' into a quarry from which one could draw ideas for contemporary questions. This treatment of the biblical text leads to taking biblical passages out of context and making them say something totally divergent from their original meaning. The serious biblical theologian senses that the vibrant, throbbing, sometimes contradictory biblical traditions evolved into the later Christian tradition, in which the same dynamics were operative. One could not serenely select a teaching from the great corpus of 'tradition' without asking the question whether this aspect of the 'tradition' was truly appropriate for the question being asked, or without understanding the sociohistorical and intellectual context that particular teaching first addressed. Biblical theologians understand that 'tradition', be it biblical or the later Christian, is a process of human experience lived in a dynamic relationship with both God and the world; it is not a serene repository of timeless truths stacked neatly like the well-shaped bricks in a magnificant cathedral. For this reason primarily, biblical theologians have found themselves so often at loggerheads with the official representatives of their own institutional denominations.

How will our new understandings of Israel's cultural identity and religious development affect our understanding of the 'tradition' process? I believe that it will only reinforce what biblical theologians have sensed for the past two centuries: 'Tradition' is a dynamic process, an evolutionary development which grows in response to human religious and social challenges. Now we perceive even more clearly that Israel emerged slowly, painfully, with people often unconscious of the transformation which was occurring, and at other times dramatically responding to a crisis situation (Elijah, Hosea, Josiah, exile). The concept of an evolving process will be impressed upon us even more clearly, and the Christian understanding of 'tradition' as a process frequently involving dialectical tensions will be affirmed even more clearly.

Hopefully, there will be a new stinging dimension added to this understanding. Perhaps Christians will realize that in a real sense the biblical tradition is still evolving, too. We have not yet unfolded totally all the implications of the monotheistic revolution. We are still part of the biblical tradition, and it is our moral imperative to continue the development of the evolutionary message found within the biblical text.

In past rhetoric, preachers and theologians often spoke of a return to the biblical tradition for inspiration. Christians, and especially Protestants, almost portrayed the scenario as though the biblical tradition had been lost, and they had to restore it. Granted, the sharp and pungent teachings of the biblical text sometimes are dulled by daily church routine and institutional concerns, but the rhetoric made it sound as though the Bible could be restored to the Church only by the biblical theologians. Our new scholarly paradigms may enable us to avoid those overstatements as we stress our continuity with the greater evolving Christian tradition.

We Jews and Christians do not really 'return' to the biblical tradition; rather, we are an extension of it—a trajectory hurtling through time into the future. At times the evolving process moves with greater clarity and vision than at other times. But we are part of a process which has never ceased and ought not to cease ever, for humanity and human religious need will be in a state of transformation forever, too. We are duty bound to continue the process, now that we have begun to see it more clearly in an evolutionary perspective. We must continue to unfold the implications which lie latent in the ethos of the Hebrew Bible and the teachings of Jesus and Paul.[16] Tradition is not a repository of belief, it is the constant working out of the implications of the monotheistic revolution. We are the tradition-making process as we proclaim the gospel or live the Torah anew in each generation.

V

The new paradigm finally may speak to another intellectual issue that often has engaged the reflection of historians and the philosophers of history. What are the significant driving forces of history and intellectual development? Are the contributions of significant individuals the true force in history, or is there an inevitable dynamic which brings about development, so that had not one individual provided a great contribution, another would have arisen to take his or her place?

Translated into issues germane to the study of the Hebrew Bible, the question becomes how significant were the contributions of people such

16. Theissen, *Biblical Faith*, p. 170 *et passim*, likewise declares that we have a moral responsibllity for continuing this cultural evolutionary process which includes the further actualization of religious values.

as Moses, Samuel, Elijah, the classical prophets, and others. This question has led scholars to undertake quests to discern what is the historical kernel connected to a particular individual. Too often the findings of a scholar tend to reflect ironically the intellectual assumptions of the person undertaking the analysis—nowhere is this more evident than in the multitude of quests for the historical Jesus. Often scholars come to the conclusion that a particular individual was really a fiction created by the biblical traditions to explain the process that arose in history. Martin Noth concluded that almost all the traditions associated with Moses were fictional.[17] Similar conclusions have been made concerning Samuel.[18] Ultimately, it is probably impossible to discover the historical kernel associated with a certain individual because the tradition process is a story-making process which stereotypes all the accounts. We may be asking the wrong question.

The seeds of the monotheistic revolution were planted in the Palestinian highlands as a people regrouped to form new social communities. Although they were unaware of where their new beginnings would take them and not consciously cognizant of being different from the predecessor culture of the lowlands at first, their embarcation on their new course was significant. In those early years there would be many individuals who would shape the direction of their community; some would contribute more dramatically than others. Their contributions would be recalled in traditions that portrayed them in stereotypic heroic fashion. Doubtless many names were forgotten. Probably the traditions recall the contributions of many individuals in a strange and idiosyncratic fashion, sometimes merged together in one hero figure. But those individuals were there and they made a difference.

To recognize that the emergence of Israel was a slow and gradual process, that the 'revolution' took centuries, especially in terms of religious values, puts a special focus upon the contributions of certain individuals. There is a tension. Their accomplishments as individuals truly were significant, yet the entire process does not stand or fall with any one individual, such as Moses. Nor can it be said that a so-called founder,

17. M. Noth, *A History of Pentateuchal Traditions* (trans. B. Anderson; Englewood Cliffs, NJ: Prentice–Hall, 1972), pp. 156-75. Cf. G. von Rad, *Old Testament Theology* (trans. D.M.G. Stalker; 2 vols.; New York: Harper & Row, 1962, 1965), I, pp. 289-96.

18. R. Gnuse, *The Dream Theophany of Samuel* (Lanham, MD: University Press of America, 1984), pp. 215-46.

such as Moses, Samuel or Elijah, is more important than a later 'perpetuator', such as Ezra, Nehemiah or the countless scribes who gave us the biblical text. They are all equally important for the development of monotheism, regardless of temporal placement. The process of emerging monotheism ought to be viewed as an organic whole. The contributions of so-called founders early in the embryonic process (Moses, Samuel, Elijah) are equal to those of the people who later developed the movement (the classical prophets) and those who preserved and systematized the movement (Ezra, Nehemiah, scribes and redactors). What the 'founders' would have accomplished would have been for naught were it not for the later 'preservers'; and the later redactors would have had nothing to shape were it not for a living tradition which had come down to them from the 'founders'. This is true no matter how small that tradition might have been. We must view the whole process holistically, as an organic trajectory through time.

Niels Peter Lemche made similar observations when he spoke of how certain individuals, such as Samuel, Saul or David, were the results of social development and not the direct agents of social change. To emphasize individual persons and their contributions, according to Lemche, would be to lose sight of the organic process of development in favor of individuals, or points on a line, rather than the line of development itself. Concentration on isolated individuals breaks the continuity of the process in our consideration.[19] Although Lemche might overstate the importance of the dynamics of the historical process and underestimate the value of key individuals, many of them nameless, nonetheless, he has issued an important warning. In its style of writing the biblical text stresses the role of epic heroes, or individuals. This contrasts with the modern understanding of history, in which the great socio-historical forces shape the flow of events, too. We must integrate both the stress upon the individual and the perception of the greater historical flow of events. The bible, in effect, speaks of the great historical flow of events by recalling the actions of many epic and heroic persons. We need to translate those perceptions into our understandings. The contributions of many individuals make the greater historical process, and no one individual can be said to have founded or created the entire process. Likewise, the socio-historical process of development could not have existed without those many named and nameless persons.

19. Lemche, 'Israel, History of', p. 541.

The contributions of any indvidual may be seen in symbolic fashion as equally significant to the total process, whether that person is early or late. Likewise, one may portray any individual in heroic or stereotypical fashion, especially since that was the style of literature in that age. For example, the particular identity of the historical Moses is not as important as the perception that he stands as a symbol for the beginning of the process—especially the legal tradition of later Israel. The image of Moses in the biblical text may be a synthesis of several people who contributed to the movement. If so, we have the storytellers' way of making the tradition manageable for the audience. There were individuals in this early age who would be recalled by later generations and lionized as great founders, and they would be characterized in the garb of later institutions. In effect, Moses and Samuel would be portrayed as prophets and priests, even though in their own era those offices had not yet come to be clearly defined in society. Figures such as Moses, Samuel or Elijah symbolize the beginning of a developmental process, and they are recalled and portrayed by authors only at the end of that process. Yet to praise them as the later traditions did was not a false endeavor, for those early individuals and many others along the way helped to unfold the implications of the monotheistic revolution/evolution. Also, to dress them in the garb of later institutions is not altogether false, since those later offices grew out of the early religious development shaped by the founders. Without them the great intellectual advance would have died, and a later era would have had to reinitiate the monotheistic evolution/revolution.

The old debate as to whether monotheism began with the classical prophets, as Julius Wellhausen suggested, or with Moses, as William Albright suggested, is misplaced. Monotheism begins with all the persons involved in the process, or more properly the emergence of monotheism is a process which lasts for six centuries from the settlement in Palestine to the Babylonian exile. The portrayal of any individual in that whole process should be seen as an attempt by the tradition to capture the spirit of the entire process. So we may forgive the heroic lionizing tendencies in the epic literature (and their anachronistic projections of later institutions onto early individuals), as we try to envision the sweep of the entire process and thus appreciate their poetic portrayals.

This mode of perception has significant philosophical implications. It attempts to mediate in the debate between the importance of the individual versus the idea of a great movement in history. It attempts to postulate that individuals all contribute to the greater historical process.

This model has been advocated by contemporary philosophers of history.[20] Highlighting the role of individual people as well as specific ages of cultural turmoil set this historical model of perception apart from nineteenth-century theories of cultural evolution. Those theories too often lost the significance of the contributions of individuals in the portrayal of a blind impersonal process of evolution. The newer model balances the factors.

The newer model resonates well with the biological paradigm of Punctuated Equilibria. For this model stresses that great advances come after the culmination of many little contributions, all by individuals, and when the breakthrough is made, the implications of that breakthrough will unfold for a number of years, again because of the contributions of many individuals. The process is an organic continuum with many persons providing significant input. This model suggests that although no one or few individuals were responsible for the evolution of monotheism, yet the contributions of significant persons drove the movement onward. It suggests that the socio-historical experiences of the people called Israel or the Jews share equally with creative individual thinkers the credit for the trajectory of emerging monotheism. Perhaps, our new perceptions concerning Israel's emergence will lead us to reflect upon such questions and to consider the possibility of using such philosophical paradigms for the understanding of biblical traditions.

VI

In conclusion, what I have attempted to undertake in this chapter is the theoretic presentation of some creative suggestions. The new scholarly view of ancient Israel and Judaism may inspire biblical theologians with a comparable vision for social reform as did older models of *Heilsgeschichte* theology in a former generation. The models may lead theologians to speak more of cultural continuity rather than dialectical tensions. That will not only affect how we view ancient Israel, it may transform our view of Church and culture in the greater world environment of our own age. We may be led to see the evolving process in ancient Israel as a process of growth that, once begun, is continuing still in our own age. This will affect our rhetoric in how we appeal to the biblical traditions to inspire action in the modern Church and society. We might see even

20. Frederick Teggart, *Theory and Processes of History* (repr.; Berkeley: University of California Press, 1960 [1918, 1925]), pp. 77-151.

more clearly the nature of tradition as a dynamic, uneven, but vibrant developmental process which will lead us to eschew static and dogmatic understandings of tradition, be they in regard to either biblical or churchly traditions. Finally, the new models may cause us to reflect more upon the philosophy of history and how such philosophical reflection may influence our perceptions of the biblical testimony.

These are all my speculative suggestions which are brought to mind when surveying the direction of biblical studies and asking the question of theological signficance. In the ensuing chapters more speculative ideas will be unfolded, which may not necessary convince the reader, but hopefully will engender some reflection and discussion among theologians, preachers and students of the Bible.

Chapter 7

THE HEBREW BIBLE AND PROCESS THEOLOGY

Our discussion of tradition, social reform, and grand intellectual paradigms leads to another topic related to this discussion. As theologians draw out images and ideas from the biblical text to weave them into some form of theological exposition, they must have some *a priori* set of systematic intellectual assumptions, or a philosophical system to create the framework of discourse into which they may work the raw materials of the biblical tradition. A theological idiom which resonates with the biblical categories as we now perceive them is process thought, a philosophical system of thought which traces its origins to the writings of Alfred North Whitehead.[1] His ideas have been explicated further by more contemporary process philosophers, most notably Charles Hartshorne, who especially addresses theological issues, as well as philosophical questions.[2] Significant theologians such as Schubert Ogden, John Cobb and Norman Pittenger, among others, have further developed Whitehead's thought in relationship to theological discourse.[3] Continued critique and discussion

1. A.N. Whitehead, *The Concept of Nature* (repr.; Cambridge: Cambridge University Press, 1964 [1920]); *idem, Science and the Modern World* (New York: Macmillan, 1925); *idem, Religion in the Making* (repr.; New York: Macmillan, 1957 [1926]); *idem, Symbolism: Its Meaning and Effect* (repr.; New York: Macmillan, 1958 [1927]); *idem, The Function of Reason* (Princeton, NJ: Princeton University Press, 1929); *idem, Process and Reality* (repr.; New York: Free Press 1978 [1929]), which was his magnum opus on process thought; *idem, Science and Philosophy* (New York: Philosophical Library, 1948), pp. 85-157.

2. C. Hartshorne, *The Divine Relativity: A Social Conception of God* (New Haven: Yale University Press, 1948); *idem, Reality as Social Process: Studies in Metaphysics and Religion* (Boston: Beacon, 1953); *idem, Creative Synthesis and Philosophic Method* (La Salle: Open Court, 1970); *idem, Omnipotence and Other Theological Mistakes* (Albany: State University of New York Press, 1984).

3. S. Ogden, *Christ without Myth* (New York: Harper & Row, 1961); *idem, The Reality of God and Other Essays* (New York: Harper & Row, 1977); *idem, On*

have led many theologians to believe that although pure philosophical process categories may not translate too well into useful theological idioms, especially in regard to portraying the personal nature of God and human finitude or sin; nonetheless, process ideas may be modified and combined with traditional theological expressions to produce a contemporary theology which addresses the Church in a more coherent and meaningful fashion.[4] In the past generation a handful of authors have speculated also upon the possible connections between process thought or process theology and biblical studies.[5] Perhaps, the directions provided by critical scholarship concerning the emergence of the Israelite religion and ethos might spark greater interest in this topic. To that end I would like to provide some creative speculations.

Theologians in the past observed that we have understood the biblical tradition in old, classical theological categories for generations, but now

Theology (San Francisco: Harper & Row, 1986); J. Cobb, Jr, *A Christian Natural Theology Based on the Thought of Alfred North Whitehead* (Philadelphia; Westminster Press, 1965); *idem, Pluralistic Age*; *idem, Process Theology as Political Theology* (Philadelphia: Westminster Press, 1982); Cobb and D.R. Griffin, *Process Theology: An Introductory Exposition* (Philadelphia: Westminster Press, 1976); N. Pittenger, *Process Thought and Christian Faith* (New York: Macmillan, 1968); *idem, The Divine Triunity* (Philadelphia: United Church Press, 1977); *idem, Catholic Faith in a Process Perspective* (Maryknoll: Orbis Books, 1981); E. Peters, *The Creative Advance: An Introduction to Process Philosophy as a Context for Christian Faith* (St Louis: Bethany, 1966), are but a few of the sources.

4.   See the critical analyses provided by the evangelical scholars in R. Nash (ed.), *Process Theology* (Grand Rapids: Baker, 1987), who point out that the view of God provided by pure process philosophy lacks the dynamic power and personal relationship to humanity that is found in the biblical portrayal of God. However, several scholars see the value in integrating modified process categories of thought with traditional classical Christian thought to produce a stronger, albeit traditional, form of theology: N. Clark, 'Christian Theism and Whiteheadian Process Philosophy: Are they Compatible?', *Process Theology* (ed. Nash), pp. 219-51; C. Pinnock, 'Between Classical and Process Theism', *Process Theology* (ed. Nash), pp. 313-27. Pittenger, a noted process theologian, clearly affirms that Process philosophical categories must be subordinated to the core beliefs and assumptions of Christian theology, *Divine Triunity*, pp. 115-17.

5.   Pittenger, *Divine Triunity*, pp. 15-31; G. Janzen, 'The Old Testament in "Process" Perspective: Proposal for a Way Forward in Biblical Theology', *Magnalia Dei, The Mighty Acts of God: Essays of the Bible and Archaeology in Memory of G. Ernest Wright* (eds. F. Cross, W. Lemke and P. Miller; Garden City, NY: Doubleday, 1976), pp. 480-509; L. Ford, *The Lure of God: A Biblical Background for Process Theism* (Philadelphia: Fortress Press, 1978).

process theism may enable us to see the biblical text in a new and living fashion. This new process focus may be a more dynamic lens by which to observe the biblical message, and the resultant theologizing may be far more congruent with the biblical perceptions of reality.[6]

All theologians use a philosophical worldview as a framework for their discourse, either consciously or unconsciously, and biblical theologians are no exception. Biblical theologians must be aware of the philosophical assumptions they use, and such a system must be relevant to modern cultural perceptions while remaining faithful to the experiences of the biblical men and women. Advocates of process thought believe their philosophical system is better suited for that task than any other contemporary reigning philosophical system,

> Process theism is the natural ally of biblical history, for process is history abstractly conceived. Process theism can provide the contemporary conceptuality by which we can appropriate this ancient literature, while the biblical tradition can provide those concrete particularities whereby our lives are given final meaning.[7]

Indeed, in my opinion process categories appear to be the best at simultaneously encapsulating both the modern worldview and the biblical worldview.

I

Several authors have noted that the biblical testimony to a sacred history in which God interacts with a chosen people over many generations is understood better by process modes of thought rather than by static, theological categories.[8] This is particularly true of the Old Testament, especially in the Pentateuch, where we have a theological document which uses the medium of historical recital, the story of the divine–human relationship, which by its very nature 'concentrates not on what God necessarily is but on what he has contingently done'.[9]

When process thought is introduced into the articulation of biblical theology a healthy synthesis results. Process thought complements the historical recital of the biblical narratives by speaking of God in such a way as to metaphysically describe a divine reality capable of interaction,

---

6. Janzen, 'Old Testament', pp. 480-509; Ford, *Lure*, p.12.
7. Ford, *Lure*, p. 135.
8. Janzen, 'Old Testament', pp. 496-97.
9. Ford, *Lure*, p. 27.

change, and even growth in relationship to the human reality. Terence Fretheim, for example, can look at biblical thought through a modern worldview and see the biblical portrayal of God's relationship to the world as 'organismic'.[10] Traditional theology, on the other hand, always had to place the abstract God of systematic theology in tension with the deity who became incarnate in the life of Israel or the person of Jesus Christ. Traditionally we spoke of the tension between divine transcendence and divine immanence. But in process thought God becomes involved with the created order more dynamically. The anthropomorphic and anthropopathic descriptions in the Hebrew Bible are not the embarrassing expressions of a primitive mind but a symbolic way of describing God's natural self-involvement with the world. As Lewis Ford notes, process complements historical recital by describing the 'necessary conditions', that is, by providing a dynamic doctrine of God for biblical theologians. Furthermore, the biblical texts complement process theology by giving 'concrete historical contours', that is, examples of the divine self-involvement in the human process of history.[11] In the Hebrew Bible God is portrayed as being bound up in time so that 'God does change in the light of what happens in the interaction between God and the world'.[12] By being in the temporal flow, God has undertaken kenosis.[13]

Salvation history paradigms and process thought are both open-ended; they are not neatly organized, closed theological systems. Process thought does not take the great symbols of salvation history, such as land, messiah, Day of the Lord, and melt them into abstract, systematic, universal truths. It lets them stand with all their historical and cultural particularity as ways in which God has become revealed or involved in the human process. Therefore, biblical theologians, especially those working with the Hebrew Bible, may feel comfortable with process thought, because it appears to respect the particularity and the original socio-historical context of the biblical symbols without forcing them to become something else in a systematic theology.

From another vantage point process theologians also perceive that categories of thought in the biblical text resonate well with process theism.

---

10. T. Fretheim, *The Suffering of God: An Old Testament Perspective* (OBT, 14; Philadelphia: Fortress Press, 1984), pp. 23, 35.

11. Janzen, 'Old Testament', p. 502; and Ford, *Lure*, p. 27.

12. Fretheim, *Suffering*, p. 35.

13. Fretheim, *Suffering*, p. 58.

Norman Pittenger noted that the metaphors and myths in the Hebrew Bible present a dynamic and pictoral image of God similar to what process thought seeks to attain,

> it would seem that there is a remarkable correspondence between the biblical insistence on the living God who is active in nature and in the affairs of men, and the recognition by process-thought that the world is a dynamic process of such a kind that whatever explanatory principle or agency there may be must be of that sort too...[14]

Pittenger also observed the open-ended nature of both systems of thought, for both recognize evolution and the emergence of new significant possibilities and symbols to inspire humanity in its quest for the divine.[15]

This recognition that new or novel theological perceptions may arise leads to another aspect of congruity between biblical thought and process theology, the acceptance of diversity. In the model of salvation history it is possible and even normal for a concept to emerge which may contradict a previous religious belief; such is the nature of progressive revelation implied by a salvation history model. Indeed, such is the reality observed by biblical scholars as they study the various tensions found in divergent traditions throughout the biblical text. Such tensions or contradictions, if we wish to use such a strong term, naturally make the classical systematic theologian nervous. But this is not so for the process theologian for whom divergent biblical traditions are natural, because they reflect different stages in the on-going process of divine involvement and interaction with the human condition with all its different socio-historical settings.

Scripture contains many different testimonies of God and the human understandings of the divine will, but process thought can accept such tensions due to what one author calls the 'lack of concern for temporal consistency' in diverse biblical traditions.[16] Process thought accepts the diverse pictures of God because they reflect different stages in an intellectual growth process, and these divergent tensions permit and promote growth by their accumulation and interaction in the greater faith community. Different viewpoints finally add up to a multi-faceted perspective of the divine–human reality,

---

14. Pittenger, *Process*, p. 20.
15. Pittenger, *Process*, p. 22.
16. Ford, *Lure*, p. 129.

> The genius of the Hebrew imagination was that it was able to accept and affirm the witness to God's former acts, even as understood from an older perspective, while at the same time proclaiming what God was about to do as grasped from a newer standpoint.[17]

Process thought may look at a presentation of biblical thought which speaks of a salvation history and a traditio-historical development of religious beliefs and affirm its basic approach to faith and ideas, because it is congruent with the notion of evolving process.

II

As previously observed in this work, the paradigms of 'salvation history' proposed by the Biblical Theology Movement have lost their lustre in the past generation among biblical scholars and theologians. However, that does not necessarily undermine the observations made in the previous section. Although not all of the Hebrew Bible may be termed a 'salvation history', part of it most certainly retains that character, and the accompanying view of a God active among the social affairs of humanity is certainly present. Process thought may still resonate with that imagery. What the new scholarship has begun to impress upon us is the even greater diversity of thought found within the biblical tradition beyond the basic salvation history imagery of the historical narratives. Again, process thought is relevant as a theological framework for biblical theologizing, because process thought does more than simply tolerate divergent theological trajectories, it affirms that diversity is an extremely important ingredient in a fuller understanding of the divine self-manifestation in the human arena. Process thought appears to be flexible in changing with the various directions in biblical scholarship, and that is more than may be said for traditional Neo-Orthodoxy.

Process thinkers also expressed some discomfort with the expressions of the old Biblical Theology Movement, perhaps because it implied that the historical arena was the chief or the only dimension for divine self-disclosure. With the current decline of the Biblical Theology Movement, some process thinkers rejoice, for now philosophical theology, and especially process thought, may be permitted to integrate more fully with biblical theology.[18] The events of sacred history may be perceived in a fuller discourse with both biblical and metaphysical categories. Biblical

---

17. Ford, *Lure*, p. 130.
18. Pittenger, *Process*, p. 5.

texts may be viewed from a broader perspective with process categories of thought.[19] Process theologians see the divine manifestation in other arenas of human activity, and thus sense the need for a 'wider conceptuality which frees theology from the ghetto of sacred history and places it within the whole sweep of human and natural history'.[20]

Therefore, process theologians can affirm not only a biblical theology which speaks of salvation history, but they may resonate even more readily with biblical theology built upon the wider concern of divine revelation in worship and cult (Psalms), human reason (Wisdom literature), the experiences of everyday life (laws and novels), as well as sacred history (narratives). Since 1965 scholars in Hebrew Bible have sensed that our lack of attention to the theology of legal, cultic and didactic biblical texts has left our biblical theology too narrow. This was one of the reasons for the increasing dissatisfaction with the traditional biblical theology systems, especially those built upon a *Heilsgeschichte* model, such as the work of Gerhard von Rad. The attempt to remedy that with more broadly based theological expositions[21] will produce models that will fit even better with an intellectual framework provided by process thought. Process theism views the divine as manifest in many ways in human culture, and now biblical theologians are stressing that the Hebrew Bible made very similar observations over two thousand years ago, particularly when we step back and look at the breadth of the entire canonical witness.

III

When I speak of introducing process categories into the discussion of biblical theology, I immediately sense the similarity between the two intellectual endeavors on a very basic level. Both stress a developmental

19. Janzen, 'Old Testament', pp. 502, 506.

20. Ford, *Lure*, p. ix.

21. S. Terrien, *The Elusive Presence: Toward a New Biblical Theology* (New York: Harper & Row, 1978); *idem, Till the Heart Sings: A Biblical Theology of Manhood and Womanhood* (Philadelphia: Fortress Press, 1985); B. Childs, *Old Testament Theology in a Canonical Context* (Philadelphia: Fortress Press, 1985); *idem, Biblical Theology of the Old and New Testaments* (Minneapolis: Fortress Press, 1993); P. Hanson, *The People Called: The Growth of Community in the Bible* (New York: Harper & Row, 1986); J. Levenson, *Creation and the Persistence of Evil: The Jewish Drama of Divine Omnipotence* (San Francisco: HarperCollins, 1988); Brueggemann, *Theology*.

process or progressive revelation. Both accept a very dynamic view of the on-going development of tradition. But there are some deeper nuances of continuity which deserve at least a limited articulation on our part.

Central to the system of process philosophy is the understanding of 'becoming', or how each present moment comes into existence. This is sometimes described as 'concrescence', or the process by which the past moment is taken up by the present moment. It is interesting to observe that process thinkers prefer not to think of the present fading into the past, rather they speak of the present drawing the past into itself. This is a more positive way of speaking. Likewise, the future is drawing the present into itself constantly, and authors prefer to say that the future is a 'lure' for the present. Similarly the metaphor is used to describe God, who lies in the future and 'lures' the present and all humanity into future possibilities, which may be described as gracious gifts or opportunities.[22]

This process of becoming is central to the entire system of process thought. Each present moment is viewed as an 'apprehension' of the past moment, each 'moment of becoming' remembers the past in a new construct. Each moment in the organic flow of time reinterprets as it uses the past and adds the dimension of the present in a new configuration. This organic notion of change sees the present flowing out of the past and into the future in the ever constant 'moment of becoming'.[23]

Biblical theologians can use the model of concrescence in several ways. A 'concrescent occasion' may be said to be the moment of dynamic presence of the divine in the human process. God 'lures' the past into the present and therefore is active in the moment of becoming, but this additionally implies that God is active in every moment of becoming, not just historical events, but also in nature, the cultic sphere and the human mind. 'God is present at every occasion, and has a hand in every event.'[24] God can be said even to suffer the experiences of violence and pain of the earthly creatures.[25] We now believe that this is what the total canon of the Hebrew Bible tells us. All these diverse 'concrescent occasions' became a sacred history. God is active in every event: rainfall, crop growth, exodus, Sinai, conquest, and even the migrations of foreign nations such as the Philistines and the Syrians (Amos 9.7).[26] Process

22. Whitehead, *Process*, pp. 46-48, 281-90.
23. Whitehead, *Science and the Modern World*, pp. 90-126.
24. Fretheim, *Suffering*, p. 75.
25. Fretheim, *Suffering*, p. 76.
26. C. Westermann, *Creation* (trans. J. Scullion; Philadelphia: Fortress Press,

thought and biblical theology combined may give us a broader and deeper natural theology.

The image of concrescence secondarily may help scholars speak of Israel's intellectual advance. The image dovetails with the new perception of Israel's social and religious development. Israelite and Jewish values do not radically break with the past, rather they 'flow' out of them. Elements of the old worldview are not negated, they are appropriated and transformed in the 'new moment of becoming' which represents the stages of Israelite and Jewish evolution. With this model one may simultaneously speak of continuity with the past and ideational advance.

This model can be used to describe not only how Israelites and Jews appropriated the values of the ancient Near East, it can describe equally the evolution of biblical traditions out of each other. For example, the laws in the Book of the Covenant in Exodus 21–23 are 'apprehended' by the Deuteronomic reform laws in Deuteronomy 12–26. For the earlier laws are selectively chosen for repetition and expanded to cover a wider range of issues in order to produce a reform code sensitive to the needs of poor and marginal people. Thus, the slave laws in the older code only permit a male debt slave to be released after six years of slavery and under the condition that the woman he married and the children he fathered while in the service of his master must remain behind in slavery (Exod. 21.2-6). The later reform oriented laws boldly mandate a universal year of slave release every seven years which permits both male and female debt slaves to be released with their families, and the law further stipulates that the master shall provision them to start a new life to prevent their relapse into debt slavery (Deut. 15.12-18). Readers of the biblical text may see this same pattern of evolution on a large scale, also. The Deuteronomic reform tradition may have developed out of the earlier epic tradition called the Elohist, the later classical prophetic movement grew out of the earlier prophetic movement, the later wisdom tradition of Job and Koheleth developed in reaction to the earlier wisdom tradition in Proverbs, and Sirach and the Wisdom of Solomon reacted to the message of Job and Koheleth.

As theologians observe this developmental process occurring on different levels in the biblical text, they sense that they are observing a

1974), pp. 1-15; Janzen, 'Old Testament', pp. 500-501; H. Schmid, 'Creation, Righteousness, and Salvation: "Creation Theology" as the Broad Horizon of Biblical Theology', *Creation in the Old Testament* (ed. B. Anderson; Issues in Religion and Theology, 6; Philadelphia: Fortress Press, 1984), pp. 102-117.

pattern of how old ideas are taken into a new religious message repeatedly over the ages. This, in turn, reflects that the Israelites and the Jews continually experienced the emergence of new levels of insight into the divine–human relationship. 'In no other culture or span of time has man's understanding of God's ways progressed so much as in ancient Israel.'[27] Any introductory study of the bible impresses upon the students that the biblical traditions reflect an intellectual and religious odyssey, and when the various traditions are isolated and studied, we gain deeper understandings of the nature of how biblical peoples evolved and changed in their perceptions of God and the world. At each stage in their religious journey the biblical traditions drew upon the teachings of past, reconfigured them and produced a powerful new message appropriate for psychological and religious needs of that age. The value of the traditio-historical critical study of the Bible is that it has focused our attention upon this process more than anything else. Consequently, the model of 'concrescence' or 'apprehension' of the past may be very useful for understanding not only God's action in the human arena but also the way in which Israelites and Jews evolved intellectually and the manner by which sacred texts were generated over a millennium of time.

IV

Other aspects of the process philosophical system may be used in helpful fashion to elucidate biblical theology. A central theme in process theism is the 'lure of God', the persuasive power of God to draw the present into the future. This theological idiom replaces the notion of the divine will acting out of pure omnipotence with the more dynamic image of a deity who is involved in the process of the world. This deity 'entices' the world and believers to move into the future in harmony with the divine will and to make the morally right decisions.

> God is not the cosmic watchmaker, but the husbandman in the vineyard of the world, fostering and nurturing its continuous growth throughout the ages; he is the companion and friend who inspires us to achieve the very best that is within us.[28]

Process thinkers often speak of such 'divine persuasion' in connection with biblical themes. The biblical traditions may be called upon to attest

27. Ford, *Lure*, p. 131.
28. Ford, *Lure*, p. 21.

to 'divine persuasion' in a way which more sensitively uses the biblical metaphors than did the old classical theological discussion of divine omnipotence. Biblical texts speak of the pathos of God, even the occasional divine repentence of the decision to destroy Israel. The rhetoric of the divine will, which comes through the prophetic demand upon people to follow God, contains the image of a God angered or agonized by the human refusal to obey the Law. Such imagery is discordant with the language of omnipotence, omniscience and omnipresence, but it flows more smoothly with process assumptions of divine self-involvement.

In biblical imagery God is not pre-determined nor has human history been foreordained, rather Israel's free response will change not only their destiny but the very nature of God. By being related to humanity in the flow of time, God does not know the future, rather God and humanity together work out the flow of history.[29]

Israel rebels against God and for a time appears to thwart the divine will in the biblical narratives. Yet process theology would have no difficulty absorbing these ancient narrative images. Process theology would say that God is active throughout the cosmos, and though the divine will might be opposed temporarily by human freedom, eventually the divine will may 'lure' or lead the creation in desired direction.[30] God serves as a 'lure for actualization, providing novel possibilities of achievement'.[31] God gives people the power to relate to the divine and interact with the divine.[32]

At times the biblical images may be rather strong, perhaps suggesting more than just a 'divine lure'. God may be portrayed as king, judge and savior, and each of these metaphors is a truly powerful image of 'divine persuasion' in the understanding of that ancient age. Such images are rather absolute and may appear more 'coercive' than 'persuasive' to us. But theologians must balance the 'coercive' and the 'persuasive' imagery.[33] Certainly images such as the divine husband, father and even mother, which we find in the oracles of Hosea, impress us as appropriately persuasive. So theologians must balance the imagery to appreciate the characterization of God as 'divine persuasion' or 'divine lure' in the entire Hebrew Bible. Nor should modern readers forget that the biblical

29. Fretheim, *Suffering*, pp. 41, 47.
30. Ford, *Lure*, p. 60.
31. Ford, *Lure*, p. 59.
32. Fretheim, *Suffering*, p. 37.
33. Ford, *Lure*, pp. 30-31.

peoples lived in the first millennium BCE, a rough-hewn age, primitive in many ways. What impresses the modern audience as strong language may be more appropriate for them in that rustic age as an image of divine persuasion. What sounds tyrannical to a post-enlightenment westerner may not be so to an ancient Palestinian.

Resonant with the general discussion of this book one might add that in the testimony of the Hebrew Bible God has been a 'lure' to Israel and the Jews, leading them toward a monotheistic faith. The new perspectives provided by scholars which stress the gradual emergence of monotheism and its corresponding linear world view certainly should tempt theologians to consider seriously the image of God 'luring' the ancient Israelites and Jews toward a deeper intellectual and religious development. Throughout the vicissitudes of monarchy and exile the prophetic minority prevailed and monotheistic faith arose due to the persistent 'enticement' of God in the life process of these ancient people. God slowly brought about the unfolding of the intellectual implications of monotheism. Ultimately, we must confess that this enticement by God is still occuring for us yet today, and the challenge for us is whether we choose to heed this divine 'enticement'.

Therefore, theologians still can speak of a salvation history, but it is an intellectual development which encompasses the entire biblical tradition and the history of the Christian faith. We are still in the dynamic process of that tradition. God is not one who dramatically intervenes in history as the old Neo-Orthodox model would have it. Rather, God is in the process, thoroughly and completely in every facet of history, nature and human consciousness. God draws, entices and 'lures' the evolutionary process ever onward toward a yet unrealized goal. Such was the exciting imagery put forth in the writings of Teilhard de Chardin, and his theological vision is very much relevant today.[34] The process is dynamic and fluid, it is forever being drawn forward by the interaction of the 'divine lure' and human free will. In this vein of thought Lewis Ford characterized the biblical tradition nicely,

---

34. P. Teilhard de Chardin, *The Phenomenon of Man* (trans. B. Wall; New York: Harper & Row, 1961); *idem, The Future of Man* (trans. N. Denny; New York: Harper & Row, 1964); *idem, The Divine Milieu* (trans. B. Wall; New York: Harper & Row, 1965); *idem, Man's Place in Nature* (trans. R. Hague; New York: Harper & Row, 1966); *idem, Toward the Future* (trans. R. Hague; New York: Harcourt Brace Jovanovich, 1975).

God has no fixed, inalterable plan here, but everywhere seeks inexorably
to urge creation beyond itself. We may interpret the biblical record as God
seeking to further this aim first with all mankind, then with his chosen
people Israel, then with the faithful remnant, finally with that individual
person willing to embody in his own life the meaning, hopes, and mission
God has entrusted to Israel.[35]

V

Another biblical category which may find a richer articulation with process thought models is the notion of prophecy. At least, process theology
will provide thought-provoking new perspectives by which to view
Israel's prophetic tradition.

Critical biblical scholars and theologians no longer describe prophets
as seers or predictors of the impending events who actually gazed into
the future, as though they were diviners using a crystal ball, in order to
predict the unalterable will of God. Although that might have been the
common understanding of many people in the ancient Near East, the
classical prophetic movement had begun to depart from that mode of
perceiving reality. Prophets did not so much predict the future as they
anticipated it in the light of their relationship with Yahweh and their
understanding of the divine will for humanity. They were more like
preachers, who proclaimed what might happen to people in the light of
their present behavior. They gave a conditional warning of what might
transpire in terms of judgment for an unrepentant people who continued
to go against the will of Yahweh, or they announced forgiveness, hope
and salvation for a responsive or oppressed people. When the prophets
uttered those oracles which later became the mainstay of messianic hopes
and the frequently quoted passages of Christians who saw them fulfilled
in Jesus Christ, the prophets were not gazing into the future. They were
anticipating a future hope for people; they were projecting into the future
their own interpretation of their experience of the living God. They sensed
that the ultimate attribute of God was grace and mercy, that forgiveness
and hope would prevail over judgment, and that ultimately God would
bring a glorious future for the people of Israel. The prophets could
not see this, but they expected it, hoped for it, and gave expression to it
with powerful symbols. Later, Christians would see that Jesus somehow
fulfilled these symbols, sometimes in most ironic fashion. Basically,

35. Ford, *Lure*, p. 76.

prophecy is not prediction, but anticipation. Into this understanding of the prophetic vision, process categories may enter and give biblical theologians richer understandings by which to describe the prophetic trajectories from the oracular expression of the prophets to the final Christ event.

Process thought concurs with critical biblical scholarship that prophecy is not merely prediction, despite the appearance of announcements concerning future events. It states that when a prophet speaks, divine intent has been declared in the human process, and that divine intent will remain until it has been brought to some form of fruition or fulfillment. The metaphor of 'divine persuasion' comes to mind most directly when speaking of such prophetic proclamations or the promise-fulfillment motif in the biblical traditions. The prophetic oracle may be viewed as a form of 'divine persuasion' by which God 'lures' the believing community into the future toward the fulfillment of the anticipated vision of hope. The final fulfillment of any prophetic vision is dependent upon the continued presence of God, who first spoke to the community of faith. God cannot be separated from the word given through a prophet, 'God is absorbed into the very life of the prophet'.[36] God will be seen by the later community of faith as having worked through the words of the prophets and the course of history to bring about the fulfillment of those promised words once given in vague and veiled fashion. There is a dynamic process which involves the divine and the human dimensions in interaction from the first ancient articulation of a prophetic anticipation to its final fulfillment, or faith-envisioned fulfillment.[37] For Christians the ultimate trajectory is the sum total of all those hopes, expectations and anticipations which are dynamically and sometimes ironically drawn together in the Christ event.

Process thought allows the prophetic tradition to be viewed in three-dimensional fashion. Biblical scholars tend to view the trajectories of promise and fulfillment from the viewpoint of the prophet in his or her ancient socio-historical context. But process thought added to critical knowledge makes theologians step back and view the prophetic trajectories from a fuller theological perspective. The trajectory from prophetic expectation to Jesus Christ for Christians may be seen as an organic continuum, and the focus is upon the 'lure of God', the 'divine persuasion', which continually works through the human condition to draw the

36. Fretheim, *Suffering*, p. 153.
37. Ford, *Lure*, p. 24.

prophetic anticipation to final fulfillment.

Biblical scholars will be quick to point out that prophetic oracles recorded in the Hebrew Bible did not always come to the originally expected fulfillment. Oracles given conditionally did not necessarily come to fulfillment, especially if they were judgment oracles and God was merciful so as to relent from the threatened punishment. In some instances the oracles uttered simply did not come true, as when Ezekiel foretold that Nebuchadnezzar would take the city of Tyre (Ezek. 26.7-14). Since God was free to change the divine intent in response to human behavior, an absolute prediction of the future could not be made at any time. All prophetic oracles which spoke of the future had to be theoretically subject to change or cancellation by God, if the appropriate response were forthcoming from people. Finally, one might suggest that the fulfillment of so many prophetic expectations by the Christ event includes many ironic fulfillments, which originally referred to something else when first spoken by the prophets, but came to be connected with the experiences of Jesus by the early Christian community in symbolic fashion. In particular, all the images which spoke of a great Jewish kingdom or empire came to be equated with a 'kingdom not of this world', and the new Jerusalem came to refer to Christian believers and not the actual restored and glorified city.

The concept of oracles which remain unfulfilled or become fulfilled only in a symbolic or ironic sense might appear to challenge process paradigms at first, but process thinkers have suggested categories for further consideration. An oracle given in the process of human development at a particular moment may be seen as contingent divine interaction with that moment which has meaning for that culture in a particular time and place, regardless of its ultimate fulfillment. For example, a judgment oracle which brings about repentence, such as Jonah's harsh message in Nineveh (Jon. 3.4), need not be fulfilled to achieve its real purpose. Rather, its true intent is not to be fulfilled, but to bring about the avoidance of the dire predictions by human repentance. The oracle has a purpose beyond its literal prediction of the future. This fits rather well with the process understanding of divine interaction with the human historical continuum which feels no obligation to maintain the concept of divine omnipotence. Biblical theologians wh owork with classical theology and the notion of divine omnipotence must feel a twinge of pain when dealing with unfulfilled oracles revealed by an all-knowing deity. Process theology can accept the unfulfilled oracle as contingent and part of the greater process of God's interaction with the world much more effectively than traditional systematic theologies. Process thought sees each oracle as an expression of the divine intent or a 'divine lure' and 'enticement' for a particular moment in the human historical process.

> Perhaps we should evaluate the truth or falsity of prophecy in terms of whether it correctly reflects God's intentions in that particular situation, not how it was in fact carried out.[38]

In the discussion of prophecy, process thought may be truly helpful in the theological task. Since the prophetic dimension is such an important part of the greater Hebrew Bible, this is not an inconsequential contribution to the overall biblical theological task.

VI

Another category of thought worthy of our consideration in the context of process thought is the notion of creation. Traditional models of classical theology generally tend to view creation in the model of creation out of nothing (*creatio ex nihilo*). However, biblical scholars are quick to point out that this thrust does not capture the dynamic spirit of the biblical text. Not only does the biblical text stress the notion of the continuing creative actions of God, which traditional theologies have encapsulated very nicely under the category of 'divine preservation', but the Bible also speaks of creation by combat and the divine suppression of chaotic forces, which more or less embarrasses traditional theological systems.

Here, process thought again may offer significant contributions. For in process thought creation is defined in dynamic and evolutionary terms. The created word is not a static entity, creation is not a singular act, but creation is a throbbing and unfinished process which is pulled forward by divine interaction with the world. Creation 'is not simply the recombination of the old, but depends upon novel structuring possibilities hitherto unrealized in the temporal world'.[39] 'Both God and the creation are involved in every ongoing creative act.'[40] The biblical tradition portrays the universe not as eternal and self-perpetuating, but as contingent upon the creative and active power of God.[41]

---

38. Ford, *Suffering*, p. 133
39. Ford, *Suffering*, p. 21.
40. Fretheim, *Suffering*, p. 74.
41. B. Anderson, 'Introduction: Mythopoeic and Theological Dimensions of Biblical Creation Faith', *Creation in the Old Testament* (ed. *idem*), p. 15.

The biblical text in subtle fashion implies that humanity helps co-create the world with God. The man and the woman are to rule creation in Genesis 1, and the man helps to name the animals in Genesis 2. The image of God and humanity together creating and sustaining world order accords well with the process image of divine interaction with humanity in the temporal process.[42]

Jon Levenson and Ronald Simkins offer an exposition of the biblical concept of creation which captures the dynamic of the biblical tradition extremely well. God did not create things out of nothing in order to bring about a nicely ordered but static universe; in the Bible God established order over the forces of chaos and evil. Further, this order must be maintained by divine action, a continuing struggle; and God's promise to keep cosmic order is foundational to the covenant relationship.[43] Levenson observes,

> The concern of the creation theology is not *creatio ex nihilo*, but the establishment of a benevolent and life sustaining order, founded upon the demonstrated authority of the God who is triumphant over all rivals... YHWH's mastery is often fragile, in continual need of reactivation and reassertion, and at times, as in the laments, painfully distant from ordinary experience, a memory and a hope rather than a current reality.[44]

Levenson's emphasis upon the importance of conflict imagery and the control of chaos in the biblical traditions can be shared by process thought. Whereas classical theology might blanch at the notion of God involved in conflict, process theism sees it as another way of describing God's involvement in the developmental process of this world. This becomes the corollary to a sacred history process model. Just as God may be said to be self-involved in the history of the world, dynamically moving people into the future, so also the biblical concept of creation sees God self-involved in the natural order, struggling to keep the forces of chaos from destroying the chosen people and the created world order. Again, process models permit the nuances of biblical language, in this

---

42. G. Yee, 'The Theology of Creation in Proverbs 8:22-31', *Creation in the Biblical Traditions* (eds. R. Clifford and J. Collins; CBQMS, 24; Washington: Catholic Biblical Association, 1992), pp. 85-96. Cf. also M. Kolarik, 'Creation and Salvation in the Book of Wisdom', *Creation in the Biblical Traditions* (eds. Clifford and Collins), p. 107.

43. Levenson, *Creation*, pp. 3-50; Simkins, *Creator*, pp. 107-17.

44. Levenson, *Creation*, p. 47.

case, the image of conflict in the natural order, to emerge in a modern theological expression.

With all these themes, divine persuasion, prophecy and creation, the language of process thought is able to bring together the distant language of the biblical age and a modern philosophical system. But the last image, that of the biblical portrayal of creation, may profit most from process models, for biblical notions of conflict between God and the created order were lost completely by classical theism, swallowed up by the perception of *creatio ex nihilo*. Process thought can preserve the imagery and the language of the biblical text and render it in intellectually acceptable form for modern theologians.

VII

A final image or metaphor virtually left untouched by classical theism is the notion of the suffering of God. The biblical tradition portrays God as personally and emotionally involved in the human dimension more clearly than systematic theology is capable of doing. The ultimate symbol is the death of Jesus, whom Christians confess as God. Instead of speaking of the suffering of God in the death of Jesus, traditional theology has chosen instead to dwell upon this action as the point at which human sin is forgiven by the ultimate sacrifice of a perfect victim. The classical expressions were articulated best by Anselm of Canterbury and Martin Luther. Any attempt to speak of God suffering in the person of Jesus was dismissed as an idea bordering on the heresy of 'Patripassionism', the heresy which harms the doctrine of the Trinity by attributing the sufferings of the second person of the Trinity to the first person of the Trinity. In the greater history of the Church theological concerns with Trinitarian formulation prevented theologians from formulating a powerful symbol of God's self-identification with the human condition. Such is the price that traditional, systematic theology sometimes forces its adherents to pay. An image of divine self-identification with human suffering could have spoken more meaningfully to countless Christians in the past two thousand years whose lives contained so much suffering, especially those mediaeval Christians haunted by the spectre of the Black Death. Instead, too many Christians have wrestled with the notion of God as the final judge or ultimate ordainer of such things as the Black Death and other afflictions of the human condition.

However, biblical theologians of late have begun to address seriously the question of divine identification with human experience in these categories. Such authors seek to redress the imbalance of theological discourse which stresses the absolute aspects of the divine nature. Christians, for example, are willing to attribute suffering to Jesus, whom they confess as God, but historically Christians would not say that Jesus suffered according to his divine nature, and they have rejected quite readily the notion that God the Father suffered, calling it the heresy of 'Patripassionism'. But now theologians are willing to speak in those categories of divine suffering and the divine identification with the human condition.[45] Imagery taken from the Hebrew Bible can help in developing such concepts in both Jewish and Christian theology.

Terence Fretheim addresses the issue most effectively in his work on divine suffering. Like process theologians, Fretheim observes that in the biblical worldview God has chosen to become involved in the world, and this implies divine self-limitation. The Bible offers metaphors concerning God's acceptance of pain, but they have been ignored, and now a 'metaphor shift seems in order', as theologians need to cultivate the 'recognition of those metaphors which have been neglected'.[46] In the Hebrew Bible God accepts the finitude of being involved in a temporal process of a particular people and the self-manifestation in their worship life.

Fretheim describes five modes of discourse in the Hebrew Bible to describe divine suffering: 1) God experiences pain when the chosen people sin and rebel against God; 2) God identifies with those who suffer and mourn; 3) God bears patiently the slow moral response of people; 4) God may suffer vicariously for people; 5) God suffers symbolically in the metaphors spoken by the prophets and in their rejection by the people.[47] God is revealed as 'one who is deeply wounded by the broken

---

45. J. Moltmann, *The Crucified God* (New York: Harper & Row, 1968), pp. 200-90, who observes that we ought to attribute divine suffering to the Triune God and not just to Jesus, as the second person in the Trinity; C. Westermann, 'The Role of the Lament in the Theology of the Old Testament' (trans. R. Soulen), *Int* 28 (1974), pp. 37-38; *idem, Elements of Old Testament Theology* (trans. D. Stott; Atlanta: John Knox, 1982), p. 174; S. Towner, *How God Deals With Evil* (Biblical Perspectives on Current Issues; Philadelphia: Westminster Press, 1976); Fretheim, *Suffering*; D. Bloesch, 'Process Theology and Reformed Theology', *Process Theology* (ed. Nash), pp. 51-53, an evangelical theologian, readily admits how traditional theology has failed to speak of God's identification with human suffering, and how process theology does come closer to the biblical text in this portrayal.

46. Fretheim, *Suffering*, p. 13.

47. Fretheim, *Suffering*, pp. 107-66.

relationship' with humanity. By these experiences of pain God has become vulnerable to humanity and has entered most fully into the process of time and the world. Ultimately, Christians see this divine pathos and vulnerability most evident in the death of Jesus in the New Testament.[48]

Fretheim's categories also resonate with Abraham Heschel's work on the prophets. Heschel, a Jewish theologian, sought to organize his discussion of the prophets around the theme of divine pathos, and he succeeded quite well.[49] His thought inspired a number of authors, including Fretheim. Heschel believed that the heart of prophetic consciousness was the awareness of God's pathos.[50]

> God does not stand outside the range of human suffering and sorrow. He is personally involved in, even stirred by, the conduct and fate of man... Whatever man does affects not only his own life, but also the life of God insofar as it is directed to man... He [man] is a consort, a partner, a factor in the life of God.[51]

Heschel reacted against theology which spoke of God as absolute and 'wholly other' and he maintained that both Jewish and Christian belief systems were influenced unfortunately by too much Greek philosophy with its antipathy to emotion.[52] For him the biblical text spoke of a deity with passion and pathos, that is, the ability to suffer with creation, and such was the result of God's covenanted relationship with Israel. 'To the biblical mind the conception of God as detached and unemotional is totally alien...God looks at the world and is affected by what happens in it; man is the object of His care and judgment.'[53] Heschel's ideas resonate excellently with process modes of discourse.

In process theology God is seen as being involved in the world and its development. This self-involvement includes the acceptance of finitude and pain by the divine. God must suffer, if the divine involvement with the world is total.[54] Classical theology has no way to speak of God's suffering, whereas the notion would be implicit in a process theological

---

48. Fretheim, *Suffering*, pp. 106, 123, 165.

49. A. Heschel, *The Prophets* (2 vols.; New York: Harper & Row, 1962), II, pp. 1-268. Cf. Moltmann, *God*, pp. 270-78, who integrates Heschel's discussion of the pathos of God into his theology of a suffering God.

50. Heschel, *Prophets*, II, pp. 2-103.

51. Heschel, *Prophets*, II, pp. 4, 6.

52. Heschel, *Prophets*, II, pp. 27-47.

53. Heschel, *Prophets*, II, pp. 37, 263.

54. Ford, *Lure*, p. 92.

system. Biblical theology and process thought thus express more adequately a portrayal of the divine nature, especially in regard to the question of suffering and theodicy, than former theological models in the classical tradition. In this regard, an alliance of biblical and process thought may produce a more meaningful form of theological discourse to undergird practical theology, especially for the pastoral dimension.

VIII

Process modes of thought lead us to view reality in a more unified or wholistic manner. As the aforegoing discussion implies, Jews and Christians may be led to see God as more totally involved in the created order. Jews and Christians may look anew at texts in the Hebrew Bible and acknowledge that God is revealed not only in sacred history, but also in the natural order (Psalms) and in the human mind (Wisdom Literature). God not only directs the human sphere of existence, God also experiences the totality of human existence.

Further insights flow from these perceptions. If God is present in the gradual flow of religious change or evolution testified to in the biblical traditions, does not comparable evolutionary advance still continue today? If we view ourselves as part of that on-going, organic continuum of change in which God is so intimately involved, we are forced to understand the dynamics of religious traditions anew. We are led to perceive that tradition is a process, not a received set of beliefs which must be faithfully and dogmatically defended. We must take our place on the continuum of religious change. Our duty is to contribute to this creative advance, not to venerate our received ideational values as icons. This reinforces the observations made earlier in this volume. Jews and Christians are part of the dynamic advance; we are the agents for unveiling the continuing implications of the millennia-long revolution of monotheism with all its attendant social implications. The monotheistic revolution continues, it is the divinely led process. Process thought will encourage us to think and speak in these categories.

There may be implications for our dialogue with the religions of the world, and the cultures in which they are found. Christians may be led to a greater openness and dialogue with our larger world neighborhood. Christians must sense that the divine is involved with this world in more ways than they had recognized previously, and that these divine manifestations may be found outside the Judaeo-Christian tradition. God may 'lure' others into a future with a deeper relationship to the divine.

If religious values are seen to emerge in a gradual process, and we no longer speak in terms of contrast and dialectical opposition, we may be more inclined to see our own culture and worldview less in opposition to other world cultures (as once we viewed Israelite values in opposition to ancient Near Eastern thought). Our feeling for the world ecumene may be enhanced, and this will deepen our sense of Christian mission to the world. We will be inspired not so much to convert others, as to share our beliefs, and we may find our mission more effective. We may develop a 'renewed appreciation for our seamless world with its diversity of cultures and cultural embodiments'.[55] A good example of this comes from a private conversation I had with the principal of a Christian dayschool in India, affiliated with a conservative Protestant American denomination. In his philosophy of Christian mission and education he believed his calling was not to convert students to Christianity, for that would isolate them from their family and society at large, thus rendering them ineffective as instruments of change in their culture. Rather, he sought to graft Christian ideals upon Hindu values so as to produce students who might influence the religious and social values of their land positively. His views reflect the role of Christian interaction in our 'seamless world culture' better than the old model of conversion. Process theology may lead Christians to a more open approach in their dealings with world cultures and other religions, especially when process thought is combined with biblical theology. We may learn to appreciate more our role in a greater religious advance for the human race which is led by the power of the divine.

IX

The critical scholarship with its new understandings concerning the Israelite conquest and the rise of monotheism dovetails nicely with the perceptions of process theology. The conquest of the land of Palestine is seen now as a gradual process, which was both peaceful and internal. The emphasis in scholarly circles is upon the continuity that the newly emerging highland Israelite villages had with predecessor Canaanite culture. Likewise, the study of emergent monotheism leads scholars to see Yahwistic monotheism developing out of the old Canaanite religion, evolving for six hundred years until the radical reconfiguration of belief

55. Hopkins, private written correspondence to author.

came to fruition in the Babylonian exile. Overall, the religion and culture of the Israelites and Jews is seen now as an evolutionary outgrowth of the previous Canaanite culture. Even though the movement is revolutionary at a certain point, one can sense that biblical scholars are describing the development as an evolutionary process. As biological models have given us leave to realize, an evolutionary model does include a moment of revolutionary breakthrough. Biblical scholars and theologians now increasingly view Israelite culture and religion in terms of a development process rather than as a contradiction to what went before. This should lead to more openness to articulating the core concepts of biblical theology in process thought categories. Hopefully, theologians might sense that these process categories ironically do justice to capturing the spirit of the thought of the ancient biblical writers of the first millennium BCE, more so than the systematizing thought of the Greek philosophers under whose mesmerizing spell people have theologized for two thousand years.

Contemporary critical thought may impress upon us the gradual nature of social and religious evolution throughout the biblical and later Judaeo-Christian tradition. If so, we will appreciate that we are part of a grand, unfolding intellectual trajectory of the human experience, and that this trajectory is still moving forward in our hands. We are the agents of continuing change. Perhaps, we may perceive the grandeur of this unfolding human condition which is led by the power of the divine. If we see ourselves as part of the 'flow of human existence', this will shape our attitudes about the Christian tradition in a new and richer fashion. I firmly believe that process thought will assist in the future direction of theologizing, and particularly in biblical theology. Hopefully, some of the paradigms and language suggested by this volume may inspire the writing of future creative theologies for consumption by theologians in the Church.

Chapter 8

PUNCTUATED EQUILIBRIA AS AN EVOLUTIONARY MODEL
FOR THE SOCIAL SCIENCES AND BIBLICAL STUDIES

Throughout this volume I have theorized an understanding of the
development of monotheism predicated upon contemporary biological
evolutionary theories which speak of rapid periods of quick evolutionary
development that punctuate periods of relative stasis. There are a number
of significant aspects to these new biological paradigms which may
provide heuristic models for studies in human cultural history. I believe
that the new language generated by these biological paradigms may be
especially helpful in future discussions concerning biblical religion. To
that end this chapter has been included in order to provide a fuller discussion of those biological models and their implications. It will provide a
more detailed clarification of many of the concepts alluded to throughout the other sections of this volume. Not all readers will find this presentation convincing, but at least most will discover something of interest
within it. This chapter is a revised and shortened version of an article
which first appeared in the journal *Zygon* several years ago.[1]

Within recent years intellectuals in diverse areas of study and research
have sought to articulate the underlying principles of reality and the
processes which circumscribe the known phenomena in our universe.
Once formulated, these heuristic paradigms could become the common
denominators for discourse in the hard sciences, social sciences and
the humanities. Authors who encourage the quest for such insights
include Ilya Prigogine, Erich Jantsch and Ervin Laszlo.[2] Some authors in
particular have encouraged the use of biological models for the study of

1. Gnuse, 'Evolutionary Theory', pp. 405-431.
2. E. Jantsch, *The Self-Organizing Universe* (New York: Pergamon Press,
1980); A. Fabel, 'The Dynamics of the Self-Organizing Universe', *Cross Currents*
37 (1987), pp. 168-77; E. Laszlo, *Evolution: The Grand Synthesis* (Boston: New
Science Library, 1987).

religion.[3] To be sure, not all thinkers concur with these assumptions. Many would challenge the attempt to articulate interdisciplinary para- digms to be used across the academic spectrum. They maintain that such over-arching metaprinciples only force the humanities into reductionistic categories, because they come from the hard sciences and are both deterministic and mechanistic. Doubtless there is truth in this accusation, especially since intellectuals have done this in the past. However, too many intellectuals are willing to permit their specific fields of research and teaching become totally isolated from other broader fields of learning and very compartmentalized specializations.

Regardless of this debate and its ultimate resolution, everyone in the discussion would admit that the biological and geological theories of evolution have exerted a far ranging influence upon thought in all the academic disciplines for more than a century. Our modern concept of progress results in part from these contributions of the hard sciences, especially the biological research and theorizing of Charles Darwin. This has been most certainly the case for the fields of history, anthropology, sociology and comparative religious study. Students of religion, espe- cially in the areas of world religions and biblical studies, have used aspects of the evolutionary paradigm to explain the history or development of human religious insight.

In biblical studies the notion of evolution has been used to describe the development of Israel's religious beliefs, social structures and socio- political values. Early nineteenth-century scholars, including Julius Wellhausen and William Robertson Smith, described Israel's faith as an evolutionary advance through various stages toward increased sophisti- cation.[4] Early twentieth-century scholars challenged the use of gradual evolutionary models to describe Israel's faith, and prefered to speak of the Mosaic revolution as bringing advanced beliefs to Israelites early in their historical experience.[5] More recently, as noted, biblical scholars occupy a moderate position which affirms both evolution and revolution, and they suggest that Israel's religious development came in several stages or 'leaps', the most significant being the exilic theological contributions.[6]

---

3.   Theissen, *Biblical Faith*, pp. 1-174; A. Clifford, 'Postmodern Scientific Cosmology and the Christian God of Creation', *Horizons* 21 (1994), pp. 62-84.

4.   Wellhausen, *Prolegomena*; and Robertson Smith, *Religion*.

5.   Albright, *Stone Age*; Kaufman, *Religion*; Wright, *Environment*.

6.   Smith, 'Religious Parties', pp. 15-56; essays in Keel (ed.), *Monotheismus*; essays in Lang (ed.), *Der einzige Gott*; *idem*, 'Yahweh-Alone', pp. 13-59.

These contemporary scholars, with the exception of Gerd Theissen, do not attend to a discussion of the role of evolutionary paradigms in the discussion, either to use or criticize them as did their predecessors. Rather, they assume that biological insights are irrelevant to their fields of study.

The experience of biblical scholars parallels that of other authors in the social sciences and the humanities. In various fields the observed phenomena attest to change which occurs in revolutionary breakthroughs rather than simple, gradual evolution. Since scholars' perception of biological evolutionary theories is one of simplistic gradualism, they politely avoid any discussion of scientific evolution in their discussion, lest it straightjacket their observations with a dogmatic theory of mere gradual change. No one seeks an overarching metaprinciple in the various disciplines.

However, within the last generation the model of evolution in biology appears to be changing, and the new model may have renewed significance for the other academic fields of learning. We may be on the verge of a major 'paradigm shift' of ideational modes of perception, which would correspond to how Thomas Kuhn describes the nature of intellectual development, especially in the sciences.[7]

Slow and gradual evolutionary theories have been replaced in some biological and palaeontological circles with the notion of quick evolutionary change in short periods of time. As this model gains acceptance in the hard sciences, it may provoke a corresponding response among thinkers in other fields.[8] Gerd Theissen calls for the renewed use of evolutionary paradigms in the field of religious studies, for they give us an 'impressive picture of the unity of all reality', for 'behind all the phenomena we have intimations of a central reality which determines and conditions everything'.[9]

I

Charles Darwin's model of evolution assumed the slow development of variegated life forms over countless aeons as the forces of natural selection

7. Kuhn, *Revolutions*. Kuhn's observations have received criticism from critical essays in G. Gutting (ed.), *Paradigms and Revolutions: Appraisals and Applications of Thomas Kuhn's Philosophy of Science* (Notre Dame: University of Notre Dame Press, 1980); and B. Barnes, *T.S. Kuhn and Social Science* (New York: Columbia University Press, 1982), but the cogency of many of his views has been acknowledged even by critics.

8. Laszlo, *Evolution*, pp. 83-109, 113-14.

9. Laslo, *Evolution*, pp. 19 *et passim*.

constantly weeded out certain individuals. Favored survivors passed on their genetic predispositions and slowly the genetic pool of a species changed and evolution occurred. Species were all part of a spectrum of life, each species evolving into the next species, proliferating into new variations. Eventually the need to adapt to various environments caused the wide range of phyla exhibited today. This theory has been called 'phyletic gradualism', the gradual evolution of all life's representatives. The model incorporated evidence from taxonomy, genetics, geology and palaeontology. The theory was stated in its most developed form by evolutionists of the previous generation: Theodosius Dobzhansky, Julian Huxley, Ernst Mayr and George Gaylord Simpson.[10] In retrospect their grand theory has been called the 'modern synthesis'. Critical reflection upon the rise of this 'synthesis' between 1936 and 1947 has been undertaken by contemporary scientists, including some of the individuals involved in its original articulation.[11]

In the past generation their model of gradual evolution has been challenged. Palaeontologists point out that the fossil record does not evince a testimony of gradual evolution, but rather periods of stasis interrupted by quick evolutionary developments.[12] Likewise, biologists are less inclined to view species as blurring into each other, rather species

10. T. Dobzhanksy, *Genetics and the Origin of the Species* (Columbia Biological Series, 11; New York: Columbia University Press, 1937); J. Huxley, *Evolution: The Modern Synthesis* (London: George Allen & Unwin, 1942); E. Mayr, *Systematics and the Origin of the Species* (Columbia Biological Series, 12; New York: Columbia University Press, 1942); G.G. Simpson, *Tempo and Mode in Evolution* (New York: Columbia University Press, 1944).

11. E. Mayr and W. Provine, *The Evolutionary Synthesis: Perspectives in the Unification of Biology* (Cambridge, MA: Harvard University Press, 1980); N. Eldredge, *Unfinished Synthesis: Biological Hierarchies and Modern Evolutionary Thought* (New York: Oxford University Press, 1985), pp. 6-83.

12. S.J. Gould, *Ever Since Darwin: Reflections in Natural History* (New York: Norton, 1977), p. 62; *idem, The Panda's Thumb: More Reflections in Natural History* (New York: Norton, 1980), pp. 182, 188; *idem, Hen's Teeth and Horse's Toes: Further Reflections in Natural History* (New York: Norton, 1983), pp. 180-81, 259; *idem, The Flamingo's Smile: Reflections in Natural History* (New York: Norton, 1985), pp. 241-42; S. Stanley, *The New Evolutionary Timetable: Fossils, Genes, and the Origin of the Species* (New York: Basic Books, 1981), pp. xv, 3, *et passim*; N. Eldredge, *Life Pulse: Episodes from the Story of the Fossil Record* (New York: Facts on File, 1987), pp. 7-11, 31; *idem, Reinventing Darwin: The Great Debate at the High Table of Evolutionary Theory* (New York: John Wiley & Sons, 1995), pp. 33-124.

are distinct entities with a life history. Evolutionary selection occurs at a species level, not at an individual plant or animal level. A species appears dramatically and disappears completely.[13]

To explain these phenomena a new theory, called 'Punctuated Equilibria' or 'Punctuated Equilibrium', has been proposed by a number of scientists, including Niles Eldredge, Stephen Jay Gould, Steven Stanley, Elisabeth Vrba and others.[14] They propose that evolution does not result from the build-up of small genetic changes gradually over long periods of time. Rather, there are long periods of stasis in the life of a species, within which there may be some genetic drift, but essentially no change of significant magnitude to create the existence of a new species.

13. Gould, *Panda's Thumb*, pp. 15, 204-13; S. Stanley, *Macroevolution: Pattern and Process* (San Francisco: Freeman, 1979), pp. 181-212; *idem, Timetable*, p. 15; N. Eldredge, *Time Frames: The Rethinking of Darwinian Evolution and the Theory of Punctuated Equilibria* (New York: Simon & Schuster, 1985), pp. 34, 150.

14. The most significant works appear to be: N. Eldredge, 'The Allopatric Model and Phylogeny in Paleozoic Invertebrates', *Evolution* 25 (1971), pp. 156-67; N. Eldredge and S.J. Gould, 'Punctuated Equilibria: An Alternative to Phyletic Gradualism', *Models in Paleobiology* (ed. T.J.M. Schopf; San Francisco: Freeman, Cooper & Co., 1972), pp. 82-115; *idem*, 'Punctuated Equilibria: The Tempo and Mode of Evolution Reconsidered', *Paleobiology* 3 (1977), pp. 115-51; Stanley, *Macroevolution*; N. Eldredge and J. Cracraft, *Phylogenetic Patterns and the Evolutionary Process: Method and Theory in Comparative Biology* (New York: Columbia University Press, 1980); S.J. Gould, 'Is a New and General Theory of Evolution Emerging?', *Paleobiology* 6 (1980), pp. 119-30; *idem*, 'The Meaning of Punctuated Equilibria and its Role in Validating a Hierarchical Approach to Evolution', *Perspectives on Evolution* (ed. R. Milkman; Sunderland: Sinauer, 1982), pp. 82-104; E. Vrba and N. Eldredge, 'Individuals, Hierarchies and Processes: Towards a More Complete Evolutionary Theory', *Paleobiology* 10 (1984), pp. 146-71; Vrba and Gould, 'The Hierarchical Expansion of Sorting and Selection Cannot Be Equated', *Paleobiology* 12 (1986), pp. 217-28. The basic ideas of the theory are presented in popular fashion in S.J. Gould, *Darwin*, pp. 56-62; *idem, Panda's Thumb*, pp. 179-93, 204-13; *idem*, 'Darwinism and the Expansion of Evolutionary Theory', *Science* 216 (1982), pp. 380-87; *idem, Hen's Teeth*, pp. 253-62; *idem, Flamingo's Smile*, pp. 230-45; S.J. Gould and N. Eldredge, 'Punctuated Equilibrium Prevails', *Nature* 332 (1988), pp. 211-12; *idem*, 'Punctuated Equilibrium Comes of Age', *Nature* 366 (1993), pp. 223-27. Their ideas were foreshadowed by Mayr, *Animal Species and Evolution* (Cambridge, MA: Harvard University Press, 1963), whose advocacy of punctuational models received little attention according to Stanley, *Timetable*, pp. 49, 78-79. An excellent summary of this model and its development is provided by P. Bowler, *Evolution: The History of an Idea* (Berkeley: University of California Press, 1984), pp. 322-26.

These periods of stasis are punctuated by short periods of rapid evolutionary development in which a new species arises and displaces the ancestral species.

How does this process of quick change occur? Through 'allopatric speciation'—the isolation of a species by geographic and climatic changes with the subsequent build-up of many genetic variations in a small animal population—the development of a new species may arise in a very short period. If better adapted to the environment, the new species will spread into the original area populated by the ancestral species and displace it.[15] This new species arises when a small portion of the ancestral population finds itself isolated at the periphery of the ancestral species' range. Since large stable central populations will dilute the emergence of new and favorable genetic mutations within individuals, the mutations must emerge in the smaller populations at the periphery of the species' range in order to surface effectively. These mutations will emerge together and create 'speciation events', and thus new species arise rapidly in small, peripheral, isolated, local populations.[16]

When the peripheral isolate develops into a new species, isolating mechanisms in the genetic structures prevent the re-initiation of genetic material into the genetic pool of the ancestral species or the new species. New forms can be fixed genetically, since offspring in small population groups tend to interbreed, thus causing genetic stabilization. In addition, animals engage in 'assortative mating', the tendency for animals to breed with those who resemble them. Therefore, a genetic change with morphological modification will be preserved. This latter principle can enable speciation to occur even when species are sympatric with the ancestral species, that is, living in the same environmental range.[17] The genetic mutation which causes significant transformation may result from chromosomal rearrangement. This rearrangement may place a 'regulatory gene' in a new position, thus creating a domino effect over many other

15. Eldredge and Gould, 'Phyletic Gradualism', pp. 82-115; Stanley, *Macroevolution*, pp. 40-74, 118-42, 272-301; *idem*, *Timetable*, pp. 5, 50, 70, 78; P.G. Williamson, 'Paleontological Documentation of Speciation in Cenozoic Mollusks from Turkana Basin', *Nature* 293 (1981), pp. 437-43; Vrba, 'What is Species Selection?', *Systematic Zoology* 33 (1984), pp. 318-28; Gould, *Flamingo's Smile*, p. 444; Eldredge, *Time Frames*, pp. 164, 183-89.

16. Gould, *Panda's Thumb*, p. 183; Eldredge, *Time Frames*, pp. 189-90, 193; *idem*, *Reinventing Darwin*, pp. 93-123.

17. Stanley, *Timetable*, pp. 121-22, 131, 136; Vrba and Gould, 'Hierarchical Expansion', pp. 217-28; Eldredge, *Reinventing Darwin*, pp. 125-66.

genes. A 'regulatory gene' in a new position activates or de-activates the performance of many other genes. The majority of genes in a life form (80%) do not function, they are 'switched-off' by a regulatory gene. A small mutation on a regulatory gene can produce a great amount of change in the species; rapid morphological change over several generations may be based upon very little genetic alteration.[18]

Morphological change continues to occur quickly as the new species adapts to its ecological niche. Sub-populations likewise may develop as the new species proliferates to fill up the environment. The species may invade new ecological territories in a non-directional or in a 'stochastic' fashion, which means multiple random explorations. If the ancestral species is encountered and the two species become territorially sympatric, then more quick morphological change may occur in the new species. Speciation requires genetic isolation until the speciation process is complete. Species appear to obtain homeostatic genetic stability in the face of disturbing influences, which is created by geographic isolation on the periphery of a territorial range and the genetic and morphological maintenance of that separate identity. Once established, change is minimal; long periods of morphological stability follow.[19]

Speciation may occur in a significant fashion after an extinction which creates a 'vacant ecological niche'. Evolution occurs rapidly as a wide variety of new species proliferate to repopulate the ecological niche.[20] Such additional speciation is called 'population flush', especially when referring to new species invading a different territory. Those species left in their original ecospace after a catastrophe will repopulate also; but they will represent a disproportionate ratio of the ancestral species' genetic pool, thus initiating further macro-evolutionary change called 'catastrophe selection'.[21] Extinctions can be local or they can be world-

---

18. Stanley, *Macroevolution*, pp. 148-64; *idem, Timetable*, pp. 127-31; Gould, *Hen's Teeth*, pp. 177-86. Cf. M. Ptashine, 'How Gene Activators Work', *Scientific American* 260.1 (1989), pp. 40-47.

19. Eldredge, 'Allopatric Model', pp. 156-67; *idem, Time Frames*, pp. 193-223; Eldredge and Gould, 'Phyletic Gradualism', pp. 82-115; Gould, *Darwin*, pp. 61, 118; *idem, Panda's Thumb*, pp. 183-213; Stanley, *Macroevolution*, pp. 65-76, 102-108, 272, 301.

20. Stanley, *Macroevolution*, pp. 65-74, 102-108; Gould, *Darwin*, p. 62; *idem, Hen's Teeth*, pp. 320-31; *idem, Flamingo's Smile*, pp. 241-42, 438-50; Vrba, 'Species Selection', pp. 318-28; Eldredge, *Reinventing Darwin*, pp. 167-97.

21. Stanley, *Macroevolution*, p. 168.

wide, as were the great extinctions in the pre-Cambrian, late Cambrian, late Ordovician, late Devonian, late Permian and late Triassic ages, which enabled a wide range of new life forms to repopulate the earth.[22] For without these extinctions to eliminate life forms and free up the ecological niches, new forms and significant change would have been impossible, and 'life would still be confined to a primitive state somewhere on the sea bottom'.[23]

What do palaeontologists mean by a short period of time? The development of a new species may take ten to fifty thousand years. Once the species has attained a new form, it will remain stable with only slight genetic variations for five to ten million years. The process of speciation is frequent, for somewhere throughout the world there always are species undergoing speciation in a changed ecological environment, although the overall global picture between worldwide catastrophes is evolutionary stability.[24]

Evolutionary change is the function of speciation rather than the old Darwinian model which saw speciation as a function of adaptive change. Evolution occurs by significant leaps at the species level.[25] Darwinian advocates of the 'modern synthesis' promulgated notions of inevitable phyletic gradualism premised upon natural selection. The corollaries of this assumption were that: 1) species arose by transformation of an ancestral species population; 2) the process was slow and regular; 3) the entire population of a species was involved in the transformation; 4) a wide geographic range was included in the transformation; and 5) breaks in the fossil record merely indicated the imperfections of that record. The mechanism of change was 6) genetic drift resulting from 7) natural selection exerted upon mutations. However, advocates of Punctuated Equilibria maintain that: 1) species arose by splitting lineages; 2) species developed quickly; 3) sub-populations also gave rise to new forms; 4) only a small part of a species' geographic range was involved; and 5) breaks in the fossil record reflect quick morphological change in limited and isolated geographic regions, since only a small animal or plant population

22. Gould, *Darwin*, pp. 62, 119-38; *idem*, *Hen's Teeth*, pp. 320-31, 346; *idem*, *Flamingo's Smile*, pp. 241-42, 348-50; Eldredge, *Life Pulse*, pp. 87, 202-212.

23. Eldredge, *Life Pulse*, p. 11.

24. Gould, *Hen's Teeth*, pp. 54, 259; *idem*, *Flamingo's Smile*, pp. 241-42; and Eldredge, *Unfinished Synthesis*, p. 128; *idem*, *Life Pulse*, pp. 31, 82.

25. Eldredge, *Time Frames*, p. 147; *idem*, *Reinventing Darwin*, pp. 167-97.

was involved. The mechanism of change was 6) phylogenetic drift resulting from 7) the directed speciation of a whole species' selection.[26]

Theorists speak of two levels of evolution in a 'nested hierarchy'. These two phenomenological levels are micro-evolution, or the change within a species, and macro-evolution, or the change in species composition within a larger phylum.[27] It is on the macro-evolutionary level that truly creative advance occurs. Subtle genetic changes in a species or micro-evolution may prepare the possibilities for later macro-evolution, but macro-evolution or true evolution occurs above the genetic level of species when ecological factors affect total species survival. To project micro-evolution to the level of macro-evolution contradicts the observation that species are distinct entities and the palaeontological record, which testifies to the stability of the species.[28] Eldredge notes,

> ...evolution emerges as a multi-level, or hierarchical affair. What goes on at one level may have little effect on the next higher or lower level. The comings and goings of entire species—and even larger groups—may have little to do with the normal processes of genetic change that go on from generation to generation within species.[29]

These scholars observe that their theory differs from earlier views of mega-evolution and macro-evolution proposed by Richard Goldschmidt and others. For those previous theories postulated fast genetic change within a single species to obtain quick processes of evolution, while the new theory postulates change due to species selection, an activity on a higher hierarchical level. In addition, Goldschmidt felt that only the chromosome mutation permitted change, while the new understanding of regulatory genes perceives that singular mutations upon genes produce great change. Old macro-evolutionary theories were merely micro-

26. Eldredge and Gould, 'Phyletic Gradualism', pp. 82-115; Stanley, *Macroevolution*, pp. 143-79; *idem, Timetable*, p. 72-109, includes a number of instances from the palaeontological record which imply the presence of 'rapid speciations' and 'adaptive radiation' of particular species; Gould, *Panda's Thumb*, pp. 194-203, 226; Eldredge, *Time Frames*, pp. 197-205.

27. Eldredge and Cracraft, *Phylogenetic Patterns*, pp. 247, 277; Eldredge, *Life Pulse*, p. 232; *idem, Reinventing Darwin*, pp. 167-97.

28. Gould, *Ontogeny and Phylogeny* (Cambridge: Belknap, 1977), pp. 209-409; *idem, Panda's Thumb*, pp. 15, 184; *idem, Hen's Teeth*, pp. 177-86; Eldredge and Cracraft, *Phylogenetic Patterns*, pp. 301-26; Eldredge, *Time Frames*, p. 145, and *Unfinished Synthesis*, pp. 139-215.

29. Eldredge, *Life Pulse*, p. 232.

evolution writ large, while the new theory of Punctuated Equilibria
assumes evolution on a multiple hierarchical level.[30]

II

There are significant implications this new theory may hold for the social
sciences. Instead of gradual change in evolution theorists speak of rapid
change between periods of long inactivity. Scholars in the social sciences
and the humanities a century ago accommodated their views to the
paradigm of slow, gradual evolutionary development, even though the
data did not warrant it, perhaps because they were reflecting the cultural
bias of that age. Critics occasionally pointed to evidence of apparent
radical change in human culture, which contradicted the model of gradual
evolution. The current model of biological evolution affirms that such
examples of radical revolution do not contradict evolution, they are
actually a form of true evolutionary advance. Consequently, scholars in
the social sciences who have ignored evolutionary models for the past
several generations may wish to reconsider the use of such models.

Is it now possible to use this new theory of Punctuated Equilibria
to discuss phenomena in the social sciences? I believe the theory has
heuristic value in a limited way, and to this end we might consider some
academic disciplines where the model merits attention and also where its
particular nuances have been anticipated. This new perspective is based
not upon new data as much as a new view of the palaeontological
and biological records. Likewise, in other fields of learning the new shift
of thought means considering the same information from a different
perspective. Some advocates of Punctuated Equilibria maintain that the
view of evolutionary gradualism in so many fields of learning, and
especially science, was a mental construct created by nineteenth-century
liberal notions of progress.[31] The new theory perceives data attesting to
leaps rather than gradualism. It appears to be causing a 'paradigm shift'
among biologists and palaeontologists; perhaps a similar shift will occur
in other fields. Ervin Laszlo has made just such a claim for Punctuated
Equilibria, for he believes it will be the 'grand synthesis' that will
'provide the basis for the next paradigm of contemporary science' and

30. R. Goldschmidt, *The Material Basis of Evolution* (New Haven: Yale
University Press, 1940), pp. 184-339; Eldredge and Cracraft, *Phylogenetic Patterns*,
p. 325; Stanley, *Timetable*, p. 135; Eldredge, *Unfinished Synthesis*, pp. 67-97, 140.

31. Gould, *Panda's Thumb*, pp. 194-203, 226.

have equal impact in the social sciences.[32]

Niles Eldredge and Stephen Jay Gould observe that the noted historian and philosopher of history, Frederick J. Teggart, postulated as early as 1918 that human culture and scientific achievement usually advanced in quantum leaps, not gradually. He criticized Darwinian evolution and its impact upon scholars, and his views foreshadowed the model of Punctuated Equilibria. Teggart theorized three patterns in history: 1) stability, which is dominant, 2) gradual change, which causes only a slight drift in human affairs, and 3) real change, accomplished quickly, all of which are major characteristics of Punctuated Equilibria theory.[33] Teggart authored two works, *Processes of History* (1918) and *Theory of History* (1925), in which he expounded that history was composed of 'events' or 'intrusions', which were sudden quantitative leaps in human experience. He criticized Darwin's uniformitarian gradualism for perpetuating the old eighteenth-century dichotomy between process and event. Eighteenth-century thinkers believed that change resulted from a natural process, an urge toward progress, and individual events were unimportant, merely accidental interference with the natural process of change. Teggart believed that change was not a natural process, but rather singular events were the *modus operandi* of change, and they represented some fundamental break with previous history. Instead of slow change and inevitable gradual progress Teggart envisioned the complementary ideas of fixity and advancement in human affairs, long periods of stability punctuated by quick change.[34] Much of what he said concurs with my philosophical perspective.

Teggart paralleled the insights of modern advocates of Punctuated Equilibria in another fashion. He suggested that intellectual and social progress resulted from the interaction of different peoples,

> ...human advancement is the outcome of the commingling of ideas through the contact of different groups...had there even been but one system of ideas common to all men, advancement would have been impossible, for progress in ideas springs from comparison.[35]

The idea of interplay in history is analogous to the notion of allopatric speciation and subsequent species diffusion. Cultural development in one environment proceeds differently than in another; subsequent contact may

32. Laszlo, *Evolution*, pp. 113-14.
33. Eldredge, *Time Frames*, pp. 143-45.
34. Teggart, *Theory*, pp. 148, 193, 198.
35. Teggart, *Theory*, pp. 285-86.

result in the extinction of one culture or it may produce a new synthesis, which is comparable to a proliferated set of variations in sympatric speciation.

In the general study of history the model of Punctuated Equilibria may provide a helpful heuristic model for viewing the process of human history. Teggart's concern was to find an ideational model which would bridge the gap between the sciences and the humanities. If one shares Teggart's concern and his view of the historical process, contemporary evolutionary theory has provided such a model. Current thinkers in 'systems analysis' are presently suggesting such a possibility for historical analysis with the model of Punctuated Equilibria.[36]

Anthropological studies may benefit from the application of models engendered by Punctuated Equilibria, and Steven Stanley, Niles Eldredge, Ian Tattersall and others propose a new understanding of human evolution using such contemporary evolutionary theory.[37] They note that the history of life and human evolution both display 'new breakthroughs followed by rapid development', and the greater patterns of cultural changes 'show stability interrupted by occasional, usually rather rapid, change, rather than linear, constant modification for the better'.[38] In human evolution new developments, like upright anthropoid posture, appeared early and spread rapidly among various human species. It seems that subsequent generations merely unfolded the dynamic potential of the initial breakthrough, while essentially the genetic make-up of the human species remained unchanged. The principle of geographic isolation played a role in human evolution as new anthropoid species arose on the remote edges of the ancestral range.[39] The various species (Australopithecus anamensis, Australopithecus ramidus, Australopithecus afarensis, Australopithecus africanus, Australopithecus robustus, Australopithecus bosei, Homo habilis, Homo rudolfensis, Homo erectus, Homo ergaster, Homo heidelbergensis, and Homo sapiens) were distinct species

36. Laszlo, *Evolution*, pp. 107-108.

37. Stanley, *Timetable*, pp. 138-64; N. Eldredge and I. Tattersall, *The Myths of Human Evolution* (New York: Columbia University Press, 1982); Tattersall, *The Human Odyssey: Four Million Years of Human Evolution* (New York: Prentice–Hall, 1993); Laszlo, *Evolution*, pp. 83-86.

38. Eldredge and Tattersall, *Myths*, pp. 3-4.

39. Stanley, *Timetable*, pp. 138-64; Eldredge and Tattersall, *Myths*, pp. 8, 59-61; Tattersall, *Odyssey*, pp. 65-67, 110-11, 133-37.

which arose in isolation, then displaced the previous species. Basically, there was not a simple, gradual, linear, evolutionary advance. Various hominid species could have overlapped each other, particularly Australopithecus africanus, Homo habilis and Homo erectus.[40]

The same pattern may be used to describe human cultural evolution, particularly in regard to tool-making capacities. A breakthrough in the archaeological record will appear and indicate that anthropoids explored all the possible uses of a tool very rapidly. Then the record will indicate a long fallow period with little change until the next critical breakthrough. The Old Stone Age and New Stone Age were cultural leaps followed by periods of stability. Each hominid species had a characteristic culture associated with it: the Acheulian culture is attributed to Homo erectus and Mousterian is connected with the Neanderthals, early Homo sapiens. In turn, Neanderthals were replaced suddenly by a new species of Homo sapiens from the periphery, perhaps Africa, who spead throughout the former Neanderthal range.[41]

Anthropologists who made these observations also extrapolated to discuss human history in general. Ancient Egypt was perceived as the best example of a society in stasis with some cultural 'drift', which remained rather unchanged until the Christian era. Greece peaked early in the first millennium BCE, but it did not continue to evolve in the later Hellenistic period, and Rome replaced Greece, but no real advance occurred. Even European history may be seen to be marked by general stasis, punctuated only by advances during the Renaissance and the industrial revolution. Similarly Punctuated Equilibria models are used to describe phenomena in history such as the rise of agriculture, the invention of writing, and the invention of steam-driven machinery.[42] Ervin Laszlo concludes,

> History's arrow of time does not fly smoothly...societies, the same as biological species, do not change at all times and in small increments. Rather, the mode of change appears saltatory and intermittent, triggered

40. Stanley, *Timetable*, p. 149; Eldredge and Tattersall, *Myths*, pp. 119-59; Tattersall, *Odyssey*, pp. 63-171; Laszlo, *Evolution*, pp. 83-86.

41. Stanley, *Timetable*, pp. 159-64; Eldredge and Tattersall, *Myths*, pp. 9-11; Laszlo, *Evolution*, p. 85.

42. E. Rivkin, *A Hidden Revolution: The Pharisees' Search for the Kingdom within* (Nashville: Abingdon Press, 1978), pp. 211-12; Braudel, *Civilization and Capitalism*, I, p. 430; Eldredge and Tattersall, *Myths*, pp. 16-17; Laszlo, *Evolution*, pp. 94-101.

by external conquests and internal discontent and by technological revolutions that change the pattern of relations between man and man and between
man and nature.[43]

Biological and social spheres seem similar—adaptation leads to stability
and non-change, so that gradual evolution does not occur. New ideas and
cultures arise in geographic isolation and then radiate into new environments. In biology isolation causes speciation, and in human cultural history
isolation creates cultural identity and social contact creates innovation.
Change results from cultural conflict and the radiation of new ideas into
an arena where the old worldview has collapsed.[44] Punctuated Equilibria
theory is used consciously by some scholars, but there are others who
appear to be using comparable models, especially theorists who discuss
the origins of the state.

Colin Renfrew postulates several models by which to understand state
formation in pre-classical Greece, ancient Britain, pre-Iron Age Europe,
and pre-Vedic India. Some of his models unconsciously parallel suggestions made by advocates of Punctuated Equilibria. For example, to explain
the rapid emergence of civilization Renfrew speaks of the 'multiplier
effect', the interaction of several social factors, such as technology, food
surplus and increased population, which by their co-development cause a
rapid increase in cultural evolution. Societies will resist change ('innate
conservative homeostasis') and maintain 'equilibrium' until a matrix of
social factors produces the multiplier effect and causes a sudden leap.
Otherwise, a few unassociated social factors may only cause 'small
random drift' in the social history of a culture. The interaction of social
factors 'lie at the root of all growth and development within the culture'.[45]
This interaction of numerous social forces compares rather well to the process of genetic reconfiguration in biological species, the rapid emergence
of cultural developments is like the breakthrough of new species into the
ecosystem or the territorial range of the ancestral species, and social

43. Laszlo, *Evolution*, p. 101.

44. Eldredge and Tattersall, *Myths*, pp. 177-80.

45. C. Renfrew, *The Emergence of Civilization: The Cyclades and the Aegean in
the Third Millennium BC* (London: Methuen, 1972); *idem*, *Before Civilization: The
Radiocarbon Revolution and Prehistoric Europe* (New York: Knopf, 1973); *idem*,
'Systems Collapse as Social Transformation: Catastrophe and Anastrophe in Early
State Societies', *Transformations: Mathematical Approaches to Cultural Change*
(eds. C. Renfrew and K. Cooke; New York: Academic Press, 1979), pp. 481-506;
idem, *Approaches to Social Anthropology* (Cambridge, MA: Harvard University
Press, 1987).

homeostasis parallels the fixity of a species once equilibrium is attained.

Michael Hoffman, ancient historian and social anthropologist, uses similar scientific evolutionary language in his assessment of state development in pre-dynastic Egypt. He describes the cultural diversity of pre-dynastic Egypt as a 'gene pool', which provided varied traits to enable a species, biological or cultural, to survive. These diverse cultures lived in a 'relationship known to biologists as "sympatric" in which members of the same or clearly related species live in the same large territory but manage to exploit different ecological niches'.[46] Hoffman's description of the rise of Menes's state reminds me greatly of Punctuated Equilibria's characterization of a biological breakthrough,

> Over the years a number of propensities develop within a social system which predispose it to a really major transformation. When that transformation does occur, it is so thorough as to convey the impression of crossing a critical threshold. The rise of Menes's state and Dynastic culture can, I believe, be understood through such an analogy.[47]

Eli Sagan provides us with another similar anthropological assessment in his description of state formation in Melanasian and African societies in recent times. He believes societies evolve through the following stages: primitive societies, early complex societies, later complex societies and archaic societies. Quantum leaps occur between stages of human social development which require a degree of energy not necessary for the gradual evolutionary process.[48] This latter movement, according to Punctuated Equilibria, would equate with simple genetic drift which produces no true evolutionary advance. Sagan suggests that slow change may occur within each of the stages of human societal development, but quantum leaps require much more energy—'universal bursts of energy... fuel the advance to the next stage'.[49] Basically, Sagan also parallels the model used by advocates of the biological theory.

Other scholars who observe the process of state formation delineate an evolutionary advance stimulated by dynamics which cause rapid social development. Experiences such as war, internal strife, class struggle, kin-group conflict, redistribution of wealth, agricultural intensification,

46. M. Hoffman, *Egypt before the Pharaohs: The Prehistoric Foundations of Egyptian Civilization* (New York: Knopf, 1979), pp. 80-82, 305-47.

47. Hoffman, *Egypt*, p. 305.

48. E. Sagan, *At the Dawn of Tyranny: The Origins of Individualism, Political Oppression and the State* (New York: Knopf, 1985), pp. 376-80 *et passim*.

49. Sagan, *Dawn*, p. 378.

resource management and others have been suggested as individual factors or productive in their tension with each other, but they all imply rapid social development brought about by human need or crisis.[50] Karl Butzer generated a hierarchy of terms to describe the modes of human cultural change in response to such dynamic forces: 1) 'Adaptive Transformation' describes radical cultural morphogenesis, such as the urban revolution in the Neolithic Age and the more recent industrial revolution. 2) 'Adaptive Modification' characterizes the phenomenon of agricultural intensification, demographic expansion, and state formation in Egypt, Mesopotamia and Mesoamerica. 3) 'Adaptive Adjustment' reflects short term limited response of cultures to natural disasters, wars and dynastic change.[51] Throughout, the assumption is that cultural change is not gradual, but a punctuated break in the general course of human history. Consciously or unconsciously social-anthropologists appear to assume a model of human development in cultural affairs remarkably similar to the biological theory of Punctuated Equilibria.

In conclusion, it appears that contemporary evolutionary theory resonates well with contemporary research in history, anthropology, sociology and the social sciences in general. Perhaps the model of Punctuated Equilibria may come to be seen as a heuristic paradigm across the disciplines.

III

In the last century of scholarly discussion concerning the nature of Israelite social and religious development there has been debate between proponents of a gradual evolutionary view (Julius Wellhausen and Robertson Smith) and those who speak of a revolutionary advance in the Mosaic period (William Albright) or the settlement era (George Mendenhall and Norman Gottwald). Using the inter-disciplinary insights generated by the theory of Punctuated Equilibria theorists may postulate a social-systems analysis which lies between these two positions. Both

---

50. K. Flannery, 'The Cultural Evolution of Civilizations', *Annual Review of Ecology and Systematics* 3 (1972), pp. 399-426; E. Service, 'Classical and Modern Theories of the Origins of Government', *Origins of the State: The Anthropology of Political Evolution* (eds. R. Cohen and E. Service; Phildelphia: Institute for the Study of Human Issues, 1978), pp. 21-34.

51. K. Butzer, *Archaeology as Human Ecology: Method and Theory for a Contextual Approach* (Cambridge: Cambridge University Press, 1982), p. 290.

Israelite identity and religious belief may be seen to evolve, but they do so in quantum leaps in response to social or religious crises. In so doing, theorists would be using scientific theory as an interdisciplinary paradigm once more, as some authors have demanded ought to be the case.[52]

Use of these models would be beneficial not only for envisioning Israel's development, but also for consideration of the wider cultural activity in the ancient Near East. Ancient Near Eastern history is divided into four periods by the textbooks: Early Bronze Age, Middle Bronze Age, Late Bronze Age and Iron Age. Between each of these eras was a period of social unrest or even political collapse over much of the ancient world, particularly in the so-called 'Dark Ages' early in the Iron Age (1200 BCE). Such observations correlate nicely with the new evolutionary model, especially the idea of local or mass extinction which opens up ecological niches to permit new species proliferation and adaptive radiation. With the collapse of urban centers, trade and social control at the end of the Late Bronze Age, there arose new societies created by the influx of new peoples and the reconfiguration of old groups of people in the Near East and Greece who had a new set of social, economic, political and technological values garnered from the old Bronze Age cultures, but which were now reconstructed into a new socio-cultural matrix. Paramount were the new entities in Assyria, Israel, Persia and Greece.

Likewise, biblical historians may look to the settlement process in Palestine as a time of creative re-adaptation of new values with a new society arising in the highlands, created by withdrawing lowland city dwellers who merged with highland pastoralists, bandits and immigrants into the land. Here they reconstituted themselves with new socio-economic structures while developing the technology from their previous social existence. This would be a definition in accord with the previously discussed settlement models of peaceful withdrawal, peaceful transition, or peaceful amalgamation. Alternatively, using the model of internal nomadic settlement, the highlanders may be viewed as a people separate from the Canaanites, who culturally interacted with them and eventually had to settle and farm the highlands following the collapse of lowland urban society and their trade relationships. With either model I would perceive the Israelites as a cultural entity which evolved on the marginal periphery of the ecosystem of Palestine after drawing heavily upon the cultural values of their predecessors, and here I rely upon the

52. Theissen, *Biblical Faith*.

evolutionary model for appropriate language.[53]

The highlanders generated social structures built on fictive kinship models of pastoral society and gradually coalesced to form a unified identity. Agricultural intensification and increased population developed together in a spiral development aided by the later development of lime-coated cisterns, iron-tipped plows and agricultural terracing (technological innovations generated in the Bronze Age, but not used until the tenth and ninth centuries BCE). Identification with the pastoralist stage of social development led the people to react against the social structures of early agrarian and advanced agrarian societies in later years, and macro-sociologists note that such societies have a proclivity toward egalitarian social values and monotheistic religion.[54] As the highlanders spread by sheer demographic expansion, they eventually exerted control over the valleys once more, and their trajectory of social and religious values began its evolutionary journey toward the Yahwistic monotheism of the exile. Although they had grown out of the valley culture of Palestine, once in the highlands they underwent some form of mutation, and as they spread back into the ancestral territory, they began to absorb and transform the population of all Palestine over a six hundred year process as the implications of the initial mutation slowly unfolded.

The Yahwistic minority spearheaded this evolutionary development and could accomplish its goals only because Israel was a peripheral people, free from the restraining social and economic forces operative in the great river valley cultures of Egypt and Mesopotamia. As a peripheral people they had access to the technological, political and social contributions of their neighbors, but they could fashion ideas together in a new matrix.[55] Their intelligentsia, the prophets, Levites and priests, articulated these new ideas, especially as they came into contact with the expanding Assyrian and Chaldean Babylonian empires and later went

53. R. de Vaux, *The Early History of Israel* (trans. D. Smith; Philadelphia: Westminster Press, 1978), pp. 532-680; Gottwald, *Tribes of Yahweh*; essays in Freedman and Graf (eds.), *Palestine in Transition*; Soggin, *History*, pp. 138-71; Frick, *Formation*; Hopkins, *Highlands*; Ahlström, *Israelites*.

54. Lenski and Lenski, *Human Societies*, pp. 237-38; L. Marfoe, 'The Integrative Transformation: Patterns of Sociopolitical Organization in Southern Syria', *BASOR* 234 (1979), pp. 32-35; Frick, *Formation*, p. 138.

55. Weber, *Judaism*, pp. xvii-xix, 252-63; Wittfogel, *Despotism*; Davisson and Harper, *Economic History*, pp. 30-85; T.F. Carney, *The Economics of Antiquity: Controls, Gifts, and Trade* (Lawrence: Coronado, 1973), pp. 20-21; Kulke, 'India's Axial Age', pp. 390-91.

into exile. As noted previously, scholars suggest that significant crises in the pre-exilic period caused the monotheistic development of this initially polytheistic or henotheistic Yahwistic faith (David's empire, Elijah and Elisha, Hosea, Hezekiah's reform, Josiah's reform, Jeremiah and Second Isaiah), and gradually transformed the religion of a small minority into the monotheistic religion of the masses. Only the Babylonian exile was capable of galvanizing these new values together and impressing them upon the people, who thereby became the Jews. These Jews returned to Palestine and made their monotheistic faith into the religion of all people in post-exilic Judah, and eventually the diaspora Jews took their new religion out into the farther reaches of the ancient world. The exile then became another moment of great evolutionary breakthrough, when monotheism finally surfaced to become the value system for all Jews, and the subsequent religious development of modern Judaism and Christianity might be said to be the unfolding of that evolutionary breakthrough in many ways.

Therefore, we might speak of two evolutionary breakthroughs capable of paradigm analysis. First, there is the highland experience in early Iron Age I (1200–1050 BCE) which is social and economic in its dynamics, for it reconstitutes a people in the highlands with a new economic base and accordingly different social values. Scholars suggest that these socio-economic differences were undergirded by redefined, but very basic, religious beliefs centered around the god Yahweh (mono-Yahwism) which was not true monotheism. Secondly, there is the religious odyssey of the pre-exilic era which culminates in the monotheistic breakthrough of the exile, when a more consistent and systematic religious value system emerges (monotheism). It is not contradictory to affirm the existence of both of these processes, for one would expect that social and economic changes necessary for existence would be manifest in the lives of people most clearly at first, and then later the ideological or religious values related to those initial social experiences would begin to develop and eventually lead to another revolutionary breakthrough. One might speak of two revolutionary breakthroughs, one social and one religious, or it might be preferable to speak of one continuous evolutionary and revolutionary breakthrough which lasted seven hundred years. In any revolution it takes time for the ideals and values to manifest themselves in terms of their fuller application among the people. One accordingly might speak of the social experience of the highlanders setting the stage for the later pre-exilic religious development, and of the exilic experience setting the stage for the later emergence of Judaism and Christianity.

This entire religio-socio-political process is reminiscent of the model of Punctuated Equilibria in several ways. First, both Israelites in the highlands of Palestine during Iron Age I (1200–1050 BCE) and the Jews in the Babylonian exile (586–539 BCE and thereafter) reconstructed social and ideational values, some of which were very ancient, in much the same way that a new species recombines genetic material in a new way, sometimes using latent or recessive genes, to produce new and rapid morphological change. There is an initial breakthrough in the early stages of development where significant social and ideational factors are reconstructed.

Secondly, Israel's withdrawal and physical isolation in the highlands of Palestine and the later self-imposed religious isolation in the Babylonian exile parallels how a new species arises as a 'geographic isolate' on the periphery of the ancestral species' territory. The isolation is necessary for the new entity to stabilize. Highlanders required separation from the valley culture in Iron Age I for their social system to emerge, and Jews in the exile consciously realized the necessity for separation from the Gentiles in order for Jewish identity to be preserved, hence the strong emphasis upon purity legislation.

Thirdly, highland Israelites expanded into the area of the old Canaanite culture (especially with the rise of David) and the later Jews expanded back into Palestine and into the greater diaspora of the world in the same way that a new species may return to live sympatrically with the ancestral species and displace it. The Israelite highlanders absorbed most of Palestine into their cultural sphere, and the later Jews (and Christians) created the most powerful missionary religion in history.

Fourthly, just as the collapse of old Bronze Age city states facilitated the spread of the Israelite social groups and the later collapse of the Judahite state permitted the creation of exilic Judaism, so also species extinction will encourage 'adaptive radiation' of a new species and further species proliferation. In the Iron Age the highland Israelites managed to create political entities which existed in Palestine as nation states, Judah and Israel, for five hundred years. In the Babylonian exile and thereafter Jews engaged in the creative production of new ideological values and a significant corpus of literature. In both situations the new cultural entity had to engage in conflict with the vestiges of the old entities thus displaced, just as a new species engages in territorial conflict with the predecessor species.

Fifthly, as new species, highland Israelites and the later exilic Jews adapted to their respective ecological niches in the middle of great and powerful civilizations in the world around them. In Palestine the Israelites had to struggle to maintain their national identity between the powers of Egypt and Mesopotamia. In exile and worldwide diaspora the Jews had to struggle to maintain their identity, and their success is evident today. The values of both highland Israel and diaspora Judaism survived, as the values of the former were preserved by the latter, and they eventually passed their social and religious heritage to the western, European culture through even later mutations, Christianity and Rabbinic Judaism.

Sixthly, the new social ethos of highland Israelites and the later religious ethos of exilic Jews both were created under pressure or crisis, just as a new species arises and spreads most successfully under the challenge of stressful changes in the ecological and geographic environment. Highland Israel emerged in the crisis of transition from the Bronze Age to the Iron Age, which saw urban centers in Palestine deteriorate greatly. Exilic Judaism was born in the crucible of national destruction, and was part of the intellectual advance of the great Axial Age.

Seventhly, the full implications of an initial breakthrough must unfold over the years, so that a particular species may be somewhat unstable for several thousand years until it attains genetic fixity and identity. Highland Israelites struggled with their pastoral, tribal identity for centuries, and exilic Jews created a monotheistic faith which still is working out the implications of its beliefs in both Judaism and Christianity.

The analogy between biological models of evolution and the development of social systems and religious beliefs among the Israelites and Jews may have value in terms of accentuating the clarity of the process, and these evolutionary categories may help us understand how early Israel and exilic Judaism came into being. We cannot apply the biological categories in a neat and strict fashion to the cultural experiences of the Israelites and Jews, but nonetheless, there are very interesting parallels. Observing these parallels will help focus upon those dynamics that created Israel and Judaism.

This analysis could be extended further to include Christianity in the paradigm. The message of the Jesus movement is like a species mutation. It drew upon the traditional teachings of Judaism and reconstructed them in a creative new fashion, integrating them around key new concepts concerning the teachings and actions of Jesus of Nazareth. The movement arose as a cultural mutation in Galilee, on the periphery of

Jewish culture in Palestine. The teachings of Jesus and belief in his death and resurrection spread outward through Jerusalem and to Rome, invading the territory of the ancestral species, Judaism. As it radiated out into the Greek world it underwent further mutation and modification in adapting to a new ecosystem. It came into conflict with and survived the struggle with pagan religions. Christianity was born under the pressure of Roman occupation and brutalization of the Jews as well as the tremendous social and religious pressures of change in Palestine wrought by Hellenism. Christianity also spread under the pressure of being persecuted in the Roman world. It spread further during an age of species die-off in that the old pagan religions had lost their ability to satisfy the religious needs of people. Finally, the Christian tradition has been unfolding the ideational and social implications of the evolutionary breakthrough ever since. There are some fascinating comparisons between early Christian growth and contemporary evolutionary theory, which might merit further further exploration.

A few authors have begun to contemplate such paradigms in their study of the Judaeo-Christian tradition. Gerd Theissen articulates ideas quite similar to these in his discussion, for he also describes Jesus as a revolutionary mutation in the greater process of human cultural evolution. Although Jesus is a 'mutation', all the elements of his ministry are very traditional. There is something new in the message of Jesus, but 'it does not lie in the individual elements but in their combination'.[56] Likewise, Anne Clifford uses evolutionary language to speak of the development of theology in the Christian tradition. She notes especially that the evolutionary process produces something greater than the component parts initially taken up, for the unfolding process often continues to manifest new potential depth. She states that, 'evolution is not just an unfolding of new forms from old materials; new forms result from a synthesis of the old and new in ways that are often unpredictable'.[57] This excellently summarizes the model that I perceive to be the process of development in both Judaism and Christianity.

IV

This new perception addresses another debate among biblical scholars. The debate over the nature of Israel's worldview has oscillated between

56. Theissen, *Biblical Faith*, pp. 85-128, especially pp. 106-107.
57. A. Clifford, 'Cosmology', p. 68.

two extremes in the past forty years. 'Salvation History' theologians have emphasized the radical uniqueness of Israel's thought in contrast to the ancient Near East, while more recently ancient Near Eastern historians and critically minded biblical scholars and theologians have stressed Israel's continuity with predecessor cultures. I have discussed this issue extensively in previous chapters. The model of Punctuated Equilibria may speak theoretically to this impasse, by providing a conceptualization that is a compromise between the two positions.

The basic characteristics of Israelite belief were gleaned from the ancient world, thus implying continuity, but the reconstruction of those values produced a radical departure from previous belief systems, especially in the thought of post-exilic Judaism. This is quite comparable to what occurs in the biological sphere, for here the creation of a new species occurs rapidly in a period of several thousand years and then endures relatively unchanged for millions of years. The species arises out of the matrix of an ancestral species in a way which would be imperceptible to human eyes over several thousand years, yet the species ultimately becomes a distinctly new identity in the process. There is both continuity and radical departure with the biological emergence of a species. We often fail to appreciate this tension, if only for the fact that we have a difficult time realizing that several thousand years is a short period of time—because as individuals we do not live very long. The same phenomenon occurs in cultural evolution, and again we often fail to get the necessary historical distance to appreciate the dynamics of the total process. One may observe that in Israel's pre-exilic experience the six hundred years of development from the highland settlements to the exile is a short span of time in relation to the total length of human cultural evolution (four million years), or the existence of our species Homo sapiens sapiens (fifty thousand years), or simply the history of village existence (thirteen thousand years). Change from the settlement to the emergence of monotheism in the exile does appear rather like a revolution in relationship to those other experiences. Israelite beliefs arose rather quickly out of the previous values of the Bronze Age world, like the recombination of genetic material in a new species. This recombination accomplished on the periphery, in highland Palestine and self-isolation in exile, produced the new cultural entity from which Jews and Christians are descended. As we observe it, we may see both the similarity and the radical differences with what had existed previously, and sense that it is not contradictory to do so. For this is the nature of species evolution; it is the nature of cultural evolution, too.

As noted before many authors in biblical studies have recognized this tension in their discussion of the Israelite or Jewish worldview. Many have spoken of Israel moving beyond the values of the ancient world while growing out of it.[58] Some suggest this was due to Israel's late arrival on the historical scene and their conscious awareness of their newness.[59] Others believe Israelites thinkers consciously reacted against old social and religious value systems and wove their own new worldview in response.[60] Stress upon the conscious decision of Israelites and Jews to re-articulate old beliefs in a new form resonates greatly with what cultural anthropologists have suggested about human consciousness being the most active agent in the on-going process of human evolution.[61] The language of biblical scholars is very reminiscent of contemporary evolutionary models, so that perhaps consideration of these models would be beneficial in this discourse.

With these evolutionary models as inspiration we might speak of Israel's ethos in a more nuanced fashion. We may regard the contributions of ancient Near Eastern thought in sympathic fashion while praising the religious and intellectual contributions of the biblical tradition. Subordinate ideas rose to become dominant in the new biblical matrix of thought— Israel 'evolved' out of the thought of the ancient world with a 'quantum leap'. If henceforth scholars no longer compare Israel's monotheism diametrically with ancient Near Eastern polytheism, we can admit more readily the existence of monolatrous and near-monotheistic tendencies in the ancient world, discussed in Chapter 3. We can see that Israelites and Jews may have drawn upon those earlier tendencies and were a part of an uneven and difficult intellectual odyssey in the ancient world. This new heuristic model will permit us to view this process both as revolutionary and as evolutionary, it is a revolutionary reconstruction of ideas which blossoms among the Israelites and Jews.

58. Malamat, 'Doctrines', p. 1; Koch, 'Der Tod', pp. 112-14; Cross, *Canaanite Myth*, p. 143; Frick, *Formation*, pp. 193-94; Miller, 'Israelite Relgion', p. 207; Eisenstadt, 'Ancient Israel', pp. 127-34; Lemche, *Ancient Israel*, p. 100.

59. Hayes, *Introduction*, p. 136; Porter, 'Historiography', p. 131.

60. Gottwald, 'Early Israel', pp. 32-33; *idem*, 'Two Models', p. 7; Brueggemann, 'A Shape', pp. 28-46.

61. Eldredge and Tattersall, *Myths*, pp. 8-11.

V

In conclusion, I believe that an overarching paradigm may provide analogs in the various disciplines of the social sciences and the humanities. This paradigm is provided by new developments in the fields of biology and palaeontology. Formerly, evolution was seen as a gradual and inevitable process, and this was the perceptual impact exerted by biological theory upon other academic fields. The new view of Punctuated Equilibria perceives the creative advance of life to be in quantum leaps produced by the reconstruction of old genetic material in a new way in geographically isolated regions under the duress of new ecological conditions. Such leaps are followed by subsequent periods of stasis and stability until a new crisis forces another alteration of the process.

The paradigms seems to be a more adequate way of describing also the processes involved in human evolution, cultural evolution, historical development and basic trends observed by sociologists and anthropologists. In particular, this model may be helpful in the discussion of ancient Near Eastern and Israelite/Jewish development. Both the social and religious dynamics of Israelites and Jews may be elucidated by paradigms related to this biological theory. The old question of evolution or revolution in Israelite thought may be resolved by recourse to this paradigm, which offers a middle position. Israel's identity evolved out of ancient Near Eastern values, but with several quantum leaps, most notably in the settlement process and the exile. With the aid of this methodological approach, theoretic perspectives may be brought closer to the observed data concerning the biblical tradition. As Gerd Theissen observes, 'the theory of evolution is the best paradigm for integrating the multiplicity of our experiences' in our modern stage of learning, especially now that we can expand the theory from the biotic realm into the 'abiotic' realm.[62]

62. Theissen, *Biblical Faith*, pp. 22-23.

CONCLUSIONS

I

The premise with which this book began was that significant new developments in contemporary biblical scholarship demand the rearticulation of themes and ideas in biblical theology. Most obviously the newly emerging perceptions concerning the settlement process of early Israel and the gradual emergence of Israelite religious values and monotheism are leading to a new understanding of the Israelite or biblical ethos. The development of that ethos contained within the Hebrew Bible arose much later and more gradually than we had assumed in our scholarly and pedagogical writings for so many years. This not only affects how we shall articulate biblical theology, but also how scholars shall write our textbooks in the future. Many authors in the field are observing how the shape of biblical studies will be altered significantly by these new scholarly conclusions.

The recognition that Israelites were not made of a people who entered the land of Palestine from the outside and thus were radically discontinuous with the native Canaanites in cultural matters is of foundational significance in reflection upon Israelite identity. In past discussions these notions of the radical differences between Israelites and Canaanites laid the groundwork for speaking of Israel's religious uniqueness in the ancient world. Now recent archaeological work has cut away that foundation. That is why, of necessity, this volume had to discuss conquest models as a prelude to the consideration of religion and emergent monotheism. Archaeology has led us to perceive that Israel emerged in the highlands of Palestine in Iron Age I in a peaceful and internal process that took centuries to accomplish. Whether that process of settlement and identity formation was peaceful withdrawal, internal nomadic settlement, peaceful transition, or peaceful amalgamation is truly an interesting debate, one which archaeologists may settle eventually. However, for our larger theological concerns, whichever model ultimately prevails is irrelevant, because the common understanding in all the current theories of settlement is that the Israelite social identity arose in a peaceful, internal and gradual process. This, in turn, implies that the social and intellectual connections between so-called Canaanite and so-called Israelite culture were very great, especially in the early formative years. This recognition leads students of the bible to acknowledge that key working concepts in future social and religious evaluations must be Israel's 'continuity' with the surrounding cultural environment and the 'gradual development' of Israelite social and religious beliefs over a long period of time. This undercuts grand old presentations of Israel as distinct from the surrounding ancient Near Eastern cultures, and as a radical breakthrough in the Mosaic age (Albright) or in the settlement process (Mendenhall and Gottwald). Archaeological research also has made biblical theologians more willing to accept a new perception of Israel's religious development, too.

In matters of religious development scholars are sensing the equally great continuity between pre-exilic Israelite religion and Canaanite religion. This seems to be a reasonable and even obvious conclusion, if the vast bulk of pre-exilic Israelites were really Canaanites who were slowly acculturating over several centuries to a new ethos. Now we sense that biblical religion represents the beliefs of only a minority of people in the pre-exilic era—the 'Yahweh-aloneists', as Morton Smith and Bernhard Lang have titled them. Biblical religion is truly an exilic or post-exilic phenomena. Israelites moved toward monotheism over a six century process until its culmination or breakthrough in the Babylonian exile.

In consideration of a number of significant scholars we observed a general consensus emerging. Significant crises or socio-historical developments in the pre-exilic period fueled this advance, so that monotheism appears to emerge as a culmination of several intellectual 'jumps' with a final major breakthrough in the exile. Authors, therefore, see this movement as both evolutionary and revolutionary in its advance. It is evolutionary in that it takes centuries to emerge. However, it is revolutionary in that the process really occurs in a relatively short period of time compared to the greater scope of human history, and the final breakthrough in the exile to radical monotheism was not the inevitable result of the gradual process, but rather it was a quantum leap prepared for by many previous smaller revolutions. Therefore, for several authors the tension of evolution and revolution is an apt metaphor to describe Israel's emerging monotheism. Unbeknown to most writers this model corresponds rather well to the reigning theory of biological evolution proposed by palaeontologists—Punctuated Equilibria.

Contemporary critical scholars have proposed a number of paradigms for our more contemporary scholarly perceptions of Israel's religious and social development. In this volume I have attempted to bring together the ideas of many of those authors in a coherent synthesis. In general, these reflective authors are focusing upon the same basic phenomena, and their suggestions make sense in a greater and more holistic survey of the religious experience of Israel. Hopefully, this text will bring their paradigms forward for greater consideration in the arena of biblical–theological reflection. Above all, the characterization of the pre-exilic monotheistic movement, or the 'Yahweh-alone' movement, suggested by Morton Smith, Bernhard Lang and others, has great merit. But even more significant for characterizing the dynamics of the evolutionary process in the pre-exilic period is the model proposed by Mark Smith of 'convergence' and 'differentiation'. This attempts to explain the phenomena observed in the biblical text as well as archaeological data wherein a process of amalgamating imagery under one deity occurs simultaneously with the exclusion of ultimately unacceptable images and practices over the period of several centuries. In a similar vein, Werner Schmidt describes a dynamic process with his concepts of 'recognition' and 'rejection'.

A number of scholars have conceptualized ways of perceiving the breakthrough to monotheism in this age, or for that matter, the other forms of intellectual and religious accomplishments which were the hallmark of this age. William Tremmel speaks of a 'kairotic moment' as the time when a religion emerges at a new level of sophistication, and thus becomes a 'consummate religion', or a high religion. Even more significant are the speculations of many scholars concerning the nature of the Axial Age (800–400 BCE), an era of intellectual and religious ferment from China or India to the Mediterranean. Too often biblical scholars have had a focus far too narrow in their observations of Israel and the ancient Near East. Recognition that significant change was afoot throughout the great cultural sphere of the Old World will give us new and dramatic insights into the nature of the Israelite and Jewish experience, especially the intellectual transformation occuring in the Babylonian exile and diaspora which would have brought Jews into contact with these greater winds of intellectual, religious and social change.

The search for terms to describe the Israelite belief phenomena has been valuable also. Terms like 'mono-Yahwism', 'intolerant henotheism', 'radical henolatry', 'national monolatry', 'incipient monotheism' and 'Yahweh-aloneism' are all very useful concepts in describing the religious feelings of Israelites who are no longer polytheists, but not quite radical monotheists. I believe the best categories in this regard were provided by Denis Baly, who uses notions such as 'pseudo-monotheism', 'proto-monotheism' and 'imperial monotheism' to describe the various mono-theistic-like movements in the ancient world up into the first millennium BCE. He should be applauded for his willingness to consider Israelite belief in a much wider context than the ancient Near East, something which I have attempted to do in this work, also. Such a wide endeavor allows additional vantage points by which to view the phenomenon of monotheism as attested in the Bible, for we then must consider religious movements which express themselves in philosophical monism as well as theistic monotheism.

Finally, an excellent methodological approach was laid out by David Petersen. He articulated the broader range of questions which need to be addressed in the discussion of monotheism. Although this volume could not do justice to all of his questions, I attempted to address some of them in detail. Any future consideration of the monotheistic phenomena ought to take into account the parameters he puts forth in his article.

Taken together the work and ideas of all these scholars, and the many others whose contributions I attempted to summarize in this volume, reflect the fact that there is indeed a 'paradigm shift' underway in bibli-cal studies. Thomas Kuhn observes that such a shift occurs when the scholarly community looks at its data but then reconfigures the informa-tion into new hypotheses. That is what is happening in biblical studies. Scholars are sensing that Israel developed socially and religiously in a way other than that envisioned for so many years. We now stress that the Israelite or Jewish ethos expressed in the Hebrew Bible arose later and more gradually than previously suspected, but its ultimate emergence was nonetheless a dramatic intellectual and cultural breakthrough. Scholars are now ready to stress the continuity Israelite thought had with the cultural and religious beliefs of the world around it, and to describe their characteristic beliefs in more nuanced fashion. We are ready to speak of how the Israelites and exilic Jews reconfigured or reconstructed the ideas of those who came before them in the ancient world—how they were able to put old wine into new bottles.

In a sense, one could say that the ancient Israelites and Jews thus experienced their own 'paradigm shift', one that has influenced the direction of western culture ever since. Successive crises in pre-exilic Israel's religious development built up to a point where the ultimate crisis of the exile brought the breakthrough to monotheism, and this process conforms very much to the pattern of intellectual behavior described by Kuhn as a revolutionary 'paradigm shift'. The 'paradigm shift' has been to recognize the dynamics of the Israelite or biblical 'paradigm shift'.

The first goal of this text is to make such ideas more available to the general reader. The creative speculations and new theories of many of the authors discussed in this text deserve a wider exposure. I would hope that the reader has found this text a valuable summary of many of the new ideas concerning the Israelite conquest and the development of monotheism. If so, then this text will contribute to the new emerging consensus in biblical studies and will aid in the future generation of textbooks and biblical theologies. That will contribute to the continuing 'paradigm shift' in biblical studies.

II

In this volume I attempted to summarize the writings of scholars on the issues of the settlement process and the development of pre-exilic Israelite religion, but I also attempted to move the discussion to the next level of reflection—the theological significance of those scholarly conclusions. In my opinion a number of important insights flow from the discussion.

1. Our deeper appreciation for Israelite religious and intellectual continuities with the ancient world should lead us to consider Israelite faith and belief in the greater matrix of religious development in the ancient world of the first millennium BCE. We should view Israelites or Jews as part of the greater spectrum of West-Semitic religious experience in the Syro-Palestinian cultural arena, and we shall profit from a more nuanced analysis which sees continuities as well as differences between Israelite and Judahite religions and those of the immediate surrounding nations in the Transjordan, Phoenicia and Syria. Then at the next level of comparison, from a wider geographical and cultural view, we may observe the differences and similarites between the Israelite religious expressions and those of Egypt and Mesopotamia. From an even later and different perspective we can see that Israelites and the later Jews were part of the great Axial Age advance in the first millennium BCE. At this level of discourse we see the religious contributions of the Jews in the context of religious developments in Persia (Zoroastrianism) and India (Vedas and the Upanishads). Consideration of monistic and monotheistic movements

in those countries, which were contemporary with the Jewish religious experience in exile and thereafter, may give us even deeper insights into the nature of the biblical monotheistic faith.

In the past biblical theologians too often contented themselves with a comparison of biblical beliefs and the texts of the first millennium BCE versus the much older Egyptian and Mesopotamian texts of the third and second millennia BCE in order to demonstrate the intellectual and moral superiority of the biblical worldview. Now that we sense the more gradual and later emergence of biblical monotheism, we realize that a better methodological approach is to compare biblical texts with authentic contemporary literature, and to perceive that several cultures were moving forward intellectually in this age, albeit in somewhat different directions.

2. There is a subtle nuance which must be maintained: Israelite and Jewish thought grows out of and has great continuity with the intellectual and religious values of the predecessor cultures in the ancient world, but at the same time it is a significant advance in the history of human culture. This was the point which the old *Heilsgeschichte* theologians sought to establish with their inspirational rhetoric. Their mistake, as we see it now, was to portray the contrasts between Israel and the ancient world too starkly, and to project too much sophistication and development too early in Israel's develomental process. For that they were criticized, and their paradigms have received much scorn. However, I believe that the idea behind their endeavor was valid and such comparisons can have a meaningful theological value, if those contrasts between the biblical tradition and the ancient world are portrayed in a more subtle fashion. This volume can in no way accomplish that task in any really developed fashion, but hopefully some of the nuanced observations generated in Chapter 5 might inspire other authors to take up this task.

Essentially, the Israelite and Jewish tradition did not invent notions such as a God who acts in history, the universal rule of one deity, ethical guidelines for living, the concept of social obligations for weaker members of society, the idea of human freedom and responsibility, and all the values associated with the linear view of reality. But in many ways the emergence of a thorough-going monotheism in the exile and beyond helped develop these ideas. Perhaps most significantly, the monotheistic movement of the Jews brought these ideas, which previously had been in the possession of the intelligentsia of the ancient world, to the fore and impressed them upon the common people. These values then could become the dominant themes in shaping the culture of a given people, rather than remaining the values of a few in a society, who could not implement these values effectively in the everyday life of that society. The simplicity of the Israelite social setting in the pre-exilic era, especially in the highlands, and the later need to reconstruct a society from the ashes in the exile, made possible the emergence of these values from a subordinate to a more dominant intellectual and social role. I am reminded of how recessive genes can surface to become dominant genes in a species undergoing a radical evolutionary transition.

In this volume I attempted to articulate those old *Heilsgeschichte* themes in a more subtle and nuanced fashion. The emphasis is upon seeing the continuity of key ideas with the thought of the great predecessor cultures, yet at the same time acknowledging that the Jewish religious experience indeed did advance the development of these ideas, so that they might become eventually the foundations for our modern worldview. In addition, we must recognize that this process of intellectual development came later in Israel's history, in the exile and beyond. Readers might wish to dispute some of the particular articulations expressed in Chapter 5, but that is irrelevant. The important insight, as far as I am concerned, is that these themes can be used meaningfully to speak of how Jewish faith advanced the intellectual heritage of the ancient world in some fashion, and that we may still use these observations in our biblical theologizing today.

3. The recognition that Israelite monotheism did not emerge fully until the exile should lead us to another insight worthy of integration into our scholarship and pedagogy—increased respect for the literary and theological accomplishments of Second Temple Judaism. Too often in the past we denigrated the worldview and values of this period, relegating to them the role of scribal collection and legalistic articulations. Too often we failed to recognize the theological accomplishments of the Priestly tradition, merely regarding their efforts as one of collating the biblical text and adding the stifling legislation found in Exodus and Leviticus. Now we should sense the Priestly tradition may have been crucial to the further development of monotheistic values, and individuals within this movement may have been the most responsible for impressing monotheistic faith and values upon the Jewish masses. Now that we sense how late some of the intellectual development and literature may have been, we can recognize how responsible the post-exilic theologians were in

terms of its development, propagation and preservation. We need to look again at Priestly texts, Wisdom Literature, and post-exilic Prophetic–Apocalyptic literature to see how they still were fighting the battle to affirm monotheism and its values in an age when the hearts and minds of the people may not yet have been won. Scholars may discern nuances in the texts which previously we had passed over unheeding.

A side effect may be the exorcism of the old subliminal demon of anti-Semitism in biblical studies. At times the denigration of post-exilic Jewish legalism and Priestly legalism in the scholarly and popular writings of Christian authors in Hebrew Bible studies directly or indirectly under-girded a negative rhetoric about Jewish beliefs. To be sure, German Protestant scholars often said critical things about cultic and Torah oriented religion because they were speaking indirectly about their own hierarchical and conservative denominations or state churches; this was probably much the reason for Julius Wellhausen's invective against post-exilic Jewish thought. But the subtle critical barbs of scholars, be they conscious or unconscious, often may strike against people other than their intended targets. Jewish beliefs were indirectly insulted by these portrayals, and those assumptions were handed on to generations of students in Christian circles. The recognition of the creative and brilliant contribution of post-exilic theologians will be a welcome remedy to our past portrayals.

4. The recognition that monotheism emerged or evolved in Israel and among the later Jews should lead us to another perception: great intel-lectual movements arise out of a process that is complex. The mono-theistic trajectory may be seen already in early henotheistic movements in the ancient Near East, which may have influenced Israel by providing some of the language and concepts by which to address a deity in exclusive fashion. The seedbed for this movement was a village society in highland Palestine which emerged slowly out of the old Late Bronze Age society, where retreating Canaanites and other population elements began a new life. This simple society unconsciously began a six century religious odyssey which would elevate an obscure regional deity to universal supremacy. This odyssey was made possible by social and reli-gious crises, the greatest of which was the Babylonian exile. Only after the total national destruction of this people could a landless people in exile reach the ultimate conclusion that their god alone existed and other deities did not. Without this final crisis could something as pure mono-theism truly have been born? Otherwise we might be looking elsewhere

for the roots of our modern monotheism or monism.

Monotheism emerges by pain. It may be the result of an evolutionary process, but it requires crises and sometimes tragedies to move it forward, and ultimately full-blown monotheism emerges as a radical leap forward. This alone is a tremendous insight concerning the nature of any religious or intellectual advance. Throughout this work I have affirmed that we should view the monotheistic advance as both an evolution and a revolution, and many scholars are beginning to use this paradigm in their discussions.

5. Closely related to this previous concept is the realization that if the monotheistic evolution/revolution took six centuries to come to fruition in the exile, perhaps the process of development is still underway. The paradigm advanced in the latter half of this volume suggests that the social implications that accompany the development of monotheism may take many years to unfold. The monotheistic breakthrough of the Babylonian exile brought with it ideals concerning the equality of people and their social and political rights. These values are exemplified in the legislation of Deuteronomy and Leviticus, from the efforts of the Deuteronomic theologians and the Priestly editors respectively. But they did not create a finished product; rather, they began an evolutionary trajectory which is still unfolding today. The teachings of Jesus are part of this on-going evolutionary process, an even deeper message of human dignity built upon the premise of radical love.

Among modern believers in the greater Judaeo-Christian tradition it is too commonplace to regard tradition as the inherited and fixed legacy of the past, which should be revered and preserved. It is my belief that this new understanding of the evolutionary monotheistic process challenges us to develop a new sense of what 'tradition' means. Tradition is a process of religious evolution; it is a trajectory of beliefs and social-ethical imperatives that change continually over the years. The trajectory remains faithful to its core message of one God and human dignity, but in each generation it must be proclaimed anew and develop some more. Jews and Christians are part of a dynamic and living trajectory of monotheistic belief and practice. They are called upon not to revere a fixed past, but to participate in the development of the on-going monotheistic revolution of the Judaeo-Christian tradition. This may be the most significant awareness which springs from the understanding of monotheism as an evolutionary and revolutionary process.

6. As we weave our biblical theological rhetoric today, we find that it

is necessary to use a foundational philosophical–theological mode of discourse to express ourselves in a meaningful fashion. I would suggest that the emphasis upon the evolutionary and revolutionary religious advance could be expressed rather well in the language and imagery of process theology. The Bible undergirds the vision of a dynamic and on-going process of religious development, and the theologian is naturally led to consider process theological models for his or her theological mode of discourse. Hopefully, the very brief chapter on process thought and the Hebrew Bible might suggest other ways in which process thought and biblical thought dovetail. Process thought might be an excellent way by which to capture the spirit of much of the language, imagery and belief found expressed in those ancient biblical texts. Above all, the use of process theological imagery reinforces the notion of an evolutionary and revolutionary monotheistic process which is developing among us yet today.

7. Finally, I believe in the value of promoting a heuristic paradigm from the sciences which may have at least some limited value in elucidating the dynamics involved in the social-historical process of emerging monotheism. The contemporary view of the biological, evolutionary process sees change resulting from the build-up of many little genetic mutations which result in an evolutionary leap as an isolated species adapts to a radically changed ecological environment. This model, called Punctuated Equilibria, posits that change occurs in rapid leaps in the developmental or evolutionary process, which only occasionally punctuates long periods of relative stasis. The idea of slow, gradual, continual, inevitable evolutionary change is being rejected in favor of this theory of 'punctuated' advances in the evolutionary process. For years students and scholars in the social sciences and the humanities chaffed under dogmatic theories of gradual change or evolution which were imposed upon their fields of research. Many authors have attacked altogether the notion of using evolution as a paradigm by which to understand social and historical processes. Now that has changed, for the contemporary theory of evolutionary advance posits the kind of developmental process which historians and social scientists have suggested for years was the actual pattern by which human culture unfolded.

Evolutionary theory now postulates that the evolutionary advance is not merely the unfolding of new forms from old materials in a gradual, upward advance, but it is an unpredictable breakthrough of old and new elements reconfigured to form a new synthesis. This language is amazingly similar to the view of monotheistic development I have advocated in this book. Furthermore, it is also the way in which process thinkers view the 'moment of becoming', or the 'apprehension of the past' by the present moment. To me it suggests that here we have a consistent pattern for viewing reality, and that both process thought and evolutionary theory may converge to provide paradigms for understanding social-scientific phenomena, such as the emergence of monotheism among the Jews in the first millennium BCE.

This is easily my most controversial thesis, and it is advanced for the reader's consideration and reflection. The notions of Punctuated Equilibria do seem to describe the process of the monotheistic evolution and revolution as I have presented them. The pre-exilic period with its stages of development wrought by socio-historical crises in Israel's existence parallels the development of potential mutations within the genetic pool of a particular species. The isolation of Israel in the highlands of Palestine as a simple society between the great river valley cultures of Egypt and Mesopotamia parallels how a new species will emerge most readily on the periphery of the ancestral species' range. The crisis of the exile, which brought radical monotheism to the fore as the organizing intellectual and religious principle for the Jews to survive, parallels how an ecological crisis or transformation will permit the new species to develop and fill the ecological niches left by other species which died off. Finally, the subsequent years in which the implications of the monotheistic evolution/revolution are unfolded parallels how a new species will spend several thousand years arriving at genetic stability as it unfolds the implications of its new genetic matrix. The parallels impress me, and it seems to be intellectually useful, or at least interesting, to propose a heuristic paradigm that appears to describe phenomena both in the biological realm and the cultural realm. The model also reinforces an understanding of the on-going monotheistic revolution which still is unfolding all of the social and ideational implications of that original breakthrough.

In conclusion, these are the arguments advanced in this small volume. It was an audacious task to treat all of these topics in a judicious fashion in such a relatively short volume. Hopefully, the reader will see that this volume is designed to inspire speculation and reflection among the readers rather than to present a systematic and definitive argument. That would be beyond my ability. This work is designed to further the direction of scholarly thought in this generation and to provide some speculative grist for the minds of scholars, theologians and students of religion.

BIBLIOGRAPHY

Ackerman, S., '"And the Women Knead Dough": The Worship of the Queen of Heaven in Sixth-Century Judah', *Gender and Difference in Ancient Israel* (ed. P. Day; Minneapolis: Fortress Press, 1989), pp. 109-24.

—'Child Sacrifice: Returning God's Gift', *Bible Review* 9.3 (1993), pp. 20-29, 56.

—'The Queen Mother and the Cult in Ancient Israel', *JBL* 112 (1993), pp. 385-401.

—*Under Every Green Tree: Popular Religion in Sixth-Century Judah* (HSM, 46; Atlanta, GA: Scholars Press, 1992).

Aharoni, Y., 'Nothing Early and Nothing Late: Rewriting Israel's Conquest', *BA* 39 (1976), pp. 55-76.

—*The Land of the Bible: A Historical Geography* (Philadelphia: Westminster Press, rev. edn, 1979 [1962]).

Ahlström, G., *A History of Ancient Palestine* (Minneapolis: Fortress Press, 1993).

—'An Israelite God Figurine from Hazor', *Orientalia Suecana* 19–20 (1970–71), pp. 54-62.

—'An Israelite God Figurine, Once More', *VT* 25 (1975), pp. 106-109.

—'Another Moses Tradition', *JNES* 39 (1980), pp. 65-69.

—*Aspects of Syncretism in Israelite Religion* (trans. E. Sharpe; Lund: Gleerup, 1963).

—'Giloh: A Judahite or Canaanite Settlement?', *IEJ* 34 (1984), pp. 170-72.

—'King Jehu—A Prophet's Mistake', *Scripture in History and Theology: Essays in Honor of J. Coert Rylaarsdam* (eds. A. Merrill and T. Overholt; PTMS, 17; Pittsburg: Pickwick Press, 1977), pp. 52-61.

—*Royal Administration and National Religion in Ancient Palestine* (Studies in the History of the Ancient Near East, 1; Leiden: Brill, 1982).

—'The Early Iron Age Settlers at Khirbet el-Msas (Tel Masos)', *ZDPV* 100 (1984), pp. 35-53

—'The Role of Archaeological and Literary Remains in Reconstructing Israel's History', *The Fabric of History* (ed. D. Edelman), pp. 116-41.

—*Who Were the Israelites?* (Winona Lake, IN: Eisenbrauns, 1986).

Albertz, R., *A History of Israelite Religion in the Old Testament Period* (trans. J. Bowden; 2 vols.; OTL; Philadelphia: Westminster Press, 1994).

—'Der Ort des Monotheismus in der israelitischen Religionsgeschichte', *Ein Gott allein* (eds. W. Dietrich and M. Klopfenstein), pp. 77-96.

Albrektson, B., *History and the Gods: An Essay on the Idea of Historical Events as Divine Manifestations in the Ancient Near East and Israel* (Lund: Gleerup, 1967).

Albright, W.F., 'Archaeology and the Date of the Hebrew Conquest of Palestine', *BASOR* 58 (1935), pp. 10-18.

—*Archaeology and the Religion of Israel* (Garden City, NY: Doubleday, 5th edn, 1968 [1941]).

—*From the Stone Age to Christianity: Monotheism and the Historic Process* (Garden City, NY: Doubleday, 2nd edn, 1957 [1940]).

—'Further Light on the History of Israel from Lachish and Megiddo', *BASOR* 68 (1937), pp. 22-26.

—*History, Archaeology, and Christian Humanism* (New York: McGraw–Hill, 1964).

—*The Archaeology of Palestine* (Baltimore: Penguin Books, 3rd edn, 1960).

—*The Biblical Period from Abraham to Ezra* (New York: Harper & Row, 1963).

—'The Israelite Conquest of Canaan in the Light of Archaeology', *BASOR* 74 (1939), pp. 11-23.

Aldred, C., *Akhenaten: King of Egypt* (London: Thames & Hudson, 1988).

—'Egypt: The Amarna Period and the End of the Eighteenth Dynasty', *The Cambridge Ancient History*. II.2. *History of the Middle East and the Aegean Region c. 1380–1000 BC* (eds. I.E.S. Edwards *et al.*; 6 vols.; Cambridge: Cambridge University Press, 1975), pp. 49-97.

Alt, A., *Kleine Schriften zur Geschichte des Volkes Israel* (3 vols.; Munich: Beck, 1953).

—'The Settlement of the Israelites in Palestine', *Essays in Old Testament History and Religion* (trans. R.A. Wilson; Garden City, NY: Doubleday, 1966), pp. 173-221.

Alter, R., *The Art of Biblical Narrative* (New York: Basic Books, 1981).

Amitai, J. (ed.), *Biblical Archaeology Today: Proceedings of the International Congress on Biblical Archaeology, Jerusalem, April 1984* (Jerusalem: Israel Exploration Society, 1985).

Anderson, B. (ed.), *Creation in the Old Testament* (Issues in Religion and Theology, 6; Philadelphia: Fortress Press, 1984).

—'Introduction: Mythopoeic and Theological Dimensions of Biblical Creation Faith', *Creation in the Old Testament* (ed. B. Anderson), pp. 1-24.

—'Mendenhall Disavows Paternity: Says he Didn't Father Gottwald's Marxist Theory', *BARev* 2.2 (1986), pp. 46-49.

—*Understanding the Old Testament* (Englewood Cliffs, NJ: Prentice–Hall, 4th edn, 1986 [1957]).

Anderson, G., *Sacrifices and Offerings in Ancient Israel: Studies in their Social and Political Importance* (HSM, 41; Atlanta: Scholars Press, 1987).

Angerstorfer, A., 'Asherah als "Consort of Jahwe" oder Asirtah?', *Biblische Notizen* 17 (1982), pp. 7-16.

Armstrong, K., *A History of God: The 4000-Year Quest of Judaism, Christianity and Islam* (New York: Knopf, 1993).

Ash, P., 'Solomon's? District? List', *JSOT* 67 (1995), pp. 67-86.

Baly, D., 'The Geography of Monotheism', *Translating and Understanding the Old Testament: Essays in Honor of Herbert Gordon May* (eds. H.T. Frank and W. Reed; Nashville: Abingdon Press, 1970), pp. 253-78.

Bardtke, H., 'Altisraelitische Erweckungsbewegungen', *Near Eastern Studies in Honor of William Foxwell Albright* (ed. H. Goedicke; Baltimore: The Johns Hopkins University Press, 1971), pp. 17-34.

Barnes, B., *T.S. Kuhn and Social Science* (New York: Columbia University Press, 1982).

Barr, J., *Old and New in Interpretation: A Study of the Two Testaments* (London: SCM Press, 1982).

—'The Interpretation of Scripture. II. Revelation through History in the Old Testament and in Modern Theology', *Int* 17 (1963), pp. 193-205.

Barrick, W.B., and J. Spencer (eds.), *In the Shelter of Elyon: Essays on Ancient Palestinian Life and Literature in Honor of G.W. Ahlström* (JSOTSup, 31; Sheffield: JSOT Press, 1984).

—'Parentheses in a Snowstorm: G.W. Ahlström and the Study of Ancient Palestine', in *In the Shelter of Elyon* (eds. B. Barrick and J. Spencer), pp. 43-65.

Bartlett, J.R, 'The Brotherhood of Edom', *JSOT* 4 (1977), pp. 2-27.

—'Yahweh and Qaus: A Response to Martin Rose (*JSOT*, 4 [1977] 28-34)', *JSOT* 5 (1978), pp. 29-38.

Bauckham, R., *The Bible in Politics: How to Read the Bible Politically* (Louisville, KY: Westminster Press, 1987).

Ben-Tor, A. (ed.), *The Archaeology of Ancient Israel* (trans. R. Greenberg; New Haven: Yale University Press, 1992).

Berlinerblau, J., 'The "Popular Religion" Paradigm in Old Testament Research: A Sociological Critique', *JSOT* 60 (1993), pp. 3-26.

Biale, D., 'The God with Breasts: El Shaddai in the Bible', *HR* 20 (1982), pp. 240-56.

Bloesch, D., 'Process Theology and Reformed Theology', *Process Theology* (ed. R. Nash), pp. 35-56.

Blum, E., *Die Komposition der Vätergeschichte* (WMANT, 57; Neukirchen–Vluyn: Neukirchener Verlag, 1984).

—*Studien zur Komposition des Pentateuch* (BZAW, 189; Berlin: de Gruyter, 1990).

Boadt, L., *Reading the Old Testament: An Introduction* (Mahwah, NJ: Paulist Press, 1984).

Boling, R., *Judges* (AB, 6A; Garden City, NY: Doubleday, 1975).

—*The Early Biblical Community in Transjordan* (Social World of Biblical Antiquity, 6; Sheffield: Almond Press, 1988).

Borowski, O., *Agriculture in Iron Age Israel: The Evidence from Archaeology and the Bible* (Winona Lake, IN: Eisenbrauns, 1987).

Bowler, P., *Evolution: The History of an Idea* (Berkeley: University of California Press, 1984).

Boyce, M., *A History of Zoroastrianism* (3 vols.; Leiden: Brill, 1975, 1981, 1991).

—'Persian Religion in the Achemenid Age', *Cambridge History of Judaism*. I. *Introduction: The Persian Period* (eds. W.D. Davies and L. Finkelstein; Cambridge: Cambridge University Press, 1984), pp. 279-307.

Braudel, F., *A History of Civilizations* (trans. R. Mayne; New York: Penguin Books, 1994).

—*Civilization and Capitalism: 15th–18th Century* (trans. S. Reynolds; 3 vols.; New York: Harper & Row, 1981, 1982, 1984).

Braulik, G., 'Das Deuteronomium und die Geburt des Monotheismus', *Gott, der Einzige* (ed. H. Haag), pp. 115-59.

Breasted, J.H., *Development of Religion and Thought in Ancient Egypt* (repr.; New York: Harper & Row, 1959 [1912]).

—*The Dawn of Conscience* (New York: Charles Scribner's Sons, 1961 [1933]).

Brelich, A., 'Der Polytheismus', *Numen* 7 (1960), pp. 123-36.

Brettler, M., *The Creation of History in Ancient Israel* (New York: Routledge, 1995).

Brichto, H.C., 'Kin, Cult, Land and Afterlife—A Biblical Complex', *HUCA* 44 (1973), pp. 1-55.

Bright, J., *A History of Israel* (Philadelphia: Westminster Press, 2nd edn, 1972 [1959]).

—*A History of Israel* (Philadelphia: Westminster Press, 3rd edn, 1981 [1959]).

—*The Kingdom of God: The Biblical Concept and its Meaning for the Church* (Nashville: Abingdon Press, 1953).

Brueggemann, W., 'A Shape for Old Testament Theology. I. Structure Legitimation', *CBQ* 47 (1985), pp. 28-46.

—*Old Testament Theology: Essays on Structure, Theme, and Text* (ed. P. Miller; Minneapolis: Fortress Press, 1992).

—'Pharaoh as Vassal: A Study of a Political Metaphor', *CBQ* 57 (1995), pp. 27-51.

—'Theodicy in a Social Dimension', *JSOT* 33 (1985), pp. 3-25.

—*The Prophetic Imagination* (Philadelphia: Fortress Press, 1978).

Butterfield, H., *The Origins of History* (New York: Basic Books, 1981).

Butzer, K., *Archaeology as Human Ecology: Method and Theory for a Contextual Approach* (Cambridge: Cambridge University Press, 1982).

Callaway, J., 'A New Perspective on the Hill Country Settlement of Canaan in Iron Age I', *Palestine in the Bronze and Iron Ages: Papers in Honour of Olga Tufnell* (ed. J.N. Tubb; London: Institute of Archaeology, 1985), pp. 31-49.

—'Respondents', *Biblical Archaeology Today* (ed. J. Amitai), pp. 72-78.

—'Village Subsistence at Ai and Raddana in Iron Age I', *The Answers Lie Below: Essays in Honor of Lawrence Edmund Toombs* (ed. H. Thompson; Lanham: University Press of America, 1984), pp. 51-66.

Carney, T.F., *The Economics of Antiquity: Controls, Gifts, and Trade* (Lawrence: Coronado, 1973).

Carpenter, E., *Theism in Medieval India* (The Hibbert Lectures, NS; London: Williams & Norgate, 1921).

Chaney, M., 'Ancient Palestinian Peasant Movements and the Formation of Premonarchic Israel', *Palestine in Transition* (eds. D. Freedman and D. Graf), pp. 39-90.

Chase, D., 'A Note on an Inscription from Kuntillet 'Ajrud', *BASOR* 246 (1982), pp. 63-67.

Childs, B., *Biblical Theology in Crisis* (Philadelphia: Westminster Press, 1970).

—*Biblical Theology of the Old and New Testaments* (Minneapolis: Fortress Press, 1993).

—*Old Testament Theology in a Canonical Context* (Philadelphia: Fortress Press, 1985).

Ciholas, P., 'Monotheisme et violence', *RSR* 69 (1981), pp. 325-54.

Clark, N., 'Christian Theism and Whiteheadian Process Philosophy: Are they Compatible', *Process Theology* (ed. R. Nash), pp. 219-51.

Clifford, A., 'Postmodern Scientific Cosmology and the Christian God of Creation', *Horizons* 21 (1994), pp. 62-84.

Clifford, R., and J. Collins (eds.), *Creation in the Biblical Traditions* (CBQMS, 24; Washington: Catholic Biblical Association, 1992).

Cobb, J., Jr, *A Christian Natural Theology Based on the Thought of Alfred North Whitehead* (Philadelphia: Westminster Press, 1965).

—*Christ in a Pluralistic Age* (Philadelphia: Westminster Press, 1975).

—*Process Theology as Political Theology* (Philadelphia: Westminster Press, 1982).

Cobb, J., and D.R. Griffin, *Process Theology: An Introductory Exposition* (Philadelphia: Westminster Press, 1977).

Cohen, M., D. Snell and D. Weisberg (eds.), *The Tablet and the Scroll: Near Eastern Studies in Honor of William W. Hallo* (Bethesda: CDL Press, 1993).

Cohn, N., *Cosmos, Chaos, and the World to Come: The Ancient Roots of Apocalyptic Faith* (New Haven: Yale University Press, 1993).

Comblin, J., 'Monotheism and Popular Religion' (trans. D. Livingstone), *Monotheism* (eds. Geffré, Jossua and Lefébure), pp. 91-99.

Coogan, M.D., 'Canaanite Origins and Lineage: Reflections on the Religion of Ancient Israel', *Ancient Israelite Religion* (eds. P. Miller, P. Hanson and D. McBride), pp. 115-24.

Coote, R., and K. Whitelam, *The Emergence of Early Israel in Historical Perspective* (Social World of Biblical Antiquity, 5; Sheffield: Almond Press, 1987).

—'The Emergence of Israel: Social Transformation and State Formation Following the Decline in Late Bronze Age Trade', *Semeia* 37 (1986), pp. 107-47.

Cornélis, E., 'The Imprecise Boundaries of Notions of the Ultimate' (trans. L.H. Ginn), *Monotheism* (eds. C. Geffré, J.-P. Jossua and M. Lefébure), pp. 3-15.

Couroyer, B., 'Le "Dieu des Sages" en Egypte, I', *RB* 94 (1987), pp. 574-603.

—'Le "Dieu des Sages" en Egypte, II', *RB* 95 (1988), pp. 70-91.

Croatto, S., *Exodus: A Hermeneutics of Freedom* (trans. S. Attanasio; Maryknoll: Orbis Books, 1981).

Cross, F.M., *Canaanite Myth and Hebrew Epic: Essays in the History of the Religion of Israel* (Cambridge, MA: Harvard University Press, 1973).

Cross, F.M. (ed.), *Symposia Celebrating the Seventy-Fifth Anniversary of the Founding of the American Schools of Oriental Research 1900–1975* (Cambridge, MA: American Schools of Oriental Research, 1979).

Cryer, F., *Divination in Ancient Israel and its Near Eastern Environment: A Socio-Historical Investigation* (JSOTSup, 142; Sheffield: JSOT Press, 1994).

Davies, P.R., 'Method and Madness: Some Remarks on Doing History with the Bible', *JBL* 114 (1995), pp. 699-705.

—*In Search of 'Ancient Israel'* (JSOTSup, 148; Sheffield: JSOT Press, 1992).

Davisson, W., and J. Harper, *European Economic History. I. The Ancient World* (New York: Appleton, Century & Crofts, 1972).

Day, J., 'Asherah in the Hebrew Bible and Northwest Semitic Literature', *JBL* 105 (1986), pp. 385-408.

—*God's Conflict with the Dragon and the Sea: Echos of a Canaanite Myth in the Old Testament* (University of Cambridge Oriental Publications, 35; Cambridge: Cambridge University Press, 1985).

—*Molech: A God of Human Sacrifice in the Old Testament* (University of Cambridge Oriental Publications, 41; Cambridge: Cambridge University Press, 1989).

—'Yahweh and the Gods and Goddesses of Canaan', *Ein Gott allein* (eds. W. Dietrich and M. Klopfenstein), pp. 181-96.

Dearman, A., *Property Rights in the Eighth-Century Prophets* (SBLDS, 106; Atlanta, GA: Scholars Press, 1988).

—*Religion and Culture in Ancient Israel* (Peabody, MA: Henrickson, 1992).

de Benoist, A., *Comment Peut-on Etre Païen?* (Paris: Michel, 1981).

—*Vu de Droite. Anthologie Critique des Idées Contemporaines* (Paris: Copernic, 1977).

de Geus, C.H.J., *The Tribes of Israel: An Investigation into Some of the Presuppositions of Martin Noth's Amphictyony Hypothesis* (Amsterdam: Van Gorcum, 1976).

de Moor, J.C., 'The Crisis of Polytheism in Late Bronze Age Ugarit', *Crises and Perspectives: Studies in Ancient Near Eastern Polytheism, Biblical Theology, Palestinian Archaeology and Intertestamental Literature* (ed. A.S. van der Woude; OTS, 24; Leiden: Brill, 1986), pp. 1-20.

—*The Rise of Yahwism: The Roots of Israelite Monotheism* (BETL, 91; Leuven: Leuven University Press/Peeters, 1990).

de Pury, A., 'Erwägungen zu einem vorexilischen Stämmejahwismus: Hos 12 und die Auseinandersetzung um die Identität Israels und seines Gottes', *Ein Gott allein* (eds. W. Dietrich and M. Klopfenstein), pp. 413-39.

de Vaux, R., 'On the Right and Wrong Uses of Archaeology', *Near Eastern Archaeology in the Twentieth Century* (ed. J. Sanders; Garden City, NY: Doubleday, 1970), pp. 64-80

—*The Early History of Israel* (trans. D. Smith; Philadelphia: Westminster Press, 1978).

Dever, W., 'Ancient Israelite Religion: How to Reconcile the Differing Textual and Artifactual Portraits?', *Ein Gott allein* (eds. W. Dietrich and M. Klopfenstein), pp. 105-25.

—'Archaeological Data on the Israelite Settlement: A Review of Two Recent Works', *BASOR* 284 (1991), pp. 77-90.

—'Archaeology, Material Culture and the Early Monarchical Period in Israel', *The Fabric of History* (ed. D. Edelman), pp. 103-15.

—'Asherah, Consort of Yahweh? New Evidence from Kuntillet 'Ajrûd', *BASOR* 255 (1984), pp. 21-37.

—'How to Tell a Canaanite from an Israelite', *Rise of Ancient Israel* (ed. H. Shanks), pp. 26-60, 79-85.

—'Iron Age Epigraphic Material from the Area of Khirbet el-Kôm', *HUCA* 40-41 (1969–1970), pp. 139-204.

—'Israel, History of (Archaeology and the Conquest)', *ABD*, III, pp. 545-58.

—'Material Remains and the Cult in Ancient Israel: An Essay in Archaeological Systematics', *The Word of the Lord Shall Go Forth: Essays in Honor of David Noel Freedman in Celebration of His Sixtieth Birthday* (eds. C. Meyers and M. O'Connor; Winona Lake, IN: Eisenbrauns, 1983), pp. 571-87.

—'Recent Archaeological Confirmation of the Cult of Asherah in Ancient Israel', *Hebrew Studies* 23 (1982), pp. 37-44.

—*Recent Archaeological Discoveries and Biblical Research* (Seattle: University of Washington Press, 1990).

—'The Contribution of Archaeology to the Study of Canaanite and Early Israelite Religion', *Ancient Israelite Religion* (eds. P. Miller, P. Hanson and D. McBride), pp. 209-47.

—'What Remains of the House That Albright Built?', *BA* 56 (1993), pp. 25-35.

Dietrich, W., 'Der Eine Gott als Symbol politischen Widerstands: Religion und Politik im Juda des 7. Jahrhunderts', *Ein Gott allein* (eds. W. Dietrich and M. Klopfenstein), pp. 463-90.

—'Uber Werden und Wesen des biblischen Monotheismus: Religionsgeschichtliche und theologische Perspektiven', *Ein Gott allein* (eds. W. Dietrich and M. Klopfenstein), pp. 13-30.

Dietrich, W., and M. Klopfenstein (eds.), *Ein Gott allein? JHWH-Verehrung und biblischer Monotheismus im Kontext der israelitischen und altorientalischen Religionsgeschichte* (OBO, 139; Göttingen: Vandenhoeck & Ruprecht, 1994).

Dijkstra, M., 'Is Balaam Also among the Prophets?', *JBL* 114 (1995), pp. 43-64.

Dion, P., 'Yahweh as Storm-God and Sun-God: The Double Legacy of Egypt and Canaan as Reflected in Psalm 104', *ZAW* 103 (1991), pp. 43-71.

Dobzhansky, T., *Genetics and the Origin of the Species* (Columbia Biological Series, 11; New York: Columbia University Press, 1937).

Dohmen, C., *Das Bilderverbot: Seine Entstehung und seine Entwicklung im Alten Testament* (BBB, 62; Frankfurt: Athenäum, rev. edn, 1987 [1985]).

—'Heisst *semel* "Bild, Statue"?', *ZAW* 96 (1984), pp. 263-66.

Drews, R., *The End of the Bronze Age: Changes in Warfare and the Catastrophe ca. 1200 BC* (Princeton, NJ: Princeton University Press, 1993).

Duchesne-Guillemin, J., *Symbols and Values in Zoroastrianism: Their Survival and Renewal* (Religious Perspectives, 15; New York: Harper & Row, 1966).

Dumas, A., 'The New Attraction of Neo-Paganism: A Political, Cultural and Spiritual Phenomenon or Epiphenomenon' (trans. D. Smith), *Monotheism* (eds. C. Geffré, J.-P. Jossua and M. Lefébure), pp. 81-90.

Duquoc, C., 'Monotheism and Unitary Ideology' (trans. R. Nowell), *Monotheism* (eds. C. Geffré, J.-P. Jossua and M. Lefébure), pp. 59-66.

Dus, J., 'Moses or Joshua? On the Problem of the Founder of the Israelite Religion', *Radical Religion* 2 (1975), pp. 26-41.

Eaton, J., *The Contemplative Face of Old Testament Wisdom in the Context of World Religions* (Philadelphia: Trinity Press, 1989).

Edelman, D.V. (ed.), *The Fabric of History: Text, Artifact and Israel's Past* (JSOTSup, 127; Sheffield: JSOT Press, 1991).

Eisenstadt, S., 'The Axial Age Breakthrough in Ancient Israel', *Axial Age Civilizations* (ed. S. Eisenstadt), pp. 127-34.

—'The Axial Age Breakthroughs—Their Characteristics and Origins', *Axial Age Civilizations* (ed. S. Eisenstadt). pp. 1-25.

Eisenstadt, S. (ed.), *The Origins and Diversity of Axial Age Civilizations* (State University of New York Series in Near Eastern Studies; Albany: State University of New York Press, 1986).

Eldredge, N., *Life Pulse: Episodes from the Story of the Fossil Record* (New York: Facts on File, 1987).

—*Reinventing Darwin: The Great Debate at the High Table of Evolutionary Theory* (New York: John Wiley & Sons, 1995).

—'The Allopatric Model and Phylogeny in Paleozoic Invertebrates', *Evolution* 25 (1971), pp. 156-67.

—*Time Frames: The Rethinking of Darwinian Evolution and the Theory of Punctuated Equilibria* (New York: Simon & Schuster, 1985).

—*Unfinished Synthesis: Biological Hierarchies and Modern Evolutionary Thought* (New York: Oxford University Press, 1985).

Eldredge, N., and J. Cracraft, *Phylogenetic Patterns and the Evolutionary Process: Method and Theory in Comparative Biology* (New York: Columbia University Press, 1980).

Eldredge, N., and S.J. Gould, 'Punctuated Equilibria: An Alternative to Phyletic Gradualism', *Models in Paleobiology* (ed. T.J.M. Schopf; San Francisco: Freeman, Cooper & Co., 1972), pp. 82-115.

—'Punctuated Equilibria: The Tempo and Mode of Evolution Reconsidered', *Paleobiology* 3 (1977), pp. 115-51.

Eldredge, N., and I. Tattersall, *The Myths of Human Evolution* (New York: Columbia University Press, 1982).

Eliade, M., *The Myth of the Eternal Return or, Cosmos and History* (trans. W. Trask; Bollingen Series, 46; repr.; Princeton, NJ: Princeton University Press, 1974 [1954]).

Elkana, Y., 'The Emergence of Second-order Thinking in Classical Greece', *Axial Age Civilizations* (ed. S. Eisenstadt) pp. 40-64.

Ellis, P., *The Yahwist: The Bible's First Theologian* (Notre Dame: Fides, 1968).

Elvin, M., 'Was There a Transcendental Breakthrough in China?', *Axial Age Civilizations* (ed. S. Eisenstadt), pp. 325-59.

Emerton, J.A., 'New Light on Israelite Religion: The Implications of the Inscriptions from Kuntillet 'Ajrûd', *ZAW* 94 (1982), pp. 2-20.

Erman, A., *Die Religion der Agypter* (Berlin: de Gruyter, 1934).

Eslinger, L., and G. Taylor (eds.), *Ascribe to the Lord: Biblical and Other Studies in Memory of Peter C. Craigie* (JSOTSup, 67; Sheffield: JSOT Press, 1988).

Esse, D., 'Review of Israel Finkelstein, The Archaeology of the Israelite Settlement', *BARev* 14.5 (1988), pp. 6-12.

Evans, C., 'Naram-Sin and Jeroboam: The Archetypal Unheilsherrscher in Mesopotamian and Biblical Historiography', *Scripture in Context II* (eds. W. Hallo, J. Moyer and L. Perdue), pp. 97-125.

Fabel, A., 'The Dynamics of the Self-Organizing Universe', *Cross Currents* 37 (1987), pp. 168-77.

Faur, J., 'The Biblical Idea of Idolatry', *JQR* 69 (1978), pp. 1-15.

Fensham, C., 'Widow, Orphan, and the Poor in Ancient Near Eastern Legal Literature', *JNES* 21 (1962), pp. 161-71.

Finkelstein, I., *The Archaeology of the Israelite Settlement* (Jersualem: Israel Exploration Society, 1988).

—'Respondents', *Biblical Archaeology Today* (ed. J. Amitai), pp. 80-83.

—'Searching for Israelite Origins', *BARev* 14.5 (1988), pp. 34-45, 58.

—'The Emergence of the Monarchy in Israel', *JSOT* 44 (1989), pp. 43-74.

—'The Great Transformation: The "Conquest" of the Highlands Frontiers and the Rise of the Territorial States', *The Archaeology of Society in the Holy Land* (ed. T. Levy; New York: Facts on File, 1995), pp. 349-65.

Finkelstein, J., 'Bible and Babel: A Comparative Study of the Hebrew and Babylonian Religious Spirit', *Commentary* 26 (1958), pp. 431-44.

Fishbane, M., *The Garments of Torah: Essays in Biblical Hermeneutics* (Bloomington: University of Indiana Press, 1989).

Flanagan, J., *David's Social Drama: A Hologram of Israel's Early Iron Age* (Social World of Biblical Antiquity, 7; Sheffield: Almond Press, 1988).

Flannery, K., 'The Cultural Evolution of Civilizations', *Annual Review of Ecology and Systematics* 3 (1972), pp. 399-426.

Fohrer, G., *History of Israelite Religion* (trans. D. Green; Nashville: Abingdon Press, 1972).

Ford, L., *The Lure of God: A Biblical Background for Process Theism* (Philadelphia: Fortress Press, 1978).

Fowden, G., *Empire to Commonwealth: Consequences of Monotheism in Late Antiquity* (Princeton, NJ: Princeton University Press, 1993).

Fowler, J., *Theophoric Personal Names in Ancient Hebrew: A Comparative Study* (JSOTSup, 49; Sheffield: JSOT Press, 1988).

Frank, H.T., *Bible, Archaeology, and Faith* (Nashville: Abingdon Press, 1971).

Frankfort, H., 'The Emancipation of Thought from Myth', *Before Philosophy* (ed. H. Frankfort; Baltimore: Penguin Books, 1949), pp. 237-63.

Freedman, D.N., 'Yahweh of Samaria and His Asherah', *BA* 50 (1987), pp. 241-49.

Freedman, D.N., and D.F. Graf (eds.), *Palestine in Transition: The Emergence of Ancient Israel* (Social World of Biblical Antiquity, 2; Sheffield: Almond Press, 1983).

Fretheim, T., *The Suffering of God: An Old Testament Perspective* (Overtures to Biblical Theology, 14; Philadelphia: Fortress Press, 1984).

Freud, S., *Moses and Monotheism* (trans. K. Jones; repr.; New York: Vintage Books, 1967 [1939]).

Frick, F., *The City in Ancient Israel* (SBLDS, 36; Missoula, MT: Scholars Press, 1977).

—*The Formation of the State in Ancient Israel* (Social World of Biblical Antiquity, 4; Sheffield: Almond Press, 1985).

Friis, H., *Die Bedingungen für die Errichtung des davidischen Reiches in Israel und seiner Umwelt* (Heidelberg: Diebner und Nauerth, 1986).

Fritz, V., 'Conquest or Settlement? The Early Iron Age in Palestine', *BA* 50 (1987), pp. 84-100.

—'The Israelite "Conquest" in Light of Recent Excavations at Khirbet el-Mishnah', *BASOR* 241 (1981), pp. 61-73.

Gadd, C.J., 'Inscribed prisms of Sargon II from Nimrud', *Iraq* 16 (1954), p. 179.

Gal, Z., 'The Late Bronze Age in Galilee: A Reassessment', *BASOR* 272 (1988), pp. 79-84.

Garbini, G., 'Gli Ebrei in Palestina: Yahvismo e religione fenecia', *Forme di Contatto e Processi di Trasformazione nelle Societá Antiche* (Rome: Ecole Française de Rome, 1983), pp. 899-910.

—*History and Ideology in Ancient Israel* (trans. J. Bowden; New York: Crossroad, 1988).

Gardiner, A., *Egypt of the Pharaohs* (New York: Oxford University Press, 1966).

Geffré, C., J.-P. Jossua and M. Lefébure (eds.), *Monotheism* (Concilium, 177; Edinburgh: T. & T. Clark, 1985).

Gese, H., 'The Idea of History in the Ancient Near East and the Old Testament', *The Bultmann School of Biblical Interpretation: New Directions?* (ed. R. Funk; New York: Harper & Row, 1965), pp. 49-64.

Glock, A., 'Early Israel as the Kingdom of Yahweh: The Influence of Archaeological Evidence on the Reconstruction of Religion in Early Israel', *CTM* 41 (1970), pp. 558-605.

Gnoli, G., *Zoroaster's Time and Homeland* (Naples: Instituto Universitario Orientale, 1979).

Gnuse, R., 'But Who is the Thief?', *Blueprint for Social Justice* 36.4 (1982), pp. 1-7.

—'Contemporary Evolutionary Theory as a New Heuristic Model for the Socio-scientific Method in Biblical Studies', *Zygon* 25 (1990), pp. 405-431.

—*Heilsgeschichte as a Model for Biblical Theology: The Debate Concerning the Uniqueness and Significance of Israel's Worldview* (College Theology Society Studies in Religion, 4; Lanham: University Press of America, 1989).

—'Holy History in the Hebrew Scriptures and the Ancient World', *BTB* 17 (1987), pp. 127-36.

—'Israelite Settlement of Canaan: A Peaceful Internal Process', *BTB* 21 (1991), pp. 56-66, 109-17.

—'Jubilee Legislation in Leviticus 25: Ancient Israel's Social Reform', *BTB* 15 (1985), pp. 43-48.

—'New Directions in Biblical Theology: The Impact of Contemporary Scholarship in the Hebrew Bible', *JAAR*, 62 (1994), pp. 893-918.

—'Reassessing Israel's Intellectual Relationship to the Ancient World: Biblical Foundations for Authority and Theology', *Raising the Torch of Good News: Catholic Authority and Dialogue with the World* (ed. B. Prusak; Annual Publication of the College Theology Society, 32 (1986); Lanham: University Press of America, 1988), pp. 147-63.

—*The Authority of the Bible: Theories of Inspiration, Revelation, and the Canon of the Bible* (New York: Paulist Press, 1985).

—*The Dream Theophany of Samuel* (Lanham: University Press of America, 1984).

—*The Jewish Roots of Christian Faith: An Introduction to the Old Testament* (New Orleans: Loyola University Press, 1983).

—*You Shall Not Steal: Community and Property in the Biblical Tradition* (Maryknoll: Orbis Books, 1985).

Goedicke, H., and J.J.M. Roberts (eds.), *Unity and Diversity: Essays in the History, Literature, and Religion of the Ancient Near East* (Baltimore: The Johns Hopkins University Press, 1975).

Goldschmidt, R., *The Material Basis of Evolution* (New Haven: Yale University Press 1940).

Gonen, R., 'The Late Bronze Age', *The Archaeology of Ancient Israel* (ed. A. Ben-Tor; trans. R. Greenberg; New Haven: Yale University Press, 1992), pp. 211-57.

—'Urban Canaan in the Late Bronze Age', *BASOR* 253 (1984), pp. 61-73.

Gottwald, N., 'Domain Assumptions and Societal Models in the Study of Pre-Monarchic Israel', *Congress Volume (Edinburgh, 1974)* (VTSup, 28; Leiden: Brill, 1975), pp. 89-100.

—'Early Israel and the Canaanite Socio-Economic System', *Palestine in Transition* (eds. D. Freedman and D. Graf), pp. 25-37

—'Israel, Social and Economic Development', *IDBSup*, pp. 465-68.

—'Nomadism', *IDBSup*, pp. 629-31.

—'Recent Studies of the Social World of Premonarchic Israel', *Currents in Research: Biblical Studies* 1 (1993), pp. 163-89.

—'Responses', *Rise of Ancient Israel* (ed. H. Shanks), pp. 70-75.

—'Sociology', *ABD*, VI, pp. 79-89.

—*The Hebrew Bible: A Socio-Literary Introduction* (Philadelphia: Fortress Press, 1985).

—'The Hypothesis of the Revolutionary Origins of Ancient Israel: A Response to A.J. Hauser and T.L. Thompson', *JSOT* 7 (1978), pp. 37-52.

—'The Israelite Settlement as a Social Revolutionary Movement', *Biblical Archaeology Today* (ed. J. Amitai), pp. 34-46.

—*The Tribes of Yahweh: A Sociology of the Religion of Liberated Israel 1250–1050 BCE* (Maryknoll: Orbis Books, 1979).

—'Two Models for the Origins of Ancient Israel: Social Revolution or Frontier Development', *Quest for the Kingdom of God: Studies in Honor of George E. Mendenhall* (eds. H. Huffmon, F. Spand A. Green; Winona Lake, IN: Eisenbrauns, 1983), pp. 5-24.

—'Were the Early Israelites Pastoral Nomads?', *Rhetorical Criticism: Essays in Honor of James Muilenburg* (eds. J. Jackson and M. Kessler; PTMS, 1; Pittsburg: Pickwick Press, 1974), pp. 223-55.

—'Were the Early Israelites Pastoral Nomads?', *BARev* 4.2 (1978), pp. 2-7.

Gottwald, N. (ed.), *The Bible and Liberation: Political and Social Hermeneutics* (Maryknoll: Orbis Books, 1983).

Gould, S.J., 'Darwinism and the Expansion of Evolutionary Theory', *Science* 216 (1982), pp. 380-87.

—*Ever Since Darwin: Reflections in Natural History* (New York: Norton, 1977).

—*Hen's Teeth and Horse's Toes: Further Reflections in Natural History* (New York: Norton, 1983).

—'Is a New and General Theory of Evolution Emerging?', *Paleobiology* 6 (1980), pp. 119-30.

—*Ontogeny and Phylogeny* (Cambridge, MA: Belknap, 1977).

—*The Flamingo's Smile: Reflections in Natural History* (New York: Norton, 1985).

—'The Meaning of Punctuated Equilibrium and its Role in Validating a Hierarchical Approach to Macroevolution', *Perspectives on Evolution* (ed. R. Milkman; Sunderland: Sinauer, 1982), pp. 83-104.

—*The Panda's Thumb: More Reflections in Natural History* (New York: Norton, 1980).

Gould, S.J., and N. Eldredge, 'Punctuated Equilibrium Comes of Age', *Nature* 366 (1993), pp. 223-27.

—'Punctuated Equilibrium Prevails', *Nature* 332 (1981), pp. 211-12.

Gowan, D., *Ezekiel* (Knox Preaching Guides; Atlanta: John Knox, 1985).

Graham, W., *Beyond the Written Word: Oral Aspects of Scripture in the History of Religion* (Cambridge: Cambridge University Press, 1987).

Gray, J., 'Israel in the Song of Deborah', *Ascribe to the Lord* (eds. L. Eslinger and G. Taylor), pp. 421-55.

Green, A., *The Role of Human Sacrifice in the Ancient Near East* (ASORDS, 1; Missoula, MT: Scholars Press, 1977).

Greenberg, R., 'New Light on the Early Iron Age at Tel Beit Mirsim', *BASOR* 265 (1987), pp. 55-80.

Gutting, G. (ed.), *Paradigms and Revolutions: Appraisals and Applications of Thomas Kuhn's Philosophy of Science* (Notre Dame: University of Notre Dame Press, 1980).

Haag, H. (ed.), *Gott, der Einzige: Zur Entstehung des Monotheismus im Israel* (Quaestiones disputatae, 104; Freiburg: Herder, 1985).

Hadley, J., 'Some Drawings and Inscriptions on Two Pithoi from Kuntillet 'Ajrûd', *VT* 37 (1987), pp. 180-213.

—'The Khirbet el-Qôm Inscription', *VT* 37 (1987), pp. 39-49.

—'Yahweh and "His Asherah": Archaeological and Textual Evidence for the Cult of the Goddess', *Ein Gott allein* (eds. W. Dietrich and M. Klopfenstein), pp. 235-68.

Halligan, J., 'The Role of the Peasant in the Amarna Period', *Palestine in Transition* (eds. D. Freedman and D. Graf), pp. 15-24.

Hallo, W., J. Moyer and L. Perdue (eds.), *Scripture in Context. II. More Essays on the Comparative Method* (Winona Lake, IN: Eisenbrauns, 1983).

Halpern, B., ' "Brisker Pipes than Poetry": The Development of Israelite Monotheism', *Judaic Perspectives on Ancient Israel* (eds. J. Neusner, B. Levine and E. Frerichs; Philadelphia: Fortress Press, 1987), pp. 77-115.

—'Doctrine by Misadventure: Between the Israelite Source and the Biblical Historian',

The Poet and the Historian: Essays in Literary and Historical Biblical Criticism (ed. R. Friedman; Harvard Semitic Studies, 26; Chico, CA: Scholars Press, 1983), pp. 41-73.

—'Erasing History—The Minimalist Assault on Ancient Israel', *Bible Review* 11.6 (1995), pp. 26-35, 47.

—'Settlement of Canaan', *ABD*, V, pp. 1120-43.

—*The Emergence of Israel in Canaan* (SBLMS, 29; Chico, CA: Scholars Press, 1983).

—'The Exodus from Egypt: Myth or Reality?', *The Rise of Ancient Israel* (ed. H. Shanks), pp. 86-117.

Hammershaimb, E., 'On the Ethics of the Old Testament Prophets', *Congress Volume (Oxford, 1959)* (VTSup, 7; Leiden: Brill, 1960), pp. 75-101.

Handy, L., 'Hezekiah's Unlikely Reform', *ZAW* 100 (1988), pp. 111-15.

Hanson, P., 'Jewish Apocalyptic against its Near Eastern Environment', *RB* 78 (1971), pp. 31-58.

—*The People Called: The Growth of Community in the Bible* (New York: Harper & Row, 1986).

Haran, M., *Temples and Temple-Service in Ancient Israel* (Oxford: Clarendon Press, 1978).

—'The Divine Presence in the Israelite Cult and the Cultic Institutions', *Bib* 50 (1969), pp. 251-67.

Hartmann, B., 'Monotheismus in Mesopotamien?', *Monotheismus* (ed. O. Keel), pp. 50-81.

Hartshorne, C., *Creative Synthesis and Philosophic Method* (La Salle: Open Court, 1970).

—*Omnipotence and other Theological Mistakes* (Albany: State University of New York Press, 1984).

—*Reality as Social Process: Studies in Metaphysics and Religion* (Boston: Beacon, 1953).

—*The Divine Relativity: A Social Concept of God* (New Haven: Yale University Press, 1948).

Hauser, A., 'Israel's Conquest of Palestine: Peasants' Rebellion?', *JSOT* 7 (1978), pp. 2-19.

—'The Revolutionary Origins of Ancient Israel: A Response to Gottwald (JSOT 7 [1978] 37-52)', *JSOT* 8 (1978), pp. 46-49.

Hayes, J., *Introduction to the Bible* (Philadelphia: Westminster Press, 1971).

Heesterman, J.C., 'Ritual, Revelation, and Axial Age', *Axial Age Civilizations* (ed. S. Eisenstadt), pp. 393-406.

Hehn, J., *Die biblische und die babylonische Gottesidee* (Leipzig: Hinrichs, 1913).

Heider, G., *The Cult of Molek: A Reassessment* (JSOTSup, 43; Sheffield: JSOT Press, 1985).

Hendel, R., 'The Social Origins of the Aniconic Tradition in Early Israel', *CBQ* 50 (1988), pp. 365-82.

—'Worldmaking in Ancient Israel', *JSOT* 56 (1992), pp. 3-18.

Hentschel, G., 'Elija und der Kult des Baal', *Gott, der Einzige* (ed. H. Haag), pp. 54-90.

Herbert, A.S., *Isaiah 40–66* (Cambridge Bible Commentary; Cambridge: Cambridge University Press, 1975).

Herrmann, S., *A History of Israel in Old Testament Times* (trans. J. Bowden; Philadelphia: Fortress Press, 1975).

—'Basic Factors of Israelite Settlement in Canaan', *Biblical Archaeology Today* (ed. J. Amitai), pp. 47-53.

Heschel, A., *The Prophets* (2 vols.; New York: Harper & Row, 1962).

Hestrin, R., 'The Lachish Ewer and the 'Asherah', *IEJ* 37 (1987), pp. 212-23.

Hodgson, M., *The Venture of Islam: Conscience and History in a World Civilization* (3 vols.; Chicago: University of Chicago Press, 1974).

Höffken, P., 'Eine Bemerkung zum religionsgeschichtlichen Hintergrund von Dtr. 6,4', *BZ* 28 (1984), pp. 88-93.

Hoffman, M., *Egypt before the Pharaohs: The Prehistoric Foundations of Egyptian Civilization* (New York: Knopf, 1979).

Holladay, J., 'Religion in Judah and Israel under the Monarchy', *Ancient Israelite Religion* (eds. P. Miller, P. Hanson and D. McBride), pp. 249-99.

Holladay, W., *Long Ago God Spoke: How Christians May Hear the Old Testament Today* (Minneapolis: Fortress Press, 1995).

Holt, E.K., *Prophesying the Past: The Use of Israel's History in the Book of Hosea* (JSOTSup, 194; Sheffield: Sheffield Academic Press, 1995).

Hopkins, D., 'Life on the Land: The Subsistence Struggles of Early Israel', *BA* 50 (1987), pp. 178-91.

—*The Highlands of Canaan: Agricultural Life in the Early Iron Age* (Social World of Biblical Antiquity, 3; Sheffield: Almond Press, 1985).

Hornung, E., *Conceptions of God in Ancient Egypt: The One and the Many* (trans. J. Baines; Ithaca, NY: Cornell University Press, 1982).

—'Monotheismus in pharaonischen Agypten', *Monotheismus* (ed. O. Keel), pp. 84-97.

Hossfeld, F.-L., 'Einheit und Einzigkeit Gottes im frühen Jahwismus', *Im Gespräch mit dem dreieinen Gott: Elemente einer trinitarischen Theologie* (eds. M. Böhnke and H. Heinz; Düsseldorf: Patmos, 1985), pp. 57-74.

Houston, W., *Purity and Monotheism: Clean and Unclean Animals in Biblical Law* (JSOTSup, 140; Sheffield: JSOT Press, 1993).

Humphreys, W.L., *Crisis and Story: Introduction to the Old Testament* (Palo Alto: Mayfield, 1979).

Hutter, M., 'Das Werden des Monotheismus im alten Israel', *Anfänge der Theologie* (ed. N. Brox; Graz: Styria, 1987), pp. 25-39.

Huxley, J., *Evolution: The Modern Synthesis* (London: Allen & Unwin, 1942).

Jacob, E., *Theology of the Old Testament* (trans. A. Heathcote and P. Allcock; New York: Harper & Row, 1958).

Jacobsen, T., *The Treasures of Darkness: A History of Mesopotamian Religion* (New Haven: Yale University Press, 1976).

Jamieson-Drake, D.W., *Scribes and Schools in Monarchic Judah: A Socio-Archeological Approach* (JSOTSup, 190; Social World of Biblical Antiquity, 9; Sheffield: JSOT Press, 1991).

Jantsch, E., *The Self-Organizing Universe* (New York: Pergamon Press, 1980).

Janzen, G., 'On the Moral Nature of God's Power: Yahweh and the Sea in Job and Deutero-Isaiah', *CBQ* 56 (1994), pp. 458-78.

—'The Old Testament in "Process" Perspective: Proposal for a Way Forward in Biblical Theology', *Magnalia Dei, The Mighty Acts of God: Essays of the Bible and Archaeology in Memory of G. Ernest Wright* (eds. F. Cross, W. Lemke and P. Miller; Garden City, NY: Doubleday, 1976), pp. 480-509.

Jaros, K., 'Zur Inscrift Nr. 3 von Hirbet el-Qôm', *Biblische Notizen* 19 (1982), pp. 31-40.

Jeppesen, K., 'Micah v 13 in the Light of a Recent Archaeological Discovery', *VT* 34 (1984), pp. 462-66.

Jeremias, J., 'Der Begriff "Baal" im Hoseabuch und seine Wirkungsgeschichte', *Ein Gott allein* (eds. W. Dietrich and M. Klopfenstein), pp. 441-62.

Johnson, R., 'The Dazzling Sun Disk: Iconographic Evidence that Amenhotep III Reigned as The Aten Personified', *KMT: A Modern Journal of Ancient Egypt* 2.2 (1991), pp. 14-23, 60-66.

Jüngling, H.-W., 'Der Heilige Israels: Der erste Jesaja zum Thema "Gott"', *Gott, der Einzige* (ed. H. Haag), pp. 91-114.

—' "Was anders ist Gott für den Menschen, wenn nicht sein Vater und seine Mutter?" Zu einer Doppelmetapher der religiösen Sprache', *Ein Gott allein* (eds. W. Dietrich and M. Klopfenstein), pp. 365-86.

Käsemann, E., 'Ministry and Community in the New Testament', *Essays on New Testament Themes* (trans. W.J. Montague; SBT, 41; London: SCM Press, 1964).

Kaufmann, Y., *The Religion of Israel: From its Beginnings to the Babylonian Exile* (trans. and abr. M. Greenberg; New York: Schocken Books, 1972).

Keel, O., 'Gedanken zur Beschäftigung mit Monotheismus', *Monotheismus* (ed. O. Keel), pp. 20-30.

Keel, O. (ed.), *Monotheismus im Alten Israel und seiner Umwelt* (BibB, 14; Fribourg: Schweizerisches Katholisches Bibelwerk, 1980).

—*The Symbolism of the Biblical World: Ancient Near Eastern Iconography and the Book of Psalms* (trans. T. Hallett; New York: Seabury, 1978).

—'Wer zerstörte Sodom?', *TZ* 35 (1979), pp. 110-17.

Keel, O., and C. Uehlinger, *Göttinnen, Götter und Gottessymbole: Neue Erkenntnisse zur Religionsgeschichte Kanaans und Israels aufgrund bislang unerschlossener ikonographischer Quellen* (Quaestiones disputatae, 134; Freiburg: Herder, 1992).

—'Jahwe und die Sonnengottheit von Jerusalem', *Ein Gott allein* (eds. D. Dietrich and M. Klopfenstein), pp. 269-306.

Kelso, J., *The Excavation of Bethel (1934–1960)* (Cambridge, MA: American Schools of Oriental Research, 1968).

Kemp, B., *Ancient Egypt: Anatomy of a Civilization* (New York: Routledge, 1994).

Kempinski, A., 'Israelite Conquest or Settlement? New Light from Tell Masos', *BARev* 2.3 (1976), pp. 25-30.

Kennedy, C., 'Isaiah 57:5-6: Tombs in the Rocks', *BASOR* 275 (1989), pp. 47-52.

Klein, H., 'Der Beweis der Einzigkeit Jahwes bei Deutero-Jesaja', *VT* 35 (1985), pp. 267-73.

Kloos, C., *Yahweh's Combat with the Sea: A Canaanite Tradition in the Religion of Ancient Israel* (Leiden: Brill, 1986).

Klopfenstein, M., 'Auferstehung der Göttin in der spätisraelitischen Weisheit von Prov 1–9?', *Ein Gott allein* (eds. W. Dietrich and M. Klopfenstein), pp. 531-42.

Knauf, E.A., 'From History to Interpretation', *Fabric of History* (ed. D. Edelman), pp. 26-64.

Knierim, R., 'The Task of Old Testament Theology', *HBT* 6 (1984), pp. 25-57.

Koch, K., 'Der Tod der Religion-stifters', *KD* 8 (1962), pp. 100-23.

—'Monotheismus und Angelologie', *Ein Gott allein* (eds. W. Dietrich and M. Klopfenstein), pp. 565-81.

—'Saddaj: Zum Verhältnis zwischen israelitischer Monolatrie und nordwest-semitischem Polytheismus', *VT* 26 (1976), pp. 299-332.

—'Wort und Einheit des Schöpfergottes im Memphis und Jerusalem: Zu Einzigartigkeit Israels', *ZTK* 62 (1965), pp. 251-93.

Kochavi, M., 'The Settlement of Canaan in the Light of Archaeological Surveys', *Biblical Archaeology Today* (ed. J. Amitai), pp. 54-60.

Kolarik, M., 'Creation and Salvation in the Book of Wisdom', *Creation in the Biblical Traditions* (eds. R. Clifford and J. Collins), pp. 97-107.

Krecher, J., and H.P. Müller, 'Vergangenheitsinteresse in Mesopotamien und Israel', *Saeculum* 26 (1975), pp. 13-44.

Kuhn, T., *The Structure of Scientific Revolutions* (Chicago: University of Chicago Press, 2nd edn, 1970 [1962]).

Kulandran, S., *Grace: A Comparative Study of the Doctrine in Christianity and Hinduism* (London: Lutterworth, 1964).

Kulke, H., 'The Historical Background of India's Axial Age', *Axial Age Civilizations* (ed. S. Eisenstadt), pp. 374-92.

Kuntz, K., *The People of Ancient Israel* (New York: Harper & Row, 1974).

Lagrange, M.-J., *Etudes sur le religions semitiques* (EBib; Paris: Lecoffre, 1903).

Lambert, W.G., 'Destiny and Divine Intervention in Babylon and Israel', *OTS* 17 (1972), pp. 65-72.

—'History and the Gods: A Review Article', *Or* 39 (1970), pp. 170-77.

—'The Historical Development of theMesopotamian Pantheon: A Study in Sophisticated Polytheism', *Unity and Diversity* (eds. H. Goedicke and J.J.M. Roberts), pp. 191-99.

Lang, A., *The Making of Religion* (New York: Longmans, Green & Co., 1898)

Lang, B., 'Afterlife: Ancient Israel's Changing Vision of the World beyond', *Bible Review* 4.2 (1988), pp. 12-23.

Lang, B. (ed.), *Der einzige Gott: Die Geburt des biblischen Monotheismus* (Munich: Kösel, 1981).

—'Der monarchische Monotheismus und die Konstellation zweier Götter im Frühjudentum: Ein neuer Versuch über Menschensohn, Sophia und Christologie', *Ein Gott allein* (eds. W. Dietrich and M. Klopfenstein), pp. 559-64.

—'Der vergöttliche König im polytheistischen Israel', *Mensch werdung Gottes— Vergöttlichung von Menschen* (ed. D. Zeller; NTOA, 7 [1988]), pp. 37-59.

—'George Orwell im gelobten Land: Das Buch Deuteronium und der Geist kirchlicher Kontrolle', *Kirche und Visitation* (eds. E. Zeeden and P. Lang; Stuttgart: Klett-Cotta, 1984), pp. 21-35.

—'Neues über die Geschichte des Monotheismus', *TQ* 163 (1983), pp. 54-58.

—'No God but Yahweh! The Origin and Character of Biblical Monotheism' (trans. J.G. Cumming), *Monotheism* (eds. C. Geffré, J.-P. Jossua and M. Lefébure), pp. 41-49.

—'Segregation and Intolerance', *What the Bible Really Says* (eds. M. Smith and J. Hoffman), pp. 115-35.

—'The Yahweh-Alone Movement and the Making of Jewish Monotheism', *Monotheism and the Prophetic Minority: An Essay in Biblical History and Sociology* (Social World of Biblical Antiquity, 1; Sheffield: Almond Press, 1983), pp. 13-59.

—'Vor einer Wende im Verständnis des israelitischen Gottesglaubens?', *TQ* 160 (1980), pp. 53-60.

—*Wisdom and the Book of Proverbs* (New York: Pilgrim, 1986).

—'Zur Entstehung des biblischen Monotheism', *TQ* 166 (1985), pp. 135-42.

Lapp, P., 'The Conquest of Palestine in the Light of Archaeology', *CTM* 38 (1967), pp. 283-300.

Laszlo, E., *Evolution: The Grand Synthesis* (Boston: New Science Library, 1987).

Lemaire, A., 'Déesses et dieux de Syrie-Palestine d'aprés les inscriptions (c. 1000-500 av. n. é.)', *Ein Gott allein* (eds. W. Dietrich and M. Klopfenstein), pp. 127-58.

—'Les inscriptions de Khirbet el-Qôm et l'ashérah de YHWH', *RB* 84 (1977), pp. 595-608.

Lemche, N.P., *Ancient Israel: A New History of Israelite Society* (The Biblical Seminar, 5; Sheffield: JSOT Press, 1988).

—*Early Israel: Anthropological and Historical Studies on the Israelite Society before the Monarchy* (VTSup, 37; Leiden: Brill, 1985).

—'Is it still Possible to Write a History of Ancient Israel?', *SJOT* 8 (1994), pp. 165-90.

—'Israel, History of (Premonarchic Period)', *ABD*, III, pp. 526-45.

—'Kann von einer "israelitischen Religion" noch weiterhin die Rede sein? Perspektiven eines Historikers', *Ein Gott allein* (eds. W. Dietrich and M. Klopfenstein), pp. 59-75.

—*The Canaanites and their Land: The Tradition of the Canaanites* (JSOTSup, 110; Sheffield: JSOT Press, 1991).

—'The Development of the Israelite Religion in the Light of Recent Studies on the Early History of Israel', *Congress Volume (Leuven, 1989)* (VTSup, 43; Leiden: Brill, 1991), pp. 97-115

—'The Old Testament—a Hellenistic Book?', *SJOT* 7 (1993), pp. 163-93.

Lenski, G., 'History and Social Change', *American Journal of Sociology* 82 (1976), pp. 548-64.

—'Review of N.K. Gottwald, The Tribes of Yahweh', *RelSRev* 6 (1978), pp. 275-78.

Lenski, G., and J. Lenski, *Human Societies: An Introduction to Macrosociology* (New York: McGraw–Hill, 3rd edn, 1978).

Levenson, J., *Creation and the Persistence of Evil: The Jewish Drama of Divine Omnipotence* (San Francisco: HarperCollins, 1988).

—*The Death and Resurrection of the Beloved Son: The Transformation of Child Sacrifice in Judaism and Christianity* (New Haven: Yale University Press, 1993).

Levine, B., 'The Balaam Inscription from Deir 'Alla: Historical Aspects', *Biblical Archaeology Today* (ed. J. Amitai), pp. 326-39.

Lewis, D.M., 'The Persepolis Tablets: Speech, Seal and Script', *Literacy and Power in the Ancient World* (eds. A. Bowman and G. Woolf; Cambridge: Cambridge University Press, 1994), pp. 17-32.

Licht, J., 'Biblical Historicism', *History, Historiography and Interpretation: Studies in Biblical and Cuneiform Literatures* (eds. H. Tadmor and M. Weinfeld; Jerusalem: Magnus, 1984), pp. 107-120.

Lichtheim, M., *Ancient Egyptian Literature* (3 vols.; Berkeley: University of California Press, 1973, 1976, 1980).

Lind, M., 'Monotheism, Power, and Justice: A Study in Isaiah 40–55', *CBQ* 46 (1984), pp. 432-46.

Lindblom, J., *Prophecy in Ancient Israel* (Phildelphia: Fortress Press, 1973).

Lipinski, E., 'The Syro-Palestinian Iconography of Woman and Goddess', *IEJ* 36 (1986), pp. 87-96.

Lohfink, N., 'Das Alte Testament und sein Monotheismus', *Der eine Gott und der dreieine Gott: Das Gottes Verständnis bei Christian, Juden, und Muslimen* (ed. K. Rahner; Schriftenreihe der Katholischen Akademie der Erzdiözese Freiburg; Munich: Schnell & Steiner, 1983), pp. 28-47.

—'Gott und die Götter im Alten Testament', *Theologische Akademie* 6 (1969), pp. 50-71.

—'The Cult Reform of Josiah of Judah: 2 Kings 22–23 as a Source for the History of the Israelite Religion', *Ancient Israelite Religion* (eds. P. Miller, P. Hanson and D. McBride), pp. 459-75.

—*Theology of the Pentateuch: Themes of the Priestly Narrative and Deuteronomy* (trans. L. Maloney; Edinburgh: T. & T. Clark, 1994).

—'Zur Geschichte der Diskussion über den Monotheismus im Alten Israel', *Gott, der Einzige* (ed. H. Haag), pp. 9-25.

London, G., 'A Comparison of Two Contemporaneous Lifestyles of the Late Second Millennium BC', *BASOR* 273 (1989), pp. 37-55.

Loretz, O., 'Das "Ahnen- und Götterstatuen-Verbot" im Dekalog und die Einzigkeit Jahwes: Zum Begriff des Göttlichen in altorientalischen und alttestamentlichen Quellen', *Ein Gott allein* (eds. W. Dietrich and M. Klopfenstein), pp. 491-527.

Luckert, K., *Egyptian Light and Hebrew Fire: Theological and Philosophical Roots of Christendom in Evolutionary Perspective* (Albany: State University of New York Press, 1991).

McCarter, K., 'Aspects of the Religion of the Israelite Monarchy: Biblical and Empirical Data', *Ancient Israelite Religion* (eds. P. Miller, P. Hanson and D. McBride), pp. 137-55.

—'The Origins of Israelite Religion', *Rise of Ancient Israel* (ed. H. Shanks), pp. 118-41.

Machinist, P., 'The Question of Distinctiveness in Ancient Israel', *A Highway from Egypt to Assyria: Studies in Ancient Near Eastern History and Historiography Presented to Hayim Tadmor* (eds. I. Eph'al and M. Cogan; Jerusalem: Magnes, 1990), pp. 420-42.

McKeating, H., *Amos, Hosea, Micah* (Cambridge Bible Commentary; Cambridge: Cambridge University Press, 1971).

McKenzie, J., *The World of the Judges* (Englewood Cliffs, NJ: Prenctice–Hall, 1966).

Macnicol, N., *Indian Theism: From the Vedic to the Muhammadan Period* (Delhi: Munshiram Manoharlal, 1915).

Malamat, A., 'Doctrines of Causality in Hittite and Biblical Historiography', *VT* 5 (1955), pp. 1-12.

—'How Inferior Israelite Forces Conquered Fortified Canaanite Cities', *BARev* 8.2 (1982), pp. 25-35.

—'Israelite Conduct of War in the Conquest of Canaan', *Symposia* (ed. F. Cross), pp. 35-55.

Marfoe, L., 'The Integrative Transformation: Patterns of Sociopolitical Organization in Southern Syria', *BASOR* 234 (1979), pp. 1-42.

Margalit, B., 'Some Observations on the Inscription from Khirbet el-Qôm', *VT*, 39 (1989), pp. 371-78.

—'The Meaning and Significance of Asherah', *VT* 40 (1990), pp. 264-97.

Mayr, E., *Animal Species and Evolution* (Cambridge, MA: Harvard University Press, 1963).

—*Systematics and the Origin of the Species* (Columbia Biological Series, 12; New York: Columbia University Press, 1942).

Mayr, E., and W. Provine, (eds.), *The Evolutionary Synthesis: Perspectives in the Unification of Biology* (Cambridge, MA: Harvard University Press, 1980).

Mazar, A., *Archaeology of the Land of the Bible 10,000–586 BCE* (Garden City, NY: Doubleday, 1990).

—'The Iron Age I', *The Archaeology of Ancient Israel* (ed. A. Ben-Tor), pp. 258-301.

—'The Israelite Settlement in Canaan in the Light of Archaeological Excavations', *Biblical Archaeology Today* (ed. J. Amitai), pp. 61-71.

Mazar, B., *The Early Biblical Period: Historical Studies* (Jerusalem: Israel Exploration Society, 1986).

Mendenhall, G., 'Ancient Israel's Hyphenated History', *Palestine in Transition* (eds. D. Freedman and D. Graf), pp. 91-103.

—'Between Theology and Archaeology', *JSOT* 7 (1978), pp. 28-34.

—' "Change and Decay in All around I See": Conquest, Covenant and the Tenth Generation', *BA* 39 (1976), pp. 152-57.

—'The Hebrew Conquest of Palestine', *BA* 25 (1962), pp. 66-87.

—*The Tenth Generation: The Origins of the Biblical Tradition* (Baltimore: The Johns Hopkins University Press, 1973).

Meshel, Z., 'Did Yahweh Have a Consort?: The New Religious Inscriptions from the Sinai', *BARev* 5.2 (1979), pp. 24-35.

—'Kuntillet 'Ajrûd', *ABD* IV, pp. 103-109.

—'Two Aspects in the Excavation of Kuntillet 'Agrud', *Ein Gott allein* (eds. W. Dietrich and M. Klopfenstein), pp. 99-104.

Meslin, M., 'The Anthropological Function of Monotheism' (trans. R. Murphy), *Monotheism* (eds. C. Geffré, J.-P. Jossua and M. Lefébure), pp. 28-37.

Mettinger, T., 'Aniconism—a West Semitic Context for the Israelite Phenomenon', *Ein Gott allein* (eds. W. Dietrich and M. Klopfenstein), pp. 159-78.

—*In Search of God: The Meaning and Message of the Everlasting Names* (trans. F. Cryer; Philadelphia: Fortress Press, 1988).

Meyers, C., *Discovering Eve: Ancient Israelite Women in Context* (New York: Oxford University Press, 1988).

Michaels, A., 'Monotheismus und Fundamentalismus: Eine These und ihre Gegenthese', *Ein Gott allein* (eds. W. Dietrich and M. Klopfenstein), pp. 51-57.

Mihalik, I., 'Some Thoughts on the Name Israel', *Theological Soundings: Notre Dame Seminary Jubilee Studies 1923–1973* (ed. I. Mihalik; New Orleans: Notre Dame Seminary, 1973), pp. 11-19.

Miller, P., 'The Absence of the Goddess in Israelite Religion', *HAR* 10 (1986), pp. 239-48.

—'Israelite Religion', *The Hebrew Bible and its Modern Interpreters* (eds. D. Knight and G. Tucker; The Bible and its Modern Interpreters; Chico, CA: Scholars Press, 1985), pp. 201-237.

Miller, P., P. Hanson and D. McBride (eds.), *Ancient Israelite Wisdom: Essays in Honor of Frank Moore Cross* (Phildelphia: Fortress Press, 1987).

Miranda, J., *Marx and the Bible: A Critique of the Philosophy of Oppression* (trans. J. Eagleson; Maryknoll: Orbis Books, 1974).

Moltmann, J., *The Crucified God* (New York: Harper & Row, 1968).

—'The Inviting Unity of the Triune God' (trans. R. Nowell), *Monotheism* (eds. C. Geffré, J.-P. Joshua and M. Lefébure), pp. 50-58.

Morenz, S., *Egyptian Religion* (trans. A. Keep; Ithaca, NY: Cornell University Press, 1973).

Moriarity, F., 'Word as Power in the Ancient Near East', *A Light unto My Path: Old Testament Studies in Honor of Jacob M. Myers* (eds. H. Bream, R. Heim and C. Moore; Philadelphia: Temple University Press, 1994), pp. 345-62.

Moyer, J., 'Hittite and Israelite Cultic Practices: A Selected Comparison', *Scripture in Context II* (eds. W. Hallo, J. Moyer and L. Perdue), pp. 19-38.

Mühlmann, W., 'Das Problem des Urmonotheism', *TLZ* 78 (1953), pp. 705-18.

Müller, H.P., 'Die aramäische Inschrift von Deir 'Alla und die älteren Bileamsprüche', *ZAW* 94 (1982), pp. 214-44.

—'Gott und die Götter in den Anfängen der biblischen Religion: Zur Vorgeschichte des Monotheismus', *Monotheismus* (ed. O. Keel), pp. 100-142.

Mullen, T., *The Assembly of the Gods: The Divine Council in Canaanite and Early Hebrew Literature* (HSM, 24; Chico, CA: Scholars Press, 1980).

Nakhai, B.A., 'What's a Bamah? How Sacred Space Functioned in Ancient Israel', *BARev* 20.3 (1994), pp. 18-29, 77-78.

Nash, R., (ed.), *Process Theology* (Grand Rapids: Baker, 1987).

Nicholson, E., *God and His People: Covenant and Theology in the Old Testament* (Oxford: Clarendon Press, 1986).

Niehr, H., *Der höchste Gott: Alttestamentlicher JHWH-Glaube im Kontext syrisch-kanaanäischer Religion des 1. Jahrtausends V. Chr.* (BZAW, 190; Berlin: de Gruyter, 1990).

—'JHWH in der Rolle des Baalsamem', *Ein Gott allein* (eds. W. Dietrich and M. Klopfenstein), pp. 307-326.

Nikiprowetsky, V., 'Ethical Monotheism', *Daedalus* 104.2 (1975), pp. 68-89.

North, R., 'Yahweh's Asherah', *To Touch the Text: Biblical and Related Studies in Honor of Joseph A. Fitzmyer, S.J.* (eds. M. Horgan and P. Kobelski; New York: Crossroad, 1989), pp. 118-37.

Noss, J., and D. Noss, *Man's Religions* (New York: Macmillan, 7th edn, 1984 [1949]).

Noth, M., *A History of Pentateuchal Traditions* (trans. B. Anderson; Englewood Cliffs, NJ: Prentice–Hall, 1972).

—'Grundsätzliches zur geschichtlichen Deutung archäologischer Befunde auf dem Boden Palästinas', *PJ* 37 (1938), pp. 7-22.

—*The History of Israel* (trans. P. Ackroyd; New York: Harper & Brothers, 2nd edn, 1960 [1958]).

Oden, R., 'The Place of Covenant in the Religion of Israel', *Ancient Israelite Religion* (eds. P. Miller, P. Hanson and D. McBride), pp. 429-47.

Ogden, S., *Christ without Myth* (New York: Harper & Row, 1961).

—*On Theology* (San Francisco: Harper & Row, 1986).

—*The Reality of God and Other Essays* (New York: Harper & Row, 1977).

Olyan, S., *Asherah and the Cult of Yahweh in Israel* (SBLMS, 34; Atlanta: Scholars Press, 1988).

Otto, E., *Theologische Ethik des Alten Testaments* (Theologische Wissenschaft, 3.2; Stuttgart: Kohlhammer, 1994).

Ottosson, M., 'The Prophet Elijah's Visit to Zarephath', *Shelter of Elyon* (eds. B. Barrick and B. Spencer), pp. 185-98.

Pardee, D., 'An Evaluation of the Proper Names from Ebla from a West Semitic Perspective: Pantheon Distribution according to Genre', *Eblaite Personal Names and Semitic Name-Giving* (ed. A. Archi; Rome: Missione Archaeologia Italiana in Siria, 1988), pp. 119-51.

Patai, R., *The Hebrew Goddess* (New York: Avon, 1978).

—*The Jewish Mind* (New York: Charles Scribner's Sons, 1977).

Patrick, D., *Old Testament Law* (Atlanta: John Knox, 1985).

Peckham, B., 'Phoenicia and the Religion of Israel: The Epigraphic Evidence', *Ancient Israelite Religion* (eds. P. Miller, P. Hanson and D. McBride), pp. 79-99.

Perdue, L., *The Collapse of History: Reconstructing Old Testament Theology* (Overtures to Biblical Theology; Minneapolis: Augsburg–Fortress, 1994).

Peters, E., *The Creative Advance: An Introduction to Process Philosophy as a Context for Christian Faith* (St Louis: Bethany, 1966).

Petersen, D., 'Israel and Monotheism: The Unfinished Agenda', *Canon, Theology, and Old Testament Interpretation: Essays in Honor of Brevard S. Childs* (eds. G. Tucker, D. Petersen and R. Wilson; Philadelphia: Fortress Press, 1988), pp. 92-107.

Pettazzoni, R., *Der altwissende Gott: Zur Geschichte der Gottesidee* (Frankfurt: Fischer, 1957).

—*Essays on the History of Religions* (trans. H.J. Rose; Studies in the History of Religion, 1; Leiden: Brill, 1967).

—*The All-Knowing God: Researches into Early Religion and Culture* (trans. H.J. Rose; London: Methuen, 1956).

—'The Formation of Monotheism', *Reader in Comparative Religion: An Anthropological Approach* (ed. W. Lessa; Evanston: Row, Peterson & Co., 1958), pp. 40-46.

Pettinato, G., 'Polytheismus und Henotheismus in der Religion von Ebla', *Monotheismus* (ed. O. Keel), pp. 32-48.

Pinnock, C., 'Between Classical and Process Theism', *Process Theology* (ed. R. Nash), pp. 313-27.

Pittenger, N., *Catholic Faith in a Process Perspective* (Maryknoll: Orbis Books, 1981).

—*Process Thought and Christian Faith* (New York: Macmillan, 1968).

—*The Divine Triunity* (Philadelphia: United Church Press, 1977).

Pixley, G., *God's Kingdom: A Guide for Biblical Study* (trans. D. Walsh; Maryknoll: Orbis Books, 1981).

—*On Exodus: A Liberation Perspective* (trans. R. Barr; Maryknoll: Orbis Books, 1987).

Polley, M., *Amos and the Davidic Empire: A Socio-Historical Approach* (New York: Oxford University Press, 1989).

Porter, J.R., 'Old Testament Historiography', *Tradition and Interpretation: Essays by Members of the Society for Old Testament Study* (ed. G. Anderson; Oxford: Clarendon Press, 1979), pp. 125-62.

Pritchard, J., (ed.), *Ancient Near Eastern Texts Relating to the Old Testament* (Princeton, NJ: Princeton University Press, 3rd edn, 1970).

—'Culture and History', *The Bible and Modern Scholarship* (ed. J. Hyatt; Nashville: Abingdon Press, 1956), pp. 313-24.

Provan, I., 'Ideologies, Literary and Critical: Reflections on Recent Writing on the History of Israel', *JBL* 114 (1995), pp. 585-606.

Ptashine, M., 'How Gene Activators Work', *Scientific American* 260.1 (1989), pp. 40-47.

Puech, E., 'L'inscription sur plâtre de Tell Deir 'Alla', *Biblical Archaeology Today* (ed. J. Amitai), pp. 354-65.

Radin, P., *Monotheism among Primitive Peoples* (New York: Bollingen, 1954).

Ramsey, G., *The Quest for the Historical Israel* (Atlanta: John Knox, 1981).

Redford, D., *Akhenaten: The Heretic King* (Princeton, NJ: Princeton University Press, 1984).

—*Egypt, Canaan, and Israel in Ancient Times* (Princeton, NJ: Princeton University Press, 1992).

—'The Monotheism of the Heretic Pharaoh: Precursor of Mosaic Monotheism or Egyptian Anomaly?', *BARev* 13.3 (1987), pp. 16-32.

Rendtorff, R., 'Die Entstehung der israelitischen Religion als relgionsgeschichtliches und theologisches Problem', *TLZ* 88 (1963), pp. 735-46.

Renfrew, C., *Approaches to Social Anthropology* (Cambridge, MA: Harvard University Press, 1987).

—*Before Civilization: The Radiocarbon Revolution and Prehistoric Europe* (New York: Knopf, 1973).

—'Systems Collapse as Social Transformation: Catastrophe and Anastrophe in Early State Societies', *Transformations: Mathematical Approaches to Cultural Change* (eds. C. Renfrew and K. Cooke; New York: Academic Press, 1979), pp. 481-506.

—*The Emergence of Civilization: The Cyclades and the Aegean in the Third Millennium BC* (London: Methuen, 1972).

Reventlow, H.G., 'Die Eigenart des Jahweglaubens als geschichtliches und theologisches Problem', *KD* 20 (1974), pp. 199-217.

Ringgren, H., *Israelite Religion* (trans. D. Green; Philadelphia: Fortress Press, 1966.

Rivkin, E., *A Hidden Revolution: The Pharisees' Search for the Kingdom within* (Nashville: Abingdon Press, 1978).

Roberts, J.J.M., 'Divine Freedom and Cultic Manipulation in Israel and Mesopotamia', *Unity and Diversity* (eds. H. Goedicke and J.J.M. Roberts), pp. 181-90.

—'Myth versus History: Relaying the Comparative Foundations', *CBQ* 38 (1976), pp. 1-13.

Robertson Smith, W., *The Religion of the Semites: The Fundamental Institutions* (New York: Schocken Books, 1972 [1889]).

Romer, J., *Testament: The Bible and History* (New York: Henry Holt, 1988).

Rose, M., *Deuteronomist und Jahwist: Untersuchungen zu den Berührungspunkten beider Literaturwerke* (ATANT, 67; Zürich: Theologisches Verlag, 1981).

—'Yahweh in Israel—Qaus in Edom?', *JSOT* 4 (1977), pp. 28-34.

Rosen, S., 'Finding Evidence of Ancient Nomads', *BARev* 14.5 (1988), pp. 46-53, 58-59.

—'Nomads in Archaeology: A Response to Finkelstein and Perevolotsky', *BASOR* 287 (1992), pp. 75-85.

Rowton, M., 'Enclosed Nomadism', *Journal of the Economical Social History of the Orient* 17 (1974), pp. 1-30.

—'Dimorphic Structure and the Parasocial Element', *JNES* 36 (1977), pp. 181-98.

—'Dimorphic Structure and the Problem of the 'Apiru-'Ibrim', *JNES* 35 (1976), pp. 13-20.

—'Urban Autonomy in a Nomadic Environment', *JNES* 32 (1973), pp. 201-215.

Ruggieri, G., 'God and Power: A Political Function of Monotheism?' (trans. P. Burns), *Monotheism* (eds. C. Geffré, J.-P. Jossua and M. Lefébure), pp. 16-27.

Russell, J.B., *The Devil: Perceptions of Evil from Antiquity to Primitive Christianity* (Ithaca, NY: Cornell University Press, 1977).

Sagan, E., *At the Dawn of Tyranny: The Origins of Individualism, Political Oppression and the State* (New York: Knopf, 1985).

Saggs, H.W.F., *Civilization before Greece and Rome* (New Haven: Yale University Press, 1989).

—*The Encounter with the Divine in Mesopotamia and Israel* (London: Athlone Press, 1978).

—*The Might that was Assyria* (London: Sidgwick & Jackson, 1984).

Sapp, J., *Evolution by Association* (New York: Oxford University Press, 1994).

Scharbert, J., 'Jahwe im frühisraelitischen Recht', *Gott, der Einzige* (ed. H. Haag), pp. 160-83.

Schmid, H., 'Creation, Righteousness, and Salvation: "Creation Theology" as the Broad Horizon of Biblical Theology', *Creation in the Old Testament* (ed. B. Anderson), pp. 102-117.

Schmidt, W., *Das Erste Gebot* (Theologische Existenz Heute, 165; Munich: Chr. Kaiser Verlag, 1969).

—*The Faith of the Old Testament: A History* (trans. J. Sturdy; Philadelphia: Westminster Press, 1983).

Schmidt, Wilhelm, *High Gods in North America* (Oxford: Clarendon Press, 1932).

—*The Origin and Growth of Religion* (London: Methuen & Co., 1931).

—*Primitive Religion* (London: Herder, 1939).

Schniedewind, W., 'History and Interpretation: The Religion of Ahab and Manasseh in the Book of Kings', *CBQ* 55 (1993), pp. 649-61.

Schottroff, W., and W. Stegemann (eds.), *God of the Lowly: Socio-Historical Interpretations of the Bible* (trans. M. O'Connell; Maryknoll: Orbis Books, 1984).

Schroer, S., 'Die personifizierte Sophia im Buch der Weisheit', *Ein Gott allein* (eds. W. Dietrich and M. Klopfenstein), pp. 543-58.

—*In Israel gab es Bilder: Nachrichten von darstellender Kunst im Alten Testament* (OBO, 74; Göttingen: Vandenhoeck & Ruprecht, 1987).

Seow, C., *Myth, Drama, and the Politics of David's Dance* (HSM, 44; Atlanta: Scholars Press, 1989).

Service, E., 'Classical and Modern Theories of the Origins of Government', *Origins of the State: The Anthropology of Political Evolution* (eds. R. Cohen and E. Service; Philadelphia: Institute for the Study of Human Issues, 1978), pp. 21-34.

Shanks, H., 'Defining the Problems: Where We Are in the Debate', *Rise of Ancient Israel* (ed. H. Shanks), pp. 1-25.

—'Frank Moore Cross: An Interview', *Bible Review* 8.4 (1992), pp. 20-33, 61-62; 8.5 (1992), pp. 18-29, 50; 8.6 (1992), pp. 18-31, 58.

Shanks, H. (ed.), *The Rise of Ancient Israel* (Washington: Biblical Archaeology Society, 1992).

Shea, W., 'The Khirbet el-Qôm Tomb Inscription Again', *VT* 40 (1990), pp. 110-16.

Shiloh, Y., 'The Casemate Wall, the Four Room House, and Early Planning in the Israelite City', *BASOR* 268 (1987), pp. 3-16.

Silberman, N.A., 'Who Were the Israelites?', *Archaeology* 45.2 (1992), pp. 22-30.

Simkins, R., *Creator and Creation: Nature in the Worldview of Ancient Israel* (Peabody, MA: Henrickson, 1994).

Simpson, G.G., *Tempo and Mode in Evolution* (New York: Columbia University Press, 1944).

Smart, N., *The World's Religions* (Englewood Cliffs, NJ: Prentice–Hall, 1989).

Smith, M., 'God and Female in the Old Testament: Yahweh and his "Asherah"', *TS* 48 (1987), pp. 333-40.

—*The Early History of God: Yahweh and the Other Deities in Ancient Israel* (San Francisco: Harper & Row, 1990).

—'Yahweh and the Other Deities in Ancient Israel: Observations on Old Problems and Recent Trends', *Ein Gott allein* (eds. W. Dietrich and M. Klopfenstein), pp. 197-234.

Smith, M., 'On the Shape of God and the Humanity of Gentiles', *Religions in Antiquity: Essays in Memory of Erwin Ramsdell Goodenough* (ed. J. Neusner; Leiden: Brill, 1968), pp. 315-26.

—'Religious Parties among the Israelites before 587', *Palestinian Parties and Politics that Shaped the Old Testament* (New York: Columbia University Press, 1971), pp. 15-56.

—'II Isaiah and the Persians', *JAOS* 83 (1963), pp. 415-21.

—'The Common Theology of the Ancient Near East', *JBL* 71 (1952), pp. 135-47.

—'The Image of God: Notes on the Hellenization of Judaism', *BJRL* 40 (1958), pp. 473-512.

—'The Veracity of Ezekiel, the Sins of Manasseh, and Jeremiah 44:18', *ZAW* 87 (1975), pp. 11-16.

Smith, M., and J. Hoffmann (eds.), *What the Bible Really Says* (San Francisco: HarperCollins, 1989).

Snell, D., 'Ancient Israelite and Neo-Assyrian Societies and Economies: A Comparative Approach', *Tablet and the Scroll* (eds. M. Cohen, D. Snell and D. Weisburg), pp. 221-24.

Soggin, A., *A History of Ancient Israel* (trans. J. Bowden; Philadelphia: Westminster Press, 1984).

—*Joshua* (trans. R.A. Wilson; OTL; Philadelphia: Westminster Press, 1972).

—*Judges* (trans. J. Bowden; OTL; Philadelphia: Westminster Press, 1981).

Sperling, D., 'Israel's Religion in the Ancient Near East', *Jewish Spirituality: From the Bible through the Middle Ages* (ed. A. Green; World Spirituality: An Encyclopedic History of the Religious Quest, 13; New York: Crossroad, 1986), pp. 5-31.

Stager, L., 'Respondents', *Biblical Archaeology Today* (ed. J. Amitai), pp. 83-87.

—'The Archaeology of the Family', *BASOR* 260 (1985), pp. 1-35.

Stähli, H.-P., *Solare Elemente im Jahweglauben des Alten Testaments* (OBO, 66; Göttingen: Vandenhoeck & Ruprecht, 1985).

Stanley, S., *Macroevolution: Pattern and Process* (San Francisco: Freeman, 1979).

—*The New Evolutionary Timetable: Fossils, Genes, and the Origin of the Species* (New York: Basic Books, 1981).

Stiebing, W., 'Climate and Collapse: Did the Weather Make Israel's Emergence Possible?', *Bible Review* 10.4 (1994), pp. 18-27, 54.

—*Out of the Desert? Archaeology and the Conquest Narratives* (Buffalo: Prometheus, 1989).

—'The End of the Mycenaean Age', *BA* 43 (1980), pp. 7-21.

Stolz, F., 'Der Monotheismus Israels im Kontext der altorientalischen Religionsgeschichte—Tendenzen neuerer Forschung', *Ein Gott allein* (eds. W. Dietrich and M. Klopfenstein), pp. 33-50.

—'Monotheismus in Israel', *Monotheismus* (ed. O. Keel), pp. 144-89.

—*Strukturen und Figuren im Kult von Jerusalem* (BZAW, 118; Berlin: de Gruyter, 1970).

Strange, J., 'The Idea of Afterlife in Ancient Israel: Some Remarks on the Iconography in Solomon's Temple', *PEQ* 117 (1985), pp. 35-40.

—'The Transition from the Bronze Age to the Iron Age in the Eastern Mediterranean and the Emergence of the Israelite State', *SJOT* 1 (1987), pp. 1-19.

Swanson, G., *The Birth of the Gods: The Origin of Primitive Beliefs* (Ann Arbor: University of Michigan Press, 1960).

Tadmor, H., 'Monarchy and the Elite in Assyria and Babylonia: The Question of Royal Accountability', *Axial Age Civilizations* (ed. S. Eisenstadt), pp. 203-24.

Tambiah, S., 'The Reflexive and Institutional Achievements of Early Buddhism', *Axial Age Civilizations* (ed. S. Eisenstadt), pp. 453-71.

Tattersall, I., *The Human Odyssey: Four Million Years of Human Evolution* (New York: Prentice–Hall, 1993).

Taylor, G., 'The Two Earliest Known Representations of Yahweh', *Ascribe to the Lord* (eds. L. Eslinger and G. Taylor), pp. 557-66.

—'Was Yahweh Worshipped as the Sun?', *BARev* 20.3 (1994), pp. 52-61, 90.

—*Yahweh and the Sun: Biblical and Archaeological Evidence for Sun Worship in Ancient Israel* (JSOTSup, 111; Sheffield: JSOT Press, 1993).

Taylor, J., 'The Asherah, the Menorah and the Sacred Tree', *JSOT* 66 (1995), pp. 29-54.

Teggart, F., *Theory and Processes of History* (repr.; Berkeley, CA: University of California Press, 1960 [1918, 1925]).

Teilhard de Chardin, P., *Man's Place in Nature* (trans. R. Hague; New York: Harper & Row, 1966).

—*The Divine Milieu* (trans. B. Wall; New York: Harper & Row, 1965).

—*The Future of Man* (trans. N. Denny; New York: Harper & Row, 1964).

—*The Phenomenon of Man* (trans. B. Wall; New York: Harper & Row, 1961).

—*Toward the Future* (trans. R. Hague; New York: Harcourt Brace Jovanovich, 1975).

Terrien, S., *The Elusive Presence: Toward a New Biblical Theology* (New York: Harper & Row, 1978).

—*Till the Heart Sings: A Biblical Theology of Manhood and Womanhood* (Philadelphia: Fortress Press, 1985).

Theissen, G., *Biblical Faith: An Evolutionary Approach* (trans. J. Bowden; Philadelphia: Fortress Press, 1985).

Thiel, W., 'Vom revolutionären zum evolutionären Israel? Zu einem neuen Modell der Entstehung Israels', *TLZ* 113 (1988), pp. 401-10.

Thompson, T., 'A Neo-Albrightian School in History and Biblical Scholarship?', *JBL* 114 (1995), pp. 683-98.

—*Early History of the Israelite People* (Studies in the History of the Ancient Near East, 4; Leiden: Brill, 1992).

—'Text, Context and Reference in Israelite Historiography', *Fabric of History* (ed. D. Edelman), pp. 65-92.

—'How Yahweh Became God: Exodus 3 and 6 and the Heart of the Pentateuch', *JSOT* 68 (1995), pp. 57-74.

—'The Background of the Patriarchs: A Reply to William Dever and Malcolm Clark', *JSOT* 9 (1978), pp. 2-43.

—*The Historicity of the Patriarchal Narratives: The Quest for the Historical Abraham* (BZAW, 133; Berlin: de Gruyter, 1974).

—*The Origin Tradition of Ancient Israel. I. The Literary Formation of Genesis and Exodus 1–23* (JSOTSup, 55; Sheffield: JSOT Press, 1987).

Tigay, J., 'Israelite Religion: The Onomastic and Epigraphic Evidence', *Ancient Israelite Religion* (eds. P. Miller, P. Hanson and D. McBride), pp. 157-94.

—*You Shall Have No Other Gods: Israelite Religion in the Light of Hebrew Inscriptions* (Harvard Semitic Studies, 31; Atlanta: Scholars Press, 1986).

Toews, W., *Monarchy and Religious Institutions in Israel under Jeroboam I* (SBLMS, 47; Atlanta: Scholars Press, 1993).

Towner, S., *How God Deals with Evil* (Biblical Perspectives on Current Issues; Philadelphia: Westminster Press, 1976).

Tremmel, W.C., *Religion, What Is it?* (New York: Holt, Rinehart & Winston, 2nd edn, 1984 [1976]).

Tylor, E.B., *Primitive Culture* (repr.; New York: Harper & Brothers, 1958 [1871]).

Uffenheimer, B., 'Myth and Reality in Ancient Israel', *Axial Age Civilizations* (ed. S. Eisenstadt), pp. 135-68.

van Beeck, F.J., 'Israel's God, the Psalms, and the City of Jerusalem: Life Experience and the Sacrifice of Praise and Prayer', *Horizons* 19 (1992), pp. 219-39.

van der Spek, R.J., 'Assyriology and History: A Comparative Study of War and Empire in Assyria, Athens, and Rome', *Tablet and the Scroll* (eds. M. Cohen, D. Snell and D. Weisberg), pp. 262-70.

van der Toorn, K., *Sin and Sanction in Israel and Mesopotamia: A Comparative Study* (Studia semitica neerlandica, 22; Assen: Van Gorcum, 1985).

van Imschoot, P., *Théologie de l'Ancien Testament*, I (Paris: Tournai, 1954).

van Selms, A., 'Temporary Henotheism', *Symbolae Biblicae et Mesopotamicae Francisco Mario Theodoro de Liagre Böhl dedicatae* (eds. M. Beck, *et al.*; Studia Francisci Scholten Memoriae Dedicata, 4; Leiden: Brill, 1973), pp. 341-48.

van Seters, J., *Abraham in History and Tradition* (New Haven: Yale University Press, 1975).

—*In Search of History: Historiography in the Ancient World and the Origins of Biblical History* (New Haven: Yale University Press, 1983).

—*Prologue to History: The Yahwist as Historian in Genesis* (Louisville, KY: Westminster/John Knox, 1992).

—*The Life of Moses: The Yahwist as Historian in Exodus–Numbers* (Louisville, KY: Westminster/John Knox, 1994).

Veyne, P., 'The Roman Empire', *A History of Private Life. I. From Pagan Rome to Byzantium* (ed. P. Veyne; trans. A. Goldhammer; Cambridge, MA: Belknap, 1987).

von Rad, G., *Old Testament Theology* (2 vols.; trans. D.M.G. Stalker; New York: Harper & Row, 1962, 1965).

von Soden, W., 'Das Fragen nach der Gerechtigkeit Gottes im Alten Orient', *MDOG* 96 (1965), p. 46.

—*Leistung und Grenze sumerische und babylonischer Wissenschaft* (Darmstadt: Wissenschaftliche Buchgesellschaft, 1965).

Vorländer, H., 'Aspects of Popular Religion in the Old Testament' (trans. G. Harrison),

Popular Religion (eds. N. Greinacher and N. Mette; Concilium, 186; Edinburgh: T. & T. Clark, 1986), pp. 63-70.

—'Der Monotheismus Israels als Antwort auf die Krise des Exils', *Der einzige Gott* (ed. B. Lang; Munich: Kösel, 1981), pp. 84-113.

—*Mein Gott: Die Vorstellungen vom persönliche Gott* (Kevelaer: Butzon & Bercker, 1975).

Vrba, E., 'What is Species Selection?', *Systematic Zoology* 33 (1984), pp. 318-28.

Vrba, E., and N. Eldredge, 'Individuals, Hierarchies and Processes: Towards a More Complete Evolutionary Theory', *Paleobiology* 10 (1984), pp. 146-71.

Vrba, E., and S.J. Gould, 'The Hierarchical Expansion of Sorting and Selection Cannot Be Equated', *Paleobiology* 12 (1986), pp. 217-28.

Wacker, M.-T., 'Spuren der Göttin im Hoseabuch', *Ein Gott allein* (eds. W. Dietrich and M. Klopfenstein), pp. 329-48.

Weber, M., *Ancient Judaism* (repr.; trans. H. Gerth and D. Martindale; Glencoe: Free Press, 1952 [1917–19]).

Weinfeld, M., *Social Justice in Ancient Israel and in the Ancient Near East* (Minneapolis: Augsburg–Fortress, 1995).

—*The Promise of the Land: The Inheritance of the Land of Canaan by the Israelites* (Los Angeles: University of California Press, 1993).

Weippert, M., 'Synkretismus und Monotheismus: Religionsinterne Konflict-bewältigung im alten Israel', *Kultur und Konflikt* (eds. J. Assman and D. Harth; Frankfurt am Main: Suhrkamp, 1990), pp. 143-79.

—'The Israelite "Conquest" and the Evidence from Transjordan', *Symposia* (ed. F. Cross), pp. 15-34.

—*The Settlement of the Israelite Tribes in Palestine* (trans. J. Martin; SBT, 2nd ser., 21; London: SCM Press, 1971).

Welcker, F., *Die griechische Götterlehre* (3 vols.; Göttingen: Dietrich, 1857–62).

Wellhausen, J., *Prolegomena to the History of Ancient Israel* (repr.; trans. A. Menzies and S. Black; Gloucester, MA: Peter Smith, 1973 [1878]).

Wenning, R., and E. Zenger, 'Ein bäuerliches Baal-Heiligtum im samarischen Gebirge aus der Zeit der Anfänge Israels', *ZDPV* 102 (1986), pp. 75-86.

Westermann, C., *Creation* (trans. J. Scullion; Philadelphia: Fortress Press, 1974).

—*Elements of Old Testament Theology* (trans. D. Stott; Atlanta: John Knox, 1982).

—'The Role of the Lament in the Theology of the Old Testament' (trans. R. Soulen), *Int* 28 (1974), pp. 20-38.

Whitehead, A.N., *Process and Reality* (repr.; New York: Free Press, 1978 [1929]).

—*Religion in the Making* (repr.; New York: Macmillan, 1957 [1926]).

—*Science and Philosophy* (New York: Philosophical Library, 1948).

—*Science and the Modern World* (New York: Macmillan, 1925).

—*Symbolism: Its Meaning and Effect* (repr.; New York: Macmillan, 1958 [1927]).

—*The Concept of Nature* (repr.; Cambridge: Cambridge University Press, 1964 [1920]).

—*The Function of Reason* (Princeton, NJ: Princeton University Press, 1929).

Whitelam, K., 'Israel's Traditions of Origin: Reclaiming the Land', *JSOT* 44 (1989), pp. 19-42.

—'The Identity of Early Israel: The Realignment and Transformation of Late Bronze-Iron Age Palestine', *JSOT* 63 (1994), pp. 57-87.

—*The Invention of Ancient Israel: The Silencing of Palestinian History* (New York: Routledge, 1996).

Widengren, G., *The Accadian and Hebrew Psalms of Lamentation as Religious Documents: A Comparative Study* (Uppsala: Almquist & Wiksell, 1936).

Wildberger, H., 'Der Monotheismus Deuterojesajas', *Beiträge zur Alttestamentlichen Theologie (Festschrift für Walther Zimmerli)* (eds. H. Donner, R. Hahnhart and R. Smend; Göttingen: Vandenhoeck & Ruprecht, 1977), pp. 506-30.

Williamson, P.G., 'Paleontological Documentation of Speciation in Cenozoic Mollusks from Turkana Basin', *Nature* 293 (1981), pp. 437-43.

Winter, U., *Frau und Göttin: Exegetische und ikonographische Studien zum weiblichen Gottesbild im Alten Israel und in dessen Umwelt* (OBO, 53; Göttingen: Vandenhoeck & Ruprecht, 1983).

Wittfogel, K., *Oriental Despotism* (New Haven: Yale University Press, 1957).

Wright, G.E., *Biblical Archaeology* (Philadelphia: Westminster Press, 2nd edn, 1962).

—*God Who Acts: Biblical Theology as Recital* (SBT, 8; London: SCM Press, 1952).

—'Introduction', *Joshua* by R. Boling (Garden City, NY: Doubleday, 1982), pp. 3-88.

—'The Literary and Historical Problem of Joshua 10 and Judges 1', *JNES* 5 (1946), pp. 105-114.

—*The Old Testament against its Environment* (SBT, 2; Chicago: Henry Regnery, 1950).

—*The Old Testament and Theology* (New York: Harper & Row, 1969).

Wright, G.E., and R. Fuller, *The Book of the Acts of God: Christian Scholarship Interprets the Bible* (Garden City, NY: Doubleday, 1957).

Yadin, Y., 'Is the Biblical Conquest of Canaan Historically Reliable?', *BARev* 8.2 (1982), pp. 16-23.

—'The Transition from a Semi-Nomadic to a Sedentary Society in the Twelfth Century BCE', *Symposia* (ed. F. Cross), pp. 57-68.

Yamauchi, E., *Persia and the Bible* (Grand Rapids: Baker, 1990).

Yee, G., 'The Theology of Creation in Proverbs 8:22-31', *Creation in the Biblical Traditions* (eds. R. Clifford and J. Collins), pp. 85-96.

Zaehner, R.C., 'Zoroastrianism', *The Concise Encyclopedia of Living Faiths* (ed. C. Zaehner; Boston: Beacon, 1959).

Zeitlin, I., *Ancient Judaism: Biblical Criticism from Max Weber to the Present* (Cambridge: Polity Press, 1984).

Zenger, E., 'Das jahwistische Werk—ein Wegbereiter des jahwistischen Monotheismus?', *Gott, der Einzige* (ed. H. Haag), pp. 26-53.

Zevit, Z., 'The Khirbet el-Qôm Inscription Mentioning a Goddess', *BASOR* 255 (1984), pp. 39-47.

Zertal, A., 'Israel Enters Canaan: Following the Pottery Trail', *BARev* 17.5 (1991), pp. 28-49, 75.

INDEXES

INDEX OF REFERENCES

INDEX OF AUTHORS